COMPUTER OBJECTIVES

COMPUTER OBJECTIVES

Dr. S. Swaminathan

KHANNA BOOK PUBLISHING CO. (P) LTD.

COMPUTER OBJECTIVES
Dr. S. Swaminathan

ISBN: 9788190675888

Published by:
Khanna Book Publishing Co. (P) Ltd.
1694-95, 1st Floor, Nai Sarak, Delhi-110006 (India)
Phone: 011-23283211 Telefax: 011-23256658
E-mail: contact@khannabooks.com
Website: www.khannabooks.com

Printed in India by:
S.P.S. Printers & Binders, Delhi

PREFACE

This book has originated from the fact that students who are preparing for various different examinations like GATE, BARC, NTPC, ONGC, HAL, C-DOT, IOCL etc., have to refer to many different books for good and conceptual objective questions in Computer Science & Engg. stream. Keeping above examinations in mind the book has been organized to provide students the best.

“Knowledge advances by steps and not by leaps.”

Lord Macaculay

CONTENTS

* means questions having solutions.

DIGITAL

1. ***$(1011001110001111000000111)_2$ in base 32 is :***

   (a) 22 14 7 16 7 (b) 11 9 23 31 8

   (c) 11 9 7 16 7 (d) 11 14 23 16 7

2. ***If $(11\ a\ 1\ b)_8 = (1\ 2\ c\ 9)_{16}$ (c stands for decimal 12) then the values of x and y are :***

   (a) 5, 1 (b) 7, 5

   (c) 5, 7 (d) None of above

3. ***The value of a and b if $(a\ 5\ 6\ 7)_8 + (2\ b\ a\ 5)_8 = (7\ 1\ b\ a)_8$ is :***

   (a) 4, 3 (b) 3, 3

   (c) 4, 4 (d) 4, 5

4. ***A decimal number has 25 digits. The number of bits needed for its equivalent binary representation is, approximately :***

   (a) 50 (b) 55

   (c) 70 (d) 75

5. ***Which of the following is the minimum error code ?***

   (a) Octal code (b) Grey code

   (c) Binary code (d) Excess-3 code

6. ***The boolean expression $A + BC$ equals :***

   (a) $(A' + B)(A' + C)$ (b) $(A + B)(A + C)$

   (c) $(A + B)(A' + C)$ (d) $(A + B')(A' + C')$

7. ***The range of numbers that can be stored in 8 bits, if negative numbers are stored in 2's complement form is :***

   (a) – 128 to + 128 (b) – 128 to + 127

   (c) – 127 to + 128 (d) – 127 to + 127

8. ***In a ripple counter using edge-Triggered JK flip-flop, the pulse input is applied to the***

   (a) Clock input of all flip-flops

Answers : **1.*** (a) **2.*** (d) **3.*** (a) **4.*** (d) **5.** (b) **6.*** (b) **7.** (b)

(b) Clock input of one flip-flops
(c) J and K input of one flip-flops
(d) J and K input of all flip-flops

9. *The output of the following circuit is given by :*

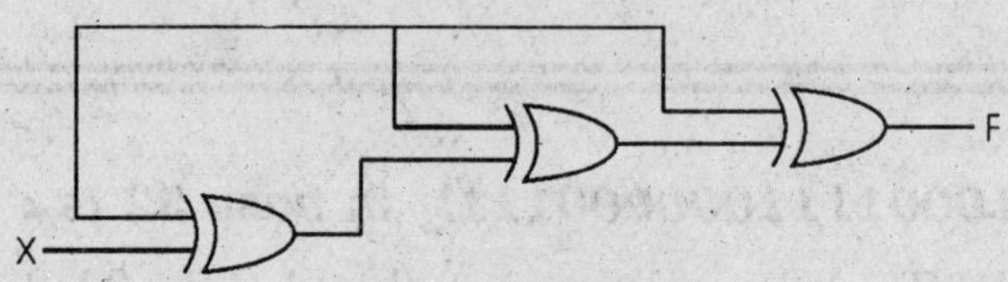

(a) 1 (b) 0
(c) X (d) X'

10. *'T' flip flops will divide the clock frequency by :*

(a) n^2 (b) n
(c) 2^n (d) $\log n$

11. *Which of the folowing 4-bit numbers equals its 1's complement ?*

(a) 1010 (b) 1000
(c) No such number (d) 0001

12. *Introducing parity bit for error detection does not imply*

(a) Increase in the length of the code
(b) Increase in the H/w of the system
(c) automatic error correction
(d) odd number of error detection

13. *How many flip flops are needed to divide by 16 ?*

(a) 2 (b) 4
(c) 8 (d) 16

14. *The number of flip flops needed to construct a binary modulo N counter is :*

(a) N (b) 2^N
(c) N^2 (d) $\log_2 N$

15. *Let * be a Boolean operation defined by*

$$C * D = CD + C'D'$$

then the value of C * C is :

(a) C (b) D
(c) 0 (d) 1

16. *Consider the following digital circuits :*

(1) Multiplexers

(2) Read only memory

(3) D-latch

(4) Circuit as shown

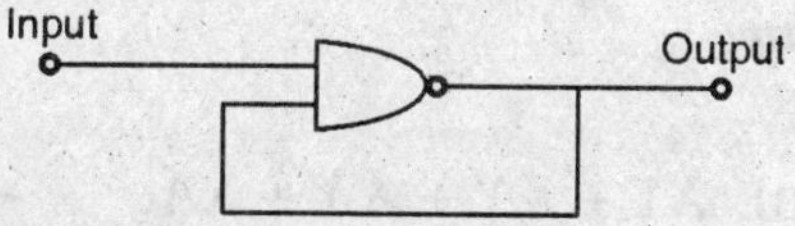

Which of these come under the class of combinational circuits ?

(a) 1 and 2 (b) 3 and 4

(c) 1, 2 and 3 (d) 1,2,3 and 4

17. ***What will be the even parity seven bit Hamming code for a word 1011 ?***

(a) 1010101 (b) 1001101

(c) 1111011 (d) 1001011

18. ***Hamming distance between two successive code groups in a cycle code is :***

(a) 4 (b) 1

(c) 2 (d) 0

19. ***Karnaugh map uses :***

(a) Hollerith code (b) Cyclic codes

(c) EBCDIC code (d) None of above

20. ***What will be the Hamming code for 2 bit message 11 in binary code ?***

(a) 10011 (b) 01111

(c) 11111 (d) 11100

21. ***Shift registers is/are used for :***

(a) Serial to parallel conversion

(b) Parallel to serial conversion

(c) Digital delay line

(d) None of above

22. ***Which of the following flip flops is free from race round problem ?***

(a) T flip flop (b) SR flip flop

(c) Master Slave JK flip-flops (d) None of above

23. ***For the input pulse train of clock period T, the delay produced by an m stage shift register is :***

(a) $(m-1)\,T$ (b) mT

(c) $(m+1)\,T$ (d) $2mT$

Answers: **8.** (b) **9.** (b) **10.** (c) **11.** (c) **12.** (c) **13.** (b) **14.** (d) **15.** (d) **16.** (b) **17.** (a) **18.** (b) **19.** (c) **20.** (b) **21.** (a),(b),(c) **22.** (c) **23.** (a)

24. *The output of the following multiplexer circuit can be represented by*

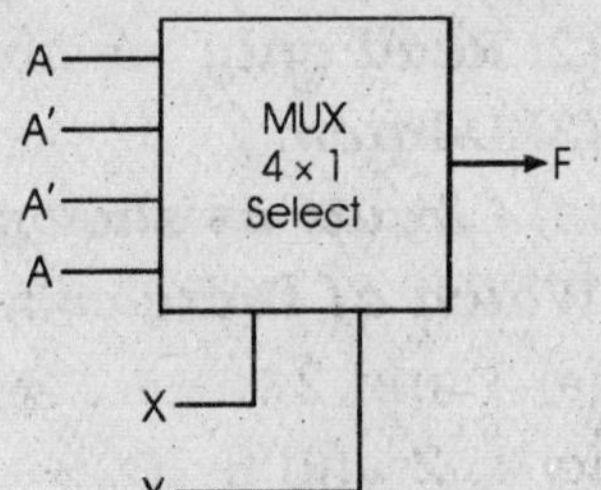

(a) $XY + XA' + A'Y + XA$
(b) $X + Y + A$
(c) $X + Y$
(d) $X'Y'A + X'YA' + XYA + XY'A'$

25. *How many 2-input multiplexers are required to construct a 2^{10}-input multiplexer :*

(a) 1023 (b) 31
(c) 10 (d) 127

26. *Highest address in a 48 K memory :*

(a) 7FFFH, 64,387 (b) BFFFH, 49,151
(c) BFFFH, 49,152 (d) None of above

27. *Which one of the following circuits converts an RS Flip Flop to T Flip Flop ?*

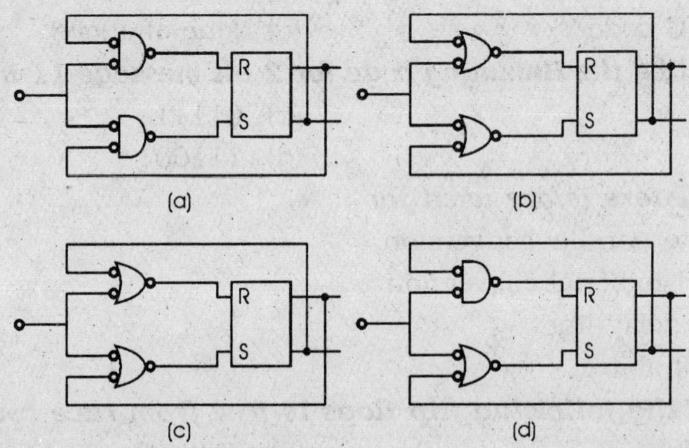

28. *The Q output of a J-K FLIP-FLOP is '1'. The output does not change when a clock-pulse is applied. The inputs J and K will be respectively (where 'x' don't care state) :*

(a) 0 and *x* (b) *x* and 0
(c) 1 and 0 (d) 0 and 1

29. *The no. of columns in a state table for a sequential circuit with 'm' flip flops and 'n' input is :*

(a) $m + n$ (b) $m + 2n$

(c) $2m + n$ (d) $2m + 2n$

30. *A computer uses trinary system instead of the traditional binary system. An 'n' bit string in the binary system will occupy :*

(a) $3 + n$ trinary digit (b) $2n/3$ trinary digit

(c) $n\log_3 2$ trinary digit (d) $n\log_2 3$ trinary digit

31. *The total no. of possible boolean functions involving 'n' Boolean variables is :*

(a) Infinitely many (b) 2^{n^2}

(c) n^2 (d) 2^{2^n}

32. *Which of the following number system has two 0's ?*

(a) Sign + magnitude (b) 1's complement

(c) 2's complement (d) None of above

33. *In a 4 bit full adder, how many half adders and OR gates are required ?*

(a) 8 & 4 (b) 4 & 7

(c) 7 & 3 (d) 8 & 3

34. *Which of the following f/f can be converted to D type (Delay) Flip-flop ?*

(a) *SR* flip-flop (b) *J–K* flip-flop

(c) Master Slave flip-flop (d) None of above

35. *With 4 boolean variables, how many boolean expressions can be formed ?*

(a) 16 (b) 256

(c) 1024 (1*k*) (d) 64 *k* (64 × 1024)

36. *The minimized expression for the given k map is :*

(a) $A + \overline{B}C$

(b) $B + AC$

(c) $C + AB$

(d) ABC

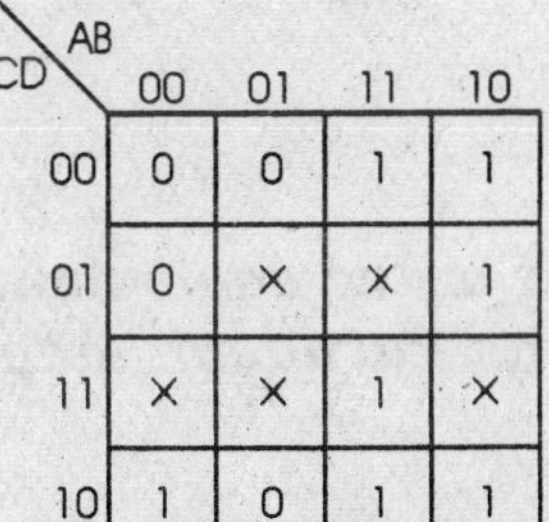

CD \ AB	00	01	11	10
00	0	0	1	1
01	0	×	×	1
11	×	×	1	×
10	1	0	1	1

37. *A number is expressed in binary two's complement as 1 00 11. Its decimal equivalent value is :*

Answers: **24.*** (d) **25.*** (a) **26.*** (b) **27.** (b) **28.*** (b) **29.*** (c) **30.** (c)
31.* (d) **32.*** (b) **33.*** (c) **34.*** (a),(b),(c) **35.** (a) **36.*** (a)

(a) 19 (b) 13
(c) – 19 (d) – 13

38. *The logic expression for the output of the following circuit is :*

(a) $\overline{AC} + \overline{BC} + CD$
(b) $A\overline{C} + B\overline{C} + \overline{C}D$
(c) $ABC + \overline{C}\,\overline{D}$
(d) $\overline{A}\,\overline{B} + \overline{B}\,\overline{C} + \overline{C}\,\overline{D}$

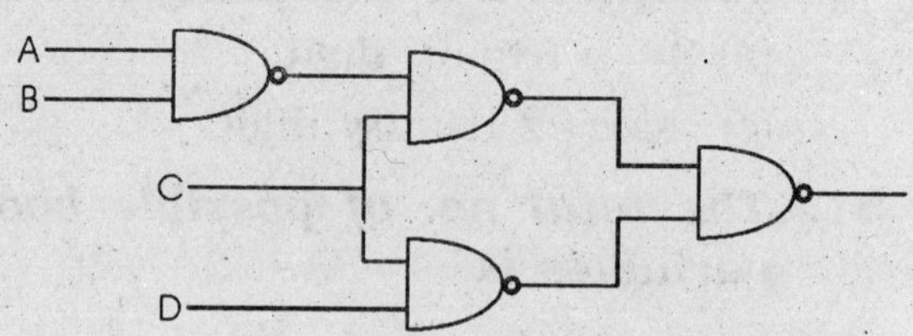

39. *What values of A, B, C must satisfy the following simultaneous boolean equations ?*

$$\overline{A} + AB = 0\ ,\ AB = AC\ ,\ AB + A\overline{C} + CD = \overline{CD}$$

(a) $A = 1$, $B = 0$, $C = 0$, $D = 1$
(b) $A = 1$, $B = 1$, $C = 0$, $D = 0$
(c) $A = 1$, $B = 0$, $C = 1$, $D = 1$
(d) $A = 1$, $B = 0$, $C = 0$, $D = 0$

40. *The number of 1s in the binary representation of* (3 ∗ 4096 + 15 ∗ 256 + 5 ∗ 16 + 3) *are :*

(a) 8 (b) 9
(c) 10 (d) 12

41. *What is the equivalent minimal boolean expression (in sum of products form) for the Karnaugh map given below ?*

(a) $BD + \overline{B}\,\overline{D}$
(b) $\overline{B}\,D + B\overline{D}$
(c) $BD + AC$
(d) $AB + C\overline{D}$

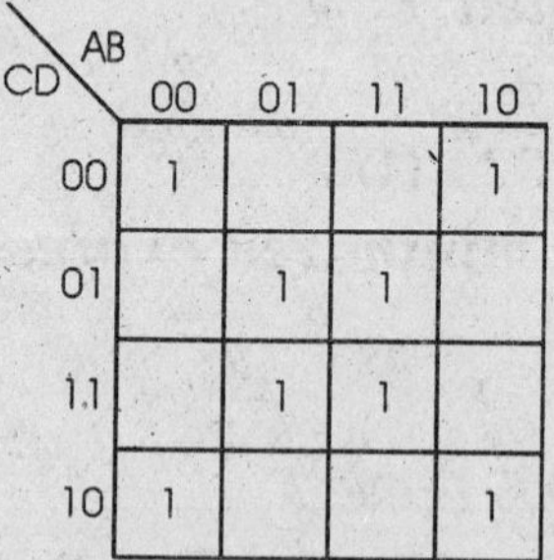

42. *What is the equivalent boolean expression in product of sums form for the karnaugh map given below ?*

(a) $B\overline{D} + \overline{B}D$
(b) $(B + \overline{C} + D)\ (\overline{B} + C + \overline{D})$
(c) $(B + \overline{D})\ (\overline{B} + D)$
(d) $(B + \overline{D})\ (\overline{B} + D)$

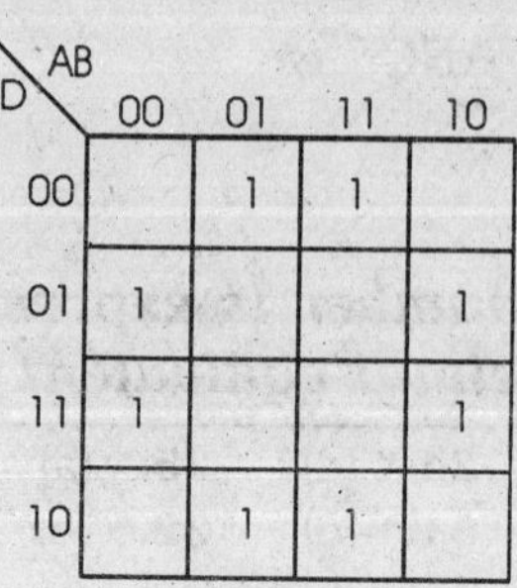

43. *A multiplexer with a 4 bit data select input is a :*

(a) 4 : 1 multiplexer (b) 2 : 1 multiplexer

(c) 16 : 1 multiplexer (d) 8 : 1 multiplexer

44. *Which of the following operations in commutative but not associative ?*

(a) AND (b) OR

(c) NAND (d) EXOR

45. *The number of binary relations on a set with n elements is :*

(a) n^2 (b) 2^n

(c) 2^{n^2} (d) None of the above

46. *Which of the following expression is not equivalent to $\overline{x}$?*

(a) *x NAND x* (b) *x NOR x*

(c) *x NAND* 1 (d) *x NOR* 1

47. *Consider a logic ckt given below. The functions f_1, f_2 and f (in canonical sum of products form) in decimal notation are*

$$f_1(w, x, y, z) = \Sigma\ 8, 9, 10$$

$$f_2(w, x, y, z) = \Sigma\ 7, 8, 12, 13, 14, 15$$

$$f(w, x, y, z) = \Sigma\ 8, 9$$

The function f_3 is :

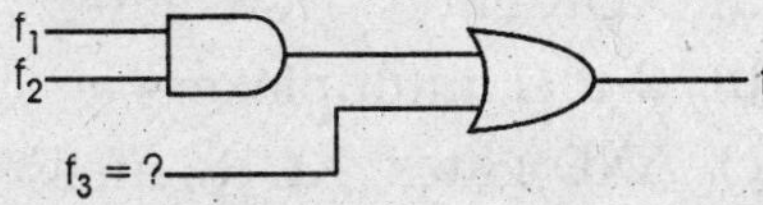

(a) Σ 9, 10

(b) Σ 9

(c) Σ 1, 8, 9

(d) Σ 8, 10, 15

48. *Which of the following are not weighted codes ?*

(a) Roman number system (b) Decimal number system

(c) Excess 3-code (d) Binary number system

49. *Which of the following does not need extra hardware for DRAM refreshing ?*

(a) 8085 (b) Motorola-6800

(c) Z-80 (d) None of the above

50. *C + D can be implemented by :*

(a) NAND gates only (b) NOR gates only

(c) AND gates only (d) None of above

Answers: **37.** (d) **38.** (b) **39.*** (a) **40.*** (c) **41.*** (a) **42.** (c) **43.** (c) **44.** (c) **45.*** (c) **46.*** (d) **47.*** (b) **48.** (a),(c) **49.** (c) **50.*** (a),(b)

51. *The simultaneous equations on the boolean variables x , y , z and w*

$$x + y + z = 1$$
$$xy = 0$$
$$xz + w = 1$$
$$xy + \overline{z}\,\overline{w} = 0$$

have the following solution for x , y , z and w respectively ?

(a) 0 1 0 0 (b) 1 1 0 1
(c) 1 0 1 1 (d) 1 0 0 0

52. *The following arrangement of master slave flip-flops has the initial state of P , Q as 0, 1 (respectively). After three clock cycles the output state P , Q is :*

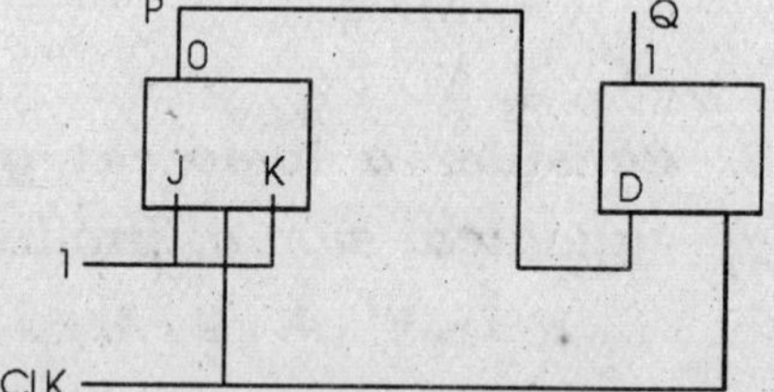

(a) 1, 0
(b) 1, 1
(c) 0, 0
(d) 0, 1

53. *Which of the following sets of components is/are sufficient to implement any arbitrary boolean function ?*

(a) XOR gates, NOT gates
(b) 2 to 1 multiplexers
(c) AND gates, XOR gates
(d) Three input gates that ouput $(A \,.\, B) \rightarrow C$ for the input A , B and C

54. *The following figure represents :*

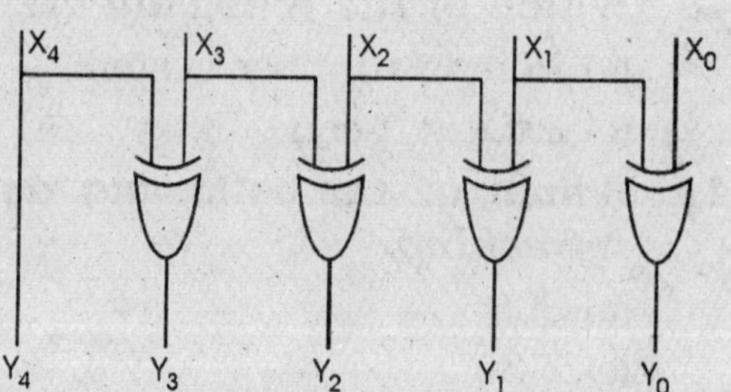

(a) Binary to grey code converter
(b) Grey to binary code converter
(c) Decimal to binary converter
(d) 2's complement to binary converter

55. *A pulse width $t_w = 50\mu sec$ (time at which high exist) is applied to one of the inputs of an XOR (Ex. OR) circuit A second + ive pulse with $t_w = 10\ \mu$ sec is applied to the other input begaining 15 μ sec after the leading edge of the first pulse. What will be the output :*

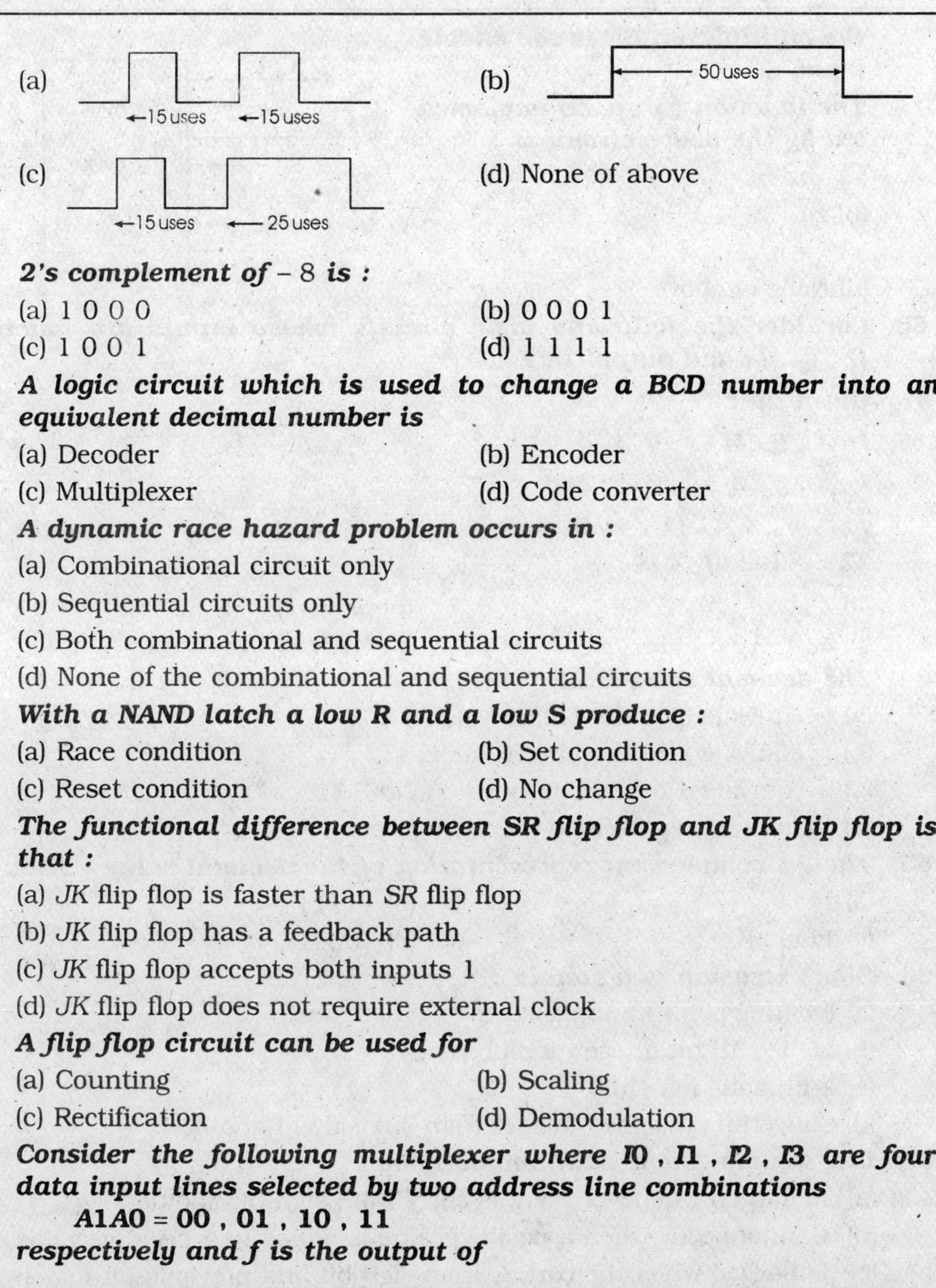

(d) None of above

56. ***2's complement of*** – 8 ***is :***

(a) 1 0 0 0 (b) 0 0 0 1

(c) 1 0 0 1 (d) 1 1 1 1

57. ***A logic circuit which is used to change a BCD number into an equivalent decimal number is***

(a) Decoder (b) Encoder

(c) Multiplexer (d) Code converter

58. ***A dynamic race hazard problem occurs in :***

(a) Combinational circuit only

(b) Sequential circuits only

(c) Both combinational and sequential circuits

(d) None of the combinational and sequential circuits

59. ***With a NAND latch a low R and a low S produce :***

(a) Race condition (b) Set condition

(c) Reset condition (d) No change

60. ***The functional difference between SR flip flop and JK flip flop is that :***

(a) *JK* flip flop is faster than *SR* flip flop

(b) *JK* flip flop has a feedback path

(c) *JK* flip flop accepts both inputs 1

(d) *JK* flip flop does not require external clock

61. ***A flip flop circuit can be used for***

(a) Counting (b) Scaling

(c) Rectification (d) Demodulation

62. ***Consider the following multiplexer where I0 , I1 , I2 , I3 are four data input lines selected by two address line combinations***

A1A0 = 00 , 01 , 10 , 11

respectively and f is the output of

Answers : **51.** (c) **52.** (a) **53.*** (b), (c) **54.** (a) **55.*** (c) **56.** (a) **57.** (a) **58.** (c) **59.** (a) **60.** (c) **61.** (a), (b)

the multiplexer. EN is the enable input.

The function f(x , y , z) implemented by the above circuit is :

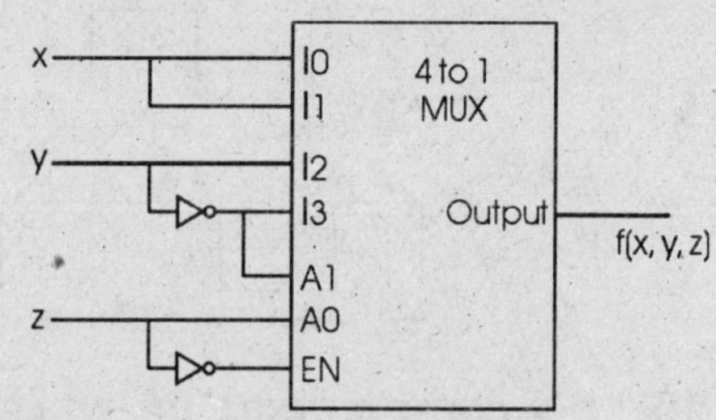

(a) xyz'

(b) $zy + z$

(c) $x + y$

(d) None of above

63. ***Consider the following logic circuits whose inputs are functions f_1, f_2, f_3 and output in F.***

Given that

$f_1 (x , y , z) = \Sigma (0, 1, 3, 5)$

$f_2 (x , y , z) = \Sigma (6, 7)$ **and**

$f (x , y , z) = \Sigma (1 , 4 , 5)$

The value of f_3 is :

(a) $\Sigma (1 , 4 , 5)$
(b) $\Sigma (6 , 7)$
(c) $\Sigma (0 , 1 , 3 , 5)$
(d) None of the above

64. ***The decimal value 0.25.***

(a) Is equivalent to the binary value 0.1

(b) Is equivalent to the binary value 0.01

(c) Is equivalent to the binary value 0.00111

(d) Cannot be represented precisely in binary

65. ***The 2's complement representation of the decimal value – 15 is :***

(a) 1111
(b) 11111
(c) 111111
(d) 10001

66. ***Sign extension is a step in :***

(a) Floating point multiplication

(b) Signed 16 bit integer addition

(c) Arithmatic left shift

(d) Converting a signed integer from one side to another

67. ***In 2's complement addition, overflow***

(a) Is flagged whenever there is carry from sign bit addition.

(b) Cannot occur when a positive value is added to a negative value

(c) Is flagged when the carries from sign bit and previous bit match

(d) None of above

68. ***Consider the circuit shown below. The output of a 2 : 1 MUX is given by te function (ac′ + bc) which of the following is true ?***

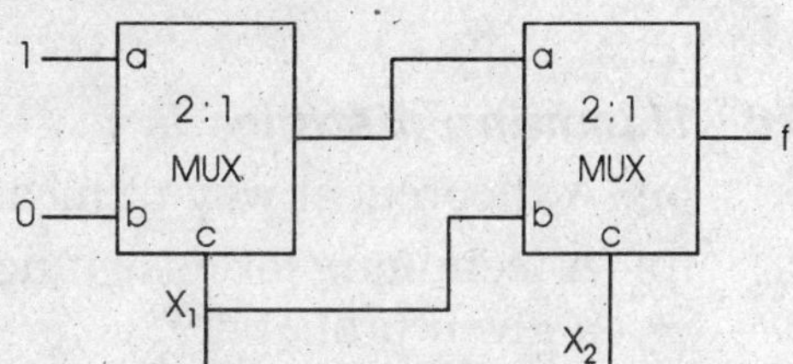

(a) $f = X1' + X2$

(b) $f = X1'X2 + X1X2'$

(c) $f = X1X2 + X1'X2'$

(d) $f = X1 + X2'$

69. ***What will be the minimal product of sum form of the b_4 output of the following excess-3 to BCD converter ?***

(a) (carry of e_2) . (e_4 + 1)

(b) (carry of e_1) . (e_2 + 1)

(c) $e_4 . e_2 . e_1$

(d) e_4

70. ***Let $F(A, B) = A' + B$ simplified expression for function $F(f(x + y, y), z)$ is :***

(a) $x' + z$ (b) xyz

(c) $xy' + z$ (d) None of the above

71. ***Ripple counter are also called***

(a) Synchronous counters

(b) Decade counters

(c) Flip flop with feedback inputs

(d) Asynchronous counters

72. ***A counter having n flip-flops will have :***

(a) 2^n states (b) $2^n - 1$ states

(c) 2^{n-1} states (d) $2^n + 1$ states

73. ***The ring counter with n flip flop has***

(a) 2^n (b) $2n$

(c) $2n - 1$ (d) $2^n - 1$

74. ***The number of clock pulse required to move data into and out of an eight bit serial-in and serial out shift register is :***

(a) 15 (b) 17

(c) 16 (d) 9

Answers : **62.*** (a) **63.*** (d) **64.** (b) **65.** (d) **66.** (d) **67.** (a) **68.*** (c) **69.*** (a) **70.*** (c) **71.** (d) **72.** (a) **73.** (c) **74.** (c)

75. *The divide-by-10 Johnson counter requires :*

(a) 5 (b) 10

(c) 4 (d) 11

76. *Hamming distance is :*

(a) A theoretical way of measuring errors

(b) A technique for assigning codes to a set of items known to occur with a given probablity

(c) A technique for optimizing the intermediate code

(d) None of the above

77. *Which of the following is/are advantages of 2's complement over 1's complement ?*

(a) Easy to implement using digital components

(b) Subtraction can be done by a single addition

(c) It has only one zero

(d) All of the above

78. *In 2's complement representation, a certain negative number – N is 1011. The representation for + N is :*

(a) 0100 (b) 0101

(c) 0110 (d) 0011

79. *Regarding complementing binary number consider the following four statements :*

(i) In the 2's complementing representation, negative numbers are stored in sign magnitude form

(ii) In the 2's complement representation, the most significant bit (MSB) is zero for a positive number

(iii) In a 4 bit binary representation of a binary number A, A + 1's complement of $A = 2^4$

(iv) Taking 2's complement is equivalent to sign change of these, the only statements true are

(a) (i) and (iii) (b) (i) and (iv)

(c) (i) and (iv) (d) (ii) and (iii)

80. *The ASCII is an :*

(a) Two bit code (b) Four bit code

(c) Seven bit code (d) Eight bit code

81. ***The exclusive OR for two inputs has the following property :***

(i) If one input is low and the other is high, the output is high

(ii) If both inputs are high, the output in high

(iii) If both inputs are low, the output is high

(iv) The output is 1 only when the input are different

(a) (i) and (ii) (b) (ii) and (iii)

(c) (iii) and (iv) (d) (iv) and (i)

82. ***The negative decimal number – M in the 2's complement representation is 1011. Then the representatin for – (N + 1) is***

(a) 1010 (b) 1100

(c) 1110 (d) 1101

83. ***In logic circuits***

(a) Sink current is greater than source current

(b) The source current is greater than sink current

(c) The sink current flows from the driver to driven gates

(d) All of the above.

84. ***Consider the following four statements :***

(i) In the 2's complement representation, – ive numbers are stored in sign magnitude form

(ii) Taking 2's compliment is equivalent to sign change

(iii) In a 4 bit binary representation of a binary number A A+1's complement of $A = 2^4$

(iv) In the 2's complement representation the most significant bit (MSB) is zero for a + ive number.

Of these, the only true statment are

(a) (i) and (iii) (b) (ii) and (iii)

(c) (i) and (iv) (d) (ii) and (iv)

85. ***In the expression A (A + B) by writing the first term A as A + 0, the expression is best simplified as :***

(a) $A + AB$ (b) AB

(c) A (d) $A + B$

86. ***How many illegitimate states has a synchronous mod-6 counter ?***

(a) 3 (b) 2

(c) 1 (d) 0

Answers : **73.** (c) **74.** (c) **75.** (a) **76.** (a) **77.** (b), (c) **78.** (b) **79.** (c) **80.** (c) **81.** (b) **82.** (a) **83.** (a) **84.** (d) **85.** (c) **86.** (b)

87. *By taking 2's complement again of the 2's complement of a binary one gets :*

(a) The 1's complement
(b) The true complement
(c) The original number
(d) The sign magnitude form of the number

88. *Which of the following flip flops is used as latch ?*

(a) TTL (b) ECL
(c) CMO (d) LSI

89. *Which of the following flip-flops is used as latch ?*

(a) *JK*-flip flop (b) *D* flip flop
(c) *RS* flip flop (d) *T* flip flop

90. *Some of MOS families are PMOS, NMOS, CMOS. The family dominating the LSI field where low power consumption is necessary is :*

(a) NMOS (b) CMOS
(c) PMOS (d) Both NMOS and CMOS

91. *The fraction 0.68_{10} is equal to*

(a) 0.01001_2 (b) 0.101_2
(c) 0.10101_2 (d) 0.10111_2

92. *A gate in which all inputs must be low to get a high output is called :*

(a) An inverter (b) A NOR gate
(c) An AND gate (d) A NAND gate

93. *Which of the following parameters is not specified for digital ICs ?*

(a) Gate dissipation (b) Propagation delay
(c) Noise margin (d) Band-width

94. *The value of the binary 1111 is :*

(a) $2^3 - 1$ (b) $2^4 - 1$
(c) 2^4 (d) None of above

95. *In MSI, a chip contains :*

(a) Less than 12 gates (b) Less than 100 gates
(c) Less than 1000 gates (d) Less than 5000 gates

96. *Given BCD number 1001 0011, its decimal equivalent is*

(a) 147 (b) 143
(c) 93 (d) 39

97. ***In the binary number 110.101 the fractional part has the value :***

(a) 0.125 (b) 0.625
(c) 0.875 (d) 0.5

98. ***To implement all functions of the basic logic functions, it suffices to have ?***

(a) OR (b) NOT
(c) AND NOT (d) None of above

99. ***Which of the following components is used for storing binary information ?***

(a) A register (b) A latch
(c) A flip flop (d) None of above

100. ***Which of the following characteristics is not true for TTL logic ?***

(a) Good speed (b) Low power dissipation per gate
(c) High cost (d) None of above

101. ***The negative decimal number $-N$ in the 2's complement representation is 1011. Then the representation for $-(N+1)$ is***

(a) 1010 (b) 1100
(c) 1110 (d) 1101

102. ***The purpose of introducing feedback loop in a digital counter ckt is :***

(a) to improve stability
(b) To improve distortion
(c) Synchronise input and output pulses
(d) To reduce the number of input pulses to reset the counter

103. ***In the 2's complement Adder-Subtractor :***

(a) Sign magnitude numbers represent –ive number
(b) Sign magnitude numbers have '1' as leading bit
(c) Sign magnitude numbers have '0' as leading bit
(d) 2's complement represents + ive numbers

104. ***BCD numbers are obtained by :***

(a) Converting decimal number to binary
(b) Converting decimal to octal numbers
(c) Each decimal digital is represented by a four bit binary
(d) Converting binary to decimal

Answers : **87.** (c) **88.** (b) **89.** (c) **90.** (b) **91.** (c) **92.** (b) **93.** (d) **94.** (b) **95.** (b) **96.** (c)
97. (b) **98.** (c) **99.** (d) **100.** (c) **101.** (a) **102.** (d) **103.** (c) **104.** (c)

105. *In segmential circuits, the output states are function of :*

(a) Present input states (b) Past input states

(c) Present and past input (d) None of above

106. *When a binary adder is used as BCD adder, the sum is :*

(a) Correct when it is < 9 (b) Correct when it is > 9

(c) Correct when it is < 16 (d) None of above

107. *Schmitt trigger can be used as a :*

(a) Comparator (b) Square-wave generator

(c) Flip flop (d) All of these

108. *For the switch ckt, taking open as 0 and closed as 1, the expression for the ckt, is Y :*

Y is given by :

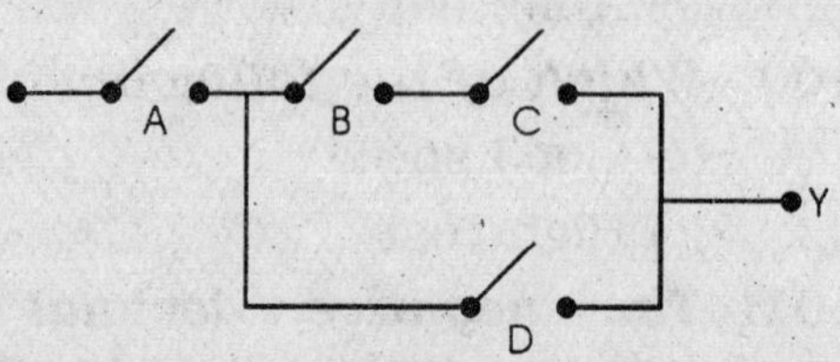

(a) $A + (B + C) D$

(b) $A + BC + D$

(c) $A (BC + D)$

(d) None of above

A B C D Y

109. *If t_p is the pulse width, At is the propagation delay, T is period of pulse Train then the following condition can avoid the race around condition :*

(a) $t_p = \Delta t = T$ (b) $2tp > \Delta t > T$

(c) $t_p < \Delta t < T$ (d) $2tp < \Delta t < T$

110. *Wired AND connection must not be used with totempole drives because :*

(a) Fanout decreases

(b) Delay is increased

(c) Noise is increased

(d) Transient current spikes occur

111. *A gate in which all inputs must be high to get a low input is called :*

(a) An inverter (b) An AND gate

(c) a NOR gat (d) A NAND gate

112. *A ring counter is same as :*

(a) Up-down counter (b) Parallel counter

(c) Shift register (d) None of these

113. *The current logging take place in :*

(a) RTL (b) HTL

(c) DCTL (d) TTL

114. *How many bytes are there in :*

1111 1011 0111 0100 1010

(a) 2 (b) 3

(c) 2 1/2 (d) 3 1/2

115. *The advantage of self-correcting code is that :*

(a) It is a weighted code

(b) It has even parity

(c) It is casy to decode electronically

(d) All of these

116. *In the circuit shown below, the outputs X_1 and X_2 are :*

(a) $X_1 = A\overline{BC} + \overline{A}B\overline{C} + \overline{AB}C + ABC$;

$X_2 = AB + AC + BC$

(b) $X_1 = (A \oplus B) \oplus C$;

$(A \oplus B) \oplus C + \overline{A}\,\overline{B}$

(c) Both A and B

(d) None of these

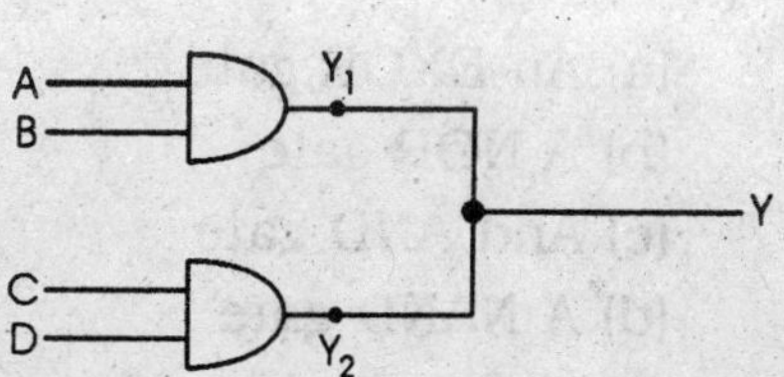

117. *The output of the following logic will be :*

(a) $Y = Y_1 + Y_2$

(b) $Y = Y_1 Y_2$

(c) $Y = 2\,(Y_1 + Y_2)$

(d) $Y = (Y_1 + Y_2)/2$

A
B
Y_1
Y
C
D
Y_2

118. *The minimum boolean expression for the circuit is :*

(a) $AB + AC + \overline{B}C$

(b) $A + BC$

(c) $A + B$

(d) $A + \overline{B} + C$

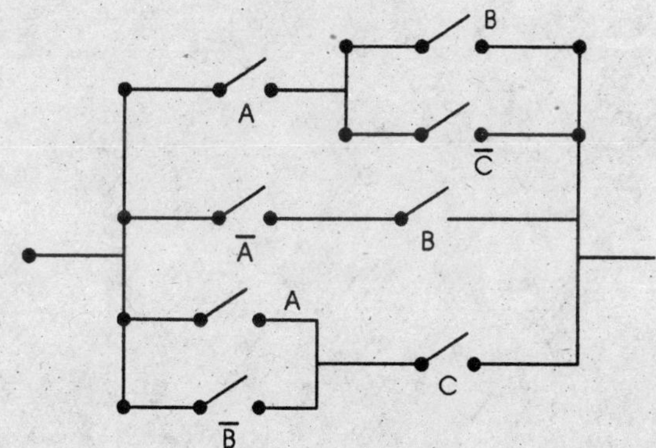

Answers : **105.** (c) **106.** (a) **107.** (d) **108.** (c) **109.** (c) **110.** (d) **111.** (d) **112.** (c) **113.** (a) **114.** (c) **115.** (c) **116.** (a) **117.** (a) **118.** (b)

119. *The negative logic AND gate shown is equivalent to a positive logic :*

(a) AND gate

(b) OR gate

(c) NAND gate

(d) NOR gate

120. *Match List I with List II and select the correct answer :*

List I	List II
(a) Zener diode	1. High speed switching
(b) Tunnel diode	2. Multivibrator circuits
(c) Gun diode	3. Voltage stablizer
(d) PIN diode	4. Microwave oscillator

(a) $A-4$ $B-1, 4$ $C-1$ $D-3$

(b) $A-4$ $B-2, 3$ $C-4$ $D-1$

(c) $A-3$ $B-1, 2$ $C-4$ $D-1$

(d) $A-3$ $B-1, 2, 4$ $C-4$ $D-1$

121. *The output f(x, y) if the multiplexer resulting from the input logical values is :*

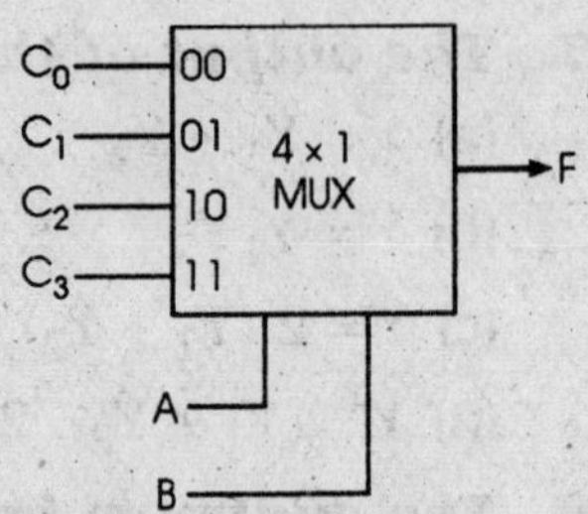

(a) An EXOR gate

(b) A NOR gate

(c) And AND gate

(d) A NAND gate

Answers : **119.** (b) **120.** (d) **121.** (a)

SOLUTIONS

1. To comment if into base 32 we need $2^5 = 32$ which is equal to 5 bits. So grouping in 5's from the right we get

$$\underset{22}{\underline{10\,11\,0}}\;\underset{14}{\underline{0\,11\,1\,0}}\;\underset{7}{\underline{0\,0\,11\,1}}\;\underset{16}{\underline{1\,00\,00}}\;\underset{7}{\underline{00\,11\,1}}$$

2. Converting to base 8 we get

$$\underline{00\,1}\;\underline{0\,0\,1}\;a\;\underline{0\,0\,1}\;b = \underline{000\,1}\;\underline{00\,1}\;\underline{0\,1\,1}\;\underline{0\,0\,1}\;\underline{0\,0\,1}$$

Compairing the values of both sides

$$1\;1\;a\;1\;b = 1\;1\;3\;1\;1$$

So the value of a and b are 3 and 1

3. Since all of them are in base 8 so adding 7 and 5 it yeilds 4 and caries 1. So $a = 4$.

$$\begin{array}{r} 4\,5\,6\,7 \\ \underline{2\,b\,4\,5} \\ 3\,4 \end{array}$$

So the value of $b = 3$

So the value of $a + 4$, $b = 3$

4.

$$2^1 = 2$$
$$2^2 = 4$$
$$2^4 = 16$$
$$2^7 = 128$$
$$2^{10} = 1024$$

So to add one decimal number we need 3 binary digit ($2^4 - 2^7$ needs 2 decimal digit to 3 decimal digit. Therefore, change in one digit)

So for 25 digit we require $25 \times 3 = 75$ binary digit.

6. Since $(A + B)(A + C)$

$$= AA + AC + BA + BC$$
$$= A + AC + BA + BC$$
$$= A + BC$$

9. Since the output of *XOR* gate depends upon the table.

x	y	F
0	0	0
0	1	1
1	0	1
1	1	0

When the input $X = 0$ then the output will be 0. So the final output will be 0.

When the input $X = 1$ then the first *XOR* gates gives the value 0. So the input of next *XOR* gates are 1, 0 which will give 1 as output. Finally the input of the last *XOR* gate is 1, 1 which is again equal to 0.

17. Parity bit is at position $2^0\ 2^1\ 2^2$

Bit position → 7 6 5 4 3 2 1

Bit → 1 0 1 P_4 1 P_2 P_1

The values of P_1 P_2 and P_4 are

P_1 is 1, 3, 5, 7

P_2 is 2, 3, 6, 7

P_4 is 4, 5, 6, 7

From first parity relation for bits, 1, 3, 5 and 7 to have even parity P_1 should be should be equal to 1.

From second parity relation for bits 2, 3, 6 and 7 to have even parity P_2 should be equal to 0.

Similarly third parity relation for bits 4, 5, 6 and 7 to have even parity P_4 should be equal to 0.

Hence, final code is D_7 D_6 D_5 P_4 D_3 P_2 P_1

1 0 1 0 1 0 1

20. Let the message code be $m_1 m_2$

The no. of parity bits required is given by

$$2^k \geq m + K + 1 \text{ where } m = 2$$

So the value of K must be equal to 3 to satisfy the relation.

Now we write code as

Bit Position	1	2	3	4	5
Code bit	P_1	P_2	m_1	P_3	m_2

For even parity value of $P_1 = P_1\ m_1\ m_2 = P_1\ 11$

so value of $P_1 = 0$.

Similarly the value of $P_2 = P_2\, m_1 = P_2\, 1$ $(\because m_1 = 1)$

$\therefore$ the value of $P_2 = 1$

for $P_3 = P_3\, m_2 = P_3\, 1$ $(\because m_2 = 1)$

so the value of $P_3 = 1$

So the hamming code for two bit message word is given as

Bit position	1	2	3	4	5
Code bit	p_1	P_2	m_1	P_3	m_2
	0	1	1	1	1

Haming code.

24. The output of the following multiplexer circuit can be represented by

$$F = C_0\, A'B' + C_1\, A'B + C_2\, AB' + C_3\, AB$$

So the output of the above will be

$$F = A\, X'Y' + A'X'Y + A'XY' + AXY$$

25. Since for 2 input we require one MUX for 4 input we require 3 MUX

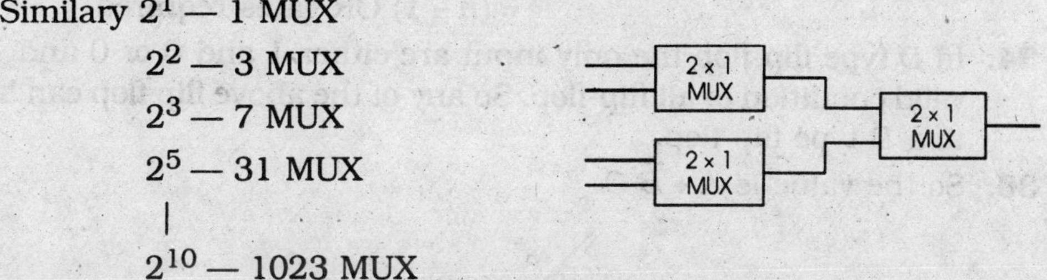

Similary 2^1 — 1 MUX

2^2 — 3 MUX

2^3 — 7 MUX

2^5 — 31 MUX

|

2^{10} — 1023 MUX

26. Because starting address is 0000H and the total address generated by 48K is 49,152 so the highest address will be 49,151.

28. The truth table of *J–K* flip-flop is

J	K	Q_{n+1}
0	0	θn
0	1	0
1	0	1
1	1	*N.A.*

According to given condition Q output is 'J' and does not change with next pulse. From truth table it is clear that this is possible if next input 0, 1 or 1, 0. In other words inputs will be x and O.

29. Because 'n' columns are needed for 'n' inputs and $2m$ columns for storing the 'm' present states and 'm' next states.

31. There are 2^n possible entries in the truth table for n Boolean variables and each having two values 0, 1.

32. For 4 bit system

$$+0 = 0000$$
$$-0 = 1111$$

33.

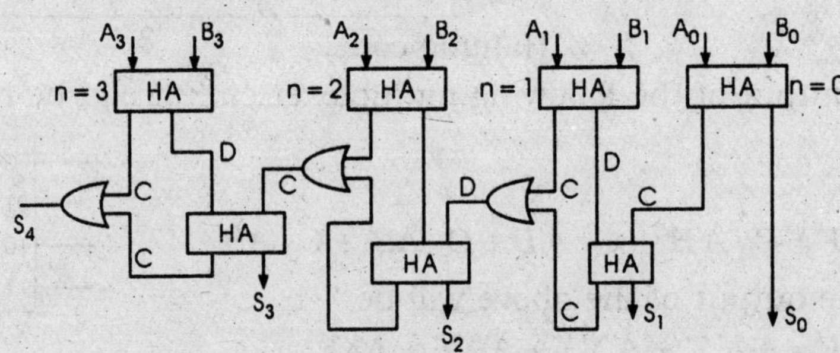

C = Carry bit

D = Data bit

Similary for n bit full adder = $(2n - 1)$ Half adder

= $(n - 1)$ OR gates required

34. In D type flip-flop the only input are either 1 and 0 or 0 and 1 which are valid condition of all flip-flop. So any of the above flip flop can be converted to a D-type flip-flop.

36. So the value is $A + \overline{B}\,C$.

CD \ AB	00	01	11	10
00	0	0	1	1
01	0	×	×	1
11	×	×	1	×
10	1	0	1	1

39. Consider second equation $AB = AC$. Clearly (B) and (C) cannot be the answer. Since $\overline{C}D = 1$ and $A\overline{C} = 1$ in (a). Therefore (a) satisfies all three conditions.

40. (3 * 4096 + 15 * 256 + 5 * 16 + 3)

$$(2^1 + 1) * 2^{12} + (2^3 + 2^2 + 2^1 + 2^0) * 2^8 + (2^2 + 2^0) * 2^4 + 2^1 + 2^0$$

$$= 2^{13} + 2^{12} + 2^{11} + 2^{10} + 2^9 + 2^8 + 2^6 + 2^4 + 2^1 + 2^0$$

= 1 1 1 1 1 1 0 1 0 1 0 0 1 1

41.

CD \ AB	00	01	11	10
00	1			1
01		1	1	
11		1	1	
10	1			1

So the minimal boolean expression for the karnaugh map is $BD + \overline{B}\,\overline{D}$.

45. The number of ordered pairs of the form (x, y) where x and y belong to the set is n^2 and since each of these pairs may either appear or not appear in any relation, so the number of possible relations is 2^{n^2}.

46. By using

NAND gates

x	x	F
0	0	1
1	1	0

so it is equivalent to $\overline{x}$

x NOR x

x	x	F
0	0	1
1	1	0

so it is equivalent to $\overline{x}$

x NAND 1

x	1	F
0	1	1
1	1	0

so it is equivalent to $\overline{x}$

47. Since f_1 and f_2 are connected by AND gate so decimal value of 8 gives the output to 1, since the value of f is 8, 9 so the final value of f_3 is 1 at decimal value 9

f_1 8

f_2 8 $\longrightarrow f(8, 9)$

so f_3 must be 9.

49. Only Z-80 has inbuilt refreshing circuit

50. Because NAND and NOR gates are universal gates that can be used to implement any gate.

53. XOR gate can be used to implement NOT by doing $A \oplus 1$. Using the AND gate and the NOT realization of XOR, we can get a NAND gate which is a universal gate. So, C is right. The 2 to 1 multiplexer gives the function

$AX + BX'$, where X is the selector input. It can be used to implement a NOT by making $A = 0$ and $B = 1$, thus we get X'. We can get an AND gate by putting $B = 0$ and thus getting $A.X$. Using NOT and AND we can get a NAND gate. We can't implement an AND gate from XOR and NOT gates so A is wrong. Similarly we can't implement a NOT gate using $A . B + C$. So D is wrong.

55. First pulse width is of 50μ*sec.* after 15μ *sec* second pulse is applied for 10 μ *sec* so the output sketch of XOR gate wil be of 15 μ *sec* pulse high followed by 10 μ *sec* line and finally 25 μ *sec* pulse respectively.

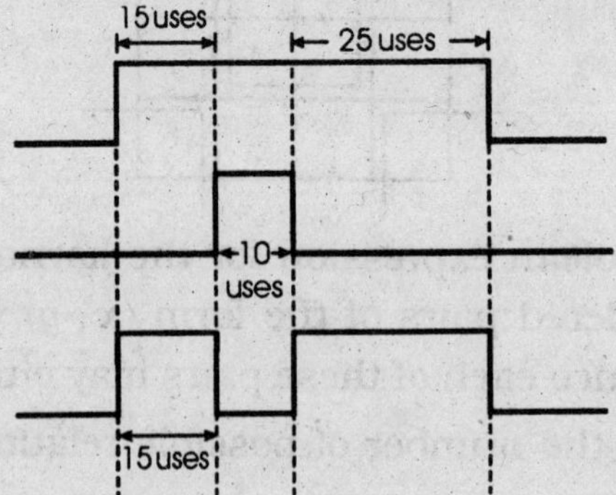

62. For all possible values of x, y, z

z	y	x	I_0	I_1	I_2	I_3	A_1	A_0	EN	F
0	0	0	0	0	0	1	1	0	1	0
0	0	1	1	1	0	1	1	0	1	0
0	1	0	0	0	1	0	0	0	1	0
0	1	1	1	1	1	0	0	0	1	1
1	0	0	0	0	0	1	1	1	0	0
1	0	1	1	1	0	1	1	1	0	0
1	1	0	0	0	1	0	0	1	0	0
1	1	1	1	1	1	0	0	1	0	0

Since the value of I_0 is active at $A_1A_0 = 00$, similarly value of I_1 is

$A_1A_0 = 01$,

$I_2 — A_1A_0 = 10$,

$I_3 — A1Ao = 11$.

Both value of I_0 and $A1Ao = 00$ are true only one time.

$$F = xyz'$$

63. Since f_1 f_2 are connected by NAND gate so decimal value of 0, 1, 3, 5, 6, 7 gives the output 1. given that value of $f(x, y, z)$ is 1, 4, 5 the value of f_3 must be 0, 3, 4 which must be in inverted form (7, 4, 3) so the value of f_3 is (3, 4, 7).

68. Since the value of a and b are given 1,0 and the possible value of C is 0.1. The output of the multiplexer is given by $(ac' + bc)$

$$x_1\ g = (ac' + bc)$$

$$\text{at } 0 = 1\,.\,1 + 0\,.\,0 = 1$$

$$\text{at } 1 = 1\,.\,0 + 0\,.\,1 = 0 \qquad \because C = x1$$

Similary there are two possible values for $x2$, and g

$x2$	$x1$	$g = a$	f
0	0	1	1
0	1	0	0
1	0	1	0
1	1	0	1

$x2$ \ $x1$	0	1
0	1	0
1	0	1

$$F = x1x2 + x1'x2'$$

69. For every value greater than 1001 we have to add 0110 to $e_8\ e_4\ e_2$ 1 in BCD so $e_2 + 1$ and $e_4 + 1$

C1 = carry of $(e_2 + 1)$ by = C1 . $(e_4 + 1)$

70. Given $F(A, B) = A' + B$, therefore

$$S = F(x + y\,,\ y) = (x + y)' + y$$

$$S = x'y' + y \qquad \because (A + B)' + A'B'$$

$$f(f(x + y)\,,\ y)\,,\ z) = f(s\,,\ z) = s' + z$$

$$= (x'y' + y)' + z$$

$$= (x'y')'y' + z = (x + y)\ y' + z \qquad \because (AB)' = A' + B'$$

$$= xy' + yy' + z = xy' + z \qquad (A')' = A \quad yy' = 0$$

■□■

CHAPTER 2

COMPUTER ARCHITECTURE

1. ***Which of the following belongs to the first generation of computer ?***
   (a) ENIAC (b) IBM 1401
   (c) IBM 8090 (d) UNIVAC
2. ***Who is called the "grandfather" of the computer ?***
   (a) Blaise Pascal (b) Charles Babbage
   (c) Joseph Jacquard (d) Dr. Herman Hollerith
3. ***The first mechanical computer designed by Charles Babbage was called :***
   (a) Abacus (b) Processor
   (c) Calculator (d) Analytical Engine
4. ***EBCDIC can code up to how many different characters ?***
   (a) 8 (b) 32
   (c) 64 (d) 256
5. ***The first generation computer system used***
   (a) Vacuum tubes (b) Transistors
   (c) Registers (d) Silicon chip
6. ***A winchester disk is :***
   (a) Disk stack (b) Removable disk
   (c) Flexible disk (d) All of above
7. ***Microprogram is :***
   (a) The name of the source program is micro Computers
   (b) The set of instructions indicating the primitive operations in a system
   (c) The general name of a 'MACROS' in assembly language programming
   (d) The name of a program of very small size
8. ***Dynamic memory cells are constructed using :***
   (a) Transistors (b) Flip-Flops
   (c) MOSFET's (d) FET's
9. ***Which of the following statements is true for dynamic memory ?***
   (a) It has low speed as compared to static memory
   (b) It has low power dissipation

(c) Its contents tend to delay over a period of time
(d) All of above

10. *Microprogramming is a technique :*
(a) For programming the microprocessors
(b) For writing small programs effectively
(c) For programming the control steps of a computer
(d) For programming output/input routines

11. *Which of the following devices should get higher priority in assigning interrupts ?*
(a) Hard disk (b) Printer
(c) Keyboard (d) Floppy disk

12. *Which of the following is True ?*
(a) Unless enabled, a CPU will not be able to process interrupts
(b) Loop instructions cannot be interrupted till they complete
(c) A processor checks for interrupts before executing a new instruction
(d) Only level triggered interrupts are possible on microprocessor

13. *Formatting of a floppy disk refers to :*
(a) Arranging the data on the disk in contiguous fashion
(b) Writing the directory
(c) Erasing the system area
(d) Writing identification information on all tracks and sectors.

14. *If R is the record, D is the recording density and G is the gap length, then the tape utilization is given by :*
(a) $F = \frac{R}{GD}$ (b) $F = \frac{R}{1 + GD}$
(c) $F = \frac{R}{R + GD}$ (d) $F = \frac{2R}{R + GD}$

15. *Which of the following is True ?*
(a) ROM is a Read/Write memory
(b) PC points to the last instruction that was executed
(c) Stock works on the principle of LIFO
(d) All instructions affects the flags

16. *Which of the following does not need extra hardware for DRAM refreshing ?*

Answers : **1.** (d) **2.** (b) **3.** (d) **4.** (d) **5.** (a) **6.** (a) **7.** (b) **8.** (c)
9. (c) **10.** (c) **11.** (c) **12.** (a) **13.** (d) **14.** (c) **15.** (c)

(a) 8085 (b) Motorola-6800
(c) Z-80 (d) None of above

17. *Which of the following are registers ?*

(a) Accumulator (b) Stack pointer
(c) Program counter (d) Buffer

18. *Which of the following remarks about BCD are true ?*

(a) It is a 8-4-2-1 weighted code
(b) Complement of a number can be found effeciently
(c) $(1\ 2\ 3\ 4\ 5\ 6\ 7\ 8)_{10}$ needs 4 bytes in BCD representation
(d) Conversion to and from the decimal system can be done easily

19. *Which of the following is/are true about ASCII ?*

(a) ASCII code is independent from Hollerith code
(b) ASCII has 128 characters, including 32 control characters
(c) American standard code for International Interchange
(d) All of above

20. *Which of the following remarks about PLA is/are true ?*

(a) It produces product of sum as the output
(b) It produces sum of product as the output
(c) It is dedicated for a particular operation
(d) It is general

21. *Choose the correct statements :*

(a) Bus is a group of information carrying wires
(b) Bus is needed to achive resonable speed of operation
(c) Bus can carry data or address
(d) A bus can be shared by more than one device

22. *Bipolar devices are desirable in the fabrication of which of the following components ?*

(a) Main memory (b) Cache memory
(c) Microprogram memory (d) Registers

23. *Which of the following are typical characteristics of a RISC machine ?*

(a) Instruction taking multiple cycles
(b) Highly pipelined
(c) Instructions interpreted by microprograms
(d) Multiple register sets

24. *Programming in a language that actually controls the path of signals of data within the computer is called :*

(a) Microprgramming
(b) System programming
(c) Assembly language programming
(d) Machine language programming

25. *The three main components of a digital computer system are :*

(a) Memory, I/O, DMA
(b) ALU, CPU, memory
(c) Memory, CPU, I/O
(d) Control circuits, ALU, registers

26. *Most of the digital computers do not have floating-point hardware because :*

(a) It is costly
(b) It is slower than software
(c) Floating point addition cannot be performed by H/w
(d) None of above

27. *Microprogram is :*

(a) Name of source program in micro computers
(b) The set of instructions indicating the primitive operations in a system
(c) Primitive form of macros used in assembly language programming
(d) Programme of very small size

28. *An index register in a digital computer is used for :*

(a) Pointing to the stack address
(b) Indirect addressing
(c) Keeping track of number of time a loop is executed
(d) Address modification

29. *Which of the following is volatile ?*

(a) Bubble memory
(b) RAM
(c) ROM
(d) Magnetic disc

30. *In a memory mapped I/o system, which of the following instructions will not be there ?*

(a) LDA
(b) IN
(c) Add
(d) Out

31. *In a virtual memory system, the address space specified by the address lines of the CPU must be _____ than the physical memory size, and _______ than the secondary storage size :*

(a) Smaller, smaller
(b) Smaller, larger
(c) Larger, smaller
(d) Larger, larger

Answers : **16.***(c) **17.** (a),(b), (c) **18.** (a), (c), (d) **19.** (a), (b) **20.** (b), (d) **21.** (a), (b), (c), (d) **22.** (b), (c) **23.** (b), (d) **24.** (a) **25.** (c) **26.** (a) **27.** (b) **28.** (d) **29.** (b) **30.** (b), (d) **31.** (c)

32. *SIMD can be used for :*

(a) Railway reservation (b) Weather forecasting

(c) Matrix multiplication (d) All of above

33. *To complete n tasks using K segments pipeline requires :*

(a) K clock cycles (b) Kn clock cycles

(c) $KX(n-1)$ clock cycles (d) $K+(n-1)$ C,/K cycles

34. *To complete 6 tasks using 4 segments pipeline requires :*

(a) 4 clock cycles (b) 10 clock cycles

(c) 9 clock cycles (d) 20 clock cycles

35. *Assuming a system having two CPU, each executing different programs. At the same time one of the CPUs tries to increment a variable x, while the other CPU tries to decrement the same x, the final value of x can never be :*

(a) Its original value (b) Its original value + 1

(c) Its original value – 1 (d) None of above

36. *Von Neumann architecture is :*

(a) SISD (b) SIMD

(c) MIMD (d) MISD

37. *To archive parallelism, one needs a minimum of :*

(a) 2 processors (b) 3 processors

(c) 4 processors (d) 1 processor

38. *In which addressing mode, the effective address of the operand is generated by adding a constant value to the contents of a register ?*

(a) Absolute mode (b) Indirect mode

(c) Immediate mode (d) Index mode

39. *Which chips are erasable by ultra-violet rays after removing them from the main circult ?*

(a) EPROM (b) EEPROM

(c) PROM (d) All of above

40. *Bubble memory is a :*

(a) Sequential access device only

(b) Direct access device only

(c) Combination of segnential and direct access devices

(d) All of above

41. *RATS stands for :*

(a) Regression analysis time series

(b) Regression analysis time sharing

(c) Real analysis series

(d) All of above

42. How many types of storage loops exist in magnetic bubble memory ?

(a) 8 (b) 4

(c) 16 (d) 2

43. Which of the following is/are true regarding ENIAC ?

(a) It was an electromechanical computer

(b) It was the first stored-program electronic digital computer

(c) It was developed by Chartes Babbage

(d) It uses vacuum tubes

44. Which is used to store firmware ?

(a) RAM (b) ROM

(c) PROM (d) EPROM

45. An index register that is automatically incremented or decremented with each use is :

(a) Shift register (b) Auto indexing

(c) Segnential indexing (d) Asynchronous

46. Which of the following statements about ROM is/are true ?

(a) Once information is placed in ROM it is permanent

(b) Once information is placed in ROM it is not premanent

(c) ROM is sometimes called firmware

(d) ROM is not used for data that changes constantly

47. The member 43 in 2's complement representation is :

(a) 01010101 (b) 11010101

(c) 00101011 (d) 10101011

48. Comparing the time T_1 taken for single instruction on a pipelined CPU with time T_2 taken on a non-pipelined but identical CPU, we can say that :

(a) $T_1 \leq T_2$

(b) $T_1 \geq T_2$

(c) $T_1 < T_2$

(d) T_1 is T_2 plus the time taken for one instruction fetch cycle

Answers : **32.** (b), (c) **33.*** (d) **34.*** (c) **35.*** (d) **36.** (a) **37.*** (d) **38.** (d) **39.** (a) **40.** (c) **41.** (a) **42.*** (d) **43.** (d) **44.** (b) **45.** (b) **46.** (a),(b),(d) **47.** (c) **48.** (b)

49. *List below are some operating system abstractions (in the left column) and the hardware components or matching of pairs is correct :*

(a) Thread	1. Interrupt
(b) Virtual address space	2. Memory
(c) File system	3. CPU
(d) Singnal	4. Disk

(a) a-2, b-4, c-3, d-1 (b) a-1, b-2, c-3, d-4
(c) a-3, b-2, c-4, d-1 (d) a-4, b-1, c-2, d-3

50. *System calls are usually invoked by using :*
(a) A software interrupt (b) Polling
(c) An indirect jump (d) A privileged instruction

51. *The main memory of a computer has 2 c.m. blocks while the cache has 2c blocks. If the cache uses the set associative mapping scheme with 2 blocks per set, then block K of the main memory maps to the set :*
(a) (k mod m) of the cache (b) (k mod c) of the cache
(c) (k mod 2c) of the cache (d) (k mod 2cm) of the cache

52. *A multiuser, multiprocessing operating system cannot be implemented on hardware that does not support :*
(a) Address translation
(b) DMA for disk controller
(c) At least two modes of CPU execution (privileged and non-privileged)
(d) Demand reguing

53. *RAID configurations of disks are used to provide :*
(a) Fault-tolerance (b) High speed
(c) High data density (d) None of above

54. *A certain processor supports only the immediate and the direct addressing modes. Which of the following programing language features cannot be implemented on this processor ?*
(a) Pointers
(b) Arrays
(c) Records
(d) Recursive procedures with local variable

55. *In serial communication employing 8 data bits, a parity bit and 2 stop bits, the minimum band rate required to sustain a transfer rate of 300 characters per second is :*

(a) 2400 band (b) 19200 band
(c) 4800 band (d) 1200 band

56. ***What will be the total time required to read 35 sectors on a 2 sided floppy disk, Assume that each track has 8 sectors and the track to track step time in 8 milli seconds. The first sector to be read is sector 3 on track 10. The diskette spins at 300 rpm and initially, the head is on track 10.***

(a) 941 msec (b) 900 msec
(c) 700 msec (d) 25 msec

57. ***Relative mode of addressing is most relevant to writing :***

(a) Co routines (b) Position-independent code
(c) Shareable code (d) Interrupt handlers

58. ***A microprogram control unit is required to generate a total of 25 control signals assuming that during any micro instruction at most two control signals are active. Minimum no. of bits required in the control word to generate the required control signal will be :***

(a) 2 (b) 2.5
(c) 10 (d) 12

59. ***The correct matching for the following pairs is :***

(a) DMA I/O	(1) High speed RAM
(b) Cache	(2) Disk
(c) Interrupt I/O	(3) Printer
(d) Condition Code Register	(4) ALU

(a) a-4, b-3, c-1, d-2 (b) a-2, b-1, c-3, d-4
(c) a-4, b-3, c-2, d-1 (d) a-2, b-3, c-4, d-1

60. ***Locality of reference implies that the page reference being made by a process :***

(a) Will always be to the page used in the previous page reference
(b) Is likely to be to one of the pages used in the last few page reference
(c) Will always be to one of the pages existing in memory
(d) Will always lead to a page fault

61. ***I/O redirection :***

(a) Implies changing the name of file
(b) Can be employed to use an existing file as input file for a program
(c) Implies connection 2 programes through a pipe
(d) None of above

Answers : **49.*** (c) **50.** (a) **51.*** (b) **52.*** (a),(b),(c) **53.*** (a) **54.*** (a),(b),(c),(d) **55.*** (c)
56.* (a) **57.** (b) **58.** (c) **59.** (b) **60.** (b) **61.** (b) (b)

62. ***a microinstruction is to be designed to specify :***

(a) none or one of the three microoperations of one kind and

(b) none or upto six microperations of another kind.

The minimum member of bits in the micro-instruction is :

(a) 9 (b) 5

(c) 8 (d) None of above

63. ***If the over head formatting a disk is 96 bytes for 4000 byte sector, what will be the no. of tracks of the disk for the following parameters ?***

no. of surfaces = 8, outer diameter of the disk = 12cm

Inner diameter of the disk = 4 cm

Inner track space = 0.1 mm

no. of sectors per track = 20

(a) 800 (b) 80

(c) 160 (d) 1600

64. ***A computer system has a 4 K word cache organized in block-set-associative manner with 4 blocks per set, 64 words per block. The number of bits in the SET and WORD field of the main memory address format is :***

(a) 15,400 (b) 6, 4

(c) 7, 2 (d) 4, 6

65. ***The capacity of a memory unit is defined by number of words multiplied by the number of bits/word. How many separate address and data lines are needed for a memory of 4 K $\times$ 16 ?***

(a) 10 address, 16 data lines (b) 11 address, 8 data lines

(c) 12 address, 16 data lines (d) 12 address, 12 data lines

66. ***The sequence of events that happen during a typical fetch operation is :***

(a) PC $\rightarrow$ MAR $\rightarrow$ Memory $\rightarrow$ MBR $\rightarrow$ IR

(b) PC $\rightarrow$ Memory $\rightarrow$ MBR $\rightarrow$ IR

(c) PC $\rightarrow$ MBR $\rightarrow$ Memory

(d) PC $\rightarrow$ MAR $\rightarrow$ Memory $\rightarrow$ IR

67. ***Property of locality of reference may fail, if a program has :***

(a) many conditional jumps (b) many unconditional jumps

(c) many operands (d) none of above

68. ***A byte addressable computer has a memory capacity of 2^p K bytes***

and can perform 2^n operations. An instruction involving 3 operands and one operator needs a maximum of :

(a) 3p bits (b) 3p + n bits

(c) p+n bits (d) 3 (p + 10) + n

69. ***The addressing modes used in an instruction of the form ADD X, Y is :***

(a) Absolute (b) Immediate

(c) Indirect (d) Index

70. ***Bubble memories are preferable to floppy disks because :***

(a) Higher transfer rate (b) Cost needed to store a bit is less

(c) They consume less power (d) Of their reliability

71. ***If memory access takes 20 n sec with cache and 110 ns without it, then the hit ratio is (cache uses a 10 n sec memory)***

(a) 93% (b) 90%

(c) 87% (d) 88%

72. ***Any instruction should have atleast :***

(a) 2 operands (b) 1 operand

(c) 3 operands (d) No operands

73. ***If the cache needs an access time of 20 n sec and the main memory 120 n sec, then the average access time of a CPU is (assume hit-ratio is 80%)***

(a) 30 n sec (b) 40 n sec

(c) 35 n sec (d) 45 n sec

74. ***The most revelant addressing mode to write position independent code is :***

(a) Direct mode (b) Indirect mode

(c) Relative mode (d) Indexed mode

75. ***The advantage of a single bus over a multibus is the :***

(a) Low cost

(b) Flexibility in attaching peripheral devices

(c) High operating speed

(d) All of the above

76. ***A microprogrammed control unit :***

(a) Is faster than a hand-wired control unit

(b) Facilitates easy implementation of new instructions

Answers : **62.** (c) **63.*** (a) **64.*** (d) **65.*** (c) **66.*** (a) **67.** (a),(b),(c) **68.*** (d) **69.** (a) **70.** (c) **71.** (b) **72.*** (d) **73.*** (b) **74.** (c) **75.** (a), (b)

(c) Is useful when very small programs are to be run

(d) Usually refers to the control unit of a microprocessor

77. *Time required to process each segment for pipe line system having 4 sepments is 20 n sec. If 100 tasks in sequence calculate time required to process 100 tasks in nonpipeline system and pipeline system :*

(a) 8000 n sec, 2060 n sec (b) 8000 n sec, 2000 n sec

(c) 2060 n sec, 8000 n sec (d) None of above

78. *The most approprite matchine for the following pairs :*

X : indirect addressing (1) Loops

Y : Immediate addresing (2) Pointers

Z : Autodecrement addressing (3) Constants

(a) X – 3,Y – 2,Z – 1 (b) X – 1, Y – 3, Z – 2

(c) X – 2, Y – 3, Z – 1 (d) Z – 3, Y – 1, Z – 2

79. *Associative memory is :*

(a) Cheap memory (b) Pointer addressable memory

(c) Content addressable memory (d) Slow memory

80. *Type of searching used in associative memory is :*

(a) Parallel search (b) Sequential search

(c) Binary search (d) Selection search

81. *Which of the following is not a form of memory ?*

(a) Instruction cache (b) Instruction register

(c) Instruction opcode (d) Translation lookaside buffer

82. *In the absolute addressing mode :*

(a) The operand is inside the instruction

(b) The address of the operand is inside the instruction

(c) The register containing the address of the operand is specified inside the instruction

(d) The location of the operand is implicit

83. *The performance of a pipelined processor suffers if :*

(a) The pipeline stage have different delays

(b) Consecutive instructions are dependent on each other

(c) The pipeline stages share hardware resources

(d) All of the above

84. *Horizontal Microprogramming :*

(a) Does not require use of signal decoders

(b) Results in large sized microinstructions than vertical micro-programming
(c) Uses one bit for each control signal
(d) All of the above

85. ***More than one word are put in one cache block to :***
(a) Exploit the temporal locality of reference in a program
(b) Exploit the spatial locality of reference in a program
(c) Reduce the miss penalty
(d) None of above

86. ***Suppose a processor does not have any stack pointer register then which of the following statements is true ?***
(a) It cannot have subroutine call instruction
(b) It can have subroutine call instruction, but not nested subroutine calls
(c) Nested subroutine calls are possible, but interrupts are not
(d) All sequences of subroutine calls and also interrupts are possible

87. ***Which of the following requires a divice drivers***
(a) Register (b) Cache
(c) Main memory (d) Disk

88. ***Where does the swap space reside***
(a) RAM (b) Disk
(c) ROM (d) On-chip cache

89. ***Which of the most appropriate match for the items in the first column with the items in the second column ?***

X. Indiret Addressing	I. Array Implementation
Y. Indexed Addressing	II. Writing relocatable code
Z. Base Register Adderessing	III. Passing array as parameter.

(a) X – III, Y – I, Z – II (b) X – II, Y – III, Z – I
(c) X – III, Y – II, Z – I (d) X – I, Y – III Z – II

90. ***Consider a 5 stage piepline-IF (Instruction fetch), ID (Intructin decode) and register read), EX (Execute), MEM (memory), and WB (Write back). All (memeory or register) reads take place in the second phase of a clock cycle and write occur in the first phase of the clock cycle. Consider the execution of the following instruction sequence.***

I_1 sub r_2, r_3, r_4 ; $r_2 \leftarrow r_3 - r_4$
I_2 sub r_4, r_2, r_3 ; $r_4 \leftarrow r_2 - r_3$

Answers :							
	76. (b)	**77.*** (a)	**78.** (c)	**79.** (c)	**80.** (a)	**81.** (c)	**82.** (b)
	83. (d)	**84.** (b)	**85.** (a)	**86.** (a)	**87.** (d)	**88.** (a)	**89.** (a)

I_3 sub r_2 , 100 r_1 ; $M[r_1 + 100] \leftarrow r_2$

I_4 sub r_3 , r_4 , r_2 $r_3 \leftarrow r_4 - r_2$

Show all data dependencies between the four instructions.

(a) r_1 , r_2 , r_3 , r_4
(b) r_1 , r_2 , r_3
(c) r_1 , r_4
(d) r_3 , r_4

91. ***After erasing, the bits of EPROM will be :***

(a) All 0's
(b) All 1's
(c) I's and o's alternately
(d) All msbs are 1 and others are 0's

92. ***The normal mode of PROM is :***

(a) Real mode
(b) Erased mode
(c) Ready to store after erased operation
(d) High-impedence in output

93. ***Three state logic circuits are used to/as :***

(a) Store data in a buffer
(b) Interface more devices through a single bus
(c) A switch
(d) Interface fast and slow devices

94. ***The mark ROM is :***

(a) ROM
(b) PROM
(c) EPROM
(d) ROM is PLA design

95. ***The 2's complement representation of $(-539)_{10}$ in hexadecimal is :***

(a) ABE
(b) DBC
(c) DE5
(d) 9E7

96. ***Effecient use of addressing modes :***

(a) Speed up execution
(b) Reduces the no. of instructions
(c) Reduces the size of instructions
(d) None of the above

97. ***The correct sequence of time delays that happen during a data transfer from a disk to main memory is :***

(a) Seek time, latency time and transfer time

(b) Seek time, access time and transfer time
(c) Latency time, seek time and transfer time
(d) Latency time, access time and transfer time

98. ***When an attempt to divide by zero is made what interrupt is generated ?***
(a) Supervisor call interrupt (SVC) (b) Program interrupt
(b) I/o interrupt (d) Timer interrupt

99. ***The various types of ROM are ROM, PROM, EPROM, E^2PROM of these, bipolar ROM's are not possible with :***
(a) SRAM (b) SRAM, DRAM
(c) DRAM (d) PROM

100. ***Which of the following is large correct ?***
(a) PROM contains a programmable AND array and a fixed OR array
(b) PROM contains a fixed AND array and a programmable OR array
(c) PLA contains a programmable OR array and a programmable OR array
(d) PLA contains a fixed AND array and a programmable OR array

101. ***The logic circuitry in ALU is :***
(a) Entirely combinational (b) Entirely sequential
(c) Combinational cum sequential (d) None of above

102. ***The difference between PLA and ROM is :***
(a) No difference
(b) PLA is combinational CKT, ROM is sequential
(c) PLA minimise the number of minterms
(d) PLA has fixed AND array, ROM has fixed OR array

103. ***Disk and Drum are the :***
(a) Hardware part of the computer (b) Software part
(c) Firmware (d) None of the above

The following information pertains to Q. 104–105.

Consider the following assembly language program for a hypothetical processor. A, B and C are 8 bit registers. The meanings of various instructions are shown as comments.

```
     MOV B, # 0      ; B ←0
     MOV C, # 8      ; C ← 8
Z :  CMP C, # 0      ; compare c with 0
```

Answers : **90.** (a) **91.** (b) **92.** (a) **93.** (b) **94.*** (a) **95.*** (c) **96.** (a),(b),(c) **97.** (a) **98.** (b) **99.** (c) **100.** (b) **101.** (a) **102.** (a) **103.** (a)

```
        JZX          ; jump to X if zero flag is set
        SUB C, # 1   ; C ← C - 1
        RRC A, # 1   ; right rotate a through carry by one it. Thus :
                     ; if the initial values of A and the carry flag
                       are a7 ... a0 and
                     ; c0 respectively, their values after te executio
                       of this
                     ; instruction will be c0a7 ... a1 and a0 and
                       respectively.
        JCY          ; jump to Y is carry flag is et
        JMP Z        ; jump to Z
    Y : ADD B , # 1  ; B ← B + 1
        JMP Z        ; jump to Z
    X :
```

104. ***If the initial value of register A is A_0, the value of register B after the program execution will be***

(a) the number of 0 bits in A_0 (b) the number of 1 bits in A_0

(c) A_0 (d) S

105. ***Which of the following instruction when inserted at location X will ensure that the value of register A after program execution is the same as its initial value?***

(a) RRC A, #

(b) NOP ; no operation

(c) LRC A, # 1 ; left rotate A through carry flag by one bit

(d) ADD A, #1

Answers : **104.** (a) **105.** (a)

SOLUTIONS

16. Because it has inbuilt refreshing cut.

33. With K segment pipeline and time t_p is used to execute n tasks. The first task requires a time equals $= K\,t_p$ to compute its operation remaining $(n-1)$ tasks enters in the pipe at the rate of 1 task/cycle and completed after a time equal $= (n-1)\,t_p$

so to complete n task using K segment

pipeline requires $= K + (n-1)$ clock cycles.

34. To complete n tasks using K segments pipeline requires

$$= K + (n-1) = 4 + (6-1) = 9$$

36. If one CPU completes the operation before the other, the result will be original value. If one CPU has already fetched the value of x and is in the process of updating it and at this point of time the order CPU fetches the value of x (which will be same as the value fetched by the first CPU), the first CPU after manipulating it will store back the result in x. After this the second CPU will store its manipulated value, overwriting what is stored by the first CPU. So, the final value may be its original value + 1 if the first CPU decremented x, is original value – 1.

37. By single processor parallelism can be achieved by overlapping instruction fetch, decode, address calculation, operand fetch and execution of different instructions simultaneously.

42. In bubble memory presence of a bubble represent a 1 while the absence represent a 0 state.

49. Thread refers to the execution of different processes simultaneously in the CPU virtual address space is implemented in memory. The file-system is the way in which data in a disk is origined. A signal is acted upon using the mechanism of interrupts.

51. Since the cache has 2c blocks and there are 2 blocks per set, the cache thus has c sets so, block K of the main memory would map to block (k mod c) of the cache.

52. Address translation is required to give different address spaces to different processes and users DMA is required to any disk transfer.

Two modes of execution are required to prevent errant users from harming one another.

Demand paging is not really required for a multiuser multiprocessing operating system, though it would help in implementing the source.

53. RAID configurations provide redundancy of data stored in the disk and thus improve fault tolerance.

54. Because Pointer require indirect addressing mode.
Arays and records require indexing modes.

55. Total no. of bits = 8 data bit + 1 Parity + 2 stop bit = 11

Transfer rate = 300 × 11 = 3300 bps

56. Time to read one sector $\frac{60}{8 \times 300}$ = 25 milli seconds to read 35 sectors starting from track 10, sector 3 we have to read track 10, side 0, track 10, side 1, track 11, side 0, track 11, side 1, track 12, side 0 and the number of sectors read are 8, 8, 8, 8, 5.
And two track steps are required

$$\text{Time} = 25 \times (8 + 8 + 8 + 8 + 5) + 2 \times 8 = 25 \times (37) + 16$$
$$= 941 \text{ millis econds.}$$

63. $\text{No of tracks} = \frac{\text{Outer diameter of the disk} - \text{Inner diameter of the disk}}{\text{Inner track space}}$

$\text{No. of tracks} = \frac{12 - 4}{0.1} \times 10 = 800.$

64. $\text{No. of word blocks} = \frac{2^2 \times 2^{10}}{2^6} = 2^6$ No. of sets = 2^4.

65. For a given memory of 4 K × 16 means it has 4 K words and 16 bit per word.

$4 \text{ K words} = 4 \times 2^{10}$ words
$= 2^{12}$ words

Hence, it requires 12 bit address line and 16 bit data line.

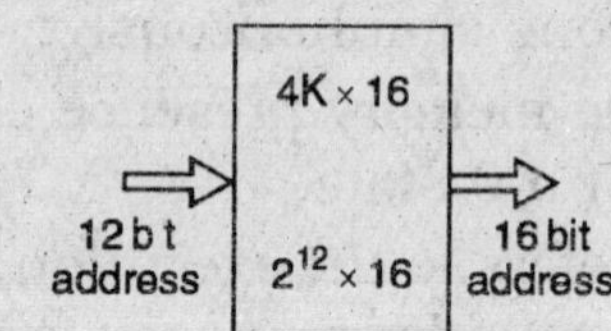

66. In fetch cycle (Instruction read from memory)
The PC contain an address of the next instruction to be fetched. This address is moved to the MAR and placed on address bus, and the result is placed on data bus and copied into the MBR and then moved to IR

MAR ← PC, MBR ← Memory IR ← MBR.

68. To specify a particular operation, out of the 2^n possible operation; one needs n bits. As the machine is byte addressable to specify a particular byte we need (p+10) bits (since $2^{(p+10)}$ bytes). So 3 addresses and 1 operation needs 3(p +10) + n bits.

71. Let p be hit ratio. then

$$20 = 10 \times p + (1 - p) \times 110$$

$$p = 90\%.$$

72. Operations on stack needed no operands address as only the top of stack can be accessed. Top of stack will be stored in a register, dedicated for this purpose.

73. Average access time = $(.8 \times 20) + (1 - .8) \times 120 = 40$ n sec.

77. For pipeline system, we know = $(K + (n - 1))\ t_p$

K = no. of segments,

n = no. of tasks.

t_p = time required to process each segment

$= (K + (n - 1))t_p = (4 + 99) \times 20 = 2060$ n sec

For non-pipeline system $t_n = Kt_p = 4 \times 20 = 80$ n sec.

$= n\ t_n = 100 \times 80 = 8000$ n sec.

94. The mask ROM is nothing but ROM.

95. ***539 = 1000011011***

– 539 = 101000011011

The leftmost digit standing for – ive sign

2's complementing of – 539 = 1101 1110 0101

D E 5

■□■

CHAPTER 3

OPERATING SYSTEM

1. ***A page fault :***
   (a) Is an error in a specific page
   (b) Occurs when a program accesses a page
   (c) Is an access to a page not currently in memory
   (d) Is a reference to a page belonging to another program
2. ***Scissoring enables :***
   (a) Entire data to be displaced
   (b) Full data display on full area of screen
   (c) No data to be displayed
   (d) A part of data to be displayed
3. ***Page stealing :***
   (a) It takes page frames from other working sets
   (b) To increase the capacity of main memory
   (c) To speed up main memory read operation
   (d) None of above
4. ***The term 'polling' is a computer system means a process by which a computer system :***
   (a) Detect/correct error
   (b) Multiplexes the inputs and updates the memory accordingly
   (c) Decides correct alternative by analysing several ones
   (d) Inquires to sec if a terminal has any transaction to send
5. ***When a computer is started, a special type of absolute Leader is executed called a :***
   (a) "Complite and go" loader (b) Boot loader
   (c) Bootstrap loader (d) Relating loader
6. ***Dijkstra's banker's algorithm is used for :***
   (a) Deadlock recovery (b) Deadlock avoidance
   (c) Mutual exclusion (d) Page fault
7. ***Operating system is :***
   (a) Collection of H/w components

(b) A collection of I/o devices
(c) A collection of software routines
(d) All of above

8. *The purpose of operating system is to :*
(a) Make computer easier to use
(b) Make most effecient use of hardware
(c) Provides a layered, user friendly interface
(d) None of above

9. *A linker :*
(a) Creates a load module
(b) Is not necessary with variable partitions
(c) Must be run after the loader
(d) Is not needed with a compiler

10. *Pass 1*
(a) Assign address to all statements in the program
(b) Save the values assigned to all labels for use in Pass 2
(c) Assemble instruction and generate data
(d) Write object program

11. *The disadvantage of "compile and go" loading scheme is/are :*
(a) A portion of memory is wasted because the core occupied by the assembler is unavailable to the object program
(b) It is necessary to retranslate the user's program deck every time it is run
(c) Requires less memory
(d) Inbuilt assembler

12. *Different phases of compiler :*
(a) Syntex analysis (b) Intermediate code generation
(c) Code generator (d) Page stealing

13. *The machine dependent operating system features :*
(a) Interrupt processing (b) File processing
(c) Process Scheduling (d) Job scheduling

14. *A compiler for a high level language that runs on one machine and produces code for a different m/c is called :*
(a) One pass compiler (b) Interpreter
(c) Cross compiler (d) None of above

Answers : **1.** (c) **2.** (d) **3.** (a) **4.** (d) **5.** (c) **6.** (a) **7.** (c)
8. (a),(b),(c) **9.** (a) **10.*** (a),(b) **11.*** (a),(b),(c) **12.** (a),(b),(c) **13.*** (a),(c) **14.** (c)

15. *Producer consumer problem can be solved using :*

(a) Semaphores (b) Moniters

(c) SCAN (d) LIFO

16. *Software that measures, monitors, analyzes and control real world events is called :*

(a) System software (b) Real time s/w

(c) Embedded software (d) Business software

17. *Transfer vector approach of linking can be access by :*

(a) External data segments

(b) External subroutines

(c) Data located in other procedures

(d) All of above

18. *Trojan-Horse programs :*

(a) Are legitimate programs that allow unauthorized access

(b) M/c languge program

(c) Are hidden programs that do not show up to the system

(d) Deadlocke avoidance program

`19. *Dispatcher is a module :*

(a) Transfer control of a processer to a process

(b) Puts tasks in I/o wait

(c) Is always small and simple

(d) Never change task priorities

20. *Virtual memory :*

(a) Simple to implement

(b) Hardware device

(c) Secondary memory allocated for swapping

(d) Main memory

21. *Which of the following is/are language processer ?*

(a) Assembler (b) Compiler

(c) Linker (d) Loader

22. *The production of object code to generate absolute machine code and load it into the physical main storage location from which it will be executed immediately upon completion of the assembly?*

(a) Two pass assembly (b) Load-and-go assembler

(c) Compiler (d) Macroprocessor

23. *Temporal locality refers to the problem that once a location is referenced :*

(a) It will not be referenced again

(b) It will be referenced again

(c) A nearby location will be referenced soon

(d) None of above

24. *Concurrent process are :*

(a) Processes that do not overlap in time

(b) Process that overlap in time

(c) Processes that are executed by the processer at the same time

(d) None of above

25. *The page replacement policy that leads to more page faults when the size of the memory is increased is :*

(a) Optimal algorithm (b) LRU Algorithm

(c) LRU approximation Algorithm (d) FIFO

26. *The only state transition that is initiated by the user process itself is :*

(a) Ready (b) Waiting

(c) Block (d) Running

27. *MSDOS support multiprogramming to some extent :*

(a) True (b) False

(c) Can't say (d) None of above

28. *A particular time, the value of a counting semaphore is 10. It will become 5 after :*

(a) 5V operations

(b) 5P operations

(c) 5V operations and 7P operations

(d) 4V operations and 9P operations

29. *At any instant the value of a counting semaphore is 10. Then 20p operations and 'x' V operations were completed on this semaphore. If the final value of the semaphore is 2 :*

(a) 10 (b) 11

(c) 12 (d) 13

30. *For memory protection which of the following regiesters are used :*

(a) Relocatable register (b) Fence register

Answers : **15.** (a),(b) **16.** (b) **17.** (b) **18.** (a) **19.** (a) **20.** (c) **21.** (a),(b) **22.** (b) **23.** (b) **24.** (b) **25.** (d) **26.** (c) **27.** (a) **28.** (b),(d) **29.** (c)

(c) Absolute register (d) Limit register

31. *Which of the following is/are true ?*

(a) Deadlock state is unsafe

(b) Unsafe state may lead to a deadlock state

(c) Unsafe state must lead to a deadlock situation

(d) Deadlock state is a subset of unsafe state

32. *Size of virtual memory depends upon :*

(a) Data bus (b) Address bus

(c) Size of main memory (d) Memory buffer register

33. *Cascading termination refers to :*

(a) termination of all child process before parent terminates normally

(b) termination of all child process before parent terminates abnormally

(c) termination of all child process before parent terminates normally or abnormally

(d) None of above

34. *6 tape drives with 'n' processes. Each process need 3 tape drive. Maximum number of n so that no deadlock occur :*

(a) 1 (b) 2

(c) 3 (d) 6

35. *Which of the following algorithm suffers from Belady's anomly ?*

(a) FIFO (b) LIFO

(c) Optimal Algo (d) None of above

36. *System having 'm' resources which are shared by 3 process x, y, z which have peak time demands of 3, 4, 6 respectively. The minimum value of 'm' that ensures that deadlock will never occur :*

(a) 13 (b) 9

(c) 10 (d) 11

37. *The main advantage of interrupt concept is elemination of :*

(a) Spooling (b) Polling

(c) Interrupt handling (d) Part of interrupt serviceing

38. *Parachor curve is a :*

(a) Curve between no. of page interrupts and physical memory available

(b) Curve between page interrupts and no. of pages

(c) Curve between CPU speed and physical memory available

(d) None of above

39. *Which of the following is used for job scheduling ?*

(a) Short term scheduling (b) Longterm scheduling
(c) Medium term scheduling (d) Dispatcher

40. ***A head of moving hard disk with 100 track numbered 0 to 99 is currently serving request to track 55. If the queue of request kept in FIFO order is***

10, 70, 75, 23, 65

Which of the following algorithms will require less head movement?

(a) FIFO (First in First out)
(b) SSTF (Shortest Seek Time first)
(c) Can't say
(d) Both of above are equal

41. ***Convoy effect :***

(a) All process waiting for the long process to complete
(b) All process waiting for the small process to complete
(c) Process is not present in main memory
(d) None of above

42. ***Aging is a technique :***

(a) Used to increase the priority of processes that are waiting for long time.
(b) Used to decrease the priority of processes that are waiting for long time
(c) Used to increase the priority of processes that are currently running
(d) used to decrease the priority of processes that are currently running

43. ***A system with a 32 bit logical address space and page size is of 4K bytes. Then a page table may consists of :***

(a) 2^{20} entries (b) 2^{32} entries
(c) 2^{12} entries (d) None of above

44. ***Following are the example of :***

A →
B → A B C
C → ⟶⟶⟶

(a) Multiprocessing and multiproframming
(b) Multiprogramming and multiprocessing
(c) Uniprogramming and multiprocessing
(d) Uniprogramming and multiprocessing

Answers : **30.** (b) **31.** (a),(b),(d) **32.** (b) **33.** (c) **34.** (b) **35.** (a) **36.** (d) **37.** (v) **38.** (a) **39.** (b) **40.** (b) **41.** (a) **42.** (a) **43.** (a) **44.** (a)

45. ***If a hit ratio is 95% and 20 n sec required to search associative registers and 100 nano sec to search the main memory then effective memory access time will be :***

(a) 140 n sec (b) 125 n sec
(c) 25 n sec (d) 122 n sec

46. ***Consider a system having four process and its arrival times are :***

Pricees	*Arrival time*	*Priority*	*CPU Time*
P1	*0.00*	*2*	*3*
P2	*1.00*	*1*	*4*
P3	*0.22*	*1*	*8*
P4	*0.48*	*3*	*12*

What will be the average turnaround time for these processes with the SJF (preemptive scheduting algorithm) ?

(a) 11.575 (b) 12.575
(c) 13 (d) None of above

47. ***For the above processes find the average turnaround time using priority preemptive scheduling algorithum :***

(a) 15.37 (b) 14.37
(c) 13.00 (d) None of above

48. ***Consider a system in which each processes runs for a average time T. A process switching requires a time S, which is effectively waisted. Find the condition for RR scheduling with time quantum Q. So that no process is executed :***

(a) Q = infinite (b) Q > T
(c) Q = S (d) Q ≃ O

49. ***In the following system :***

Processes	*Allocation*	*Maximum*	*Available*
	ABC	*ABC*	*ABC*
P0	*012*	*012*	*152*
P1	*000*	*750*	
P2	*354*	*356*	
P3	*632*	*652*	

If the request from processes P2 is for (0, 2, 2) can the requested granted?

(a) Yes
(b) No
(c) Can't say

(d) Initally system is not in safe state

50. ***For the memory partitions of 100 K, 500 K, 200 K, 300 K and 600 K which of the following algorithm places the processes 210 K, 410 K, 110 K and 420 K effeciently ?***

(a) First fit
(b) Best fit
(c) Worst fit
(d) None of above

51. ***In Bit vector algorithm for free space management the free space bit map for free disk blocks of 1, 2, 3, 7, 9 would be :***

(a) 0111000101
(b) 1000111010
(c) 1111000101
(d) 0000111010

52. ***Consider a memory in which blank regions are free space. The sequence of requests for blocks of size 300, 25, 125, 50 can be satisfied if we use :***

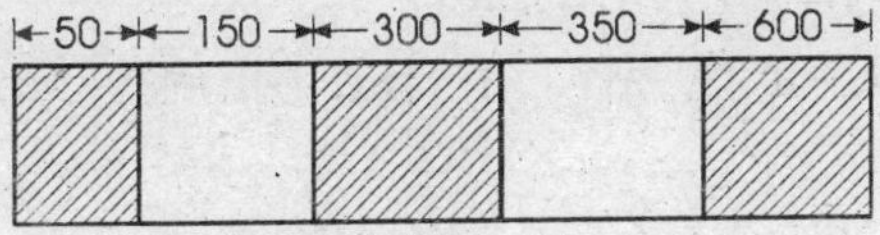

|←50→|←150→|←300→|←350→|←600→|

(a) Either first fit or best fit policy (any one)
(b) First fit but not best fit policy
(c) Best fit but not first fit
(d) None of above

53. ***Listed below are some operating system abstractions and the hardware components or matching of pairs is correct?***

(a) Thread — 1. Interrupt
(b) Virtual address space — 2. Memory
(c) File system — 3. CPU
(d) Signal — 4. Disk

(a) a-2, b-4, c-3, d-1
(b) a-1, b-2, c-3, d-4
(c) a-3, b-2, c-4, d-1
(d) a-4, b-1, c-2, d-3

54. ***Which of the following disk scheduling strategies is likely to give the best throughput ?***

(a) Farthest cylinder next
(b) Nearest cylinder next
(c) FCFS
(d) Elevator algorithm

55. ***Which of the following statements is true ?***

(a) Macro definations cannot appear within other macro definations in assembly language programs

Answers :					
	45.* (b)	**46.*** (b)	**47.*** (a)	**48.** (c),(d)	**49.*** (a)
	50.* (b)	**51.** (a)	**52.*** (b)	**53.** (c)	**54.** (a)

(b) Overlay is used to run a program which is longer than the address space of a computer
(c) Virtual memory address can be used to accommodate a program which is longer than the address space of a computer
(d) It is not possible to write interrupt service routines in a higher level language

56. ***The problem of Fragmentation arises in :***
(a) Static storage allocation
(b) Stack allocation of storage
(c) Stack allocation with dynamic binding
(d) Heap allocation

57. ***Memory refreshing may be done :***
(a) By the CPU, which contains a special refresh counter
(b) By an external refresh controller
(c) Either by the CPU or by an external refresh controller
(d) None of the above

58. ***The process of organizing the memory into two banks to allow both 8 and 16 bit data operations is called :***
(a) Bank switiching (b) Two-way memory interleaving
(c) Indexed mapping (d) None of above

59. ***Allocation of space for a file in a disk is :***
(a) Pre-allocated
(b) Done as one cluster at a time
(c) Done as a pair of cluster at a time
(d) Done as a sectors at a time

60. ***Race round condition occurs when :***
(a) Two processes unknowingly wait for resources that are held by each other
(b) Two process wait for the same resources
(c) All resources are shared
(d) Two processes share the same shared resource

61. ***BIOS = Basic input/output system and IOCS = Input/output Control System. Which one of the following is true :***
(a) BIOS and IOCS are same
(b) BIOS controls all devices and IOCS controls only certain devices
(c) BIOS is not a part of operating system and IOCS is a part of operating system

(d) BIOS is stored in ROM and IOCS is stored in RAM

62. *Which one of the following is more responsible for loading operating system from FD/HD into RAM?*

(a) Power on self text (POST) (b) Boot strap loader (BSL)
(c) Boot record (d) CPU

63. *DOS maintains :*

(a) One stack (b) Two stacks
(c) Three stacks (d) Four stacks

64. *The DOS area was the following sections :*

(a) Boot record, root directory, DTA
(b) Partition table, boot record, 2 copies of FAT, root directory data area
(c) Boot record, root directory, MDB, DDD, FAT
(d) Root directory, PSP, boot record, FAT, environment area

65. *Which of the following statements is false ?*

(a) Virtual memory implements the translation of a program's address space into physical address space
(b) Virtual memory allows each program to exceed the size of the primary memory
(c) Virtual memory increases the degree of multiprogramming
(d) Virtual memory reduces the context switching overhead

66. *A processer needs software interrupt to :*

(a) Test the interrupt system of the processor
(b) Implement co-routines
(c) Obtain system services which need execution of privileged instructions
(d) Return from subroutine.

67. *A CPU has two modes privileged and non-privileged. In order to change the mode from privileged to non-privileged :*

(a) A hardware interrupt is needed
(b) A software interrupt is needed
(c) A privileged instruction (which does not generate an interrupt) is needed
(d) A non-privileged instruction (which does not generate an interrupt) is needed

68. *Consider a set of n tasks with known runtimes $r_1, r_2 ...... r_n$ to be run*

Answers : **55.*** (b) **56.** (d) **57.** (c) **58.** (b) **59.** (b) **60.** (b) **61.** (a)
62. (d) **63.** (c) **64.** (b) **65.** (c) **66.** (c) **67.** (d)

on a uniprocessor machine. Which of the following processor scheduling algorithms will result in the maximum throughput ?

(a) Round Robin (b) Shortest Job-first

(c) Highest-Response-Ratio-Next (d) First-Come-First-Served

69. ***Consider a virtual memory system with FIFO page replacement policy. For an arbitrary page access pattern, increasing the number of page frames in main memory will :***

(a) Always decrease the number of page faults

(b) Always increase the number of page faults

(c) Sometimes increase the number of page faults

(d) Never effect the number of page faults.

70. ***Which of the following does not interrupt a running process ?***

(a) A device (b) Timer

(c) Schedular process (d) Power failure

71. ***Consider a mechine with 64 MB physical memory and a 32-bit virtual address space. If the page size is 4 KB, what is the approximate size of the page table ?***

(a) 16 MB (b) 8 MB

(c) 2 MB (d) 24 MB

72. ***The optimal page replacement algorithm will select the page fault that :***

(a) Has not been used for the longest time in the past

(b) Will not be used for the longest time in the future

(c) Has been used least number of times

(d) Has been used most number of times

73. ***To evaluate an expression without any embedded function calls :***

(a) One stack is enough

(b) Two stack are needed

(c) As many stacks as the height of the expression are needed

(d) A turing machine is needed in the general case

74. ***Which combination of the following features will suffice to characterize an OS as a multiprogrammed OS ? (a) more than one pragram may be loaded into main memory at the same time for execution. (b) If a program waits for certain events such as I/o, another program is immediately scheduled for execution (c) If the execution of a program terminates, another program is immediately scheduled for exccution :***

(a) a (b) a and b
(c) a and c (d) a, b and c

75. ***In the index allocation scheme of blocks to a file, the maximum possible size of the file depends on :***

(a) The size of the blocks, and the size of the address of the blocks
(b) The number of blocks used for the index and the size of the blocks
(c) the size of the blocks, the number of blocks used for the index, and the size of the address of the blocks
(d) None of the above

76. ***The process table transition diagram represents :***

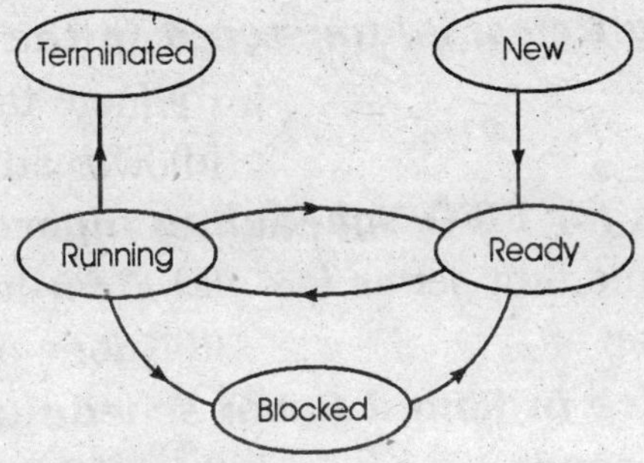

(a) A batch operating system
(b) An operating system with a preemptive schedular
(c) An operating system with a non-preemtive schedular
(d) A uniprogrammed operating system

77. ***The root directory of a diok should be placed :***

(a) At a fixed address in main memory
(b) At a fixed location on the disk
(c) Anywhere on the disk
(d) At a fixed location on the system disk

78. ***Writing a software in assembly language is prefered to writing in a high level language when :***

(a) Memory space is limited
(b) Optimal use of hardware resources
(c) Programmer's productivity is important
(d) Portablity is important

79. ***The machine independent operating system features :***

Answers : **68.** (a) **69.*** (c) **70.*** (b) **71.** (a) **72.** (b) **73.** (a) **74.** (d) **75.** (c) **76.** (b) **77.** (b) **78.** (a), (b)

(a) I/O supervision (b) File processing
(c) Management of real memory (d) Job scheduling

80. ***Two uses of semaphores is/are :***
(a) Mutual exclusion
(b) Scheduling constaints
(c) Producer-consumer with a bounded buffer
(d) none of above

81. ***Semaphores are like integers, except :***
(a) No negative values (b) Only operations are P and V
(c) Operations must be atomic (d) none of above

82. ***Of the following items, is/are stored in the thread control block :***
(a) CPU registers (b) Page table pointer
(c) Stack pointer (d) Thread priority

83. ***Different names for FIFO Scheduling algorithm is/are :***
(a) FCFS–first come first serve (b) FIFO–first in first out
(c) Run until done (d)Nnone of above

84. ***Typical time slice in Round Robin scheduling is between ?***
(a) 10-100 milliseconds (b) 1-10 milliseconds
(c) 10-100 microseconds (d) 10-10 microseconds

85. ***System calls are usually invoked by using***
(a) A software interrupt (b) Polling
(c) An indirect jump (d) A priviliged instruction

86. ***A uni-processor computer system only hastwo processes, both of which alternate 10ms CPU burstswith 90ms I/O burstts. Both he processes werecreated at nearly the same time. The I/O of both processes can proceed in parallel. Which of the following scheduling strategies will result in the least CPU utilization (over a long period oftime) for his system?***
(a) First come first served scheduling
(b) Shortest remaining time first scheduling
(c) Static priority scheduling with differenttpriorities for the two processes
(d) Round robin scheduling with a time quantum of 5 ms.

87. ***Assuming hat no page faults occur, the average time taken to access avirtual address is approximately (to he nearest 0, 5 ns)***
(a) 1.5 ns (b) 2 ns
(c) 3 ns (d) 4 ns

88. ***Suppose a processhas only the following pages in its virtual address space : two contiguous code pagesstarting at virtual address 0 × 00000000, two coniguous data pages sharting at virual address 0 × 00400000, and a stac page starting at virtual address 0 × FFFFF000. The amount of memory required for storing the page tables of this process is***

(a) 8 KB (b) 12 KB

(c) 16 KB (d) 20 KB

The Following Information to Q. 89-90

Suppose we want to synchronise wo cuncurrent process P and Q using binary semaphores S and T. The code for the procesess P and Qis shown below :***

Synchronization satements can be insered only at points W, X, Y and Z

89. ***Which of the following will always lead to an output starting with '001100110011'?***

(a) P(S) at W, V(S) at X, P(T) at Y, V(T) at Z, S and T unitially 1

(b) P(S) at W, V(T) at X, P(T) at Y, V(S) at Z, S initially 1, and T intially 0

(c) P(S) at W, V(T) at X, P(T) at Y, V(S) at Z, S and T initially 1

(d) P(S) at W, V(S) at X, P(T) at Y, V(T) at Z, S initially 1, and T inittially 0

90. ***Which of the following will ensure that the output string never contains a substring of the form 0.1"0 or 10"1 where n is odd?***

(a) P(S) at W, V(S) at X, P(T) at Y, V(T) at Z, S and TT initially 1

(b) P(S) at W, V(T) at X, P(T) at Y, V(S) at Z, S and T initially 1

(c) P(S) at W, V(T) at X, P(T) at Y, V(S) at Z, S initially 1

(d) P(S) at W, V(S) at X, P(T) at Y, V(T) at Z, S and TT initially 1

91. ***Using a larger block size in a fixed block size file system leads to***

(a) better disk throughput but pooer disk space utilization

(b) better disk throughput and better disk space utilization

(c) poorer disk throughput but better disk space utilizaiton

(d) poorer disk throughput and poorer disk space utilization

92. ***In a system with 32 bit virtual addresses and 1 KB page size, useofone-level page tables for virtual to physical address translation is not practtical because of***

Answers : **79.** (d) **80.*** (a),(b),(c) **81.*** (a),(b),(c) **82.** (a),(c),(d) **83.*** (a),(b),(c) **84.*** (b) **85.** (a) **86.** (a) **87.*** (b) **88.** (b) **89.** (a) **90.** (c) **91.*** (d)

(a) the large amount of internal fragmentation
(b) the large amount of external framgentation
(c) the large memory overhead in maintaining pagetables
(d) the large computaion overhead in the translation process

Answers : **92.*** (c)

SOLUTIONS

10. Phase I is an analysis phase in this it analyise all instructions and generate relative address, data and instructions.

11. It has an inbuilt assembler which is placed in memory and executed with source program as input. Assembler places the object code file in another part of the memory and works as a loader and transfers the control of execution to the begaining of object code.

13. Different phases of compiler are

Lexical analysis (scanning)

Sybtax analysis

Sementic analysis

Intermediate code generation

Code optimization

Code generator.

15. In bit map or bit vector algorithm each block is represented by 1 bit. If the block is free the bit is 1, if the block is allocated the bit is zero.

19. Dispatcher is the module that gives control of the *CPU* to a process selected by the short term schedular.

23. Locality of reference states that if the page is referenced it is likely to be referenced again soon. Temporal locality of reference states that once a location, data or instruction is referenced it is often referenced very soon. Ex.—loops

Spatial locality of reference states that once the location is referenced a nearly location will be referenced very soon.

Ex. → Sequential instruction.

25. Belady's anomaly states the fact that, for some page replacement algorithms, the page fault rate may increase as the memory size increases. If consider a reference string

4, 3, 2, 1, 4, 3, 5, 4, 3, 2, 1, 5

When the no. of frames are 3 then the no. of page faults are 9 and if we increase the size of memory to 4 then the no. of page faults also increases.

27. Example of multiprogramming in *MSDOs* is print utility and *TSR* programs.

28. *P* operation decreases the semaphore value by 1. Similarly each V operation increases the semaphore value by 1.

34. 2 process never lead to deadlock because the peak time demand of 3 tape drives by each process can be satisfied by 6 (3 + 3) tape drives available.

36. 11 resources ensures that atleast 1 process will have no pending reguest alloting

	A B C		A B C
fullfilling demand	3 4 6	OR	2 3 5
	= 11		= 11

11 resources moves lead to a dead lock.

40. **Case I** FIFO in this the track moves from the current track 55 to

$$55 \rightarrow 10 \rightarrow 70 \rightarrow 75 \rightarrow 23 \rightarrow 65$$

Hence, the no. of tracks the head moved

$$= (55 - 10) + (70 - 10) + (75 - 70) + (75 - 23) + (65 - 23)$$
$$= 45 + 60 + 5 + 52 + 42$$
$$= 204$$

In case of *SSTF* the head moves from

$$55 \rightarrow 65 \rightarrow 70 \rightarrow 75 \rightarrow 23 \rightarrow 10$$

Hence, the number of tracks the head moves

$$= (65 - 55) + (70 - 65) + (75 - 70) + (75 - 23) + (23 - 10)$$
$$= 85$$

Hence, *SSTF* is better than *FIFO*.

43. Since the page size of 4*k* bytes which is 2^{12} so the page table entry are of

$$2^{32}/2^{12} = 2^{20}.$$

45. If the page is present in associative registers then 20 nsec to search the associative registers and 100 nsec to access memory so the total of 120 nsec required, if the page is not present in associative registers then we must access the page table from main memory required 100 nsec then other 120 nsec required to access the page so the total 220 nsec required effective memory access time

$$= .95 \times 120 + .05 \times 220$$
$$= 125 \text{ nsec.}$$

46.

P_1	P_2	P_3	P_4

0 3 7 15 27

Turn around time is the waiting time + execution time, so for process

$P_1 = 0 + 3 = 3$

$P_2 = (3 - 1) + 4 = 6$

$P_3 = (7 - .22) + 8 = 14.78$

$P_4 = (15 - .48) + 12 = 14.52 + 12 = 26.52$

$= \frac{3 + 6 + 14.78 + 26.52}{4}$

$= \frac{50.30}{4} = 12.575$

47.

P_1	P_3	P_1	P_4

0 .22 8.22 12.22 15 27

Using preemptive priority schedulig initialy the processes $p1$ is present so $p1$ is executed for .22 unit after that a p_2 of high priority is entered in ready queue so the processes. $p1$ is preempted and $p3$ is get assigned to CPU for execution. Similarly after completion of process $P3$ another processes $P2$ is assigned.

So turnaround time of $P1 = (12.22 - .22) + .22 + 2.78 = 15$

$P_2 = (8.22 - 1.00) + 4 = 11.22$

$P_3 = 0 + 8 = 8$

$P_4 = (15 - .48) + 12 = 26.52$

$= \frac{26.52 + 15 + 11.22 + 8}{4}$

$= \frac{60.74}{4} = 15.37$

49. Initially the system is in the safe state for the safe sequence of $\langle P_0, P_2, P_3, P_1 \rangle$ so on granting the reguest of (0, 2, 2) to process P_2 the safe sequence can be generated $\langle P_0, P_3, P_2, P_1 \rangle$.

50. Let $P_1 = 210$ K, $P_2 = 410$ K, $P_3 = 110$ K and $P_4 = 420$K

For frist fit algo

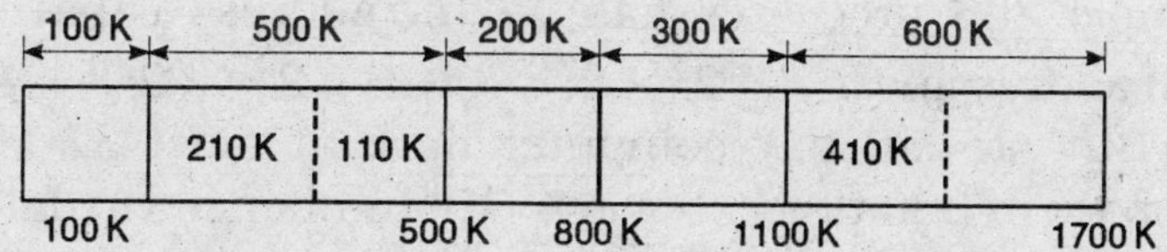

In this case there is no space left for the processes of 420 K, therefore so the first fit algo can't places all processes into memory.

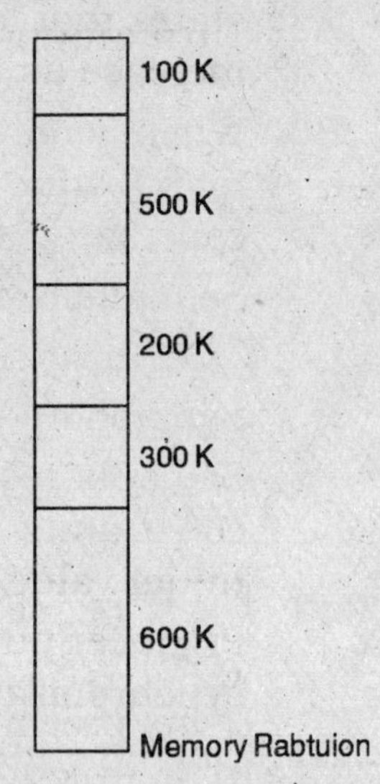

Memory Rabtuion

Using Best fit algo

So by using best fit algorithm we can allocate all processes into memory

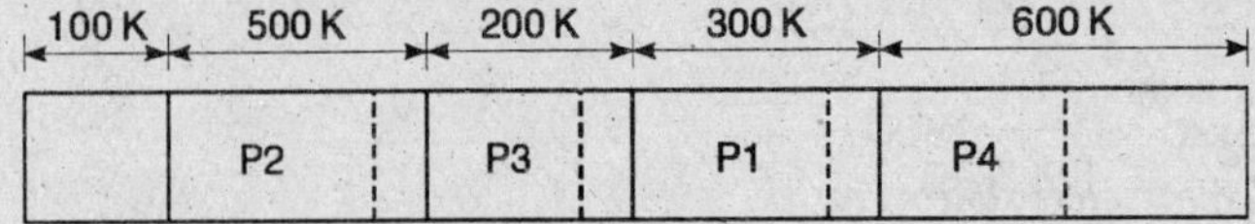

Using Worst fit algo

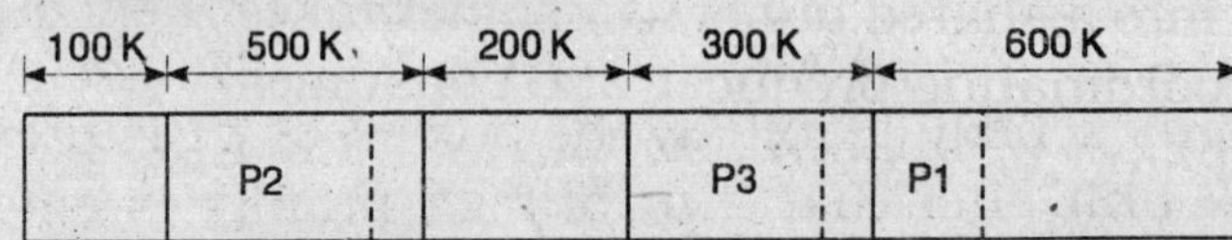

So by using worst fit algrithem all processes cannot be alocated into memory.

At any instant the value of semaphore is 10, it will become 5 after 5P operations (each p operation decreases the value by 1, similarly 4V operations and 9P operations make the value 5.

52.

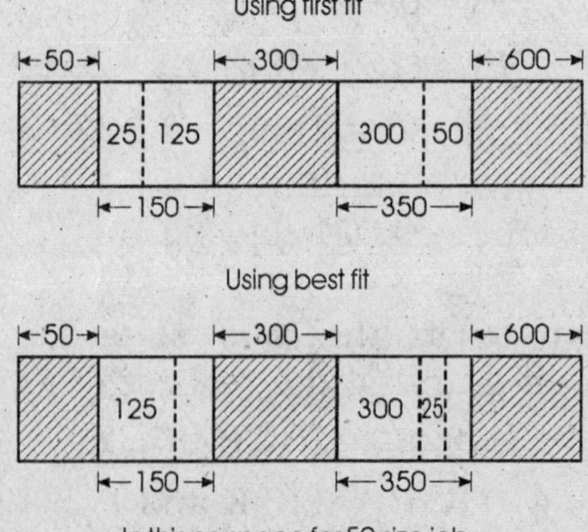

In this no space for 50 size job.

55. For Example 386 processer has 32 bit address capacity. Hence its is capable of addressing $2^{32} = 2^2 \times 2^{30}$ = 4GB = $2^{12} \times 2^{20}$ = 4096 MB of main memory. But present day computer have at most 32 MB of RAM. The address space of 386 processer is 4 GB and hence virtual memory can be at most 4 GB. If the program is of 6 GB, we have to use only overlay technique.

69. FIFO page replacement algorithm suffers from Belady's anomaly. Which states that for some page replacement algorithms, the page fault rate may increase as the number of allocated frames increases.

80. When semaphores are used for mutual exclusion, the semaphore has an initial value of 1, and P( ) is called before the critical section, and V( ) is called after the critical section.

```
Semaphore->P( );
 //critical section goes here
Semaphore->V( );
```

Semaphores can also be used to express generalized scheduling constraints–semaphores provide a way for a thread to wait for something. Initial value of the semaphore is 0.

Producer puts things into a shared buffer, consumer takes them out. Need synchronization for coordinating producer and consumer.

81. Only operations are P and V - can't read or write value, except to see it initially.

Operations must be atomic - two P's that occur together can't decrement the value below zero. Similarly, thread going to sleep in P won't miss wakeup from V, even if they both happen at about the same time.

83. FIFO meant, one program kept CPU until it completely finished.

FIFO pros & cons :

+ simple

–short jobs get stuck behind long jobs

84. If time slice is too big Response time suffers

If time slice is too small than throughput suffers. Spend all your time context switching, none getting real work done.

87. hit ratio (TLB) = 96%

t - access time (TLB) = 1 nsec

hit ratio (virtual page) = 90%

T = M. memory access time = 10 nsec

Average access time

$$= \text{hit ratio} \times \text{TLB access time} + (1 - \text{hit ratio}) \times T$$

$$= 0.9 \times 1 + 0.1 \times 10 = 1.9 \text{ nsec} \simeq 2\text{n sec.}$$

91. In case of large block size and fixed block size file system, CPU utlization is poorer and thoughput is also decreased.

92. Number of pages $= \frac{2^{32}}{2^{12}} = 2^{20}$.

■□■

CHAPTER 4

DATA STRUCTURE

1. ***Which one of the following permutations can be obtained in the output using a stack assuming that the input is the sequence 1, 2, 3, 4, 5 in that order?***

(a) 3, 4, 5, 1, 2 (b) 3, 4, 5, 2, 1

(c) 1, 5, 2, 3, 4 (d) 5, 4, 3, 1, 2

2. ***The no. of substring, (or all lengths) that can be formed from a character string of length n is :***

(a) n (b) n^2

(c) $\frac{n(n-1)}{2}$ (d) $\frac{n(n+1)}{2}$

3. ***Linked lists are not suitable data structures of which one of the following problems ?***

(a) Insertion sort (b) Binary search

(c) Radix sort (d) Polynomial manipulation

4. ***Which of the following algorithm design techniques is used in the quicksort algorithm?***

(a) Dyanamic programming (b) Backtracking

(c) Divide and conquer (d) Greedy method

5. ***Which one of the following statements is false ?***

(a) Optimal binary search tree construction can be performed efficiently usign dynamic programming

(b) Breath first search cannot be used to find converted components of a graph

(c) Given the prefix and postfix walks over a binary tree. The binary tree cannot be uniquely constructed.

(d) Depth-first search can be used to find connected components of a graph.

6. ***Merge sort uses :***

(a) Divide and conquer strategy (b) Backtracking approach

(c) Heuristic search (d) Greedy approach

7. *For merging two sorted lists of sizes m and n into a sorted list of size m + n, we require comparisons of :*

(a) $O(m)$ (b) $O(n)$

(c) $O(m+n)$ (d) $O(\log m + \log n)$

8. *A binary tree T has 'n' leaf nodes. The number of degree 2 in T is :*

(a) $\log_2 n$ (b) $n-1$

(c) n (d) 2^n

9. *The minimum number of edges in a connected cyclic graph on n vertices is :*

(a) $n-1$ (b) n

(c) $n+1$ (d) None of above

10. *The postfix expression for the infix expression* $\dfrac{A+B*(C+D)}{F+D*E}$ ***is :***

(a) $AB + CD + * F/D + E*$ (b) $ABCD + *F/DE* + +$

(c) $A * B + CD/F * DE ++$ (d) $A + * BCD/F * DE ++$

11. *Which of the following statements is true ?*

I. As the number of entries in a hash table increases, the number of collosions increases

II. Recursive programs are effecient

III. The worst case complexity for quicksort is $O(n^2)$

IV. Binary search using a linear linked list is effecient

(a) I and II (b) II and III

(c) I and IV (d) I and III

12. *What is the number of binary trees with three nodes which when traversed in postorder give the sequence A, B, C ?*

(a) 3 (b) 4

(c) 5 (d) 6

Solution : In post order sequence → Left right root

13. *How many minimum spanning trees does the following graph has ?*

(a) 1

(b) 2

(c) 3

(d) 11

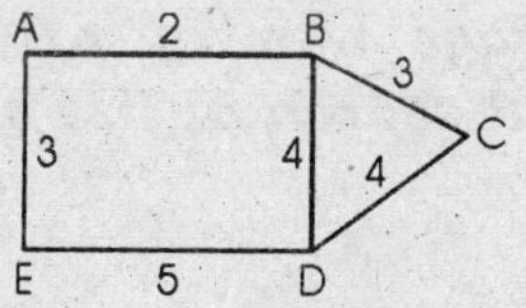

14. *Consider the following statements*

Answers : **1.*** (b) **2.*** (d) **3.*** (b) **4.** (c) **5.** (a) **6.** (a) **7.** (c) **8.** (b) **9.*** (b) **10.** (b) **11.** (d) **12.*** (d) **13.*** (b)

I. FIFO types of computation are efficienctly supported by stacks

II. Implementing LISTS on liked lists is more effecient than implementing LISTS on an array for almost all the basic LIST operation

III. Implementing QUEUES on a circular array is more effecient than implementing QUEUES on a linear array with two indices.

IV. LIFO type of computations are effeciently supported by QUEUES.

(a) II and III are true

(b) I and II are true

(c) III and IV are true

(d) II and IV are true

15. ***In the balanced binary tree given below which of the following sequences denotes the post order traversal sequence ?***

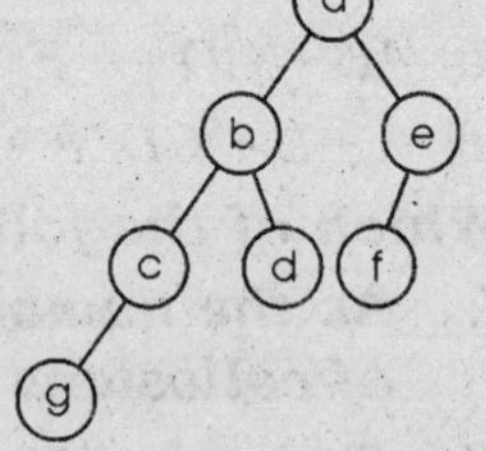

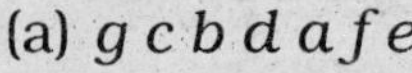

(a) *g c b d a f e*

(b) *g c d b f e a*

(c) *f e d g c b a*

(d) *f e g c d b a*

16. ***An advantage of chained hash table (external hashing) over the open addressing scheme is :***

(a) Worst case complexity of search operations is less

(b) Space used is less

(c) Deletion is easier

(d) None of above

17. ***The minimum number of interchanges needed to convert the array 89, 19, 40, 17, 22, 10, 2, 5, 7, 11, 6, 9, 70 into a heap with minimum element at the root is :***

(a) 0 (b) 1

(c) 2 (d) 3

18. ***The average number of key comparision done on a successful sequential search in list of length n is :***

(a) $\log n$ (b) $\frac{n-1}{2}$

(c) $\frac{n}{2}$ (d) $\frac{n+1}{2}$

19. ***A binary search tree is generated by inserting in order the following integers :***

50, 15, 62, 5, 20, 58, 91, 3, 8, 37, 60, 24.

The number of nodes in the left subtree and right subtree of the root respectively is :

(a) (4, 7) (b) (7, 4)

(c) (8, 3) (d) (3, 8)

20. ***Quick sort is run on the two inputs shown below :***

I. 1, 2, 3, ..., n

II. n, n – 1, n – 2 , ... 2, 1

To sort is ascending order.

Let M_1 and M_2 be the number of comparisons made for the inputs (i) and (ii) respectively. Then :

(a) $M_1 < M_2$ (b) $M_1 > M_2$

(c) $M_1 = M_2$ (d) $M_1 \neq M_2$

21. ***Let G be the directed, weighted graph shown below. What will be the sequence of vertices for single source shortest path by Dijkstra's algorithm (starting from node A) ?***

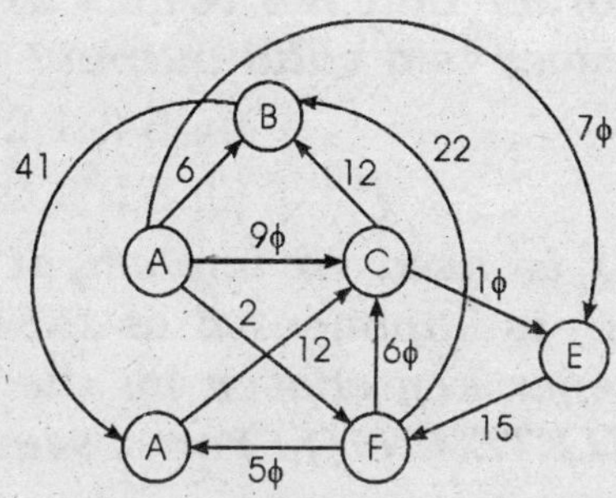

(a) *AFBDCE*

(b) *AEFDCB*

(c) *ABDCEF*

(d) None of above

22. ***From the above figure what will be the cost of the path from A to E ?***

(a) 60 (b) 65

(c) 69 (d) 70

Answers : **14.** (a) **15.** (b) **16.** (c) **17.** (c) **18.** (b) **19.*** (b) **21.** (c) **21.** (a) **22.** (c)

23. ***The concentration of two costs is to be performed in O(1) time. Which of the following implementations of a list should be used?***

(a) Singly linked list (b) Doubly linked list

(c) Circular doubly linked list (d) Array implementation of list

24. ***The correct matching for the following pairs is :***

(a) All pair shorest path	***(1) Greedy***
(b) Quick sort	***(2) Depth-First Search***
(c) Minimum weight spanning tree	***(3) Dynamic programming***
(d) Connected components	***(4) Divide and conquer.***

(A) $a - 2, b - 4, c - 1, d - 3$ (B) $a - 3, b - 4, c - 1, d - 2$

(C) $a - 3, b - 4, c - 2, d - 1$ (D) $a - 4, b - 1, c - 2, d - 3$

25. ***Which of the following is essential for connecting an infix expression to the postfix from effeciently ?***

(a) An stack operator

(b) And operand stack

(c) An operand stack and an operator stack

(d) A parse tree

26. ***A binary search tree contains the value 1, 2, 3, 4, 5, 6, 7, 8, the tree is traversed in preorder and the values are printed out. Which of the following sequences is a valid output?***

(a) 5 3 1 2 4 7 8 6 (b) 5 3 1 2 6 4 8 7

(c) 5 3 2 4 1 6 7 8 (d) 5 3 1 2 4 7 6 8

27. ***A priority queue Q is used to implement a stack S that stores characters. PUSH (C) is implmented as INSERT (Q, C, K) where K is an appropriate integer key chosen by the implementation. POP is implemented as DELETEMIN (Q). For a sequence of operations, the keys chosen are in :***

(a) Non increasing order (b) Non-decreasing order

(c) Strictly increasing order (d) Strictly decreasing order

28. ***Give the correct matching for the following pairs :***

(A) **O (log n)**	***(P) selection***
(B) **O (n)**	***(Q) Insertion sort***
(C) **O (n log n)**	***(R) Binary search***
(D) **O (n^2)**	***(S) Merge sort***

(a) $A - R, B - P, C - Q, D - S$ (b) $A - R, B - P, C - S, D - Q$

(c) $A - P, B - R, C - S, D - Q$ (d) $A - P, B - S, C - R, D - Q$

29. ***Which of the following statements is false ?***

(a) A tree with n nodes has $(n - 1)$ edges

(b) A labelled rooted binary tree each be uniquely constructed given its postorder and preorder traversal results

(c) A complete binary tree with n internal nodes has $(n + 1)$ leaves

(d) The maximum number of nodes is a binary tree of height h is $(2^{h+1} - 1)$

30. *The Inorder and postorder traversal is in the following sequences?*

Inorder ***a f b c d g e***

Postorder ***a f c g e d b***

What will be the sketch of a binary tree ?

(a)

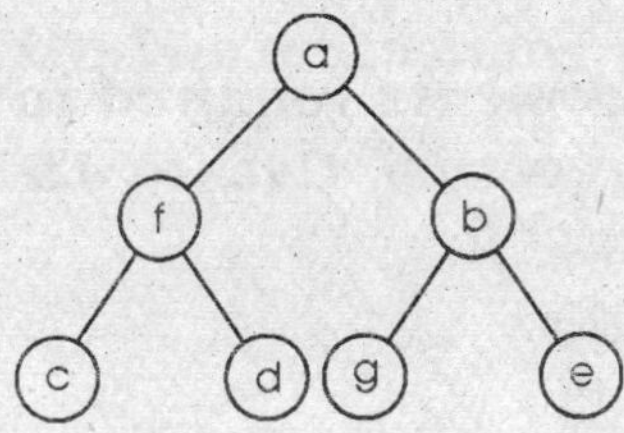

(b)

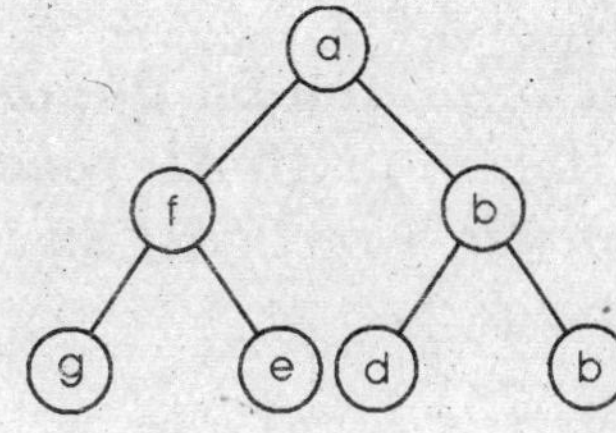

(c)

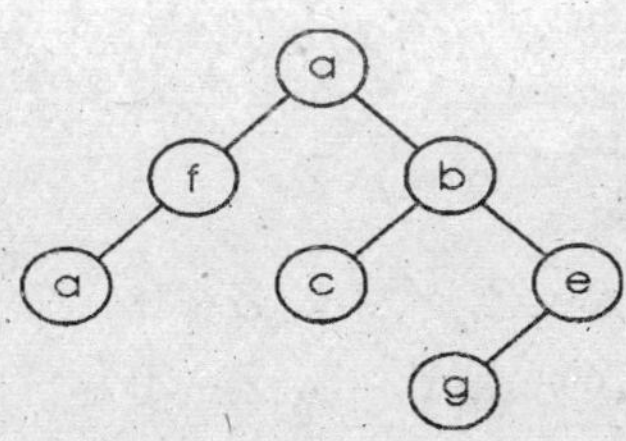

(d)

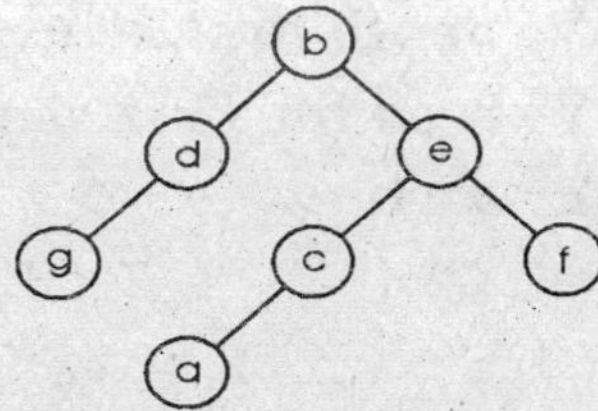

31. *A sorting technique is called stable if :*

(a) It takes $O(n \log n)$ time

(b) It maintains the relative order of occurrence of non-distant elements

(c) It uses divide and conquer paradigm

(d) It takes $O(n)$ space.

32. *To array n numbers stored in an array such that all negative values occur before all positive ones. Minimum number of exchanges required in the worst case is :*

(a) $n - 1$ (b) n

(c) $n + 1$ (d) $\frac{n}{2}$

Answers :

23. (c)	**24.** (b)	**25.** (a)	**26.** (d)	**27.** (d)
28. (b)	**29.*** (c)	**30.*** (c)	**31.** (b)	**32.** (d)

33. *The member of articulation points of the following graph is :*

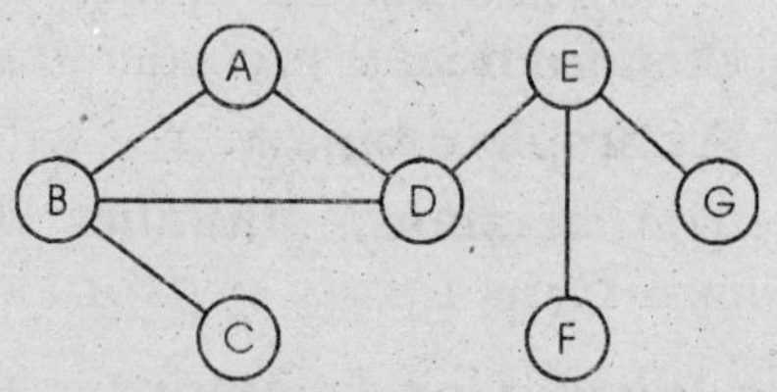

(a) 0
(b) 1
(c) 2
(d) 3

34. *If n is a power of 2, then the minimum number of multiplication needed to compute a^n is :*

(a) $\log_2 n$ (b) $\sqrt{n}$
(c) $n - 1$ (d) n

35. *The minimum number of records movements required to merge five files A (with 10 records), B (with 20 records), C (with 15 records), D (with 5 records) and E (with 25 records) is :*

(a) 165 (b) 90
(c) 75 (d) 65

36. *The most appropriate matching for the following pairs :*

X : depth-first search ***1 : heap***
Y : breadth first search ***2 : queue***
Z : sorting ***3 : stack***

(a) $X-1$, $Y-2$, $Z-3$ (b) $X-3$, $Y-1$, $Z-2$
(c) $X-3$ $Y-2$, $Z-1$ (d) $X-2$, $Y-3$, $Z-1$

37. *Let G be an undirected connected graph with distant edge weights. Let e_{max} be the edge with maximum weight and e_{min} the edge with minimum weight. Which of the following is false ?*

(a) Energy minimum spanning tree of G must contain e_{min}
(b) If e_{max} is in a minimum spanning tree, then its removal must disconnect G
(c) No minimum spanning tree contains e_{max}
(d) G has a unique minimum spanning tree

38. *The topological sorting for the following graph is :*

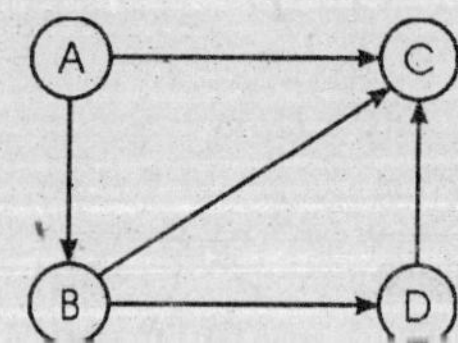

(a) *ABDC*
(b) *ADCB*
(c) *ACDB*
(d) *BDCA*

39. A data structure is stored in a circular array with N memory cells, find number of elements in terms of front and Rear (If front ≤ Rear) :

(a) Front + Rear
(b) Front + Rear + 1
(c) Front – Rear + 1
(d) Rear – Front + 1

40. If in the above question Rear < Front then find the number of elements in terms of front and rear :

(a) Front – Rear – 1
(b) N – Front + Rear + 1
(c) N + Front + Rear + 1
(d) N – Front – Rear + 1

41. Evaluate an arithmetic expression P, written in Postfix notation P : 12, 7, 3 –, 1, 2, 1, 5, +, *, + :

(a) 15
(b) 14
(c) 10
(d) None of above

42. A height balanced tree is a binary tree in which the difference in heights between the left and the right subtree is not more than :

(a) 0
(b) 2
(c) 1
(d) –1

43. Each node of a balanced binary tree must have a balance of :

(a) 0
(b) –1
(c) 1
(d) 2

44. The tree is rotated such that which traversal of the transformed tree is same as that of original tree and the transformed tree is balanced :

(a) Preorder
(b) Inorder
(c) Post order
(d) All of above

45. Multilevel search tree of order 4 means :

(a) 4 nodes and max 3 keys
(b) 4 nodes and max 4 keys
(c) 4 nodes and any no. of keys
(d) 3 nodes and max 4 keys

46. What will be the depth of binary search tree with n sorted elements $d_1, d_2, d_3 \dots d_n$?

(a) n
(b) $n - 1$

Answers : **33.*** (d) **34.*** (a) **35.*** (d) **36.** (c) **37.** (c) **38.*** (a) **39.*** (d) **40.*** (b) **41.*** (a) **42.** (c) **43.*** (a),(b),(c) **44.*** (b) **45.** (a)

(c) $\frac{n(n-1)}{2}$ (d) $\frac{n(n+1)}{2}$

47. ***The following sequence of operations is performed on a stack push (A), Push (B), Pop, Push (A), Push (B), pop, pop, pop, push (B), pop. The sequence of popped out values are :***

(a) B, B, A, A, B (b) B, B, A, B, B

(c) B, A, B, B, A (d) B, A, B, B, B

48. ***Depth of binary tree with 'n' nodes is :***

(a) $\log(n+1) - 1$ (b) $\log(n)$

(c) $\log(n-1) + 1$ (d) $\log(n) + 1$

49. ***A hash function h defined as h (key) = key mod 7 with liner probing, is used to insert the keys 37, 38, 72, 48, 11, 56 into a table indexed from 0 to 6. 48 will be stored in the location :***

(a) 4 (b) 3

(c) 5 (d) 6

50. ***The eccentricity of node E in the graph is :***

(a) 4 (b) 5

(c) 2 (d) 7

51. ***The principle of locality of reference justifies the use of***

(a) Interrupts (b) DMA

(c) Polling (d) Cache memory

52. ***A machine needs a minimum of 100 sec to sort 1000 names by quick sort. The minimum time needed to sort 100 names will be approximately :***

(a) 50.2 sec (b) 6.7 sec

(c) 72.7 sec (d) 11.2 sec

53. ***X and Y are non-negative integers. Suppose a function F is recursively defined as follows :***

$$a\,F(X, Y) = \begin{cases} f(Y, X) & \text{if } X < Y \\ X & \text{if } Y = 0 \\ F(Y, \text{mod}(X, Y)) & \text{otherwise} \end{cases}$$

What will be the value of **(6, 15) ?**

(a) 2 (b) 3

(c) 4 (d) 5

54. ***R be an integer array with N elements. Suppose Y is an integer function defined by***

$$Y(S) = Y(R, N, S)$$

$$Y(S) = \begin{cases} 0 & \text{if } S = 0 \\ Y(S-1) + R(S) & \text{if } 0 < S \leq N \\ Y(S'-1) & \text{if } S > N \end{cases}$$

What will be the value of Y(5) for N = 3 and value of array R : 2, 7, –4 ?

(a) 3 (b) 4

(c) 5 (d) 6

55. ***In the above question, what does this function do ?***

(a) Add the contents of an array

(b) Multiply contents of an array

(c) Substraction the contents of an array

(d) None of above

56. ***A character set a, b, c, d, e each occuring with the probability .12, .4, .15, .08, .25 respectively. The optimal coding technique will have the average length of :***

(a) 2.00 (b) 2.15

(c) 0.80 (d) 0.15

57. ***If the data is already sorted which of the following should be avoided ?***

(a) Quick sort (b) Bubble sort

(c) Merge sort (d) Radix sort

58. ***If the record are small and keys are difficult to compare then which of the following shorting is recommended ?***

(a) Insertion sort (b) Quick sort

(c) Merge sort (d) Bubble sort

59. ***Which of the following sorting methods will be the best if number of swappings done, is the only measure of efficiency?***

(a) Selection sort

(b) Bubble sort

(c) Merge sort

(d) Insertion sort

Answers : **46.*** (a) **47.*** (a) **48.*** (a) **49.*** (d) **50.*** (d) **51.** (d) **52.*** (b) **53.*** (b) **54.*** (c) **55.** (a) **56.*** (b) **57.** (a) **58.** (a) **59.*** (a)

60. ***If the work of rearranging the library books in a shelf in proper order, at the end of each day which of the following sorting algorithm is best ?***

(a) Merge sort (b) Bubble sort

(c) Quick sort (d) Insertion sort

61. ***Which of the following lists of nodes correspond to a postorder traversal of the binary tree in the figure shown ?***

(a) *ABDEHCFIGJ*

(b) *DHEBIFJGCA*

(c) *DBEHAIFCJG*

(d) *ABCDEFGHIJ*

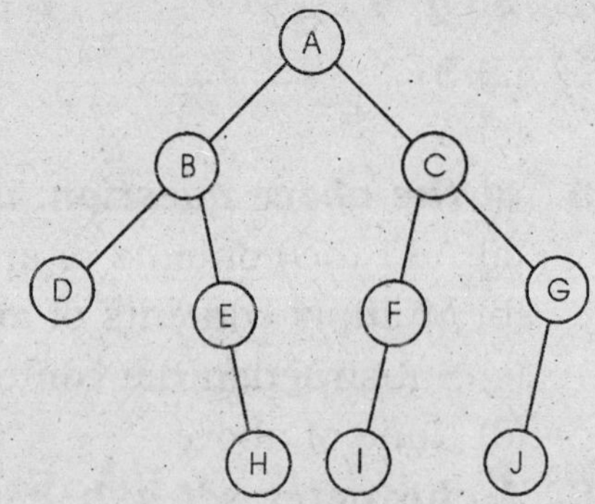

62. ***The corresponding binary tree of the expression*** **$(A + B * C)/(A - C)$** ***is:***

(a)

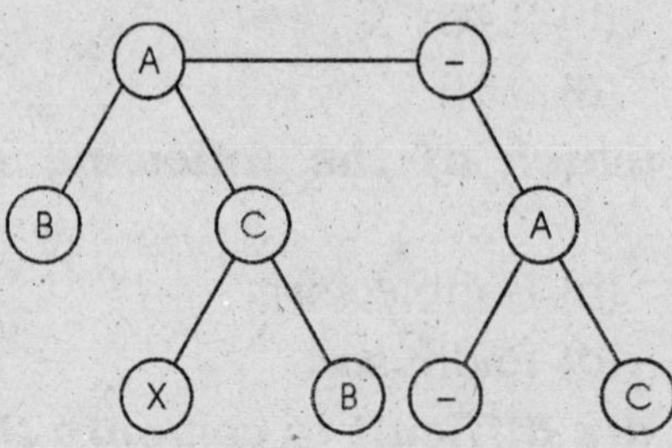

(b)

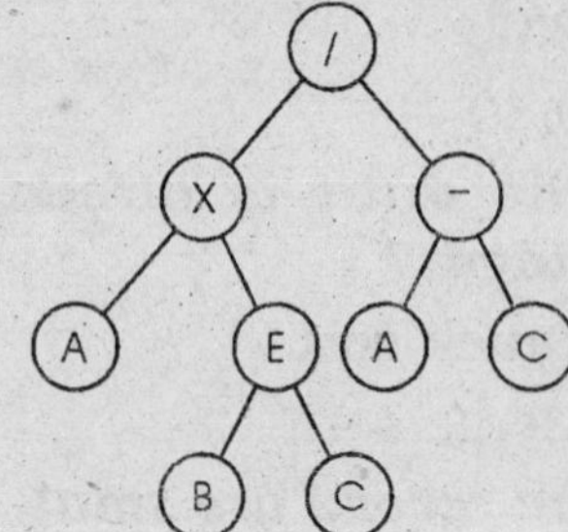

(c)

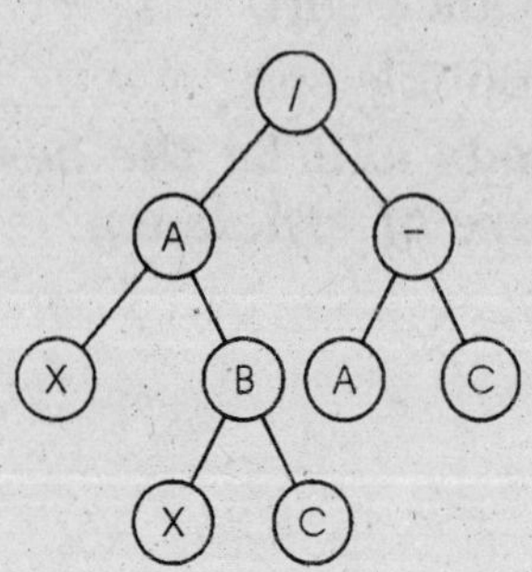

(d) none of above

63. *Let the incidence matrix of a graph be* $M = \begin{bmatrix} 1 & 0 & 0 \\ 1 & 0 & 1 \\ 1 & 1 & 0 \end{bmatrix}$***. The corresponding graph is given as :***

(a)

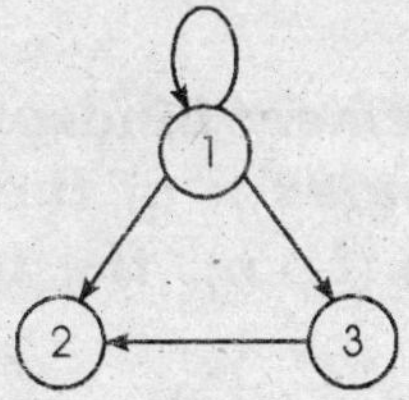

(b)

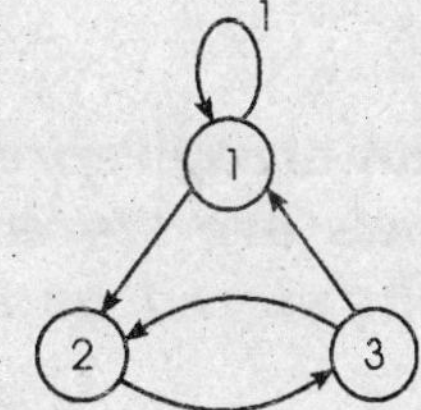

(c)

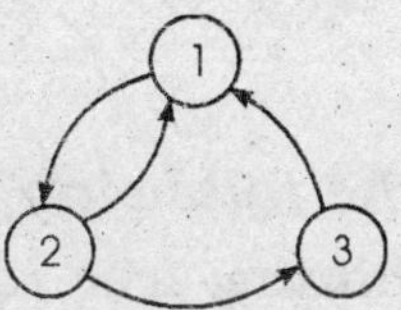

(d) None of above

64. *In evaluating the infix expression* $4 - (3 + 5)$***, which stack is immpossible ?***

(a)

5	
4	
3	
2	
1	4

(b)

5	
4	
3	8
2	–
1	4

(c)

5	
4	
3	5
2	+
1	1

(d)

5	
4	3
3	(
2	–
1	4

65. *Which of the following sorting algorithms yield approximately the same wort-case and average case running time behaviour in* $O(n \log n)$**?**

(a) Bubble sort and selection sort
(b) Heap sort and merge sort
(c) Quick sort and radix sort
(d) Tree root and Quick sort

Answers : **60.** (d) **61.** (b) **62.** (b) **63.** (b) **64.** (c) **65.** (b)

66. ***Randomized quicksort is an extension of quicksort where the pivot is chosen randomly. What is the worst case complexity of sorting n numbers using randomized quicksort?***

(a) $O(n)$ (b) $O(n \log n)$

(c) $O(n^2)$ (d) $O(n!)$

67. ***Consider an array representation of an n element binary heap where the elements are stored from index 1 to index n of the array. For the element stored at index i of the array (i ≤ n), the index of the parent is :***

(a) $i - 1$ (b) $\lfloor i/2 \rfloor$

(c) $\lceil i/2 \rceil$ (d) $\frac{(i+1)}{2}$

68. ***What will be the value of S_1, S_2 and S_3 in the following function so that the function computes the depth of a binary tree rootes at it.***

Type def struct tnode {

int key

struct tnode * right, * left;

} * tree;

int depth (tree t)

{ int x, y;

if (t = NULL) return 0;

x = depth (t → left);

S_1

if (x > y) return S_2

else return S_3;

(a) y = depth ($t \to$ right), x, y (b) y = depth ($t \to$ right), y, x

(c) x = depth ($t \to$ right), x, y (d) y = depth ($t \to$ left), y, x.

69. ***Let A be a sequence of B distinct integer sorted in ascending order. How many distant pairs of sequences, B and C are there such that (i) each is sorted in ascending order (ii) B has 5 and C has 3 elements, and (iii) the result of merging B and C gives A?***

(a) 2 (b) 30

(c) 56 (d) 256

70. ***Suppose the numbers 7, 5, 1, 8, 3, 6, 0, 9, 4, 2 are inserted in that order into an initially empty binary search tree. The binary search tree uses the usual ordering on natural numbers. What is the inorder traversal sequence of the resultant tree?***

(a) 7 5 1 0 3 2 4 6 8 9 (b) 0 2 4 3 1 6 5 9 8 7
(c) 0 1 2 3 4 5 6 7 8 9 (d) 9 8 6 4 2 3 0 1 5 7

71. ***Consider the following graph :***

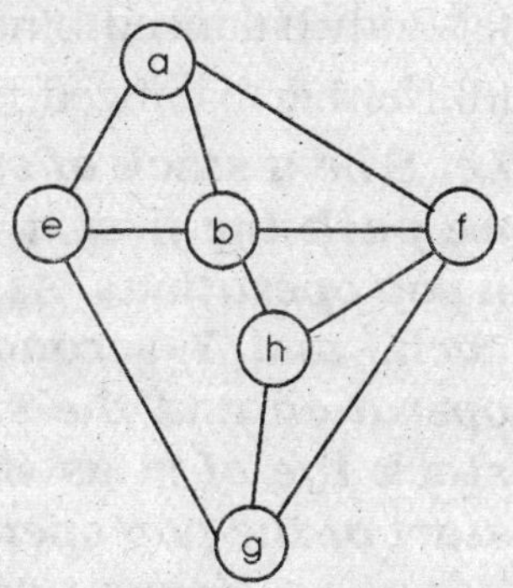

Among the following sequences :

I a b e g h f

II a b f e h g

III a b f h g e

IV a f g h b e

Which are depth first traversals of the above graph?

(a) I, II and IV only
(b) I and IV only
(c) II, III and IV only
(d) I, III and IV only

72. ***The usual θ(n²) implementation of inertion sort to sort an array uses linear search to identify the position where an element is to be inserted into the already sorted part of the array. If, instead, we use binary search to identify the position, the worst case running time will***

(a) remain $\theta(n^2)$ (b) become $\theta(n(\log n)^2)$
(c) become $\theta(n \log n)$ (d) become $\theta(n)$

73. ***In a heap with n elements with the smallest element at the root, the 7th smallest element can be found in time***

(a) $\theta(n \log n)$ (b) $\theta(n)$
(c) $\theta(\log n)$ (d) $\theta(1)$

74. ***How many perfect matchings are there in a complete graph of 6 vertices?***

(a) 15 (b) 24
(c) 30 (d) 60

75. ***A data structure is required for sorting a set of integers such that each of the following operations can be done in (log n) time, where n is the number of elements in the set.***

I Deletion of the smallest element.

II Insertion of an element if it is not already present in the set.

Which of the following data structures can be used for this purpose?

Answers : 66. (a) 67. (b) 68. (a) 69. (d) 70. (c)
71. (d) 72. (c) 73. (c) 74. (a)

(a) A heap can be used but not a balanced binary search tree

(b) A balanced binary search tree can be used but not a heap

(c) Both balanced binary search tree and heap can be used

(d) Neither balanced binary search tree nor heap can be used

76. *Let S be a stack of size n ≥ 1. Starting with the empty stack suppose we push the first n natural numbers in sequence and then perform n pop operations. Assme that push and pop operation take X seconds each, and Y seconds elapse between the end of one such stack operation and the start of the next operation. For n ≥ 1, define the stack life of m as the time elapsed from the end of Push (m) to the start of the pop operation that removes m from S. The average stack life of an element of this stack is*

(a) n (X + Y)

(b) 3Y + 2X

(c) n (X + Y) - X

(d) Y + 2X

77. *Let T (n) be the number of different binary search trees on n distant elements.*

These $T(n) = \sum_{k=1}^{n} T(K-1)\,T(x)$ ***where x is***

(a) n - k + 1

(b) n - k

(c) n - k - 1

(d) n - k - 2

78. *Consider the following 2 - 3 - 4 tree (i.e., B-tree with a minimum degree of two) in which each data item is a letter. The usual alphabetical ordering of letters is used in constructing the tree.*

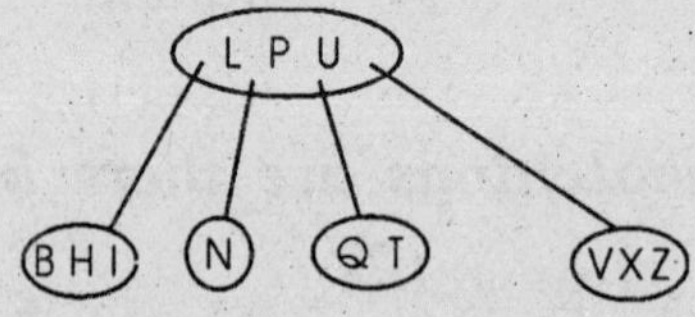

What is the result of inserting G in the above tree?

(a)

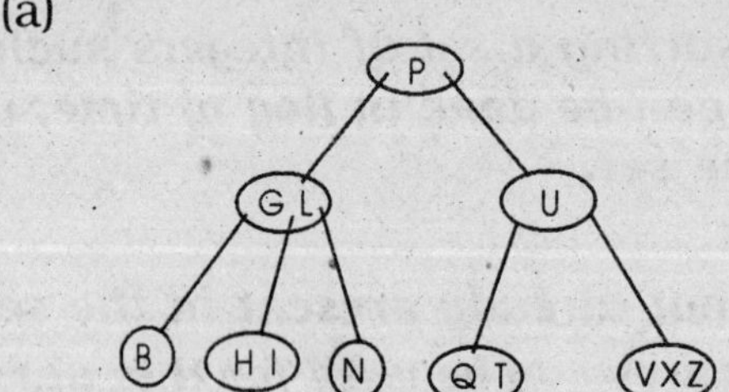

(b)

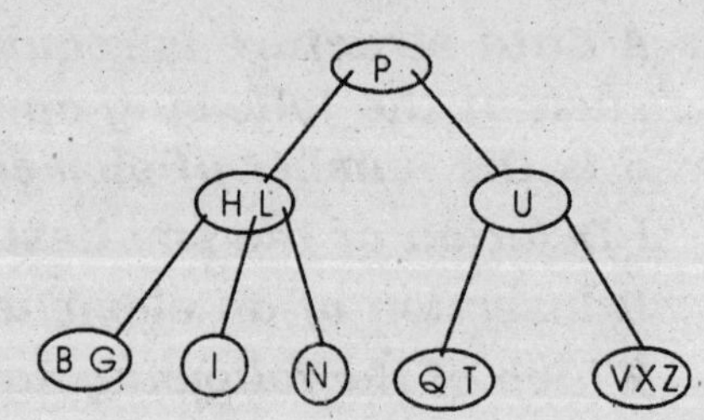

(c)

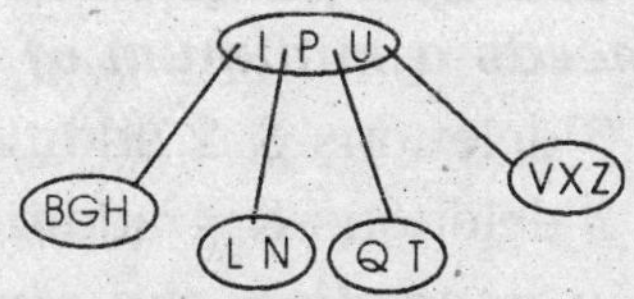

(d) None of the above

79. *What is the time taken by binary search algorithm to search a key in a stored aray of n element ?*

(a) $0(\log_2 n)$ (b) $0(n)$

(c) $0(n \log_2 n)$ (d) $0(n^2)$

80. *Which of the following operations is performed more efficiently doubly linked list than by a linear linked list ?*

(a) deleting a node whose location is given

(b) searching an unsorted list for a given item

(c) inserting anode after the node with a given location

(d) traversing the list reverely to process each node

81. *A linear list of elements, in which deletion can be done from one end, insertion can take place only at the other end is known as*

(a) queue (b) stack

(c) tree (d) deque

82. *The five items : A,B,C,D and E are pushed in stack the other starting from A. The stack is popped four items and each element is insered in a queue. Then two elements are deleted from the queue and pushed back on the stack. Now one item is popped from the stack. The popped item is:*

(a) A (b) B

(c) D (d) D

83. *If each node in a tree has value than every value in its left subtree and has value less than every value in its right subtree, the tree is known as*

(a) Complete tree (b) full binary tree

(c) binary search tree (d) unthread tree

84. *Pre-order is nothing but*

(a) depth first order (b) breadth first order

(c) topological order (d) liner order

Answers : **75.** (b) **76.*** (d) **77.*** (a) **78.** (c) **79.** (a) **80.** (d) **81.** (a) **82.** (d) **83.** (c) **84.** (c)

85. ***The initial configuration of queue is a, b, c, d ('a' is at the front). To get the configuration d, c, b, a one needs a minimum of***

(a) deletion & 3 additions (b) 3 deletions & 2 additions

(c) 3 deletion & 3 additions (d) 3 deletions & 4 additions

86. ***Which of the following is not true in regarding the singly linked list?***

(a) Nodes are linked in one direction

(b) Address of the list is the addres of last node

(c) The last node is pointing to NULL indicate the end of the list

(d) Searching for a node always starts at the first node and traverses through every subequent bodes

87. ***Which of the following is false regarding doubly link list ?***

(a) Nodes are linked in both forward and backward direction

(b) It can not reuse its memory

(c) The first nodes next pointer is NULL

(d) Traversing can be dne in either way

88. ***Which of the following is the feature of stack ?***

(a) All operations are at one position

(b) It cannot reuse its memory

(c) All element are of different types

(d) Any element can be accessed from it

89. ***By using which data structure, we can convert in fix arithmetic expression into postfix expression ?***

(a) Doubly link list (b) Queue

(c) Stack (d) Graph

90. ***Partition exchange sort is also known as***

(a) Heap sort (b) Bubble sort

(c) Radix exchange sort (d) Quick sort

91. ***The performance of quick sort is best when***

(a) The input array is not sorted

(b) The input array is relatively sorted

(c) The number of elements in the array is very small

(d) (b) & (c)

92. ***Consider the following statements :***

1. Stack is a LIFO 2. Stack is a FIFO

3. Queue is LIFO 4. Queue is a FIFO

(a) Only 1 & 3 are true
(b) Only 2 & 3 are true
(c) Only 1 & 4 are true
(d) Only 2 & 4 are true

93. ***How many elements we can accesses in regards to queue***

(a) 1 (b) 2
(c) 3 (d) all elements

94. ***Prefix form of*** (A + B*C)) $ ((A + B)*C

(a) $ + A*BC* + ABC (b) $ + A*BC +* ABC
(c) +A * BC$* + ABC (d) +A * BC$ + AB*C

95. ***New > data = 20***

New > next = temp > next

temp > next = new

This will .... the item (New) in the list

(a) Insert (b) Modify
(c) Delete (d) Traverse

96. ***Which is not the operation of a queue, if queue is Q & X is item ?***

(a) empty (Q) (b) deque (Q, X)
(c) enque (Q, X) (d) push (Q, X)

97. ***Which path we will never get if we traverse graph in DFS***

(a) v1 v2 v4 v8 v6 v3 v7 (b) v1 v3 v6 v8 v7 v5 v2 v4
(c) v1 v3 v2 v7 v6 v4 v5 v8 (d) v1 v2 v5 v8 v6 v v7 v4

98. ***last > next = first;***

first > prev = last;

This notation is used in

(a) Circular Link List (b) Singly Link list
(c) Doubly Circular Link List (d) Linked Stack

99. ***Which data structure grows or shrinks during run time ?***

(a) Stack (b) Queue
(c) Tree (d) Array

100. ***Each node on the adjacent list represents...........of the graph***

(a) Loop (b) Edge
(c) Relation (d) Degree

Answers :							
85. (c)	**86.** (b)	**87.** (c)	**88.** (a)	**89.** (c)	**90.** (d)	**91.** (d)	**92.** (c)
93. (b)	**94.** (a)	**95.** (a)	**96.** (d)	**97.** (c)	**98.** (c)	**99.** (a)	**100.** (b)

101. ***Consider an array adj2 such that adj2 [i] [j] is the value of the foregoing expression .adj2 is said to be the .... of adj with itself***

(a) Division (b) Addition

(c) Subtraction (d) Boolean product

102. ***BST has a special property***

(a) it is always CBT

(b) It has always exactly 2 links NULL

(c) L child < parent < R child

(b) It has no leaf node

103. 7th ***iteration of bubble sort for nos. 25, 48, 34, 12, 57, 86, 33, 92 will give***

(a) 12, 25, 33, 37, 86, 57 92

(b) 12, 25, 37, 33, 48, 57, 86, 92

(c) 12, 25, 33, 37, 48, 57, 86, 92

(d) 25, 28, 37, 57, 12, 86, 92

104. ***The basic idea underlying the .... sort is to pass through the file sequentially several times. Each pass consists of comparing each element in the file with successor***

(a) Bubble Sort (b) Insertion Sort

(c) Heap Sort (d) Quick Sort

105. ***Which is correct sequence of line complixities in ascending order ?***

(a) Linear, logarithmic, polynomial, exponential

(b) Logarithmic, linear, polynomial, exponentia

(c) Logarithmic, linear, exponential, polynomial

106. ***In a singly linked list, if a new node is to be inserted between two consecutive nodes how many links have to be modified ?***

(a) 1 (b) 2

(c) 3 (d) 4

107. ***At compile time***

(a) An object is bound of its function for member function call

(b) An object is not bound to its function at compile time

(c) An object is linked to its function dynamically

(d) Virtual function calls are resolved

108. ***An undirected graph G with n vertices and e edges are represented by Adjacency list. What is the time required to determine the total number of edges in G ?***

(a) O(e) (b) O(n)

(c) $O(n^2)$ (d) O(e + n)

109. ***Which of the following statements is false ?***

(a) every tree is a bipartite graph

(b) a tree contains a cycle

(c) a tree with n nodes contains n-1 edges

(d) a tree is a connected graph

110. ***A binary tree with the property that the value at each node is at least as large as the values as its children are known as***

(a) binary search tree (b) AVL tree

(c) Completely tree (d) Heap

111. ***There cannot be a circular***

(a) Singly link list (b) Queue

(c) Stack (d) Doubly linked list

112. ***A threaded binary tree is better than a binary tree because***

(1) It refuses the null links

(2) Traversal is easier for it using the threads

(3) A non-recursive traversal can be implemented for it and the same cannot be implemented for a binary tree

(a) Aall are true (b) Only 1 & 2 are true

(c) Only 2 & 3 are true (d) Only 1 & 3 are true

Answers :						
	101. (d)	**102.** (c)	**103.** (c)	**104.** (a)	**105.** (b)	**106.** (b)
	107. (a)	**108.** (d)	**109.** (b)	**110.** (d)	**111.** (c)	**112.** (d)

SOLUTIONS

1. There are two operations on stack PUSH and POP.
The input string is 1, 2, 3, 4, 5.

Applying push operation 3 times the position of stack will be applying the pop operation one time, we set 3 as an output.

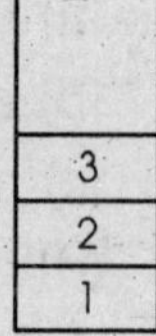

Similarly by applying another push operation
We get the output string 3, 4, 5, 2, 1.

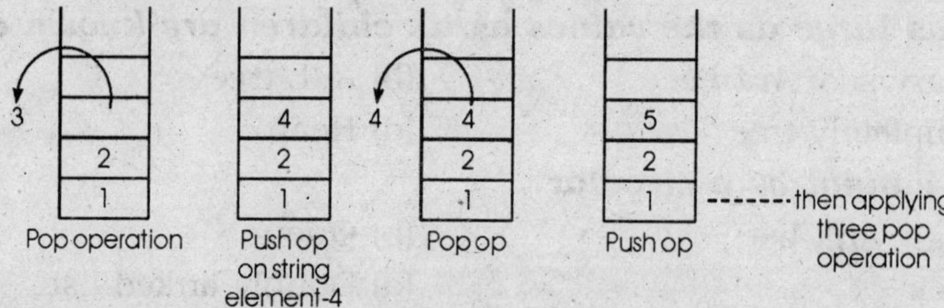

2. Let $S = x_1, x_2 \dots x_n$ be the given string of length n.
The no. of possible string starting with x_1 is n
The no. of possible string starting with x_2 is $(n - 1)$
The no. of possible string starting with x_n is 1
Hence, the number of substrings of S is

$$1 + 2 + 3 \dots (n - 1) + n = \frac{n(n+1)}{2}.$$

Example : $S = xyz$

$x \quad y \quad z$

No. of substring $= 3 + 2 + 1$

$$= \frac{3(3+1)}{2} = 6$$

$x \quad y \quad z$
$xy \quad yz$
xyz

3. In linked list there is no way to find the middle element.

9. Any connected acylic graph is a tree having $n - 1$ edges, Hence minimum number of edges in a connected cyclic graph is $(n - 1) + 1 = n$. By adding an edges to a tree we will get a minimal connected cyclic graph

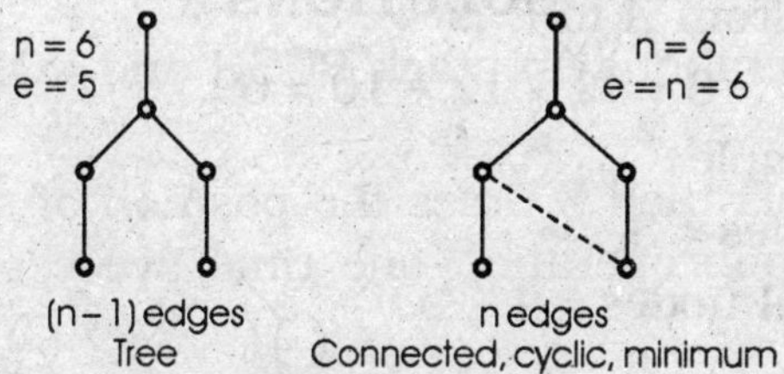

12. In post order sequence → left right root.

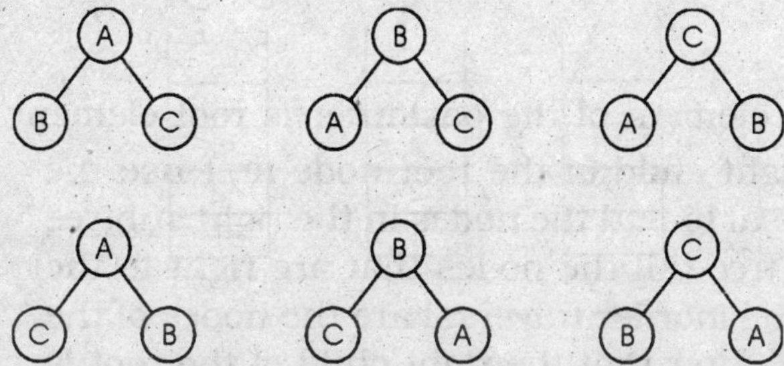

13. There are two minimum spannings trees with 12 as weights its weights.

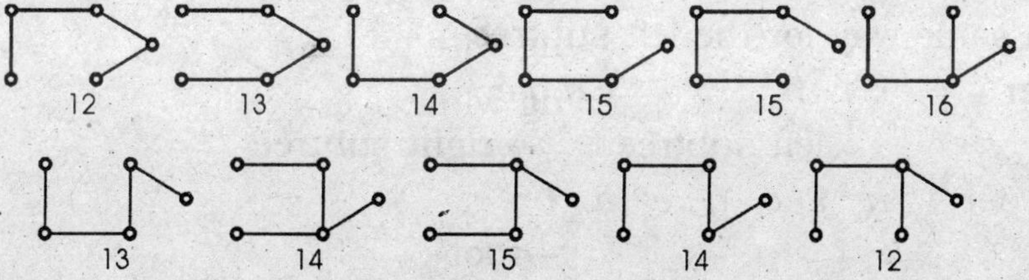

19. The binary search tree generated by inserting in order the following integers are 50, 15, 62, 5, 20, 58, 91, 3, 8, 37, 60, 24.

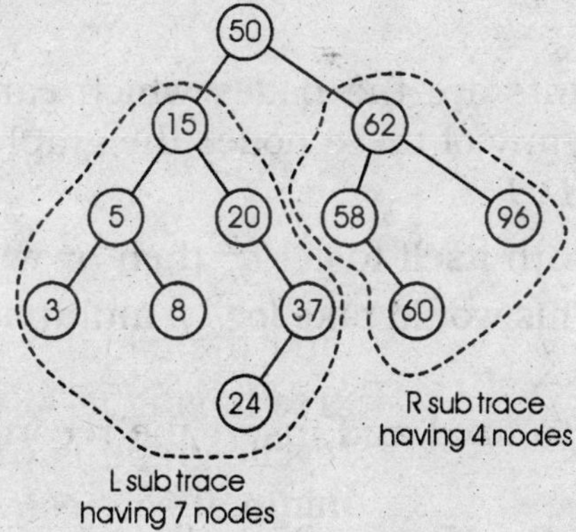

22. Cost of the path from A to E is

$$6 + 41 + 12 + 10 = 69.$$

29. Consider an example

Here Internal nodes = 3

Leaves = External nodes = 4

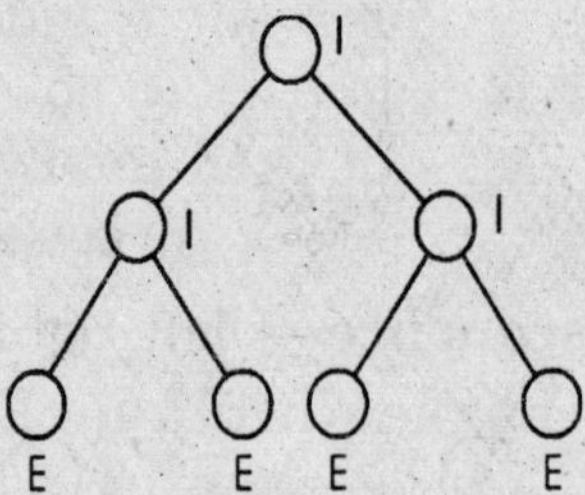

30. We know last element of the postorder is root element of the binary tree. To find the right child of the root node first use the inorder traversal to find the nodes in the right subtree of the binary tree (All the nodes that are right to the root node in the inorder traversal are the nodes of the right subtree). After that the right child of the root is obtained by selecting the last node in the postorder traversal of the right subtree.

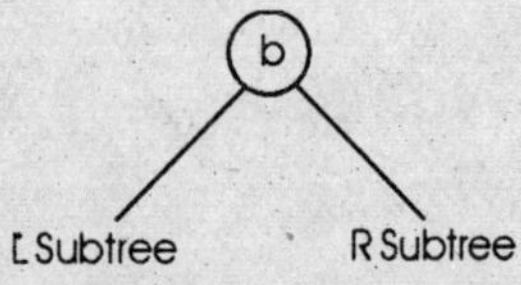

In the same way for the left subtree

Inorder $a\,f\;\;b\qquad c\,d\,q\,e$

↓ left subtree → right subtree

postorder $a\;\; f\;\; c\;\; g\;\; e\;\; d\;\; b$

→root

32. Minimum number of exchanges required in the worst case would be $\frac{n}{2}$ as the worst case would be one where all the +ive numbers occur before the negative ones.

33. The articulation points are the nodes which can't be removed from the graph. On removing any of these nodes the graph is no longer connected. These nodes are B, D, F.

34. We first multiply a with itself to get a^2 then a^2 with itself to get a^4 and so on until we get a^n. This would take $\log_2 n$ multiplication since n is a power of 2.

35. Keep the records of A fixed and insert the records of the other files in A in sorted order.

This would require $20 + 15 + 5 + 25 = 65$ record movements.

38. For topological sorting the graph must be

Irreflexive—Means having no loops

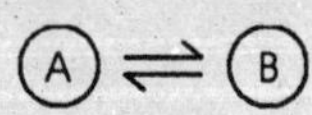

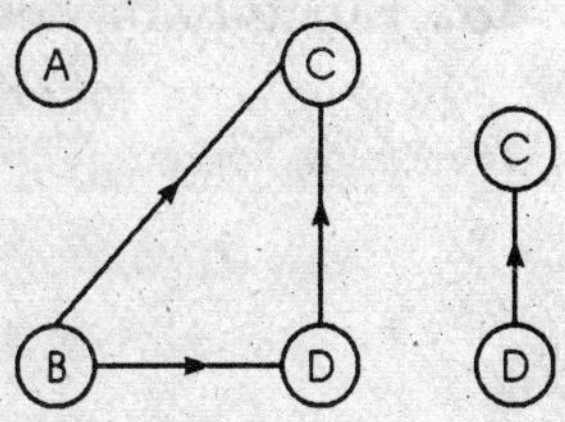

Antisymmetry—No parallel paths.

Transitive —If $A \to B \to C$ then A must $A \to C$

First we take the nodes whose indegrees are zero. Since A has all indegrees zero so A node is cut first after that B is cut then finally D.

$A\ B\ D\ C$

39. Consider an example when front ≤ Rear

No. = Rear – Front + 1

= 6 – 3 + 1 = 4

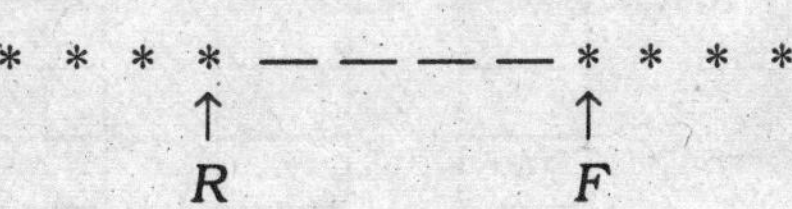

40. Rear = 4 Front = 9

No. = N – Front + Rear + 1

= 12 – 9 + 4 + 1 = 8

* * * * — — — — * * * *
↑ ↑
R F

41. To evaluate an arithmetic expression written in postfix notation we have to first convert it into infix notation.

12, 7, 3, –, 1, 2, 1, 5, +, *, +

Start scanning from the left

= 12[7.3]/2 [1 + 5] * +

= 12/[7 – 3] 2 * [1 + 5] +

$$P = \frac{12}{4} + 2 * 6 = 15$$

43. When left subtree is heavier than right subtree → 1

When right subtree is heavier than left subtree → –1

When left subtree is equal to right subtree → 0

44. Consider an example

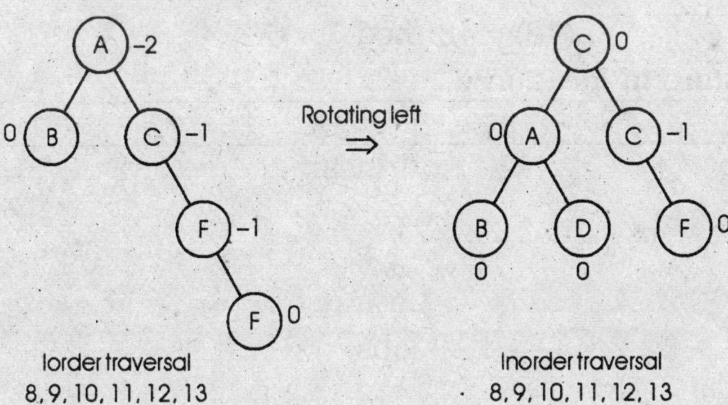

46. Since data items are already sorted.

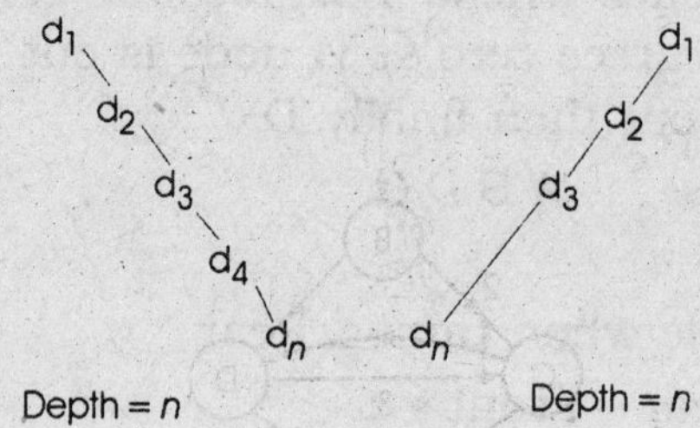

47. The sequence generatd after the following operations :

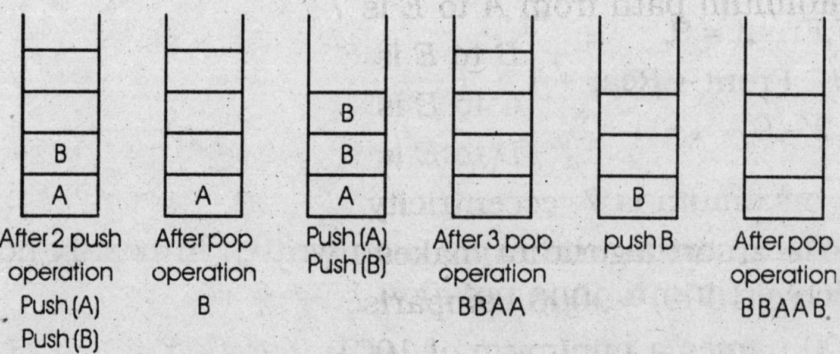

Sequence generated :

So final sequence generated after all operation *BBAA*.

48. For depth d the no. of nodes n will be

$$n = 2^{(d+1)} - 1$$

$$n + 1 = 2^{d+1}$$

$$d = \log (n + 1) - 1.$$

49. h (37) = 37 mod 7 = 2, so 37 will be store in location 2. h(38) = 3, so it will store in location 3. h(72) = 72 mod 7. This result in a collision with linear probing the alternate location for 72 will be location 4.

$$h(48) = 48 \bmod 7 = 6$$

So 48 will store in location 6.

		37	38	72		48
0	1	2	3	4	5	6

50. The ecentricity of a mode is the maximum of minimum path from other nodes to the given node.

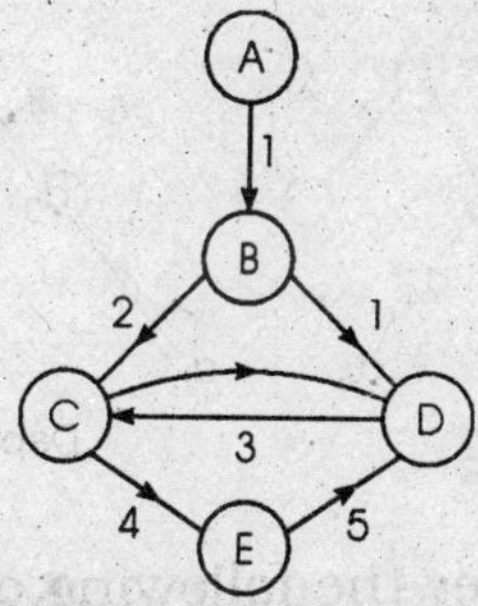

Cost of minimum path from A to E is 7

" " " " " " B to E is 6

" " " " " " C to E is 4

" " " " " " D to E is 7

Since the maximum is 7, eccentricity of node E is 7.

52. The best quick sort algorithm makes $n \log n$, comparisons.

So $1000 \times \log(1000) = 9000$ comparisons, which takes 100 sec.

To sort 100 names a minimum of $100(\log 100) = 600$

Comparisons are needed.

This takes $100 \times 600/9000 = 6.7$ sec

53. Since $X < Y$

$$\begin{aligned} F(15, 6) &= F(6, \text{MOD}(15, 6)) \\ &= F(6, 3) \\ &= F(3, 0) = 3 \text{ if } Y = 0\ F(X, Y) = X. \end{aligned}$$

54. Since $Y(5)\ \ S > N$

$$\begin{aligned} S(5) &= Y(R, 3, 5) = Y(4) = Y(3) \\ Y(R, N, 3) &= Y(3-1) + R(3) \\ &= Y(1) + R(2) + R(3) \\ \\ &= Y(0) + R(1) + R(2) + R(3) \\ &= 0 + 2 + 7 + (-4) = 5 \end{aligned}$$

It adds the contents of an array.

55. The average binary search for the different binary seach trees.

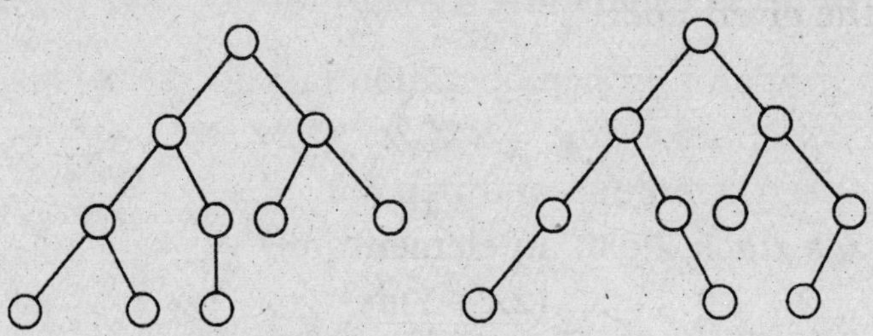

56. By using Hoffman coding

Average code length

$$= \frac{.12 \times 4 + .08 \times 4 + 2 \times .25 + 3 \times .15 + 1 \times .4}{5}$$

$= 2.15$

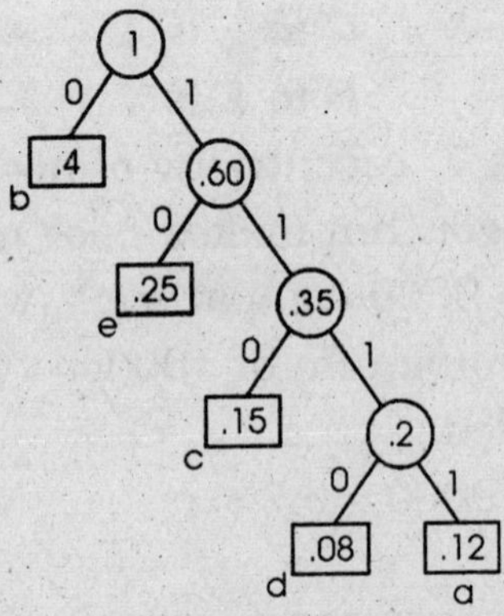

59. Because selection sort requries less swappings but more comparisons.

In a Binary search tree left child is less than right child

so by inserting numbers we get

So the inorder traversal of this tree is

In inorder traversal we first traverse left tree then root and finally right sub tree tree.

So the sequence generated by inorder traversal is

0, 1, 2, 3, 4, 5, 6, 7, 8, 9

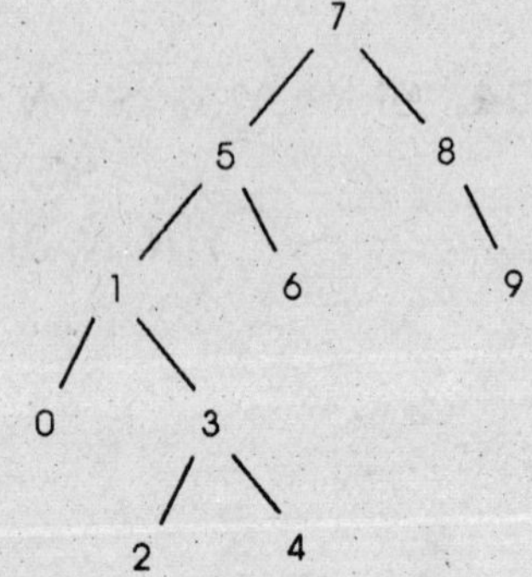

73. Any element can be found in time θ(log *n*).

74. For complete graph of 6 vertices

Number of perfect matching $= \frac{n(n-1)}{2} = \frac{6 \times 5}{2} = 15.$

76. Since each push and pop operation takes X seconds.

So push & pop take time = 2 X

delay between one push and pop = Y

So, average stack life of an element (m)

$$= \frac{(2X + Y)m}{m} = Y + 2X$$

77. $T(n) = T(x)\,[T(0) + T(1) + T(2) \ldots T(n-1)]$.

Therefore, $x = n - k + 1$

CHAPTER 5

8085 MICROPROCESSOR

1. ***No. of externally initiated operations that 8085 can respond is :***
   (a) 2 (b) 3
   (c) 4 (d) None of above
2. ***Flags are :***
   (a) Flip flops (b) Register
   (c) AND gates (d) Tristate devices
3. ***Number of ports in 8085 are restricted to 256 in peripheral I/O because :***
   (a) μP has 8 bit data interface
   (b) IN and OUT instructions uses 8 bits address
   (c) All devices are either serial or 8 bit parallel
   (d) μP can access at most 256 interrupts.
4. ***The content of output port with address OC H after execution of the following program is :***
   MVI, B, 2A H
   MOV A, B
   MOV C, A
   SUB C
   MOV A, B
   OUT OC H
   (a) *00 H* (b) 01 *H*
   (c) 2 *AH* (d) *FF H*
5. ***It is given that the clock input frequency of 8085 μP 1 is 8 MHz and CLKOUT of 8085 μP 2 is 8 MHz. This means that :***
   (a) μp 1 will be faster than μp 2
   (b) μp 2 will be faster than μp 1
   (c) Both will be at the same speed
   (d) None of the above.
6. ***Lower order nibble of an accumulator can be complemented by :***
   (a) ANI 0FH (b) XRI 0FH

(c) ORI 0FH (d) CMA

7. ***The μp issues ALE during first T-state is :***

(a) Fetch cycle only (b) Memory read cycle

(c) Memory write cycle (d) Every M/C cycle

8. ***The data lines of 8085 processor are multiplexed with :***

(a) High order address lines

(b) Low order address lines

(c) States lines

(d) None of the above

9. ***The output of the following program***

MVI A, xH

ORA A

JP NEXT

XRA

NEXT : OUT OPI

HLT :

(a) Any x (b) x if x is negative

(c) x if x is positive (d) $x + x$

10. ***Find the odd man out :***

(a) CMC (b) ANA

(c) INX (d) RAL

11. ***Number of times the loop is repeated is***

NEXT : MVI B, 1AH

DCR B

HN2 NEXT :

(a) 1 AH (b) IAH +1

(c) 01 (only once) (d) Infinite

12. ***When CALL is executed, the stack pointer register is decremented by :***

(a) 1 (b) 2

(c) 0 (d) Off set value

13. ***The instruction RET transfers the contents of the top two locations of the stack to the :***

(a) Accumulator (b) H and L registers

(c) Any two register pair (d) Program counter

Answers : **1.** (c) **2.** (a) **3.** (b) **4.*** (c) **5.** (b) **6.** (b) **7.** (d) **8.** (b) **9.** (c) **10.** (c) **11.*** (d) **12.*** (b) **13.** (d)

14. *Match the following :*

(1) LHLD	***(A) Copy HL register into stack pointer***
(2) XCHG	***(B) Load HL register***
(3) SPHL	***(C) Interchange HL and DE***

(a) 1 – *B*, 2 – *C*, 3 – *A* (b) 1 – *A*, 2 – *B*, 3 – *C*
(c) 1 – *A*, 2 – *C*, 3 – *B* (d) 1 – *B*, 2 – *A*, 3 – *C*

15. *8085 has ...... number of RST instructions :*

(a) 4 (b) 2
(c) 8 (d) 6

16. *8085 has 4 interrupts in which ...... is/are maskable and ...... is/are non-maskable :*

(a) 1, 3 (b) 2, 2
(c) 3, 1 (d) 0, 4

17. *RST 7.5 interrupt in 8085 microprocessor executes the interrupt service routine from interrupt vector location :*

(a) 0000H (b) 0075H
(c) 003CH (d) 0034H

18. *Purpose of a start bit in RS232 serial communication protocol is :*

(a) To synchronise receiver for receiving every byte
(b) To synchronise receiver for receiving a sequence of bytes
(c) A parity bit
(d) To synchronise receiver for receiving the last byte

19. *The correct matching for the following pairs is :*

(A) DMA I/O	***(1) High speed RAM***
(B) Cache	***(2) Disk***
(C) Interrupt I/O	***(3) Printer***
(D) Condition Code Register	***(4) ALU***

(a) *A* – 4, *B* – 3, *C* – 1, *D* – 2 (b) *A* – 2, *B* – 1, *C* – 3, *D* – 4
(c) *A* – 4, *B* – 3, *C* – 2, *D* – 1 (d) *A* – 2, *B* – 3, *C* – 4, *D* – 1

20. *Contents of a register after the execution of the following 8085 microprocessor program is :*

MVI A, 55 H

HVI C, 25 H

ADD C

DAA

(a) 74 H (b) 80 H

(c) 50 H (d) 22 H

21. *Find the odd man out :*

(a) RIM (b) SOD

(c) SIM (d) ADD

22. *Find the odd man out :*

(a) 6502 (b) 8086

(c) Z-80 (d) 8748

23. *To put the 8085 μp in the wait state :*

(a) Lower the HOLD input (b) Lower the READY input

(c) Raise the HOLD input (d) Raise the Ready input

24. *The 8085 μp responds to the presence of an interrupt :*

(a) As soon as the TRAP pin become 'high'

(b) By checking the TRAP pin for 'high' status at the end of each instruction fetch

(c) By checking the TRAP pin for 'high' status at the end of each execution of each instruction

(d) By checking the TRAP pin for 'high' status at regular intervals.

25. *Consider a 8085 instruction IN 09 H stored as follows :*

Memory Address	***M/C Code***
3050	***DA***
3051	***09***

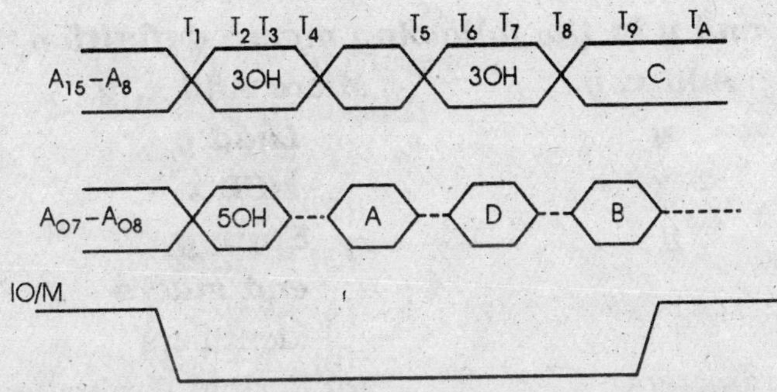

What are the conents of A, B, C and D in hexadecimal

(a) $A = DAH,\ B = 09H,\ C = 09H,\ D = 51H$

(b) $A = 09H,\ B = DAH,\ C = 09H,\ D = 51H$

(c) $A = DAH,\ B = 09H,\ C = 51H,\ D = 09H$

(d) $A = 09H,\ B = DAH,\ C = 09H,\ D = 51H$

Answers : **14.** (a) **15.** (c) **16.*** (c) **17.** (c) **18.** (b) **19.** (b) **20.** (a) **21.** (b) **22.*** (b) **23.** (b) **24.** (c) **25.** (a)

26. *The octal representation of an integer is 3428. If this were to be treated as the eight bit integer in an 8085 based computer, the decimal equivalent is :*

(a) 226 (b) – 98
(c) 76 (d) – 30

27. *Address space of 8086 CPU is :*

(a) 1 M byte (b) 256 K byte
(c) 1 KM byte (d) 64 K bytes

28. *Number of machine cycles required for RET instruction in 8085 μp is :*

(a) 1 (b) 2
(c) 3 (d) 5

29. *A single instruction to clear the lower four bits of the accumulator in 8085 assembly language is :*

(a) XRI OFH (b) ANI FOH
(c) XRI FOH (d) ANI OFH

30. *In a vectored interrupt :*

(a) The branch address is assigned to a fixed location in memory
(b) The interrupting source supplies the branch information to the processor the through an interrupt vector
(c) The branch address is obtained from a register in the processor
(d) None of above

31. *What are x and y in the following macro definition*

Macro	***Add x, y***	***Micro Add x, y***
Load	***y***	***Load y***
MUL	***x***	***MUL x***
Store	***y***	***Store y***
end macro		***end macro***

(a) Variables (b) Identifiers
(c) Actual parameters (d) Formal Parameters

32. *A sequence of two instructions that multiplies the contents of the DE register pair by 2 and stores the result in the HL regiester pair (8085 μp) is :*

(a) XCHG and DAD B (b) XTHL and DADH
(c) PCHL and DAD D (d) XCHG and DAD H.

33. *A slow memory can be connected to 8085 by using :*

(a) INTR (b) $\overline{\text{RESET IN}}$

(c) HOLD (d) READY

34. *A device employing INTR line for device interrupt puts the CALL instruction on the data bus while :*

(a) $\overline{INTA}$ is active

(b) HOLD is active

(c) READY is active

(d) None of the above

35. *In 8085 which of the following modifies the program counter ?*

(a) Only PCHL instruction

(b) Only ADD instruction

(c) Only JMP and CALL instruction

(d) All instructions

36. *What are the status of the auxillary carry (AC) and carry flag (CY) after executing the following 8085 program ?*

MV1 H, 5DH

MU1 L, 6B H

MOV A, H

ADD L

(A) AC = 0 and CY = 0

(B) AC = 1 and CY = 1

(c) AC = 1 and CY = 0

(d) AC = 0 and CY = 1

37. *RLC instruction is equivalent to :*

(a) STC (b) DAD H

(c) CMC (d) ADC C

38. *The 8085 μp will enter into 1 NA cycle after the recognition of :*

(a) Any interrupt (b) TRAP only

(c) INTR only (d) RST 7.5, 6.5, 5.5 only

39. *Which of the following lists the interrupts in increasing priority ?*

(a) INTR, RST 7.5, RST 6.5, RST 5.5, TRAP

(b) RST 5.5, RST 6.5, RST 7.5, TRAP, INTR

(c) INTR, RST 5.5, RST 6.5, RST 7.5, TRAP

(d) INTR, TRAP, RST 5.5, RST 6.5, RST 7.5

40. *The interrupt vector address for TRAP is :*

Answers : **26.*** (b) **27.*** (a) **28.*** (a),(c) **29.** (b) **30.** (b) **31.** (d) **32.** (d) **33.** (b) **34.** (a) **35.** (c) **36.** (c) **37.** (b) **38.** (c) **39.** (c)

(a) 0000 H (b) 0024 H
(c) 0018 H (d) 002C H

41. ***In order to reset carry without affecting accumulator content, one was to use :***
(a) SUB A (b) XRA A
(c) ORA A (d) CMC

42. ***Stack pointer will not be affected by the instructions :***
(a) Push PSW (b) CALL ADDRESS
(c) XTHL (d) RST n

43. ***Content on the temp loction after the execution of the above program is :***

MVI B, 00H
MVI A, 1C H
DCR B
DAA
STA TEMP
HLT

(a) 1 CH (b) 22 H
(c) 82 H (d) 12 H

44. ***Which of the following require maximum T-states?***
(a) MOV A, B (b) MOV A, M
(c) LDAX B (d) DAD D

45. ***The μp may be made to exist from HALT state by asserting :***
(a) RESET (b) Any of the five interrupt lines
(c) READY line (d) HOLD line by (a) or (b)

46. ***The number of RAM chips of size*** **(245 *k* × 1)** ***required to build 1 M byte memory is :***
(a) 8 (b) 32
(c) 10 (d) 24

47. ***Alter RESET, the CPU begains execution from meomory location :***
(a) 0000 H (b) 0001 H
(c) FFFFH (d) B000H

48. ***Which one of the following interrupt is non-maskable ?***
(a) TRAP (b) RST 7.5
(c) INTR (d) RST 6.5

49. ***The interrupt which is edge triggered ?***

(a) INTR (b) TRAP
(c) RST 7.5 (d) RST 5.5

50. ***In vectored interrupt :***
(a) The branch address is assigned to a fixed location in memory
(b) The interrupting source supplies the branch in formation to the processor through an interrupt vector
(c) The branch address is obtained from a register in the processor
(d) None of the above

51. ***Pick the class of interrupt with highest priority :***
(a) Supervisor call interrupt (SVC)
(b) Program interrupt
(c) I/O interrupt
(d) Time interrupt

52. ***Pick the class of interrupt with lowest priority :***
(a) Supervisor call interrupt (SVC)
(b) Program interrupt
(c) I/O interrupt
(d) Time interrupt

53. ***In 8085 μp, after the execution of XRA A instruction :***
(a) The carry flag is set
(b) The accumulator contains FF_H
(c) The zero flag is set
(d) The accumulator contents are shifted left by one bit.

54. ***In a microprocessor, the address of the next instruction to be executed, is stored in :***
(a) Stack pointer (b) Address latch
(c) Program counter (d) General purpose register

55. ***In order to enable RST 5.5, RST 6.5 and RST 7.5 interrupts, which of the following instruction are needed?***
(a) EI only (b) SIM only
(c) EI and SIM only (d) None of above

56. ***What do the contents of instruction regiser specify ?***
(a) Operand for the instruction being executed
(b) Op code for the instruction being executed

Answers : **40.** (b) **41.** (c) **42.** (c) **43.** (b) **44.** (d) **45.** (d) **46.** (b) **47.** (a)
48. (a) **49.** (c) **50.** (a) **51.** (a) **52.** (c) **53.** (c) **54.** (c) **55.** (c)

(c) Op code for the instruction to be executed next

(d) Operand for the instruction to be executed next

57. *What is the purpose of using ALE signal high ?*

(a) To latch low order address from bus to separate $A_0 - A_7$ lines

(b) To latch data $D_0 - D_7$ from bus to separate data bus

(c) To disable data bus latch

(d) All of the above

58. *The first machine cycle of an instruction is always :*

(a) A memory read cycle

(b) A fetch cycle

(c) A I/O read cycle

(d) A memory write cycle

59. *What is the purpose READY signal?*

(a) It is used to indicate to user that μp is working and ready for use

(b) It is used to provide for proper WAIT states when μp is communicating with slow peripheral devices ?

(c) It is used to provide for proper showing down of fast peripheral devices so as to communicated to μp's speed.

(d) None of above

60. *How many interrupts control lines are there in 8085 μp?*

(a) 6 (b) 8

(c) 12 (d) 16

61. *The PC contains 0450 H and SP contains 08D6H. What will be the content of PC and SP following a call to subroutine at location 02 AFH ?*

(a) 0453 H, 08D8 H (b) 0453 H, 08D4 H

(c) 02AFH, 08D 8H (d) 02AFH, 08D4 H

62. *How many and what are the machine cycles needed for execution of Push B ?*

(a) 2, Fetch and memory write

(b) 3, Fetch and 2 memory write

(c) 3, Fetch, memory write and read

(d) 3, Fetch and 2 memory read

63. *Shifting a register to left by one bit position is equivalent to (Binary code) :*

(a) Divison by 2

(b) Multiplication by 2

(c) Addition of 2

(d) Subtraction of 2

64. ***Parallel operation is preferred because :***

(a) It is faster than series operation

(b) If requires less memory

(c) Circuitary is simple

(d) All the above

Answers : **56.** (b) **57.** (a) **58.** (b) **59.** (b) **60.** (a) **61.** (d) **62.** (b) **63.** (b) **64.** (a)

SOLUTIONS

4. The contents of regsiter *B* is *2AH* after *MVI* operation which is move to *A*, and then *C*. Finally *A* is subtracted by *B* which is same *2AH* – *2AH* = *00H* (contents of *A*) Again the contents of *B* (*2AH*) is moved to *A*.

10. For all instruction CMC, ANA and RAL, the Flags are affected but for INX flags are not affected.

11. Loop will run infinite times becasue at every jump condition the contents of register are initilized.

12. Before the transfer of control to specified address, the address of the next instruction to CALL is pushed on the stack.

16. RST 7.5, 6.5, 5.5 are maskable interrupts TRAP is a non-maskable interrupt.

21. SOD is serial out data, not in instruction. All others RIM, SIM, and ADD are instructions.

22. 8086 is 16-bit and all others are 8-bit.

26.

D_7	D_6	D_5	D_4	D_3	D_2	D_1	D_1
1	1	1	0	0	0	1	0

Binary equivalent of 342

Which is equivalent to – 98

∵ D_7 bit is sign bit.

27. Address bus of 8086 μp is of 20 bits. So address space is of 2^{20} = 1 MB.

32. XCHG instruction changes the conents of DE with HL.

28. If condition is true-3(opcode fetch, memory read stack), memory read (stack)).

If condition is false-1 (opcode fetch).

DAD operation odds the contents of HL pair with register pair (HL).

CHAPTER 6

AUTOMATA THEORY

1. ***Let S and T be languages over $\Sigma = \{a, b\}$ represented by the regular expresions $(a + b^*)^*$ and $(a + b)^*$, respectively. Which of the following is true ?***

   (a) $S \subset T$ (b) $T \subset S$
   (c) $S = T$ (d) $S \cap T = \phi$

2. ***Let L denote the language generated by the grammer S → OSO/OO. Which of the following is true ?***

   (a) $L = O^+$ (b) L is regular but not O^+
   (c) L is context free but not regular (d) L is not context free

3. ***What can be said about a regular language L over {a} whose minimal finite state automation has two states ?***

   (a) L must be $\{a^n \mid n \text{ is odd}\}$
   (b) L must be $\{a^n \mid n \text{ is even}\}$
   (c) L must be $\{a^n \mid n \geq 0, 0\}$
   (d) Either L must be $\{a^n \mid n \text{ is odd}\}$, or L must be $\{a^n \mid n \text{ is even}\}$

4. ***Consider a regular expression (0 + 1) (0 + 1) ... n times. The minimum state finite automation that recognises the language represented by this regular expression contains :***

   (a) n states (b) $n + 1$ states
   (c) $n + 2$ states (d) None of above

5. ***Context free language are closed under :***

   (a) Union, intersection (b) Union, kleene closure
   (c) Intersection, complement (d) Complement, kleene closure

6. ***Let L_D be the set of all languages accepted by a PDA by final state and L_E the set of all languages accepted by empty stack. Which of the following is true ?***

   (a) $L_D = L_E$ (b) $L_D \supset L_E$
   (c) $L_D \subset L_E$ (d) None of above

Answers : **1.** (c) **2.** (b) **3.** (d) **4.*** (c) **5.** (a) **6.** (a)

7. *If L_1 is context free language and L_2 is a regular language, which of the following is/are false ?*

(a) $L_1 - L_2$ is not context free (b) $L_1 \cap L_2$ is context free

(c) $\sim L_1$ is context free (d) $\sim L_2$ is regular

8. *Two of the following four regular expressions are equivalent which two ? (ε is the empty string) ?*

(i) $(00)^* (\varepsilon + 0)$ (ii) $(00)^*$ (iii) 0^* (iv) $0(00)^*$

(a) (i) and (ii) (b) (ii) and (iii)

(c) (i) and (iii) (d) (iii) and (iv)

9. *Which of the following statements is false ?*

(a) The Halthing problem of Turing machines is undecidable

(b) Determining whether a context free grammar is ambiguous is undecidable

(c) Given two arbitrary context free grammars G_1 and G_2 it is undecidable whether $L(G_1) = L(G_2)$

(d) Given two regular grammars G_1 and G_2 it is undecidable whether $L(G_1) = L(G_2)$

10. *Let $L \subseteq \Sigma^*$ where $\Sigma = \{a, b\}$: Which of the following is true ?*

(a) $L = \{x \mid x$ has an equal number of a's and b's$\}$ is regular

(b) $L = \{a^n b^n \mid n \geq 1\}$ is regular

(c) $L = \{x \mid x$ has more a's than b's$\}$ is regular

(d) $L = \{a^m b^n \mid m \geq , n \geq 1\}$ is regular

11. *If the regular set A is represented by $A = (01 + 1)^*$ and the regular set 'B' is represented by $B = ((01)^* 1^*)^*$, which of the following is true ?*

(a) $A \subset B$

(b) $B \subset A$

(c) A and B are incomparable

(d) $A = B$

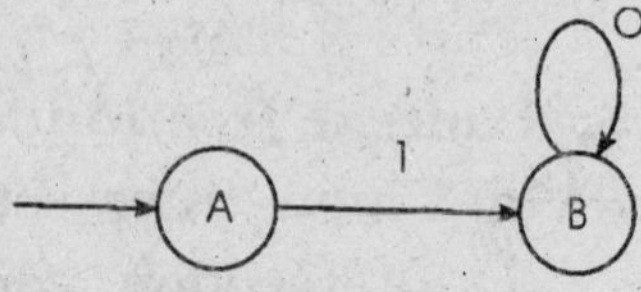

Determinaticautomaticfor serves

12. *Which of the following set can be recognized by a Deterministic Finite-state Automaton ?*

(a) The number 1, 2, 4, 8, ..., 2^n , ... written in binary

(b) The number 1, 2, 4, ..., 2^n , ... written in unary

(c) The set of binary string in which the number of zeros is the same as the number of ones

(d) The set {1, 101, 11011, 1110111, ... }

13. ***Regarding the power of recognition of languages, which of the following statements is false ?***

(a) The non-deterministic finite-state automata are equivalent to deterministic finite-state automata.

(b) Non-deterministic Push-down automata are equivalent to deterministic Push-down automata.

(c) Non-deterministic Turing machines are equivalent to deterministic Push-down automata.

(d) Multi-tape Turing machines are equivalent to Single-tape Turing machines.

14. ***The string 1101 does not belong to the set represented by :***

(a) $110^* (0 + 1)$ (b) $1(0 + 1)^* 101$

(c) $(10)^* (01)^* (00 + 11)^*$ (d) $(00 + (11)^* 0)^*$

15. ***Let L be the set of all binary strings whose last two symbols are the same. The number of states in the minimum state deterministic finite. automata accepting L is :***

(a) 2 (b) 5

(c) 8 (d) 3

16. ***Which one of the following regular expressions over {0, 1} denotes the set of all strings not containing 100 as a substring ?***

(a) $0^* (1 + 0)^*$ (b) $0^* 1010^*$

(c) $0^* 1 {}^*01$ (d) $0^*(10 + 1)^*$

17. ***Which of the following languages over {a, b, c} is accepted by a deterministic pushdown automaton ?***

(a) $\{wcw^R \mid w \in \{a, b\}^*\}$ (b) $\{ww^R \mid w \in \{a, b, c\}^*\}$

(c) $\{a^n b^n c^n \mid n \geq 0\}$ (d) $\{w \mid w$ is a palindrome over $\{a, b, c\}\}$

18. ***If L_1 and L_2 are context free languages and R a regular set, one of the languages below is not necessarily a context free languages ?***

(a) L_1L_2 (b) $L_1 \cap L_2$

(c) $L_1 \cap R$ (d) $L_1 \cup L_2$

19. ***In some programming languages, an indentifier is permitted to be a letter followed by any number of letter or digits. If L and D denote the sets of letters and digits respectively, which of the following expressions defines an identifier ?***

Answers : **7.** (a),(c) **8.** (c) **9.** (d) **10.** (d) **11.*** (d) **12.** (a) **13.** (b) **14.** (c) **15.** (b) **16.** (b) **17.** (a) **18.** (b)

(a) $(L \cup D)^+$ (b) $L(L \cup D)^*$

(c) $(L, D)^*$ (d) $L.(L.D)^*$

20. ***Consider a grammer with the following productions ?***

$S \rightarrow a \alpha b \mid b \alpha c \mid aB$

$S \rightarrow \alpha S \mid b$

$S \rightarrow a\,bb \mid ab$

$b\alpha \rightarrow b\,d\,b \mid b$

The above grammer is :

(a) Context free (b) Regular

(c) Context sensitive (d) $LR(K)$

21. ***Let $\Sigma = \{0, 1\}$, $L = \Sigma^*$ and $R = \{0^n 1^n$ such that $n > 0\}$ then the languages $L \cup R$ and R are respectively :***

(a) Regular, Regular (b) Nor Regular, Regular

(c) Regular, Not Regular (d) Not Regular, Not Regular

22. ***Which of the following conversions is not possible ?***

(a) Regular grammer to context free grammer

(b) Non-deterministic *FSA* to determinstic *FSA*

(c) Non-deterministic *PDA* to deterministic *PDA*

(d) Non-deterministic Turing Machine to determinitic Turing Mechine

23. ***Which of the following features cannot be captured by context-free grammers ?***

(a) Syntex of if-than-else statements

(b) Syntex of recursive procedures

(c) Whether a variable has been declared before it use

(d) Variable names of arbitrary length

24. ***If the state machine described below should have a stable state, the restriction on the inputs is given by :***

(a) $a \cdot b = 1$

(b) $a + b = 1$

(c) $\bar{a} + \bar{b} = 1$

(d) $\overline{a \cdot b} = 1$

(e) $\overline{a + b} = 1$

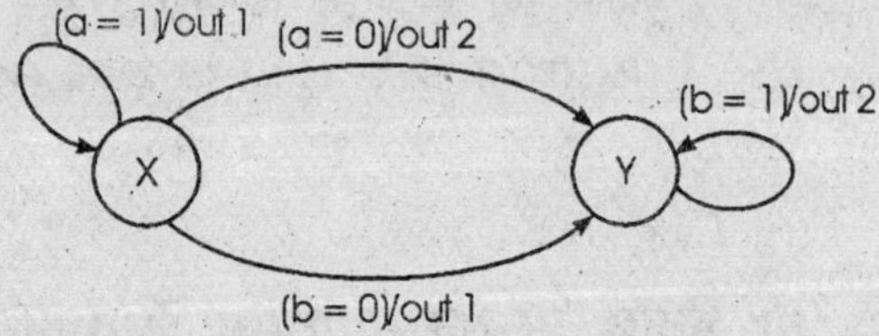

25. ***If Σ is finite non-empty set of symbols, then the language is a subset:***

(a) Σ^+ (b) Σ^*

(c) $\Sigma^+ + \{\lambda\}$ (d) None of above

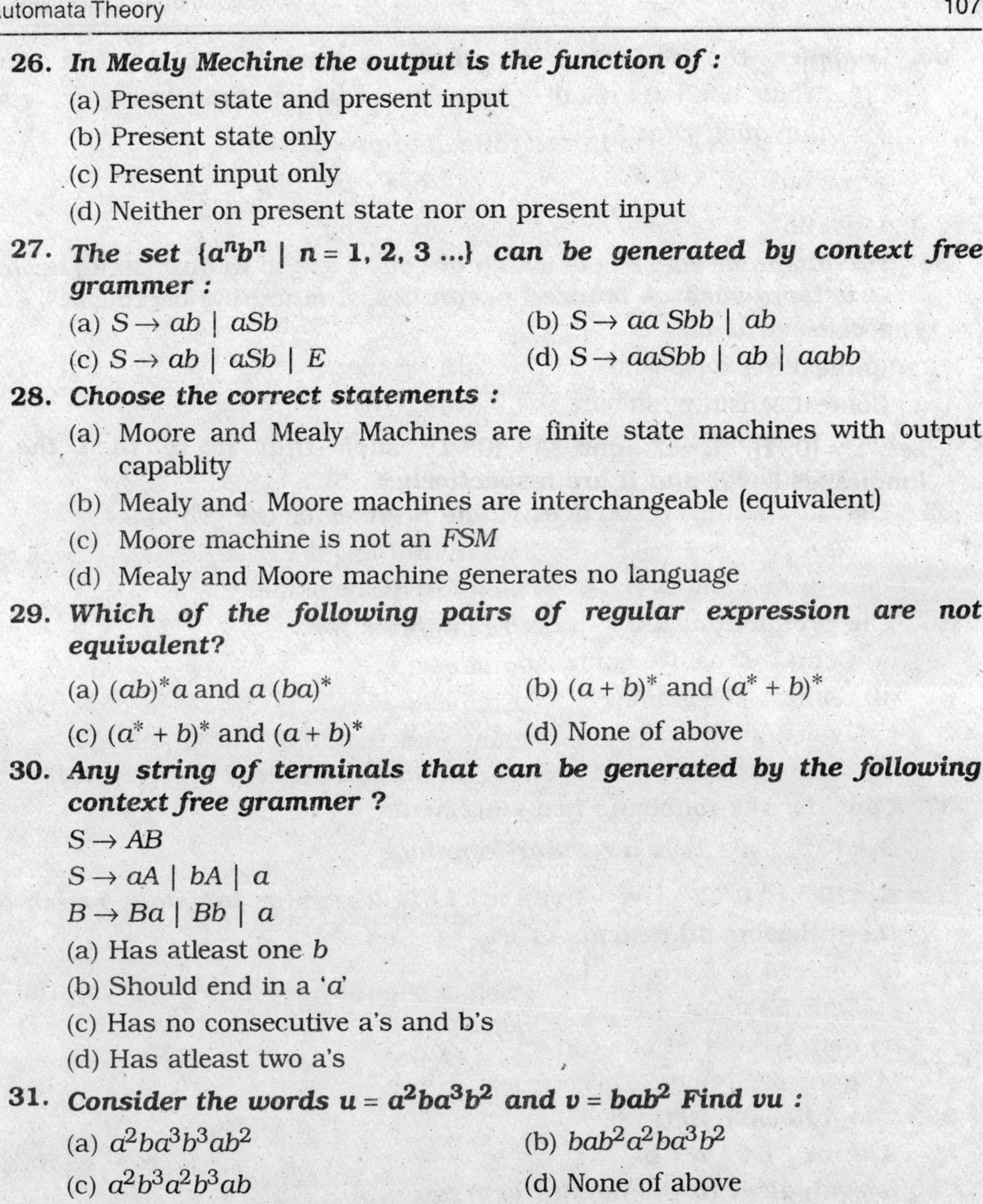

26. *In Mealy Mechine the output is the function of :*

(a) Present state and present input

(b) Present state only

(c) Present input only

(d) Neither on present state nor on present input

27. *The set $\{a^n b^n \mid n = 1, 2, 3 \ldots\}$ can be generated by context free grammer :*

(a) $S \to ab \mid aSb$ (b) $S \to aa\,Sbb \mid ab$

(c) $S \to ab \mid aSb \mid E$ (d) $S \to aaSbb \mid ab \mid aabb$

28. *Choose the correct statements :*

(a) Moore and Mealy Machines are finite state machines with output capablity

(b) Mealy and Moore machines are interchangeable (equivalent)

(c) Moore machine is not an *FSM*

(d) Mealy and Moore machine generates no language

29. *Which of the following pairs of regular expression are not equivalent?*

(a) $(ab)^* a$ and $a\,(ba)^*$ (b) $(a + b)^*$ and $(a^* + b)^*$

(c) $(a^* + b)^*$ and $(a + b)^*$ (d) None of above

30. *Any string of terminals that can be generated by the following context free grammer ?*

$S \to AB$

$S \to aA \mid bA \mid a$

$B \to Ba \mid Bb \mid a$

(a) Has atleast one *b*

(b) Should end in a '*a*'

(c) Has no consecutive a's and b's

(d) Has atleast two a's

31. *Consider the words $u = a^2ba^3b^2$ and $v = bab^2$ Find vu :*

(a) $a^2ba^3b^3ab^2$ (b) $bab^2a^2ba^3b^2$

(c) $a^2b^3a^2b^3ab$ (d) None of above

32. *In the above question find the value of $|uv|$:*

(a) 10 (b) 11

(c) 12 (d) 14

Answers : **19.** (b) **20.** (c) **21.** (c) **22.** (c) **23.** (b) **24.** (b) **25.** (b),(c)
26.* (a) **27.*** (a),(d) **28.** (a),(b),(c) **29.** (d) **30.*** (d) **31.** (b) **32.** (c)

33. Consider the following language r over $A = \{a, b\}$ such that $L_1 = \{b^m ab^n : m > 0, n > 0\}$ find a regular expression r over $A = \{a, b\}$ such that $L_1 = L(r)$:

(a) $r = aa^* \, bb^*$
(b) $r = bb^* \, abb^*$
(c) $r = ab^*$
(d) $r = ba^*$

34. The language constructs which are most useful in describing nested structures such as balaced parantheses, matching begin-end's etc. are :

(a) Regular expressions
(b) Context free grammars
(c) Non-context free grammers
(d) None of above

35. The .... recognizes viable prefixes of the grammer ?

(a) *NFA*
(b) *DFA*
(c) both *NFA* and *DFA*
(d) None of above

36. The production $aAb \to acccb$ is defined for :

(a) Context sensitive grammer
(b) Context free grammer
(c) Type-3 grammer
(d) Linear grammer

37. Consider the following two statements

$S_1 : \{0^{2n} \mid n \geq 1\}$ is a regular language

$S_2 : \{0^m \mid^n 0^{m+n} \mid m \geq 1 \text{ and } n \geq 1\}$ is a regular language which of the following statements is true :

(a) Only S1 is correct
(b) Only S2 is correct
(c) Both S1 and S2 one correct
(d) None of S1 and S2 is correct

38. The following CFG

$A \to aA \mid bA \mid a \mid b$

is equivalent to the regular expression :

(a) $(a^* + b)^*$
(b) $(a + b)^+$
(c) $(a + b)(a + b)^*$
(d) $(a + b) * (a + b)$

39. ***Which of the following CFG's can't be simulated by an FSM ?***

(a) $S \to S\,a \mid a$

(b) $S \to abA$
$A \to cB$
$B \to d \mid a\,A$

(c) $S \to aSb \mid ab$

(d) None of above

40. ***What will be regular expressions for the set of all strings of 0's and 1's ending in 00 ?***

(a) $0\,(0 + 1)^*\,1$

(b) $(0 + 1)^*\,00$

(c) $0\,(0 + 1)^*\,1$

(d) $(0 + 1)^*\,01$

41. ***Regular expression for $L = \{\lambda, 11, 1111, 111111 \ldots\}$:***

(a) $(00)^*$

(b) $(0 + 1)^*$

(c) $(11)^*$

(d) 1^*

42. ***If ϕ be the regular expression then the value of $(\phi^*)^*$:***

(a) ϕ

(b) 0

(c) 1

(d) λ

43. ***What will be the regular expression for $L = \{a^n \mid n$ is divisible by 2 or 3 or $n = 5\}$?***

(a) $(a^2)^* + a^5$

(b) $(a^2)^* + (a^3)^* + (a^5)^*$

(c) $(a^2)^* + (a^3)^* + a^5$

(d) $(a^5)^* + (a^3)^*$

44. ***Which of the following pairs are regular ?***

(a) $L = \{a^{i^2} \mid i \geq 1\}$

(b) $L = \{ww^R : w \in \Sigma^*\}$

(c) $L = \{a^{2n} \mid n \geq 1\}$

(d) None of above

45. ***Which of the following statements is true ?***

(a) If a language is context tree it can always be accepted by a deterministic push down automation

(b) The union of two context free languages is context free

(c) The intersection of two context free languages is context free

(d) The complement of a context free language is context free

46. ***Given an arbitrary non-deterministic finite automation (NFA) with N states, the maximum number of states in an equivalent minimized DFA is at least :***

(a) N^2

(b) 2^N

(c) $2N$

(d) $N!$

Answers : **33.** (b) **34.** (b) **35.** (b) **36.*** (a) **37.*** (a) **38.** (b),(c),(d) **39.*** (c) **40.** (b) **41.** (c),(d) **42.*** (d) **43.** (b) **44.*** (b),(c) **45.** (a) **46.** (c)

47. *Consider a DFA, over $\Sigma = \{a, b\}$ accepting all strings which have number of a's divisible by 6 and number of b's divisible by 8. What is the minimum number of states that the DFA will have ?*

(a) 8 (b) 14

(c) 15 (d) 48

48. *The finite state machine described by the following state diagram with A as starting state, where an label is $\frac{x}{y}$ and x stands for 1-bit input and y stands for 2-bit output :*

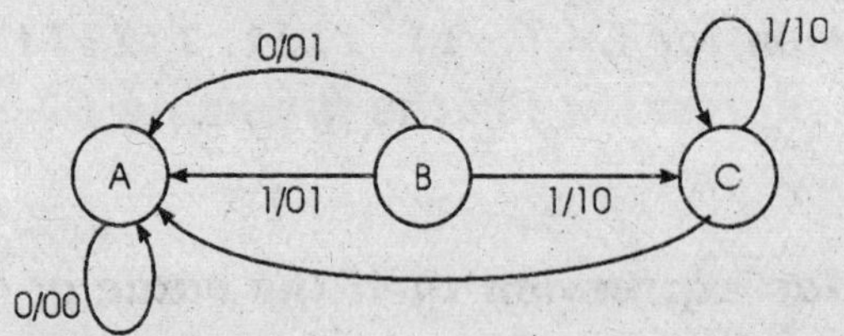

(a) Outputs the sum of the present and the previous bits of the input

(b) Output 01 whenever the input sequence contains 11

(c) Outputs 00 whenever the input sequence contains 10

(d) None of the above

49. *The smallest finite automaton which accepts the language $\{x \mid$ length of x is divisible by 3$\}$ has :*

(a) 2 states (b) 3 states

(c) 4 states (d) 5 states

50. *Consider the following languages*

$L1 = \{ww \mid w \in \{a, b\}^*\}$

$L2 = \{ww^R \mid w \in \{a, b\}^*$, w^R is the reverse of $w\}$

$L3 = \{o^{2i} \mid i$ is an integer$\}$

$L4 = \{O^{i^2} \mid i$ is an integer$\}$

Which of the languages are regular ?

(a) Only $L\,1$ and $L\,2$ (b) Only $L\,2$, $L\,3$ and $L\,4$

(c) Only $L\,3$ and $L\,4$ (d) Only $L\,3$.

51. *Consider the following problem X*

Given a Turing machine M over the input alphabet Σ, any state q of M and a word $w \in \Sigma^*$, does the computation of N on w visit the state q ?

Which of the following statements about X is correct ?

(a) X is decidable
(b) X is undecidable but partially decidable
(c) X is undecidable and not even partially decidable
(d) X is not a decision problem

52. ***The language accepted by a pushdown Automaton in which the stack is limited to 10 items is best described as :***
(a) Context free
(b) Regular
(c) Deterministic context free
(d) Recursive

53. ***The regular expression for the following DFA is :***
(a) $(a^* + b^*)\ abb$
(b) $(ab)^*\ ab$
(c) $a^*\ ab^*\ ba$
(d) $(a \mid b)^*\ abb$

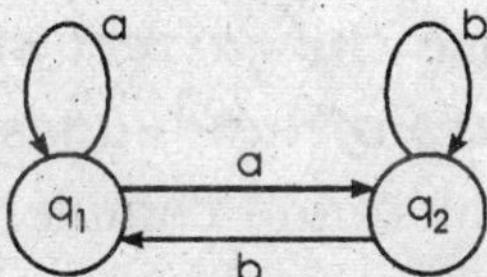

54. ***CSG can be recognized by a :***
(a) *FSM*
(b) *DPDM*
(c) *NDPDM*
(d) linear bounded memory machine

55. ***Choose the correct statements :***
(a) An *FSM* with 1 stack is more powerful than an *FSM* with no stack
(b) An *FSM* with 3 stack is more powerful than an *FSM* with 2 stacks
(c) An *FSM* with 2 stacks is more powerful than a *FSM* with 1 stack
(d) All of above

56. ***The number of states of the FSM, required to simulate a computer, with a memory capable of storing 'm' words, each of length 'n' bits is :***
(a) $m \times 2^n$
(b) 2^{mn}
(c) 2^{m+n}
(d) None of the above

57. ***The language English is a :***
(a) Regular language
(b) Context free language
(c) Context sensitive language
(d) None of the above

Answers : **47.** (b) **48.** (a) **49.** (b) **50.** (a) **51.** (c) **52.** (c) **53.** (d) **54.** (d) **55.** (a),(c) **56.*** (b) **57.** (b)

58. X, Y, W are three languages. If X and W are regular and if XY = W, then :

(a) Y has to be regular
(b) Y cannot be regular
(c) Y need not be regular
(d) Y has to be a CFL

59. Consider the grammer

$S \to PQ \mid SQ \mid PS$

$P \to x$

$Q \to y$

To get a string of n terminals, the number of productions to be used is :

(a) n^2
(b) $n + 1$
(c) $2n$
(d) $2n - 1$

60. Choose the correct statements.

A class of languages that is closed under :

(a) Union and complementation has to be closed under intersection
(b) Intersection and complementation has to be closed under union
(c) Union and intersection has to be closed under complementation
(d) All of the above

61. Which of the following definitions generates the same language as L, where $L = \{x^n y^n, n \geq 1\}$?

(i) $E \to xEy \mid xy$

(ii) $xy \mid x^+ xyy^+$

(iii) $x^+ y^+$

(a) (i) only
(b) (i) and (ii)
(c) (ii) and (iii)
(d) (ii) only

62. Let $A = \{0, 1\}$ and $L = A^*$. Let $R = \{0^n 1^n, n > 0\}$, then the languages LUR and R are respectively :

(a) Regular, regular
(b) Not regular, regular
(c) Regular, not regular
(d) Not regular, not regular

63. Which of the following is not possible algorithmically ?

(a) Regular grammar to context free grammar
(b) Non-deterministic FSA to deterministic FSA
(c) Non-deterministic PDA to deterministic PDA
(d) Non-determinists Turing machine to deterministic Turing machine

64. An FSM can be used to add two given integers. This is :

(a) True (b) False

(c) May be true (d) None of the above

65. *A CFG is said to be in Chosky Normal Form (CNF), if all the productions are of the form A → BC or A → a. Let G be a CFG in CNF. To derive a string of terminals of langth x, the number of productions to be used is :*

(a) $2x - 1$ (b) $2x$

(c) $2x + 1$ (d) 2^x

66. *Which of the following statements is false ?*

(a) Every type 3 grammar is a type 2 grammar

(b) English is a language (of automaton) on the alphabet $(a, b, c, ..., z)$.

(c) Any word of $\Sigma^* = \bigcup_{k=0}^{\infty} \Sigma^k$ is of finite length

(d) Accepted words only can form a language

67. *From the set of production*

S → ABSc, S → Abc, BA → AB, Bb → bb, Ab → ab and Aa → aa

(i) it is possible to derive the word abc

(ii) it is possible to derive the word aabc

Of the two statements (i) and (ii),

(a) Both are frue (b) Both are false

(c) (i) is true and (ii) is false (d) (i) is false and (ii) is true

68. *Consider the following statements (i), (ii), (iii) and (iv) :*

(i) It is enough, if a FSM which can perform binary addition is equipped with three states, namely, carry (c), not carry (n) and stop (s)

(ii) The concept of an algorithm is an idealization of the underlying logic of an actual program.

(iii) An algorithm is a single list of instructions for a computation

(iv) The grammar

S → AB, B → ab, A → aa, A → a, B → b is unambiguous.

Then

(a) All the statements are true

(b) Only (i), (ii), (iii) are true

(c) Only (ii) , (iii), (iv) are true

(d) Only (i), (iii), (iv) are true

Answers : **58.*** (c) **59.** (d) **60.*** (a),(b) **61.*** (a) **62.*** (c) **63.*** (c) **64.*** (b) **65.*** (a) **66.** (d) **67.** (c) **68.** (b)

69. Let $\Sigma = \{a, b\}$. Then an automaton A accepting only those words from Σ having an even number of a's requires

(a) Only one state
(b) Only two states
(c) Only three states
(d) More than three states

70. $(a \mid b)^*$ denotes the set of all strings :

(a) With zero or more instances of a or b
(b) With one or more instances of a or b
(c) Equal to $(a^* b^*)^*$
(d) Only $a^n b^n$ where $n \geq 0$

71. $(a) \mid ((b)^*(c))$ is equivalent to :

(a) The set of strings with either a or zero or more b's and one c
(b) The set of strings with either a or one or more b's and one c
(c) $b^* c \mid a$
(d) Both (b) and (a)

72. Using top-down parsing determine which of the following strings belongs to the languages generated by the grammer G = (V, T, S, P) where

V = (a, b, c, A, B, C, S)

T = (a, b, c)

S = starting symbol

and the productions P are given by

$S \rightarrow AB$, $A \rightarrow Ca$, $B \rightarrow Ba$, $B \rightarrow Cb$, $B \rightarrow b$, $C \rightarrow Cb$, $C \rightarrow b$

(i) baba ***(ii) abab*** ***(iii) cbaba***

(a) (i) only
(b) Both (i) and (ii)
(c) Both (ii) and (iii)
(d) None of the above

73. Find, if G = (V, T, S, P) is a type 3 grammar given that V = {S, A, B, a, b} and T = {a, b}, S is the start symbol. The productions P are given by

(i) $S \rightarrow aAB$, $A \rightarrow Bb$, $B \rightarrow \lambda$
(ii) $S \rightarrow ABA$, $A \rightarrow aB$, $B \rightarrow ab$
(iii) $S \rightarrow bA$, $A \rightarrow b$, $S \rightarrow \lambda$
(iv) $S \rightarrow aA$, $A \rightarrow bB$, $B \rightarrow b$, $B \rightarrow \lambda$

(a) (i) only
(b) (ii) only
(c) (iii) only
(d) (iv) only

74. An automaton is a .... device and a grammar is a .... device :

(a) Generative, cognitive
(b) Generative, acceptor
(c) Acceptor, cognitive
(d) Cognitive, generative
(e) Cognitive, acceptor

75. Pushdown machine represents :

(a) Type 3 regular grammar (RG)

(b) Type 2 context-free grammar (*CFG*)
(c) Type 1 context-sensitive grammar (*CSG*)
(d) Type 0 phrase-structured grammar (*PSG*)

76. ***If L (G_i) represents the class of languages that can be generated by the class of grammars G_i, where G_0 is unrestricted grammar, G_1 is context-sensitive grammar, G_2 is context-free grammar and G_3 is regular grammar, then which of the following is true ?***

(a) $L(G_0) \subset L(G_1) \subset L(G_2) \subset L(G_3)$ (b) $L(G_0) \supset L(G_1) \supset L(G_2) \supset L(G_3)$
(c) All context-free are regular (d) None of the above

77. ***Two finite state machines are said to be equivalent if :***

(a) They have the same member of states
(b) They have the same member of edges
(c) They have the same member of states and edges
(d) They recognize the same set of tokens

78. ***Consider the NFA M shown below :***

Let the language accepted by M be L. Let L_1 be the language accepted by the NFA M_1, obtained by changing the accepting state of M to a non-accepting state and by changing the non-accepting state of M to accepting states. Which of the following statements is true?

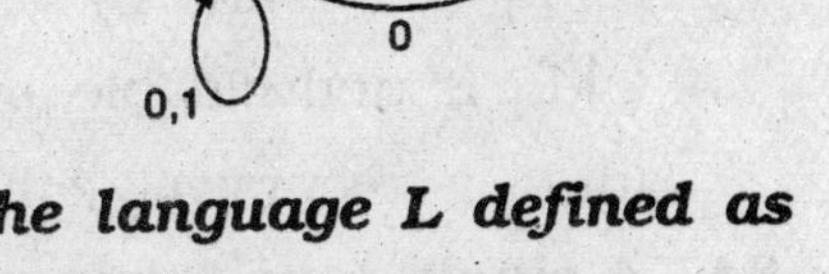

(a) L_0 = (0, 1)* - L
(b) L_1 = (0, 1)*
(c) $L_1 \subseteq L$
(d) L_1 = L

79. ***Nobody knows yet if P = NP. Consider the language L defined as follows:***

$$L = \begin{cases} (0+1)^* \text{ if } P = NP \\ \phi \text{ otherwise} \end{cases}$$

Which of the following statemnts is true?

(a) L is recursive
(b) L is recursively enumerable but not recursive
(c) L is not recursively enumerable
(d) Whether L is recursive or not will be known after we find out if P = NP

Answers : **69.** (b) **70.** (a),(c) **71.** (a),(c) **72.** (a) **73.** (c) **74.** (d)
75. (b) **76.** (b) **77.** (d) **78.*** (c) **79.*** (d)

80. *The regular expression O$_*$ (10$_{**}$ denotes the same set as*

(a) (1*0)*1*
(b) 0 + (0 + 10)*
(c) (0 + 1)*10(0 + 1)*
(d) none of the above

81. *If the strings of a language L can be effectively enumerated in lexicographic (i.e., alphabetic) order, which of the following statements is true?*

(a) L is necessarily finite
(b) L is regular but not necessarily finite
(c) Le is context free but not necessarily regular
(d) Le is recursive but not necessaily context free

82. *Let G = ((S), (a, b) R, S) be a conect free grammer where he rule set R is S * a S b | SS | s***

Which of he following statements is true?
(a) G is not ambiguous
(b) There exits z, y, ** L (G) such hatt xy ** L(G)
(c) There is a deterministic pushdown automation that accepts L(G)
(d) We can find adeterministic finite state automation that accepts L(G)

83. *Consider two language L_1 and L_2 each on the alphabet * Let F : **** be a polynomial time computable bijection such that (**) Further, let f^{-1} be also polynomial time computable.***

Which of he following CANNOT be true?
(a) L_1 ** P and L_2 is finite
(b) L_1 *** NP and L_2 ****P
(c) L_1 is undecidable and L_2 is decidable
(d) L_1 is recursively enumerable and L_2 is recursive

84. *A single tape Turing Machine M has two states q_0 and q_1 of which q_0 is the starrting state. The tape alphabet of M is (, 1, B) and its nput alphabet is (0, 1). The symbol B is the blank symbol usedto indicate end of an input string. The transtion function of M is described in the following table ****

he tableisinterpreted as illustrated below.

The entry (q1, 1, R) in row q_0 and column 1 signifies that if M is in state q_0 and reads 1 on the current tape square, then it writes 1 on the same tape square, moves its tape head one position to the right and transitions to state q_1.

Which of the following statements is true about M?

(a) M doesnot halt on any string in $(0 + 1)_+$

(b) M does not halt on any string in $(00 + 1)_*$

(c) M halts on all string ending in a 0

(d) M halts on all string ending in a 1

85. ***Define languages L_0 and L_1 as follows :***

$$L_0 = (, w, 0 \mid M \text{ halt on } w)$$

$$L_1 = (, w, 1 \mid M \text{ does no halts on } w)$$

Here , w, i is a triple, whose first component. M is an encoding of a Turing Maching, second component, w, is a string, and hirdcomponent, i, is a bit.

Let L = L_0 *** L_1. Which of the following is true?

(a) L isrecursively enumerable, but L** is no

(b) L is recursively enumerable, but L** is not

(c) Both L and L** are recursive

(d) Neither L nor L** is recursively enumerable

86. ***Consider the following deterministic finite stateautomaion M.***

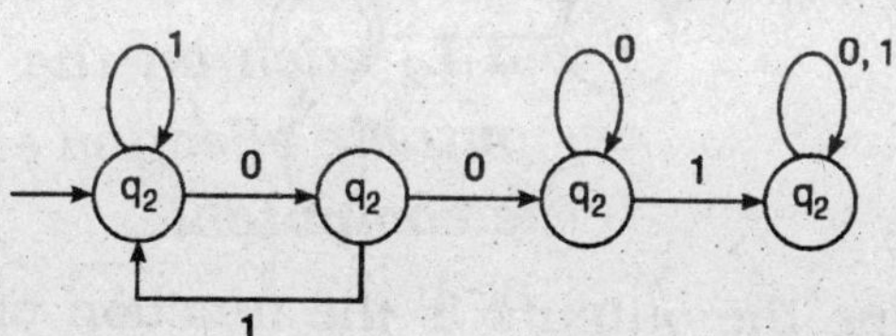

Let S denotethesetofseven bit binary stringsin which the first, the fourth, and he last bits are 1. The number of strings in S that are accepted by M is

(a) 1 (b) 5

(c) 7 (d) 8

Answers : **80.*** (d) **81.*** (d) **82.*** (d) **83.** (c) **84.** (d) **85.** (a) **86.*** (a)

SOLUTIONS

4. The finite state automation must basically accept any n bit string so, we nead $n + 1$ states for counting through 0 to n and finally a termination state. Totally, we need $n + 2$ states.

7. Intersection of a context free language and a regular language is context freee. $L_1 - L_2$ is the same as $L_1 \cap \sim L_2$. Also $\sim L_2$ is regular (as complement of a regular language is regular).

So $L_1 - L_2$ is context free. so A is false.

11. $(R_1 + R_2)^* = R_1{}^* R_2{}^*$

$(R_1{}^*) = R_1{}^*$, R_1 and R_2 are regular expressions.

15.

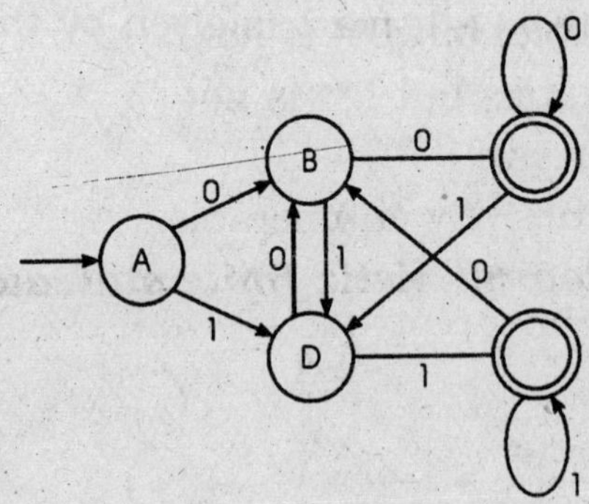

26. In mealy mechine the outputs is the function of the present state $q(t)$ and present input $x(t)$

$$z(t) = \lambda(q(t), x(t))$$

27. Because production $S \to aaSbb \mid ab$ can't produce $aa\,bb$ and $S \to ab \mid aSb \mid E$ cannot be possible due to $S \to E$.

30. Starting symbol is S, and $A \to a$, $B \to a$ are the only productions that could terminate a string variable from A and B respectively. So, atleast two a's have to come any way.

36. In type I grammer (context sensitive grammer) Productions will be of the form

$$aAb \to a\,\alpha\,b$$

where A is between two letters type grammer (context free grammer) is of the type $A \to aacb$

Type 3 grammer (linear or regular) is of the type $A \to aA/a$ or

$$A \to aC \mid Bc \mid b.$$

37. The state diagram for finite state automaton M accepting S_1. Therefore $S_1 = L(M)$ is thus a regular language.

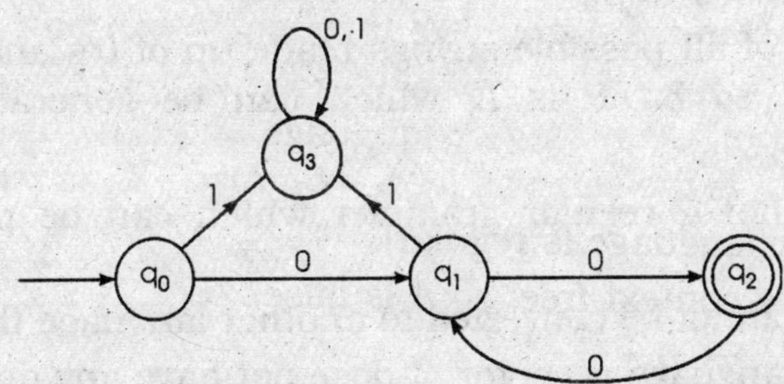

The language S_2 generated by grammer G which consists of all words of the form $0^m \mid {}^n0^{m+n}$ with $m \geq 1$, $n \geq 1$ is given by the productions.

$S \to 0S0$, $X \to 1\,X0$

$S \to 0X0$, $X \to 10$ with S as start symbol. Since the productions are not of the form $A \to a$, $A \to aB$. $A \to \lambda$. So G is not a regular grammer.

39. Generates the set $\{a^m b^m, m = 1, 2, 3 \ldots\}$ which in not regular. (a) and (b) being left linear and right liner respectively, should have equivalent regular expressions.

42.

Since $\phi^* = \lambda$ then

$$(\phi^*)^* = (\lambda)^* = \lambda$$

Value of $\lambda^* = \lambda$.

56. Totally these are mn bits. Each bit can be in one of the two possible states- 1 or 0. So the entire memory made up of mn bits will be in one of the possible 2^{mn} states.

58. For example

$$X = a^*$$

$$Y = a^n b^n b^*$$

$$W = XY = a^*\ b^*$$

60. By De Morgan's laws the first two options can be proved easily. Let the universal set U be $\{1, 2, 3, 4\}$. Let $A = \{\{1\}, \{4\}, \{1, 4\}, \{2, 4\}, \{1, 2, 4\}, \{\lambda\}\}$. A is closed under and intersection but is not closed under complementation. For example, complement of $\{1, 4\}$ is $\{2, 3\}$ which is not a member of A.

61. II generates strings like

xxyyy which are not supposed to be III generates strings like *xyy*, which are not supposed to be.

62. *L* be the set of all possible strings made up of 0's and 1's (including the null string). So $L \cup R$ is *L*, which can be generated by the regular expression $(a + b)^*$

where *R* is not a regular grammer which can be proved by pumping Lemma.

63. A language cannot be converted to another language that is less powerful.

64. All *FSM* are language acceptor, it dose not have any output capability. So, it cannot add or subtract and output result.

65. Proved by induction.

78.

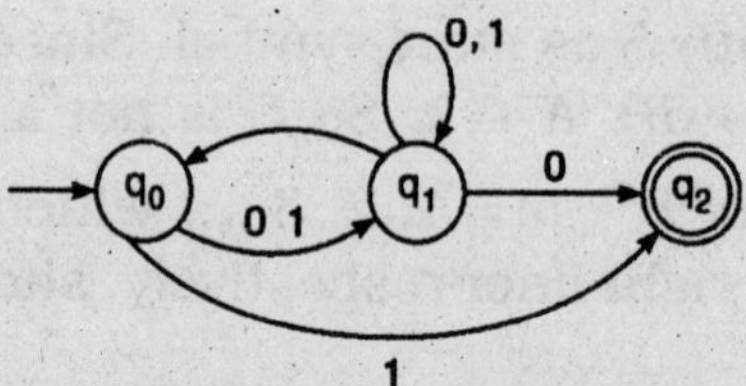

By changing the non accepting state to accepting state and changing the accepting state to non accepting state known as L_1

$$L_1 = (0/1)\ (0,\ 1)^*$$

$$= 0(0/1)\ (0,\ 1)^*$$

So $L_1 \subseteq L$

79. P = NP or P ≠ NP

This is an unsolved problem in computer science.

80. $0^*\ (10^*)^* = 0^*\ (1^*\ 0^*)$

So by $(1^*\ 0)^*\ |\ ^* = (1^*\ 0^*)|^*$

∴ First option is wrong

$$0 + (0 + 10)^* = 0 + (0^*\ |^*\ 0^*)$$

This option is also wrong

$$(0 + 1)^*\ 10\ (0 + 1)^* = 0^*\ |^*\ 10\ (0^*\ |^*)$$

Therefore fourth option is correct.

81. Therefore fourth opion is correct. It is a sequence of number with no repetation.

82. Hence, S is ambiguous, therefore we can find a deterministicfinie state automata that accepts (G).

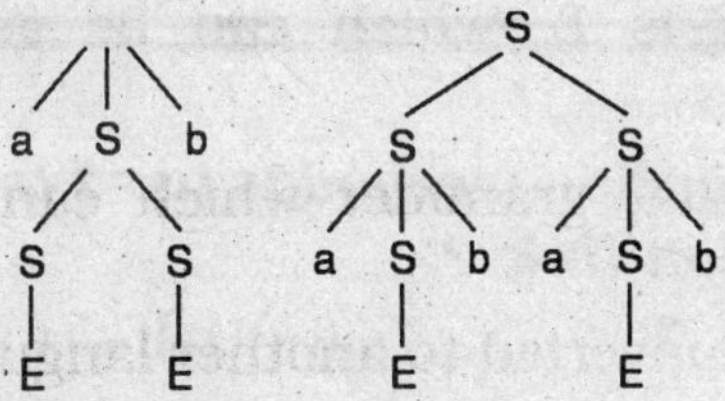

84.

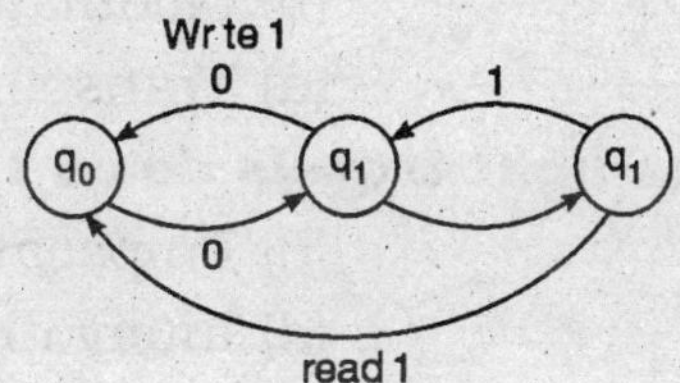

86. The number of strings in S hat are accepted by M is one

Position	1	2	3	4	5	6	7
	1	0	0	1	0	0	1

CHAPTER 7

COMPUTER NETWORKS

1. ***Which data communication method is used to transmit the data over a serial communication link ?***

(a) Simplex (b) Half-duplex

(c) Full duplex (d) All of above

2. ***In communication satellite, multiple repeaters are known as :***

(a) Detector (b) Modulator

(c) Stations (d) Transponders

3. ***Loss in signal power as light travels down the fibre is called :***

(a) Attenuation (b) Propagation

(c) Scattering (d) Interruption

4. ***In OSI model, dialogue control and token management are responsibilities of :***

(a) Session layer (b) Network layer

(c) Transport layer (d) Data link layer

5. ***Under mark parity, each parity bit is :***

(a) Alternated between 0 and 1 (b) Always set to 0

(c) Always set to 1 (d) Not used

6. ***half-duplex protocol :***

(a) Exceeds that of a full-duplex protocol

(b) Is less than that of a full-duplex protocol

(c) Equals throughput on a full-duplex protocol

(d) Is faster than all other types of protocols

7. ***Synchronous modems are more costly than the asynchronous modems because :***

(a) They produce large volume of data

(b) They contain clock recovery circuits

(c) They transmit the data with stop and start bit

(d) Capable of operating large bandwith

8. ***Which of the following is an important characteristic of LAN ?***

(a) Application independent interfaces

(b) Parallel transmission

(c) Unlimited expansion

(d) More cheaper

9. ***The basic Ethernet design does not provide :***

(a) Access control

(b) Addressing

(c) Automatic retransmission of a message

(d) Multiple virtual networks

10. ***Which of the following is possible in a token passing bus networks ?***

(a) In-service expansion

(b) Unlimited number of stations

(c) Unlimited distance

(d) None of above

11. ***Which of these protocols is a sliding window protocol ?***

(a) XMODEM (b) YMODEM

(c) YMODEM-G (d) WXMODEM

12. ***Difference between DDCMP and SDLC is :***

(a) DDCMP does not have a transparent mode

(b) SDLC does not use a CRC

(c) DDCMP has a message header

(d) DDCMP does not require special hardware to find the beginning of a message

13. ***Which of the following transmission systems provides the highest data rate to an individual device?***

(a) Voiceband modem (b) Local area network

(c) Computer bus (d) Digital PBX

14. ***Main characteristic of a LAN ?***

(a) Parallel transmission

(b) Unlimited expansion

(c) Low-cost access for low-bandwidth channels

(d) Application-independent interfaces

15. ***Which of the following transmission media is not readily suitable to CSMA operation ?***

(a) Radio (b) Optical fibers

(c) Coaxial cable (d) Twisted pair

Answers : **1.** (c) **2.** (d) **3.** (a) **4.** (a) **5.** (c) **6.** (a) **7.** (b) **8.** (a) **9.** (c) **10.** (a) **11.** (d) **12.** (a) **13.** (c) **14.** (d) **15.** (b)

16. *Which of the following functions is not provided as part of the basic Ethernet design?*

(a) Access control

(b) Addressing

(c) Automatic retransmission of a message

(d) Multiple virtual networks

17. *Which of the following data communications functions is generally provided for in a LAN ?*

(a) Data link control
(b) Applications processing

(c) Flow control
(d) Routing

18. *Minimum length of an Ethernet frame ?*

(a) 64 bytes
(b) 72 bytes

(c) 1500 bytes
(d) 1700 bytes

19. *What is the function of the preamble in an Ethernet network?*

(a) Clock synchronization
(b) Error checking

(c) Collision avoidance
(d) Broadcast

20. *What is the difference between the Ethernet frame Preamble field and the IEEE 802.3 Preamble and Start of Frame Delimiter fields ?*

(a) 1 byte
(b) 1 bit

(c) 8 bits
(d) 16 bits

21. *An Ethernet hub :*

(a) Functions as a repeater

(b) Connects to a digital PBX

(c) Connects to a token-ring network

(d) Functions as a gateway

22. *Which of the following is a key characteristic of an FDDI network ?*

(a) Self-healing capability
(b) 10 Mbps operating rate

(c) Ring enable capability
(d) IEEE standardization

23. *A bridge operates at which layer ?*

(a) The data link layer
(b) The application layer

(c) The network layer
(d) The segmentation layer

24. *A major advantage associated with the use of a LAN switch is its capability to :*

(a) Convert frames

(b) Support multiple simultaneous connections

(c) Enable cut-through storage

(d) Connect file servers

25. ***What is ARPANET ?***

(a) Computer program

(b) A network funded by DARPA

(c) Collection of networks

(d) A connectionless protocol network

26. ***TCP/IP :***

(a) Is restricted to use on LANs

(b) Operates only on IBM PCs

(c) Is in the public domain

(d) Was developed by Dr. Ethernet

27. ***What authority is responsible for assignning the network portion of an IP address?***

(a) NetCen (b) Network Centre

(c) Nicnet (d) InterNIC

28. ***The largest range of addresses available for assignment to a host computer is obtained by which of the following ?***

(a) A Class A address (b) A Class B address

(c) A Class C address (d) A Class D address

29. ***The network 198.78.41.0 is a :***

(a) Class A network (b) Class B network

(c) Class C network (d) Class D network

30. ***The subnet mask 255.255.255.192 :***

(a) Extends the network portion to 16 bits

(b) Extends the network portion to 26 bits

(c) Extends the network portion to 36 bits

(d) None of above

31. ***Which of the following Transmission system provides the highest data rate to an individual devices ?***

(a) Computer bus (b) Telephone lines

(c) Voice band modem (d) Leased lines

32. ***In a synchronous modem, the digital-to-analog converter transmits signal to the :***

(a) Equalizer (b) Modulator

Answers : **16.** (c) **17.** (a) **18.** (b) **19.** (a) **20.** (b) **21.** (a) **22.** (a) **23.** (c) **24.** (b) **25.** (b) **26.** (c) **27.** (d) **28.** (a) **29.** (c) **30.** (b) **31.** (a)

(c) Demodulator (d) Terminal

33. ***In geosynchronous orbit, satellite :***

(a) Remain in a fixed position so that as earth rotates, it can fully cover the earth

(b) Remains in a fixed position related to points on earth.

(c) Moves faster than the earth's rotation so that it can cover larger portion of earth

(d) Moves simultaneously

34. ***The Address Resolution Protocol translates :***

(a) A physical address into a hardware address

(b) An IP address into a logical address

(c) A hardware address into a physical address

(d) An IP address into a hardware address

35. ***The TCP sliding window :***

(a) Can be used to control the flow of information

(b) Always occurs when the field value is 0

(c) Always occurs when the field value is 1

(d) Occurs horizontally

36. ***A key advantage of using a GUI—based TCP/IP application is that it :***

(a) Glues the application to an HP address

(b) Hides the complexity of commands

(c) Allows file transfers

(d) Initiates server protection

37. ***The first level of protection between the Internet and a corporate network :***

(a) A proxy service (b) A corporate administrator

(c) The security policy (d) A router access list

38. ***A firewall feature that can protect against repeated attempts to illegally log on to a computer :***

(a) Authentication (b) The buddy system

(c) Proxy services (d) Stateful inspection

39. ***Infoseek is a :***

(a) A Web browser

(b) A TCP/IP protocol

(c) A Web search tool

(d) A network layer protocol

40. ***Frequency of failure and network recovery time after a failure are measures of :***

(a) Performance (b) Reliability

(c) Security (d) Feasibility

41. ***Which topology requires a central controller or hub ?***

(a) Mesh (b) Star

(c) Bus (d) Ring

42. ***Communication between a computer and a keyboard involves transmission :***

(a) Simplex (b) Half-duplex

(c) Full-duplex (d) Automatic

43. ***Which of the following topology is most reliable ?***

(a) Mesh (b) Star

(c) Bus (d) Ring

44. ***A television broadcast is an example of ______ transmission :***

(a) Simplex (b) Half-duplex

(c) Full-duplex (d) Automatic

45. ***In a ________ topology, if there are n devices in a network, each device has n – 1 ports for cables.***

(a) Mesh (b) Star

(c) Bus (d) Ring

46. ***The OSI model consists of _________ layers :***

(a) Three (b) Five

(c) Seven (d) Eight

47. ***The location of synchronization points is decided by :***

(a) Transport (b) Session

(c) Presentation (d) Application

48. ***The end-to-end delivery of the entire message is the responsibility of the ________ layer.***

(a) Network (b) Transport

(c) Session (d) Presentation

49. ***In the _________ layer, the data unit is called a frame :***

(a) Physical (b) Data link

(c) Network (d) Transport

Answers : **32.** (a) **33.** (a) **34.** (d) **35.** (a) **36.** (b) **37.** (d) **38.** (d) **39.** (c) **40.** (b)
41. (b) **42.** (a) **43.** (a) **44.** (a) **45.** (a) **46.** (c) **47.** (b) **48.** (b) **49.** (b)

50. *Decryption and encryption of data are the responsibility of the _______ layer :*

(a) Physical (b) Data link
(c) Presentation (d) Session

51. *Dialog control is a function of the _________ layer :*

(a) Transport (b) Session
(c) Presentation (d) Application

52. *Node-to-node delivery of the data unit is the responsibility of the _________ layer :*

(a) Physical (b) Data link
(c) Transport (d) Network

53. *As the data packet moves from the upper to the lower layers, headers are _________ :*

(a) Added (b) Removed
(c) Rearranged (d) Modified

54. *translations from one character code to another occur in :*

(a) Transport (b) Session
(c) Presentation (d) Application

55. *The amount of uncertainty in a system of symbol is called :*

(a) Bandwidth (b) Entropy
(c) Loss (d) Quantum

56. *Synchronous protocol :*

(a) Trammit characters one at a time
(b) Allow faster transmission than asynchronous protocol do
(c) Are generally used by personal computers
(d) Are more reliabile

57. *The geostationary satellite used for communication systems :*

(a) Rotates with the earth
(b) Remains stationary relative to the earth
(c) Is positioned over equator
(d) All of above

58. *Coaxial cable has conductors with :*

(a) Equal resistance (b) The same diameter
(c) Common axis (d) None of above

59. *If the bandwidth of a singal is 5 kHz and the lowest frequency is 52 kHz, what the highest frequency ?*

(a) 5 kHz (b) 10 kHz
(c) 47 kHz (d) 57 kHz

60. ***As frequency increases, the period :***

(a) Decreases (b) Increases
(c) Ramains the same (d) Doubles

61. ***HDLC is :***

(a) High-duplex line communication
(b) High-duplex data link control
(c) High-duplex digital link combination
(d) Host double level circuit

62. ***When data and acknowledgement are sent on the same frame, this is called :***

(a) Piggybacking (b) Backpacking
(c) Piggypacking (d) A good idea

63. ***In token ring, where is the token when a data frame is in circulation ?***

(a) At the receiving station (b) At the sending station
(c) Circulating in the ring (d) None of these

64. ***Which Project 802 standard provides for a collision-free protocol ?***

(a) 802.2 (b) 802.3
(c) 802.5 (d) 802.6

65. ***Another term for CSMA/CD and the IEEE 802.3 standard is :***

(a) Ethernet (b) Token ring
(c) FDDI (d) Token bus

66. ***FDDI :***

(a) Fast data delivery interface (b) Fiber distributed data interface
(c) Fibre distributed digital interface (d) Fast distributed data interface

67. ***The application layer of a network :***

(a) Establishes, maintains, and terminates virtual circuits
(b) Defines the user's port into the network
(c) Consists of software being run on the computer connected to the network
(d) All of the above

68. ***How many pairs of stations can simultanesusly communicate on Ethenet LAN ?***

(a) 1 (b) 2

Answers : **50.** (c) **51.** (b) **52.** (b) **53.** (a) **54.** (c) **55.** (b) **56.** (b) **57.** (d) **58.** (c)
59. (d) **60.** (a) **61.** (b) **62.** (a) **63.** (b) **64.** (c) **65.** (a) **66.** (b) **67.** (c)

(c) 3 (d) Multiple

69. *FDDI is a :*

(a) Ring network (b) Star network
(c) Mesh network (d) Bus network

70. *In which OSI layers does the FDDI protocol operate ?*

(a) Physical (b) Data link
(c) Network (d) (a) and (b)

71. *Which OSI layer corresponds to the TCP-UDP layer ?*

(a) Physical (b) Data link
(c) Network (d) Transport

72. *Which of the following is an example of a client-server model ?*

(a) DNS (b) FTP
(c) TELENT (d) All of these

73. *What are the components of a browser ?*

(a) Retrieval method, host computer, pathname
(b) Controller, client program, interpreter
(c) Hypertext, hypermedia, HTML
(d) All of the above

74. *Which type of Web document is run at the client site?*

(a) Static (b) Dynamic
(c) Active (d) All of these

75. *Java is :*

(a) A programming language (b) A runtime environment
(c) A class library (d) All of these

76. *The difference between a multiplexer and statistical multiplexer is :*

(a) Statistical multiplexers need buffers while multiplexers do not need buffers
(b) Multiplexer uses X.25 protocol, while statistical multiplexers use the Aloha protocol
(c) Multipliexers use TDM while statistical multiplexers uses FDM
(d) None of above

77. *Which of the following is not an example of network layer ?*

(a) X.25 level - 2 - ISO layer
(b) Source routing and Domain naming—Usenet
(c) X.25 packet level Protocol (PLP) - ISO
(d) Internet protocol (IP) - ARPANET

78. *Ethernet transmits data in :*

(a) Continuous streams of 0's and 1's
(b) Frames
(c) Blocks of 256 byts
(d) None of the above

79. *A workgroup is a set of users that :*

(a) Share common properties (b) Use the same printer
(c) Work as a term on projects (d) None of the above

80. *Flow control is used to prevent :*

(a) Bit errors
(b) Overflow of the sender buffer
(c) Overflow of the receiver buffer
(d) Collision between sender and receiver

81. *For a sliding window of buffer size n, what will be a maximum number of frame sent but unacknowledged ?*

(a) 0 (b) n – 1
(c) n (d) n + 1

82. *ARQ stands for ________ :*

(a) Automatic repeat quantization
(b) Automatic repeat request
(c) Automatic retransmission request
(d) Acknowledge repeat request

83. *Sending a file from your personal computer's primary memory or disk to another computer is called :*

(a) Uploading (b) Downloading
(c) Logging on (d) Hang on

84. *Demodulation is a process of :*

(a) Converting digital signals to analog signals
(b) Connerting analog signals to digital signals
(c) Combining many low speed channels into one high speed channel
(d) Dividing the high speed signals into frequency bands

85. *Which of the following is used for modulation and demodulation ?*

(a) Protocols (b) Gateway
(c) Modern (d) Multiplexer

Answers : **68.** (a) **69.** (a) **70.** (d) **71.** (d) **72.** (d) **73.** (d) **74.** (c) **75.** (d) **76.** (a) **77.** (a) **78.** (b) **79.** (a) **80.** (c) **81.** (a) **82.** (b) **83.** (a) **84.** (b) **85.** (c)

86. *Difference between synchronous and asynchronous trammission is :*

(a) The clocking is derived from the data in synchronous transmission

(b) The clocking is mixed with the data in asynchronous transmission

(c) Pulse height is different

(d) Bandwidth is different

87. *Maximum data rate of a channel for a noiseles 3 - KHz binary channel is*

(a) 3000 bps (b) 6000 bps

(c) 1500 bps (d) None of the above

88. *Maximum data rate of a channel of 3000 Hz bandwidth and SNR of 30 dB is*

(a) 15,000 bps (b) 60,000 bps

(c) 30,000 bps (d) 3,000 bps

89. *Asuming that for a given network layer inplementation connection establishment overhead is 100 bytes and disconnection overhead is 28 bytes. What would be the minimum size of a packet the transport layer needs to keep up, if it wishes to implement a datagram service above the network layer and needs to keep its overhead to a maximum of 12.5% (Ignore transport layer overhead)*

(a) 512 bytes (b) 768 bytes

(c) 1152 bytes (d) 1024 bytes

90. *The topology with linghest reliability is*

(a) bus topology (b) star topology

(c) ring topology (d) mesh topology

91. *How many characters per sec. (7 bits + 1 parity) can be transmitted over a 2400 bps line if the transfer of synchronous (1 start and 1 stop bit)?*

(a) 300 (b) 240

(c) 250 (d) 200

92. *How many characters per sec. (7 bits + 1 parity) can be transmitted over a 2400 bps line if the transfer is asynchronous (1 start and 1 stop bit)?*

(a) 300 (b) 240

(c) 250 (d) 275

93. *Which of the following assetions is FAlse about the Internet Protocol (IP)?*

(a) It is possible for a computer to have multiple IP addresses

(b) IP packets from the same source to the same destination can take different routes in the network

(c) IP ensures that a packetr is discarded if it is unable to reach its destination within a given number of hops

(d) The packet source cannot set the route of an outgoing packets; the route is determined only by the routing tables in the routers on the way

94. ***Which of the following functionalities must be implemented by a transpor protocol over and above the network protocol?***

(a) Recovery from packet losses

(b) Detection of duplicate packets

(c) Packet delivery in the correct order

(d) End to end connectivity

95. ***Which of the following scenarious may lead to an irrecoverable error in a database system?***

(a) A transaction writes a data item after it is read by an uncommitted transaction

(b) A transaction reads a data item after it is read by an uncommitted transaction

(c) A transaction reads a data item after it is written by a committed transaction

(d) A transaction reads a data item after it is written by an uncommitted transaction

96. ***The subnet mask for a particular network is 255.255.31.0. Which of the folowing pair of IP addresses could belong to this network?***

(a) 172.57.88.62 and 172.56.87.233

(b) 10.35.28.3 and 10.35.29.4

(c) 191.203.31.87 and 191.234.31.88

(d) 128.129.43 and 128.8.161.55

97. ***A 2km long broadcast LAN has 10 roman nothing sup 7 bps bandwidth and uses CSMA/CD. The signal travels along the wire at 2 × 10 roman nothing sup 8 m/s. What is the minimum packet size that can be used on this network?***

(a) 50 bytes

(b) 100 bytes

(c) 200 bytes

(d) None of the above

Answers :

86. (a)	**87.*** (b)	**88.*** (c)	**89.** (d)	**90.** (d)	**91.*** (a)
92.* (b)	**93.*** (a)	**94.** (d)	**95.** (d)	**96.*** (c)	**97.*** (d)

98. ***Host A is sending data to host B over a full duplex link. A and B are using the sliding window protocol for flow control. The send and receive window sizes are 5 packets eac. Data packets (sent only from A to B) are all 1000 bytes long and the transmission time for such a packet is 50 ***. Acknowledgement packets (sent only from B to A) are very smal land require negligible transmission time. The propagation delay over the link is 200 ***. What is the maximum achievable throughput in this communication?***

(a) 7.69 × 10 roman nothing sup 8 bps
(b) 11.11 × kk10 roman nothing sup 6 bps
(c) 12.33 × 10 roman nothing sup 6 bps
(d) 15.00 × 10 roman nothing sup 6 bps

Answers : **98.*** (b)

SOLUTIONS

87. Maximam data rate = $2H \log_2 V$ bps

where H is bandwidth,

V is the discrete levels

$= 2 \times 3 \log_2 2 = 6$ kbs = 6000 bps.

88. Maximum number of the bps = ***

= 3 log roman nothing sub 2 (1 + 30) = 30,000 bps.

91. No. of characters transmitted : 2400/8 = 300

Start and stop bits are not needed in synchronous transfer of data.

92. No. of characters transmitted

$$= \frac{2400}{(8+1+1)} = \frac{2400}{10} = 240$$

93. Rvery computer has a fixed IP addresses.

96. Subet mask 255.255.31.0

Shows class C network

So IP address in class C is 191.203.31.87 and 191.234.31.88.

97. l = 2km = 2000 mts.

$\lambda = 10^7$ bpsec

$V = 2 \times 10^8$ m/sec

$$t = \frac{S}{V} = \frac{2 \times 10^3}{2 \times 10^8} = 10\ \mu \text{ sec}$$

Total no. of packets = $10^7 \times 10\ \mu$ sec = 100 bits.

98. Size of window = 5 packet

Size of packet = 1000 bytes

Size of window = 5000 bytes

Transmisstion time = 5 × 50 = 250 *** sec

Propagation delay = 200 *** sec

Therefore total time delay = 250 + 200 = 450 ** μ sec

$$\text{Maximum thoughput} = \frac{500}{450} \times 10^8$$

$= 11.11 \times 10^6$ bpsec.

■□■

CHAPTER 8

COMPILERS

1. ***Assembler is a machine dependent, because of :***
   (a) Macro definition table (MDT)
   (b) Pseudo operation table (POT)
   (c) Argument list array (ALA)
   (d) Mnemonics operation table (MOT)
2. ***Macro processor is an inbuilt function of :***
   (a) Loader (b) Editor
   (c) Linker (d) Assembler
3. ***Storage mapping is done by :***
   (a) Loader (b) Linker
   (c) Operating system (d) Compiler
4. ***Forward reference table (FRT) is arranged like :***
   (a) Stack (b) Queue
   (c) Linked list (d) Double linked list
5. ***Which of the following derivations a top-down parser use while parsing an input string? The input is assumed to be scanned in left to right order :***
   (a) Leftmost derivation
   (b) Leftmost derivation traced out in reverse
   (c) Rightmost derivation
   (d) Rightmost derivation traced out in reverse
6. ***In what module, multiple instances of execution will yield the same result even if one instance has not terminated before the next one has begun ?***
   (a) Nonreusable module (b) Serially module
   (c) Reenterable module (d) Recursive module
7. ***Which of the following system software does the job of merging the records from two files into one ?***
   (a) Documentation system (b) Utility program
   (c) Networking software (d) Security software

8. ***Which of the following is/are loop optimization technique?***
(a) Jamming (b) Unrolling
(c) Induction variable elimination (d) All of above

9. ***Which of the following can be used to identify loops ?***
(a) Dominators (b) Reducible graphs
(c) Depth first search (d) All of the above

10. ***Which table is a permanent database that has an entry for each terminal symbol ?***
(a) Terminal table (b) Literal table
(c) Identifier table (d) Reductions

11. ***The table created by laxical analysis to describe all literal used in the source program is :***
(a) Terminal table (b) Literal table
(c) Identifier table (d) Reductions

12. ***In absolute loading scheme, which loader function is accompished by assembler ?***
(a) Reallocation (b) Allocation
(c) Linking (d) Loading

13. ***Non-relocatable program is one which :***
(a) Cannot be made to execute in any area of storage other than the one designated for it at the time of its coding or translation
(b) Consists of a program and relevant information for its relocation
(c) Can itself perform the relocation of its address-Sensitive portions
(d) All of the above

14. ***The graph showing the inter-dependencies of the attributes of different nodes in a parse tree is called :***
(a) Flow graph (b) Dependency graph
(c) Karnaugh's graph (d) Steffi graph

15. ***Three address code involves :***
(a) Exectly three address (b) No unary operators
(c) At most 3 address (d) None of above

16. ***Symbol table is used for :***
(a) Checking type compatibility
(b) Suppressing duplication of error messages
(c) Storage allocation

Answers : **1.** (d) **2.** (d) **3.*** (d) **4.** (c) **5.** (a) **6.** (c) **7.** (b) **8.** (d)
9. (d) **10.** (a) **11.** (b) **12.** (a) **13.** (a) **14.** (b) **15.** (c)

(d) None of above

17. ***Main advantage of panic mode of error recovery is :***

(a) Simple to implement (b) It is very effective

(c) Never gets into infinite loop (d) None of above

18. ***Which of the following statements is false ?***

(a) An unambiguous grammer has the same leftmost and rightmost derivation

(b) An LL(1) parser is a top-down parser

(c) LALR is more powerful than SLR

(d) An ambiguous grammer can never be LR(K) for any K.

19. ***Optimizing compiler :***

(a) Is optimized to occupy less space

(b) Is optimized to take less time for execution

(c) Optimizes the code

(d) None of above

20. ***Phase structured grammers is/are :***

(a) Regular (b) Context free

(c) Context-sensitive (d) None of above

21. ***Synthesized attribute can be easily simulated by a :***

(a) LL grammer (b) Ambiguous grammer

(c) LR grammer (d) None of above

22. ***Bottom up parser generates :***

(a) Leftmost derivation (b) Rightmost derivation

(c) Rightmost derivation in reverse (d) Leftmost derivation

23. ***An ideal compiler should :***

(a) Be smaller in size

(b) Take less time for compiling

(c) Be written in a high level language

(d) Produce object code that is smaller in size and executes faster.

24. ***An ideal compiler should :***

(a) Detect error

(b) Detect and repair error

(c) Detect, repair and correct error

(d) None of above

25. ***Optimization techniques whch are typically applied on loops :***

(a) Peephole optimization

(b) Constant folding

(c) Elimination of induction variables

(d) Removal of invariant computation.

26. ***Which of the following statements is true ?***

(a) SLR parser is more powerful than LALR

(b) LALR parser is more powerful than canonical LR parser

(c) Canonical LR parser is more powerful than LALR parser

(d) The parser SLR, cononical CR, and LALR have the same power

27. ***Cross-compiler is a compiler :***

(a) Which is written in a language that is different from the source language

(b) That generates object code for its host machine

(c) Which is written in a language that is same as the source language

(d) That runs on one machine but produces object code for another machine.

28. ***Which of the following is/are true ?***

(a) Debugging can be faster and easier in interpreter than compiler

(b) Interpreter takes less time to execute than compiler

(c) Compiler can generate stand-alone programs that often take less time for execution

(d) Interpreter needs less computer resources than compiler

(e) Interpreter is helpful in the initial stages of program development than compiler

29. ***Given the following expression grammer***

E → E * F | F + E | F

F → F-F | id

Which of the following is true ?

(a) * has higher precedence than +

(b) – has higher precedence than *

(c) + and – have same precedence

(d) + has higher precedence than *

30. ***Which of the following is the most powerful parsing method ?***

(a) LL(1)

(b) Canonical LR

(c) SLR

(d) LALR

Answers : **16.** (a),(b),(c) **17.** (a),(c) **18.** (d) **19.** (c) **20.** (a),(b),(c) **21.** (c) **22.** (c) **23.** (a),(b),(c),(d) **24.** (c) **25.** (c),(d) **26.** (c) **27.** (d **28.** (a),(c),(e) **29.** (b) **30.** (b)

31. *A grammer that is both left and right recursive for a non-terminal, is :*

(a) Ambiguous

(b) Unambiguous

(c) Information is not sufficient to decide whether it is ambiguous or unambiguous

(d) None of above

32. *Shift Reduce parsers are :*

(a) Top down parsers (b) Bottom up parsers

(c) May be top down or bottom up (d) None of the above

33. *Recursive descent parsing is an example of :*

(a) Top-down parsing (b) Bottom-up parsing

(c) Predictive parsing (d) None of above

34. *LR stands for :*

(a) Left to right

(b) Left to right reduction

(c) Right to left

(d) Left to right and right most derivation in reverse

35. *A programming language is to be designed to run on a machine that has small memory. The language should :*

(a) Prefer a 2 pass compiler to a 1 pass compiler

(b) Prefer a 1 pass compiler to a 2 pass compiler

(c) Prefer an interpreter to a compiler

(d) Not support recursion

36. *Which of the following is/are correct :*

(a) Loader brings object program into memory for execution

(b) Linkage editors perform linking after loading

(c) Dynamically linking schemes delay linking until execution time

(d) Absolute loader modifies the object program to be loaded at any address location

37. *A compiler compiler is an :*

(a) Compiler which compiles a compiler program

(b) Software tool used in automatic generation of a compiler

(c) Compiler written in the same language it compiles

(d) Another name for cross compiler

38. ***A compiler which allows only the modified section of the source code to be recompiled is called as :***

(a) Incremental compiler (b) Reconfigurable compiler
(c) Dynamic compiler (d) Selective compiler

39. ***Which of the following system software resides in main memory always ?***

(a) Text editor (b) Loader
(c) Linker (d) Assembler

40. ***The machine independent phases of the compiler :***

(a) Syntax analysis (b) Code generation
(c) Lexical analysis (d) Intermediate code generation

41. ***Which of the following is/are correct ?***

(a) Any s/w can be simulated by Hardware
(b) Any hardware can be simulated by software
(c) Firmware is nothing but hardware implementation of s/w
(d) Firmware is nothing but software implementation of hardware

42. ***A software is to be developed for a system which has small memory. The s/w should have***

(a) Use recursion whenever possible
(b) Avoid using recursion
(c) Use macros instead of functions
(d) Not use macros insead of functions

43. ***Which of the following suffices to convert an arbitrary CGF to an LL (1) grammar?***

(a) Removing left recursion alone
(b) Factoring the grammar alone
(c) Removing left recursion and factoring the grammar
(d) None of the above

44. ***Assume that the SLR parser for a grammer G has n roman nothing sub 1 states and the LALR parser for G has n roman nothing sub 2 states. The relationship between n_1 and n_2 is***

(a) n_1 is necessarily less than n_2
(b) n_1 is necessarily equal to n_2
(c) n_1 is necessarily greater than n_2
(d) none of the above

Answers : **31.*** (c) **32.*** (b) **33.** (a) **34.** (d) **35.*** (a),(b),(d) **36.** (b),(d) **37.*** (b)
38. (a) **39.** (b) **40.** (a),(c),(d) **41.*** (a),(b),(c) **42.** (b),(d) **43.*** (c) **44.*** (b)

45. *In a bottom up evaluation of a sytax directed definition, inherited attributes can*

(a) always be evaluated

(b) be evaluated only if the definition is L-attributed

(c) be evaluted only if the definition has synthesized attributes

(d) never be evaluated

46. *Consider the grammer shows below*

$$S \rightarrow i\,E\,t\,S\,S' \mid a$$
$$S' \rightarrow e\,S \mid \varepsilon$$
$$E \rightarrow b$$

In the predictive parse table. M, of this grammer, the entries M[S', e] and M[S', $] respectively are

(a) (b)

(c) (d)

47. *Consider the grammer show below*

$$S \rightarrow CC$$
$$C \rightarrow c\,C\,d$$

The grammer is

(a) LL (1) (b) SLR (1) but not LL (1)

(c) LALR (1) but not SLR (1) (d) LR (1) but not LALR (1)

48. *Consider the translation scheme shown below*

S → TR

R → T {print ('+');} R | ε

T → numb {print (num.val);}

Here num is a taken that represents an integer and num.val reresents the corresponding integer value. For an input string '9 + 5 + 2', this translation scheme will print

(a) 9 + 5 + 2 (b) 95 + 2 +

(c) 952 + + (d) ++ 952

Answers : **45.** (c) **46.** (a) **47.*** (d) **48.** (d)

SOLUTIONS

3. Compiler generates 'storage mapping' to access real data stored in memory.

31. The grammar A → AA, A → a is ambiguous. It is left and right recursive.

The grammer A → A × B, B→YB, A→a, B→b is not ambiguous through it is left or right recursive.

32. Any shift reduce parser typically works by shifting entries onto the stack. If a handle is found in the top of the stack, it is popped and replaced by the corresponding left and side of the production, If ultimately we have only the starting non-terminal on the stack, when there are no more tokens to be scanned, the parsing will be successful. So, it is bottom-up.

35. In two pass compiler, the space occupied by the first pass can be used by the second pass. Since an interpreter translates and executes one line at a time, it is less complex than a compiler. So, it should occupy less space. Recursion needs run time stack, whose size changes dynamically and often increases exponentially with respect to the associated paramter.

37. These are tools that can be used to automatically generate modules of a compiler. *e.g*, YACC (yet another compiler-compiler) generates the parser when the syntax of the language, in the form of CFG, is given as input.

41. S/w and H/w are logically equivalent. The function of the hardware can be simulated by the software and the function of the s/w can be simulated by the hardware.

42. Each time macro is called, it will expanded, thus increasing the code size. Using functions instead of macros increases the execution time because of the function call overhead, but the size of the source code will not increase.

43. Grammer is top down parsing. It is used in left recursion.

44. Number of tates in SLR and LALR parser are always same.

47.

S → CC
C → c C d
S → c C/d

is an example of canonical LR grammer. Cannonical LR grammer is called LR (1) grammer. Every SLR (1) is in LR (1) grammer.

■□■

CHAPTER 9

DBMS

1. ***The way a particular application views the data from the database that the application uses is a :***

   (a) Module (b) Relational model

   (c) Schema (d) Subschema

2. ***A network schema permits :***

   (a) Many-to-many relation-ships

   (b) One-to-many relation-ships

   (c) Many-to-one relation-ships

   (d) None of above

3. ***In a database the smallest entity to be processed as a single unit is called :***

   (a) Data field (b) Data record

   (c) Data file (d) Data base

4. ***Locking can be used for :***

   (a) Deadlock (b) Lost update

   (c) Uncommitted dependency (d) Inconsistant data

5. ***In relational model column is referred to as :***

   (a) Tuple (b) Entity

   (c) Degree (d) Attribute

6. ***ER model comes under :***

   (a) Physical data model

   (b) Record based logical model

   (c) Object based logical model

   (d) All of above

7. ***If we delete a record to which another record contains a pointer, then that pointer is called a :***

   (a) Pinned pointer (b) Dangling pointer

   (c) Pointless fointer (d) None of above

8. ***A computer file can be best described as :***

   (a) A single data item.

(b) A general collection of data item

(c) An orderly collection of data items

(d) A random collection of data items

9. *Report generators can :*

(a) Print row-oriented reports

(b) Perform arithmetic operations

(c) Selectively retrive and print lists

(d) All of the above

10. *Which of the following is/are problems of file management system?*

(a) Update

(b) Lack of data independences

(c) Data redundancy

(d) All of the above

11. *Which of the following is not a logical database structure ?*

(a) Tree

(b) Network

(c) Chain

(d) Relational

12. *Consider the following set of functional dependencies on the schema R (A, B, C, D, E, F)*

$$A \rightarrow BC$$
$$E \rightarrow CF$$
$$B \rightarrow E$$
$$CD \rightarrow EF$$

Then $(AB)^+$ is equal to :

(a) {A, B, C}

(b) {A, B, E}

(c) {A, B, C, E, F}

(d) {A, B, C, D, E, F}

13. *Relation R = (L, M, N, O, P) the following dependencies hold : $M \rightarrow O$, $NO \rightarrow P$, $P \rightarrow L$ and $L \rightarrow MN$, R is decomposed into R_1 = (L, M, N, P) and R_2 = (M, O)*

Is the above decomposition a lossless join decomposition?

(a) Yes

(b) No

(c) Can't say

14. *In the above question what is the highest normal form satisfied by the above decomposition ?*

(a) 1 NF

(b) 2 NF

(c) 3 NF

(d) 4 NF

Answers :	**1.** (c)	**2.** (a)	**3.** (a)	**4.** (b),(c),(d)	**5.** (d)	**6.** (c)	**7.** (b)
	8. (c)	**9.** (d)	**10.** (d)	**11.** (c)	**12.*** (c)	**13.*** (a)	**14.** (b)

15. ***In the above question which are the dependencies that are not preserved ?***

(a) M →O, P→ L
(b) L → MN, M → O
(c) M → O, NO → P
(d) M → O, NO → P, P → L

16. ***An audit trail :***

(a) Is used to make back-up copies
(b) Is the recorded history of operations performed on a file
(c) Can be used to restore lost information
(d) None of the above

17. ***If a data is stored in two places in the database, then :***

(a) Storage space is wasted
(b) Changing the data is one spot will cause data inconsistency
(c) It can be more easily accessed
(d) Both (a) and (b)

18. ***In order to use a DBMS, it is important to understand***

(a) The physical schema
(b) All subschemas that the system supports
(c) One subschema
(d) Both (a) and (b)
(e) None of the above

19. ***The index consists of :***

(a) A list of keys
(b) Pointers to the master list
(c) Both (a) and (b)
(d) None of the above

20. ***Report generators are used to :***

(a) Store data input by a user
(b) Retrieve information from files
(c) Answer queries
(d) Both (b) and (c)

21. ***A file produced by a spreadsheet :***

(a) Is generally stored on disk in an ASCII text format
(b) Can be used as it by the DBMS
(c) Can be used for graphic
(d) All of the above

22. ***A data dictionary doesn't provide information about :***

(a) Where data is located
(b) The size of the disk storage device
(c) Who owns or is responsible for the data
(d) How the data is used

(e) Security and privacy limitations

23. *Software packages that used for business is a :*

(a) Special purpose packages

(b) Custom made programs

(c) Single function application packages

(d) Data management packages

24. *Periodically adding, changing and deleting file records is called file:*

(a) Updating
(b) Upgrading

(c) Restructuring
(d) Renewing

(e) None of the above

25. *Which of the following is a relational database ?*

(a) 4th dimentions
(b) Foxpro

(c) d base IV
(d) All of the above

26. *Data Flow model mainly shows :*

(a) Decision and control information

(b) Processing requirements and the flow of data

(c) Relationships

(d) None of above

27. *A trigger is :*

(a) A statement that enables to start any DBMS

(b) A statement that is executed by the user when debugging an application program

(c) A condition the system tests for the validity of the database user

(d) A statement that is executed automatically by the system as a side effect of a modification to the database

28. *Which of the following query transformations (i.e. replacing) the l.h.s expression by the r.h.s. expression) is incorrect? R_1 and R_2 are relations, C_1 and C_2 are selection conditions and A_1, A_2 are attributes of R_1 :*

(a) $\sigma_{C_1}(\sigma_{C_1}(R_1)) \rightarrow \sigma_{C_2}(\sigma_{C_2}(R_1))$

(b) $\sigma_{C_1}(\Pi_{A_1}(R_1)) \rightarrow \Pi_{A_1}(\sigma_{C_1}(R_1))$

(c) $\sigma_{c_1}(R_1 \cup R_2) \rightarrow \sigma_{c_1}(R_1) \cup \sigma_{c_1}(R_2)$

(d) $\Pi_{A_2}(\sigma_{C_1}(R_1)) \rightarrow \sigma_{C_1}(\Pi_{C_1}(\Pi_{A_2}(R_1)))$

Answers: **15.** (c) **16.** (b) **17.** (d) **18.** (c) **19.** (c) **20.** (d) **21.** (a) **22.** (b) **23.** (d) **24.** (a) **25.** (d) **26.** (b) **27.** (d) **28.*** (a)

29. ***The following database relations containing the attributes :***
Book—id
Subject—Category-of-book
Name—of-Author
Nationallity—of-Author
with book-id as the primary key
What is the highest normal form satisfied by this relation?
(a) INF (b) 2NF
(c) 3NF (d) BCNF

30. ***In a relational schema, each tuple is divided into fields called :***
(a) Relations (b) Domains
(c) Queries (d) None of above

31. ***The set of permitted values for each attribute is called its :***
(a) Attribute set (b) Attribute range
(c) Domain (d) Group

32. ***Which of the following is/are correct ?***
(a) Relational algebra and relational calculus are both procedural query language
(b) Relational algebra and relational calculus are both non-procedural query language
(c) Relational algebra is a procedural query language and relational calculus is a non-procedural guery language
(d) Relational algebra is a non-procedural guery language and relational calculus is a procedural guery langauge

33. ***E-R modelling technique is a :***
(a) Top-down approach
(b) Bottom-up approach
(c) Left-right approach
(d) None of above

34. ***Relations produced from an E-R model will always be in :***
(a) First normal form
(b) Second normal form
(c) Third normal form
(d) Fourth normal form

35. ***In Railway reservation system, the entities are data, train number,***

place of departure, destination, type of train and seats available. The primary key is :

(a) Train number

(b) Train number + place of departure

(c) Train number + date

(d) Train number + destination

36. ***Transaction X holds a shared lock R. If transaction Y also requests for a shared lock on R :***

(a) Result in a deadlock situation

(b) Immediately granted

(c) Immediately rejected

(d) Granted as soon when it is released by X

37. ***A database management system consist of application programs called :***

(a) FORTRAN
(b) AUTOFLOW
(c) BPL
(d) TOTAL
(e) None of the above

38. ***Which two files are used during operation of the DBMS?***

(a) Query language and utilities

(b) Data manipulation language and query language

(c) Data dictionary and transaction log

(d) Data dictionary and query language

39. ***A locked file can be :***

(a) Accessed by only one user

(b) Modified by users with the correct password

(c) Is used to hide sensitive information

(d) None of the above

40. ***Canonical cover on the schema (A, B, C) with the set of functional dependencies :***

$$A \rightarrow BC$$
$$A \rightarrow B$$
$$AB \rightarrow C$$
$$B \rightarrow C$$

(a) $A \rightarrow BC$ and $B \rightarrow C$
(b) $A \rightarrow BC$ and $AB \rightarrow C$
(c) $A \rightarrow BC$ and $A \rightarrow B$
(d) $A \rightarrow B$ and $B \rightarrow C$

Answers : **29.*** (b) **30.** (b) **31.** (c) **32.** (c) **33.** (a) **34.** (c)
35. (c) **36.** (b) **37.** (c) **38.** (c) **39.** (d) **40.*** (d)

41. ***Consider the following set of functional dependencies on the scheme R (A, B, C, D, E, F)***

$$A \rightarrow B$$
$$BC \rightarrow DE$$
$$AEF \rightarrow G$$

find closure X^+ of set of attributes {AC}

(a) {B} (b) {B, D, E, G}

(c) {A, B, C, D, E} (d) None of the above

42. ***Consider a schema R (A, B, C, D) and functional dependencies A → B and C → D. Then the decomposition of R into R_1 (AB) and R_2 (CD) is :***

(a) Dependency preserving and lossless join

(b) Lossless join but not dependency preserving

(c) Dependency preserving but not lossless join

(d) Not dependency preserving and not lossless join

43. ***Let r and s be two relations over the relation schemas R and S respectively, and let A be an attribute in R. Then the relational algebra expression $\sigma_{A=a}(r \times s)$ is always equal to :***

(a) $\sigma_{A=a}(r)$ (b) r

(c) $\sigma_{A=a}(r) \infty s$ (d) None of above

44. ***Relation R is decompased using a set of functional dependencies F, and relation S is decomposed using another set of functional dependencies, G. One decomposition is definitely BCNF, the other is definitely 3 NF, but it is not known which is which. To make a guaranteed identification, which one of the following tests should be used on the decompositions? (Assume that the closures of F and G are available)***

(a) Dependency-preservation (b) Lossless join

(c) BCNF defination (d) 3NF defination

45. ***From the following instance of a relation schema R (A, B, C), we can conclude that :***

(a) A functionally determines B and B functionally determines C

(b) A functionally determines B and B does not functionally determine C

(c) B does not functionally determine C

A	B	C
1	1	1
1	1	0
2	3	2
2	3	2

(d) A does not functionally determine B and B does not functionally determine C

46. ***Given the relations***
employee (name, salary, dept no), and
departent (dept no, deptname, address)
Which of the following queries cannot be expressed using the basic relational algebra operations (σ, Π, X, $\times$ $\times$, $\cup$, $\cap$, $-$) ?

(a) Deptt. address of every employee
(b) Employees whose name is the same as their department name
(c) The sum of all employee salaries
(d) All employees of a given department

47. ***Given the following relation instance***

X	Y	Z
1	4	2
1	5	3
1	6	3
3	2	2

Which of the following functional dependencies are satisfied by the instance ?

(a) X Y $\to$ Z and Z $\to$ Y
(b) Y Z $\to$X and Y $\to$ Z
(c) Y Z $\to$ X and X $\to$ Z
(d) X Z $\to$Y and Y $\to$ X

48. ***Given relation r (w, x) and s (y,z) the result of select distinct w,x from r,s is guaranteed to be the same as r, provided :***

(a) r has no duplicates and s is non-empty
(b) r and s have no duplicates
(c) s has no duplicates and r is non-empty
(d) r and s have the same number of tuples

49. ***In S Q L, relations can contain null values, and comparisons with null values are treated as unknown. Suppose all comparisons with a null value are treated as false. Which of the following pairs is not equivalent?***

(a) x = 5 not (not (x = 5))
(b) x = 5 x > 4 and x < 6, where x is an integer
(c) x $\neq$ 5 not (x = 5)
(d) None of the above

Answers : **41.*** (c) **42.** (a) **43.** (c) **44.** (a) **45.** (a)
46. (c) **47.** (b) **48.** (a) **49.** (c)

50. ***Consider the join of a relation R with a relation S. If R has m tuples and S has n tuples, then the maximum and minimum sizes of the join respectively are :***

(a) m + n and 0 (b) mn and 0

(c) m + n and |m − n| (d) mn and m + n

51. ***The relational algebra expression equivalent to the following tuples calculus expression***

$$\{t \mid t \in r \wedge (t[A] = 10 \wedge t[B] = 20)\} \text{ is :}$$

(a) $\sigma_{(A = 10 \vee B = 20)}(r)$ (b) $\sigma_{(A = 10)}(r) \cup \sigma_{(B = 20)}(r)$

(c) $\sigma_{(A = 10)}(r) \cap \sigma_{(B = 20)}(r)$ (d) $\sigma_{(A = 10)}(r) - \sigma_{(B = 20)}(r)$

52. ***Let R = (A, B, C, D, E, F) be a relation scheme with the following dependencies***

$$C \to F,\ E \to A,\ EC \to D,\ A \to B$$

Which of the following is a key for R?

(a) CD (b) EC

(c) AE (d) AC

53. ***Consider a schema R (A, B, C, D, E) and functional dependencies :***

$$A \to BC$$
$$CD \to E$$
$$B \to D$$
$$E \to A$$

Then the decomposition of R into R_1 (A, B, C) and R_2 (A, D, E) is lossless decomposition :

(a) Yes (b) No

(c) Can't say (d) Incomplete data

54. ***Consider the schema R = (S T U V) and the dependencies S →T, T → U, U → V and V → S. Let R = (R1 and R2) be a decomposition such that R1 ∩ R2 = ϕ. The decomposition is :***

(a) Not in 2 NF (b) In 2 NF but not in 3 NF

(c) In 3 NF but not in 2 NF (d) In both 2 NF and 3 NF

55. ***Which of the following is/are correct ?***

(a) An SQL query automatically eliminates duplicates

(b) An SQL query will not work if there are no indexes on the relations

(c) SQL permits attribute names to be repeated in the same relation

(d) None of the above

56. *Given two union compatible relations R_1 (A, B) and R_2 (C, D). What is the result of the operation R_1 A = C AB = D R_2 ?*

(a) $R_1 \cup R_2$ (b) $R_1 \times R_2$

(c) $R_1 - R_2$ (d) $R_1 \cap R_2$

57. *The command used to select only one copy of each set of duplicable rows :*

(a) Select distant (b) Select unique

(c) Select different (d) None of above

58. *Which of the following is/are DML commands ?*

(a) Delete (b) Select

(c) Update (d) Create

59. *Which command is used to remove rows from a table ?*

(a) Delete (b) Remove

(c) Truncate (d) Both (a) and (c)

60. *Grant command is used in SQL to :*

(a) Allow user to access databases

(b) Allow user to create databases

(c) Grant system privileges, roles and object privileges to uses and roles

(d) Choose auditing for specific SQL command

61. *Which command is used to remove a table or index from the database in SQL ?*

(a) Delete table (b) Drop table

(c) Erase table (d) None of above

62. *A logical schema :*

(a) Is the entire database

(b) Is a standard way of organizing information into accessible parts

(c) Describe how data is actually stored on disk

(d) None of the above

63. *Which of the following is/are the characteristies of a relational database model ?*

(a) Tables (b). Treelike structure

(c) Complex logical relationship (d) Records

64. *Data security threats include :*

(a) Hardware failure (b) Privacy invasion

Answers : **50.** (b) **51.** (c) **52.*** (b) **53.*** (a) **54.** (d) **55.** (d) **56.** (d)
57. (a) **58.** (a),(b),(c) **59.** (d) **60.** (c) **61.** (b) **62.** (a) **63.** (a),(c),(d)

(c) Fraudulent manipulation of data (d) None of above

65. *A report generator is used to :*

(a) Update files (b) Print files on paper

(c) Data entry (d) None of above

66. *The command is used to create a database user :*

(a) Make user (b) Create user

(c) ADD user to Database (d) All of above

67. *Which of the following is/are record based logical model(s)?*

(a) Network model (b) Object-oriented model

(c) Relational model (d) E-R model

68. *Student and courses enrolled, is an example of :*

(a) One-to-one relationship (b) One-to-many relationship

(c) Many-to-one relationship (d) Many-to-many relationship

69. *A data dictionary is a special file that contains :*

(a) The names of all field in all fields

(b) The data types of all fields in all files

(c) The width of all fields in all files

(d) All of the above

70. *DBMS are used to :*

(a) Eliminate data redundancy

(b) Maintain data integrity

(c) Establish relationships among different files

(d) All of the above

71. *R (A, B, C, D) is a relation. Which of the following does not have a lossless-join dependency preserving BCNF decomposition?*

(a) A→B, B→CD (b) A→B, B→C, C→D

(c) AB→C, C→AD (d) A→BCD

72. *Which of the following relational calculus expressions is not safe ?*

(a) $\{t \mid E\ u \in R_1 (t[A] = u[A]) \land \neg \exists S \in R_2 (t[A] = S[A])\}$

(b) $\{t \mid \forall u \in R_1 (u[A] = \text{"X"} \Rightarrow \exists S \in R_2 (t[A] = S[S] \land S[A] = u[A]))\}$

(c) $\{t \mid \neg (t \in R_1)\}$

(d) $\{t \mid E\ u \in R_1 (t[A] = u[A]) \land \exists S \in R_2 (t[A] = S[A])\}$

73. *With regard to the expressive power of the formal relational query languages, which of the following statements is true ?*

(a) Relational algebra is more powerful than relational calculus
(b) Relational algebra has the same power as relational calculus
(c) Relational algebra has the same power as safe relational calculus
(d) None of the above

74. ***A B^+-tree index is to be built on the Name attribute of the relation STUDENT. Assume that all student names are of length 8 bytes, disk blocks are of size 512 bytes, and index pointers are of size 4 bytes. Given this scenario, what would be the best choice of the degree (i.e., the number of pointers per node) of the B^+ Tree ?***

(a) 16 (b) 42
(c) 43 (d) 44

75. ***Director's salary details are hidden from the employee. That is :***

(a) Conceptual level data hiding (b) Physical level data hiding
(c) External level data hiding (d) None of the above

76. ***If every non-key attribute is functionally dependent on the primary key, then the relation will be in :***

(a) First normal form (b) Second normal form
(c) Third normal form (d) Fourth normal form

77. ***The modify operation is likely to be done after :***

(a) Delete (b) Look-up
(c) Insert (d) None of the above

78. ***The database environment has all of the following components except :***

(a) Users (b) Separate files
(c) database (d) Data-base administrator

79. ***Two files may be joined into a third file if :***

(a) They have a row in common
(b) They have a field in common
(c) They have no records with the same value in the common filed
(d) Both (b) and (c)

80. ***Consider the following functional dependencies in a database :***

Data_of_Birth → Age ***Age → Eligibility***
Name → Roll_number ***Roll_number → Name***
Course_number → Course_name ***Course_number → Instructor***
(Roll_number, Course_number) → Grade

Answers : **64.** (b) **65.** (b) **66.** (c) **67.** (a),(c) **68.** (d) **69.** (a),(b),(c) **70.** (d) **71.** (b)
72. (a) **73.** (b) **74.** (a) **75.** (c) **76.** (c) **77.** (b) **78.** (b) **79.** (b)

The relation (Roll_number, Name, Data_of_Birth, Age) is

(a) in second normal form but not in third normal form

(b) In third normal form but not in BCNF

(c) in BCNF

(d) in none of the above

Consider the set of relations shows below and the SQL query that follows :

Students : (Roll_number, Name, Data_of_Birth)

Courses : (Course_number, Course_name, Instructor)

Grades : (Roll_number, Course_number, Grade)

select distinct Name

from Students, Courses, Grades

where Students. Rool_number = Grades. Roll_number

and Courses. Instructor = Korth

and Courses. Course_number = Grades.Courses_number

and Grades.grade = A

81. ***Which of the following sets is computed by the above query?***

(a) Names of students who have got an A grade in al courses taught by Korth

(b) Names of students who have got an A grade in all courses

(c) Name of studens who have got an A grade in at least one of the courses taught by Korth

(d) None of the above

82. ***Consider the data items D1, D2, and D3, and the following execution schedule of transaction T1, T2, and T3. In the diagram, R(D) and W(D) denote the actions reading and writing the data items D respectively.***

	T1	T2	T3
		R (D3);	
		R (D2);	
		W (D2);	
			R (D2);
time			*R (D3);*
	R (D1);		
	W (D1);		
			W (D2);
			W (D3);
		R (D1);	
	R (D2);		
	W (D2);		
		W (D1);	

(a) The schedule is serializable as T2; T3; T1

(b) The schedule is serializable as T2; T1; T3

(c) The schedule is serializable as T3; T2; T1

(d) The schedule is not serializable

Answers : **80.** (a) **81.** (c) **82.** (c)

SOLUTIONS

12. Let **result** be temp variable

result = AB

A → BC **result** = ABC

B → E = ABCE

E → CF = ABCEF

Therefore, value of $(AB)^+$ = {A B C E F}

13. Because no spurious tuples arises from R_1 and R_2.

28. Condition C_1 may be different from C_2.

29. Nationality of the author transitively depends on Book-id, primary key, So it can't be in the 3 NF.

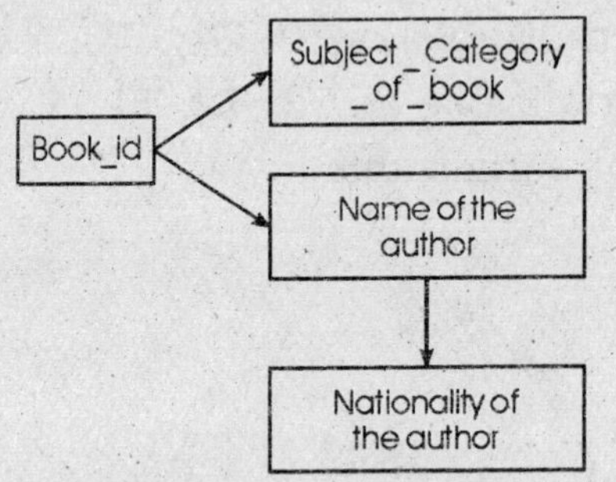

Functional Dependency diagram

40. Since there are two FD's with same set of attributes on left side

A → BC A → B

So we get A → BC

A is extrancous in AB → C because

(F – {AB – C}) U {B → C} ∵ B → C already exist

So FD's are A → BC and B → C

C is extraneous in A → BC such that on removing C there exists A → B

(F – {A → BC)}) U {A – B}

A → BC is removed by A → B

So the canonical cover is –

A → B and B → C.

41. Let result is an temp variable

result = AC

result = ABC Since $A \to B$

= ABCDE Since $BC \to DE$

Therefore, $X^+ = \{A, B, C, D, E\}$.

52. EC is the key as :

$$E \to A \to B,$$

So $EC \to AB$.

$$C \to F,$$

So $EC \to F$

Also, $EC \to D$ and $EC \to EC$

Hence, taking all the above, $EC \to ABCDE$.

53. For lossless decomposition

$$R_1 \cap R_2 = A$$

So either $A \to BC$ or $A \to DE$ must be present in FD's for lossless decomposition ($A \to BC$) is present in FD's so the decomposition is lossless).

■□■

CHAPTER 10

C LANGUAGE

1. ***What will be the value of y in the following program fragment ?***

   int y = 10;

   if(y ++ >9 && y ++! = 10 && y ++> 10)

   (a) 10 (b) 11

   (c) 12 (d) 13

2. ***What will be the value of y in the following program fragment ?***

   int x = 7;

   if (x ++ > 6 && x ++ ! = 8 && x ++ > 9)

   (a) 7 (b) 8

   (c) 9 (d) 10

3. ***In the following progrm fragment***

   int a = 10 , b = 5 , c = 3 , d = 3;

   if (a > b && (c = d ++))

   print f(" % d % d % d % d", a , b , c , d);

   else

   print f(" % d % d % d % d", a , b , c , d);

   What will be the output ?

   (a) a = 10 , b = 5 , c = 2 , d = 3 (b) a = 10 , b = 5 , c = 3 , d = 3

   (c) a = 10 , b = 5 , c = 4 , d = 3 (d) a = 10 , b = 5 , c = 3 , d = 4

4. ***lint is :***

   (a) C compiler (b) C interpreter

   (c) An IDE (d) A tool for analyzing a C program

5. ***What will be the value of i?***

   int i=1;

   i=i+2*i++;

   printf ("%d",i);

   (a) 4 (b) 1

   (c) 3 (d) 2

6. ***int e=3; switch (c)***

```
{
case 2:
c=3;
case 3:
c=4;
case 4;
c=5;
case 5:
c=6;
default:
c=0;
}
```

What will be the value of c in the following program fragment after the end of switch?

(a) 4 (b) 5
(c) 3 (d) 0

7. ***By default any real number is treated as :***
(a) Float (b) Double
(c) Long double (d) Compiler dependent

8. ***What will be the output of the following***

```
main( )
{
printf("%d%d%d', size of(2.13f), size of(2.12), size of(2.14L)) ?
}
```

(a) 4 4 4 (b) 4 8 10
(c) 4 4 8 (d) 4 4 10

9. ***Are these expressions same ?***
null pointer, NULL macro, ASCII NULL character and a null string
(a) Yes (b) No
(c) Can't say (d) Compiler dependent

10. ***What will be the value of c in the following program fragment?***

```
int c, b=4;
c=b+NULL;
```

(a) 4 (b) 0
(c) NULL (d) Compiler dependent

Answers :

1.* (d)	**2.*** (c)	**3.*** (d)	**4.** (d)	**5.** (a)
6.* (d)	**7.** (b)	**8.*** (b)	**9.*** (b)	**10.** (a)

11. *What will be the output of the following program fragment?*

```
main( )
{
char s1[ ]="wood";
char s2[ ]="wood";
if (s1= =s2)
        printf ("equal");
else
        printf("unequal");
}
```

(a) Equal (b) Unequal
(c) Compiler dependent (d) Can't say

12. *What will be the value of element in the following program fragment?*

```
int c=20;
main( )
{
static int element =c;
}
```

(a) 20 (b) 0
(c) Compiler dependent (d) Error message

13. *What will be the output of the following ?*

```
void main( )
{
static char k;
if(k=='0')
printf("0");
else if (k==48)
printf ("48")
else if ((k==0)&& (k=='\x0))
printf ("1"); }
```

(a) 0 (b) 48
(c) 1 (d) NULL

14. *What will be the output of the following program fragment?*

```
#define GOOD 100
void main( )
```

```
{
typedef500 BAD;
printf ("%d %d", BAD, GOOD);
}
```

(a) 500 100
(b) 100 500
(c) Compiler error
(d) Can't say

15. ***What will be the output of the following program fragment?***

```
void main( )
{
char far*p=0x0000FFFF
printf("%Fp\n",p);
p++;
printf ("%Fp\n",p);
}
```

(a) 0000:FFFF 0000:0000
(b) 0000:FFFF 1000:0000
(c) 0000:FFFF 0001:0000
(d) 0000:FFFF 00010000

16. ***What will be the output of the following program fragment?***

```
const int d1=200;
d1 ++;
printf ("%d", d1);
```

(a) 200
(b) 201
(c) 202
(d) Compiler error

17. ***What will be the output of the following program fragment?***

```
int i=20;
char j=20;
float k=20;
double 1=20;
printf ("%d", sizeof(i));
printf ("%d", sizeof(20))
printf ("%d", sizeof(j))
printf ("%d", sizeof(k))
printf ("%d", sizeof(l))
```

(a) 2 2 1 4 8
(b) 2 1 1 4 8
(c) 2 1 1 4 4
(d) 2 2 1 8 4

Answers : **11.*** (b) **12.*** (d) **13.*** (c) **14.*** (c) **15.*** (a) **16.*** (d) **17.*** (a)

18. *What will be the value of d1 and d2 in the following program fragment?*

int d1, d2;

for(d1=1,d2=;1;d1=<=10,d2<=7;d1++,d2++)

printf("%d%d",d1,d2);

(a) 10 10 (b) 10 7

(c) 7 7 (d) 7 10

19. *If the integer needs 1 byte storage, then maximum value of an unsigned integer is :*

(a) 2^8 (b) 2^7

(c) 2^8-1 (d) 2^7-1

20. *If 1 2 4 are the inputs then what will be the output of the following program fragment?*

int a, b, c;

printf ("%d", scanf("%d%d%d", &a, &b, &c));

(a) 1 (b) 2

(c) 3 (d) 4

21. *Coercion*

(a) Takes place across assignment operator

(b) Takes place if an operator has operands of different data types

(c) Casting

(d) Refers to bitwise operations

21. *Which of the following is not correct?*

(a) // it is valid (b) /* it is valid*/

(c) /*it/*is valid*/*/ (d) /*it// is valid */

22. *What will be the output of the following loop?*

for (putchar('d'); putchar('o'); putchar('b'))

putchar('g')

(a) dogbog

(b) dobgbo

(c) dogbogbogbog.......

(d) Syntex error

23. *What will be the output of the following loop?*

while (printf("%d", printf(11ab")))

printf("cd");

(a) abcdcdcdcd.....
(b) abcdabcd.......
(c) Syntex error
(d) None of above

24. *What will be the output of the following?*
printf("%d", printf("dd", "aa", "ss"));
(a) dd 2
(b) aa 1
(c) ddaa 2
(d) ddaass 3

25. *C is a :*
(a) Machine level language
(b) High level language
(c) Low level language
(d) High level language with some low level features

26. *Which of the following are/is syntactically correct?*
(a) for();
(b) for(;)
(c) for(;;);
(d) for(;;){}

27. *The value of an automatic variable that is declared but not initialized is :*
(a) 0
(b) Can't say
(c) -1
(d) Compiler dependent

28. *What will be the output of the following?*

```
static int i[ ]={0, 1, 2, 3, 4};
static int *ip[ ]={i, i+1, i+2, i+3, i+4}
int **ptr=p;
ptr ++;
*p++;
*++ptr;
printf ("%d %d %d %d", ptr - p, *ptr -i, **ptr);
```

Answers : **18.*** (c) **19.** (c) **20.*** (c) **21.** (c) **22.** (c)
23.* (d) **24.*** (a) **25.** (d) **26.** (c), (d) **27.** (b)

(a) 1 1 1

(b) 2 2 2

(c) 3 3 3

(d) 1 2 3

29. *Which of the following is/are correct?*

(a) 0 stands for false condition

(b) Value other than zero stands for false conditon

(c) 1 stands for false condition

(d) Value other than zero stands for true condition

30. *The following program will print "hi" if*

if (c >d)
if (d >e)
printf ("hello");
elso
printf ("hi");

(a) c<=d (b) d>e

(c) d<=e && c<=d (d) c>d &&d<=e

31. *The order in which actual arguments are evaluated in function call?*

(a) Can't say

(b) From left

(c) From right

(d) None of above

32. *If m=10 then the statement arr[++n]=n++assigns :*

(a) 10 to arr[12]

(b) 4 to arr[12]

(c) 4 to arr[11]

(d) Compiler dependent

33. *Which of the following is/are correct?*

(a) C supports 1 dimensional array

(b) Aray element may be an array by itself

(c) Carry element need not occupy contiguous memory location

(d) All are correct

34. *Void can be used :*

(a) As a data type of a function that returns nothing to its calling environment

(b) Inside the brackets of a function that does not need any argument

(c) inn a printf statement

(d) in an expression

35. ***What will be the output of the following?***

```
main ( )
{
printf ("hello");
main ( );
}
```

(a) Syntax error (b) Print hello infinite times

(c) Prints hello (d) None of above

36. ***The default parameter passing scheme is :***

(a) Call by value (b) Call by reference

(c) Can't say (d) None of above

37. ***What will be the output of the following?***

```
main ( )
{
fun ( ); funB; funB;
}
fun ( )
{
static int y;
printf ("%d", y++);
}
```

(a) 0 1 2 (b) 1 2 3

(c) 3 3 3 (d) 0 0 0

38. ***C supports array bound checking :***

(a) True (b) False

(c) Can't say (d) Compiler dependent

39. ***What will be the output of the following?***

```
main( )
{
intx=10, y=2;
printf ("%d",x+++++y);
}
```

Answers : **28.*** (c) **29.** (a),(d) **30.** (d) **31.*** (a) **32.** (d) **33.*** (a),(b) **34.** (a), (b) **35.*** (b) **36.** (a) **37.*** (a) **38.*** (b)

(a) Prints 12
(b) Prints 12
(c) Prints 14
(d) Compiler error

40. *What will be the output of the following ?*

```
main ( )
{
int x=10y, y=2;
printf ("%d", x+++y);
}
```

(a) Prints 12
(b) Prints 13
(c) Prints 10
(d) Compiler error

41. *What will be the output of the following?*

```
man ( )
{
int inc ( );
inc( );
(*inc) ( ); }
int abc( )
{
printf ("hello");
}
```

(a) Prints hellohello
(b) Prints hello
(c) Compiler error
(d) Prints hello hello

42. *Which of the following is/are correct regarding pointers?*

(a) Integer data type
(b) Char data type
(c) Passed to a function as argument
(d) Returned by a function

43. *Which of the following is/are correct?*

```
char m[ ]="ILOVEINDIA";
char *n="ILOVEINDIA";
```

(a) Puts (m) and puts (n) will be same
(b) Puts (m) and puts (n) will be different
(c) Can't say
(d) Compiler dependent

44. *What will be the output of the following?*

```
main( )
```

```
{
float x=.5, y=.7;
if (y<.7)
if (x<.5)
printf ("hello");
else
printf ("India");
else
printf ("great");
}
```

(a) hello (b) India
(c) great (d) can't say

45. ***Bit field :***

(a) Is a field having many sub fields
(b) Is subroutine declaring the size of the members in terms of bits
(c) Is a member of a structure whose size is specified in terms of bits
(d) None of above

46. ***Which of the following is/are correct regarding the use of macro in place of functions?***

(a) Reduces execution time
(b) Reduces code size
(c) Increases code size
(d) Increases execution time

47. ***Which of the following is/are correct?***

(a) 'd' same as "d" (b) Length of "d" is 2
(c) Can't say (d) None of above

48. ***What will be the output of the following program fragment ?***

```
char ch='A';
while (ch='F')
{
switch (ch)
{
case'A':
case'B':
```

Answers : **39.*** (a) **40.*** (a) **41.*** (a) **42.** (c), (d) **43.** (a) **44.** (b) **45.** (c) **46.*** (a), (c) **47.*** (d)

```
case'C':
case'D':
ch++;
continue;
case'E':
case'F':
ch++;
}
putchar(ch);
}
```

(a) CD (b) EF
(c) EG (d) FG

49. *What will be the output of the following program fragment prints?*

```
main ( )
{
float x=.6;
printf ("%d, %f ", x, x);
```

(a) 0 0.00000 (b) 0 0.6
(c) 0 0.60000 (d) Syntax error

50. *puts (argv [0]); prints*

(a) The name of source file
(b) Argv
(c) The number of command line arguments
(d) Name of executable file

51. *In which of the following cases is it possible to obtain different result for call-by-reference and call-by-name parameter passing methods?*

(a) Passing a constant value a parameter
(b) Passing the address of an array as a parameter
(c) Passing an array as a parameter
(d) Passing an array elements as a parameter

52. *The three common methods of passing parammeters are :*

(a) Call-by-reference, call-by-address, call-by-location
(b) Call-by-reference, call-by-value, call-by-name
(c) Call-by-reference, call-by-value, call-by-address
(d) Call-by-value, call-by-address, call-by-location

53. ***Call-by-reference is also known as***

(a) Call-by-address or call-by-location

(b) Call-by-address or call-by-value

(c) Call-by-value or call-by-name

(d) None of above

54. ***The methods of parameter passing used in the language C is :***

(a) Call-by-value (b) Call-by-name

(c) Call-by-reference (d) Call-by-address

55. ***In the C language :***

(a) At most one activation record exists between the current activation record and the activation record for the main

(b) The number of the activation record exists between the current activation record and the activation record for the main depends on the actual function calling sequence

(c) The visibility of the global variables depend on the actual function calling sequence

(d) Recursion requires the activation record for the recursive function to be saved on a different stack before the recursive function can be called

56. ***The results returned by funnctions under value-result and reference parameter passing conventions :***

(a) Do not differ

(b) Differ in the presence of loops

(c) Differ in all cases

(d) May differ in the presence of exceptions

57. ***Consider the following declaration of a two-dimensional array in C char a[100][100];***

assuming that the main memory is byte-addressable and that the array is stored starting from memory address 0, the address of a[40][50] is :

(a) 4040 (b) 4050

(c) 5040 (d) 5050

58. ***The C language is :***

(a) A context free language

(b) A context sensitive language

Answers : **48.*** (d) **49.** (c) **50.*** (d) **51.** (b) **52.** (b)
53. (a) **54.** (a) **55.** (d) **56.** (b) **57.** (b)

(c) A regular language

(d) Parsable fully only by a turing machine

59. *What will be the output of the following statements assuming call by reference parameter passing?*

```
{
x-10;
y=3;
func1(y, x, x);
print x;
print y;
}
func1 (x, y, z)
{
y=y+4;
z=x+y+z;
}
```

(a) 10, 3
(b) 31, 3
(c) 27, 7
(d) None of above

60. *Consider the following three C functions :*

```
[P1]
int*g(void)
{
intx=10;
return (&x);
}
[P2]
int*g(void)
{
int*px;
*px=10;
return px;
}
[P3]
int*g(void)
{
int*px;
```

```
px=(int*)malloc (size of (int));
*px=10;
return px;
}
```

Which of the above three functions are likely to cause problems with pointers?

(a) Only P3 (b) Only P1 and P3
(c) Only P1 and P2 (d) P1, P2 and P3

61. Consider the following C program:

```
void abc (char*s)
{
if (s[0]=='\0')
return;
abc(s+1);
abc(s+1);
printf("%c",s[0])'
}
main( )
{
abc("123");
}
```

What will be output of the following program?

(a) 3 2 1 3 2 1 1 (b) 3 3 2 3 3 2 1
(c) 3 2 1 1 (d) 3 2 1 1 2 3 3

62. Consider the followig C function

```
float f (float x, int y) {
float p, s; int i;
    for (s = 1, p = 1, i = 1; i  < y; i++)
    {
    p * = x/i;
    s+ = p;
    }
    return s;}
```

for large values of y, the return value of the function f best approximates

Answers : **58.** (a) **59.** (a) **60.** (a) **61.** (b)

(a) x^y (b) e^x

(c) log (1 + x) (d) x^x

63. ***Assume the following C variable declaration***

int * A[10], B[10] [10];

of the following expression.

I A [2] II A [2][3] III B [1] IV B [2][3]

which will not give compile-time errors if used as left hand sides of assignment statements in a C program?

(a) I, II and IV only (b) II, III and IV only

(c) II and IV only (d) IV only

64. ***The following program fragment is written in a programming language that allows vairables and does not allow nested declarations of functions.***

```
global int i=100, i=5;
void P(x) {int i=10;
print (x+10);
i=200; j=20;
print(x);
}
main (){p(i+j);]
```

The programming language used static scoping and call by need parameter parsing machanism, the values printed by the above programme are

(a) 115, 220 (b) 25, 220

(c) 25, 15 (d) 115, 105

65. ***If the language uses dynamic scoping and call by name parameter passing mechanism, the values printed by the programme are***

(a) 115, 220 (b) 25, 220

(c) 25, 15 (d) 115, 105

66. ***Consider a C program shown below :***

```
# include <stdio.n>
# define print (x) print f ("%d", x)
        int x;
        void Q (int Z)
        {
        z + = x; print (z);
```

```
{
void p (int * y)
{
int x = * y + 2;
Q (x);
* y = x - 1;
print (x);
}
main (void){
x = 5;
p (&x);
print (x);
{
```

The outputs of this program is

(a) 12 76 (b) 22 12 11
(c) 14 66 (d) 766

67. *What will be the storage size of the following union?*

```
union un
{
int i;
char ch[2];
double b;
}
```

(a) 12 (b) 8
(c) 10 (d) Can't say

68. *What will be the output of the following?*

```
for(i=3; i<15;i+3)
{
printf("%d", i);
++i;
}
```

(a) 3 6 9 12 (b) 2 15 12 11
(c) 3 7 11 (d) 2 7 11 15

Answers : **62.** (c) **63.** (d) **64.** (d) **65.** (a) **66.** (a) **67.** (b) **68.** (c)

SOLUTIONS

1. The value of $y = 13$ because both the above conditions are satisfied. Because after checking y ++ >9 the value of y is incremented and becomes $y = 10$ so second condition becomes true (y ++ ! = 10 since value of y is 11) and the value of y after checking becomes 12, similarly after checking last condition the value of y becomes 13.

2. In this case value of x increases two times because after checking frist condition the value of x is 8 wich does not satisfies second condition and fail but the value of x is incremented.

3. The value of d is incremented because the condition a > b and $c = d$ ++ both are satisfied due to which the other condition is not checked. Therefore the values of a , b , c , d are $a = 10$ $b = 5$ $c = 3$ $d = 4$*/

6. The value of e becomes 0 because we are not using break statement so after jumping to case 3 it passes through all the case conditions including default condition. Therefore, we always use break statements after each case statements.

8. In first case the size of first real no. is 4 because f represent float value, in case second we know by default the real numbers are treated as double so the size of double is 8. in case third L presents long double which is of 10 bytes.

9. A NULL macro is used to represent the null pointer in source code it has the value 0 associated with it. A null pointer is a pointer which doesn't point anywhere. ASCII NULL character has all its as 0 but does n't have any relationship with the null pointer. The null string is just an empty string.

11. In if condition we are comparing the address of two char array not the values of the array.

12. Variable c and element are present in the data area. The static variable element is initialized by the value of the global variable 'c', which is not possible because 'static' variables can only be initialized by either constants or the addresses of variables.

13. Value of k is automatically initialized to zero (ASCII value 48) which is not equal to '0' and nor is it equal to 48 but is equal to the ASCII value zero or the hexadecimal constant '\x0' known as the NULL character.

14. Keyword typedef can only be used with data types, whereas the preprocessor #define directives can be replace any C statements.

Another difference between these two concepts is that 'typedef' statements are compiled by the C compiler while the preprocessor #define directives are handled by preprocessor.

15. The absolute address is generated by the microprocessor depending upon the segment and the offset registers.

Far pointer arithmetic is applied only to the offset and not to the segment. If we try to increment the maximum value of an offset, it simply overflows without affecting the segment address.

16. We can't modify the value of a constant object. We can change the value by using pointers.

17. In the first case the size in bytes of integer variable (2 bytes). In second case the size in bytes of character constant '20' whose ASCII value is 53 is an integer (2 bytes). In third case the size in bytes of a character variable (1 bytes). In fourth case the size in bytes of a float variable which is of 4 bytes. In fifth case the size in bytes of a double which is of 8 bytes.

18. The comma operator plays a important role inside a for loop. It always considers the value of the last variable. Here in condition 'd2' appears after 'd1' and so the for loop considers only the value if d2 ignoring d1 for testing the conditions.

20. We know any function returns a value to a calling environment. In the case of scanf it is the number of variables it scans. So the output will be 3 since it scans 3 variables.

23. First printf prints "ab" and returns a value 2 since it prints two characters. So the condition results ab2 and runs for an infinite times so the output will be ab2cdab2cd......

24. As explained above.

26. A union is a single memory location that is shared by two or more variables. The variables that share the memory may be of different types. Only one variablle may use at a time. So the size of sample is the maximum size of the data type.

28. In first case ptr is incremented by 1 pointing to location first of array p[]. In second case* and ++ are both urinary operators so associativity is from right to left hence ++is performed before*, so ptr is again incremented by 1 pointing to location 2 of array p[]. In the third case ptr is again incremented by 1 pointing to location 3 of array p[].

31. As in following function we can't say what will be the output int i=10; printf ("%d %d", i++, ++i);

33. C support one dimensional arrays only. But the array element can be an array by itself. A declaration like char [3] [4], will be interpreted as a 1 dimensional array of size 3 (rather than 4) each element being a character array of length 4.

35. Recursive call for function main ( ).

37. By default y is initialized to 0. Since it is static class storage it preserves its value so the value is incremented each time.

38. C does not support auto bound checking so we can access 4th element of an array that is declared to be of lesser size.

39. The compiler will tokenize as x, ++, ++, +, y the compiler while grouping the tokens to expression, finds the second ++ applied x. Hence, produces an error message L value required.

So to evaluate this expression we require parenthesis or blank.

(x++)+(++y) or x++ + ++y.

40. Same as above.

41. Since (*inc)( ) is a pointer to a function so we can invoke inc( ) by any of the two ways (*inc)( ); or by inc( );

46. Function call involves storing the current contents and jumping to its starting address which increases the execution time on the other hand macro increases the code size.

47. "d" is of 2 characters d and '\0' and its length is 1.

48. Continue statement takes the control to while for A, B, C and D so putchar run only two times for 'e' and 'f'.

50. Its an pointer to an executable code file.

62. For higher vlaue of y

$$p = P * x/i = x/i$$

$$S = s + p = 1 + x/i$$

when i < Y and i++

$$S = 1 + x/i + x/i+1 + ... = 1 + x + x/2 + x/3.....$$

Hence the larger value of y, In(1 + x)

63. B[2][3] gives the element of second rows from third column.

64. x = i+j = 100 + 5 = 105 (global value)

print (x + 10) = 115

print (x) = 105 *** static value

66.

```
* y = 5
x = * y + 2 = 7
Q (x);
z = x = 7
z = z + x = 7 + 5 = 12
* y = z - 1 = 6
```

■□■

CHAPTER 11

OBJECT ORIENTED PROGRAMMING WITH C++

1. *Which of the following is false about C++?*

(a) is block structured language

(b) is not block structured language

(c) aids in object oriented programming

(d) is an extension of C

2. *Which of the following is true about argv?*

(a) it is an array of character ptr

(b) it is pointer to an array of character pointers

(c) it is an array of strings

(d) None of the above

3. *Polymorphism is implemented through which mechanism in C++?*

(a) Late Interpretation (b) Late Binding

(c) Early Interpretation (d) Overloading

4. *Dragons have wings like a bird and scales like a lizard. In object-oriented verabage, we would say this is an example of __________.*

(a) Multilevel inheritance (b) Polymorphism

(c) Multiple Inheritance (d) Aggregation

5. *The vector class is a*

(a) template class (b) container class

(c) virtual class (d) abstract base class

6. *Class A {*

protected:

void setName( );

virtual void showName( )= 0;

private:

Answers : **1.** (a) **2.** (a) **3.** (d) **4.** (c) **5.** (a)

```
std :: string name;
};
```

What can be said about class A above?

(a) It cannot be derived from

(b) It has virtual derivation

(c) Descedants of this class could use its member function showName( ) to display contents of "name"

(d) It contains an illegal statement statement (the initialiser list for Show Name)

7. *A class cannot be*

(a) Virtual (b) Generic

(c) Inline (d) Friend

8. *Objects of the same class share the values of _________ while they maintain separate values for ________.*

(a) Static variables,non static variables#

(b) Non static variables, static variables

(c) Global variables, static variables

(d) Static variables register variables.

9. *Exception handling in C++ can be achieved using keywords*

1) try 2) look 3) throw 4) catch 5) raise

Which of the following statement is most appropriate?

(a) 1,2 and 4 (b) 1,3 and 4

(c) 2,3 and 4 (d) 2,4 and 5

10. *Which of the following keywords cannot appear inside a class definition?*

(e) a) friend (b) static

(c) template (d) virtual

11. *The C++ keywords*

(a) must be in lower case

(b) must be in uppercase

(c) first letter must be capital

(d) can be in uppercase or lowercase

12. *Consider following code segments*

(1)

```
int a, b, c [1000];
for (a=0;a;a++)
c[a] = b+ a;
```

(2)
```
int a,b,c[1000];
int *p =c;
        for(a=0;a;a++)
{ *p=b+a;
        p++; }
```
(a) First is faster than second
(b) Second is faster than first
(c) Both are equally faster
(d) Cannot be ascertained

13. ***Find odd man out***
(a) break
(b) return
(c) exit
(d) continue

14. ***':: m' will refer to***
(a) Global variable m
(b) Local variable m
(c) Variable m, in class where it is declared
(d) Extern variable m

15. ***Given void *gp, int *ip, char *cp, float *fp Which of the following is false***
(a) gp = ip
(b) gp = cp
(c) gp = fp
(d) *gp = *fp

16. ***If program file contains following code-***
```
main( )
{
}
```
(a) Program will give compilation error
(b) Program will get compiled, but cant be converted into executable file
(c) Program will give runtime error
(d) None of above

17.
```
#include
am.h
        void main( )
        {       int x =8;
                x< 1;
                cout < x;
                x>1;
                cout <x;
```

Answers : **6.** (c) **7.** (c) **8.** (a) **9.** (b) **10.** (c) **11.** (a) **12.** (a) **13.** (d) **14.** (a) **15.** (d) **16.** (d)

```
        }
```
(a) 16 8 (b) 8 8
(c) 8 16 (d) Linked Error

18. ***void main ( )***
```
{       int x=20, y=35;
        x=y++ + x++;
        y = ++y + ++x;
        cout< x <" "< y;
}
```
(a) 55 55 (b) 58 95
(c) 57 94 (d) 55 93

19. ***include***
```
        g
        #include
        am
        using namespace std;
int main( )
        {       string s1,s2;
                string s3 = "Abcd" ef";
                string s4("opqr");
                s2="xyz";
                s1=s3+ " "+s4;
                s1 += "p";
                cout < s1+s2+ " ||" < endl;
        }
```
(a) Abcd ef opqr.xyz!! (b) Abcd ef xyz!!
(c) Abcd ef opqr p xyz !! (d) Compilation error

20. ***union packed***
```
{char i;  short j;  int k;  long l;  float f;   double m;  long double d;
};
int main( )
{cout < sizeof(packed) < endl;
}
```
(a) 23 (b) 24
(c) 8 (d) 10

21.
```
#define mul(x) (x++ *x++ *x++)
void main( )
{     int i = 3; int j;
j= mul(i);
cout< j;
cout < i;
getch( );
}
```
Predict the value of i and j repectively

(a) 3 & 60 (b) 6 & 27
(c) 6 & 120 (d) 4 & 50

22. *Which is most appropriate about the pointer to a constant?*

(a) it points to the variables
(b) It can not point to any other constants of same type
(c) The contents of what it points to can not be changed.
(d) It can point to any other constants of any type

23. *Which of the following is false?*

(a) Variable has scope & visibility
(b) Variable having scope may not be visible
(c) Variables having visibility may not have scope
(d) None of these

24. *To create new datatype we can use*

(a) Union (b) Enum
(c) Typedef (d) New

25. *> is used to*

(a) accept only basic data types provided by C++
(b) accept any data types provided by C++
(c) accept any object
(d) accept only standard data types provided by C++*

26. *Which operator cannot be overloaded through friend?*

(a) * = (b) = =
(c) = (d) + =

Answers : **17.** (b) **18.** (c) **19.** (d) **20.** (d) **21.** (b) **22.** (c)
23. (c) **24.** (c) **25.** (d) **26.** (d)

27. *Which of the following operators are used as both unary & binary operators*

(1) + (2) ++

(3) || (4)

(5) &

(a) 1,4,5 (b) 2,4,5

(c) 1,2,5 (d) 2,3,6

28. *What is false for operator overloading?*

(a) Precedence & associativity of the operator must remain the same

(b) Overloaded operator should not have an operand of the User Derived Data Type

(c) Syntax of the operator usage must be the same

(d) Existing operators can not be overloaded

29. *In C++, function call can appear on the LHS of the assignment operator when*

(a) function is returning pointer

(b) function is returning reference

(c) function is returning void*

(d) function is accepting references as formal parameters

30. *The signature of function is its ________*

(a) .. function code (b) prototype

(c) call (d) parameter list

31. *What is true about inline functions?*

(a) It's a compulsion on the compiler to make function inline

(b) It's a request to the compiler to make the function inline*

(c) It's the indication to the compiler that the function is recursive

(d) It's the indication to the compiler that the function is member function.

32. *Member functions that return the value of an attribute of an object are called*

(a) Destructors (b) Inspector

(c) Facilitator (d) Mutators

33. *Static member function*

(a) can access any other member function & member variables

(b) can access only static member variables & member functions

(c) can be only called through object of the class

(d) Returns only static data.

34. ***A friend function***

(a) is declared as a friend & defined elsewhere in the program

(b) is always an inline function

(c) creates objects without initialization

(d) May be a static member function of the class.

35. ***If a base class member access is public, and an inherited class accesses specifier is private, which of the following statements is true?***

(a) The base class members can be accessed by derived class objects

(b) The base class members cannot be accessed by the derived class members

(c) The derived class members can be accessed by the base class objects.

(d) The base class members can be accessed by the derived class

36. ***class professor {};***

```
class teacher :public virtual professor{};
class researcher : public virtual professor{};
class myprofessor : public teacher, public researcher{};
```

Referring to the sample code above, if an object of class "myprofessor" was created, how many instances of professor will it contain?

(a) 0 (b) 1

(c) 2 (d) 3

37. ***Choose most appropriate statement***

(a) An abstract base class can have pure virtual destructor

(b) An abstract base class can have only virtual destructor

(c) An abstract base class can have non virtual destructor

(d) An abstract base class cannot have destructor

38. ***The conversion from basic data to class type can be done by***

(a) Writing constructor

(b) Is not possible

(c) Overloaded casting operator

(d) Object of a class

39. ***What is used to terminate a function?***

Answers :

27. (a)	**28.** (d)	**29.** (b),(c)	**30.** (b)	**31.** (b)	**32.** (c)
33. (b)	**34.** (a)	**35.** (a),(d)	**36.** (b)	**37.** (d)	**38.** (a)

(a) break (b) return
(c) exit (d) halt

40. ***If n bits are allocated for storage then it can store _____ to _______ range of signed numbers.***

(a) -2n-1, 2n-1 -1 (b) -2n-1, 2n-1
(c) -2n, 2n (d) -2n, 2n-1

41. ***Which of the following is false with respect to inheritance?***

(a) When a base class is privately inherited, public members of the base class becomes private members of derived class.
(b) When a base class is publically inherited, public members of base class becomes public members of derived class.
(c) When a base class is privately inherited, a private member of base class becomes private members of derived class.
(d) When a base class is publically inherited protected members of base class becomes protected members of derived class.

42. ***When a base class pointer points to derived class object***

(a) It can access only base class members.
(b) It can access only derived class members.
(c) Both base class & derived class members,
(d) None

43. ***Which one is appropriate?***

(a) '\n' is used in C & endl is used in C++
(b) '\n' is used in C++ & endl is used in
(c) '\n' & endl both can be used in C
(d) '\n' & endl both can be used in C++.

44. ***Which way is wrong to invoke function f( ) of namespace C of namespace B ?***

(a) B::C::f ( );
(b) C:: f( );
(c) Using namespace B C:: f( );
(d) Using namespace B::C f( );

45. ***Which is false***

(a) Default constructor does not contain any arguments
(b) A constructors must be a public member
(c) A parameterised constructor constructor must not return anything
(d) All are false

```
void main( )
{       switch(3,2,1)
        {       case 1:cout< "one";
                case 2:cout<"two";
                case 3:cout<"three";
                default :cout<"*";
        }
}
```

What is the output of the above code?

(a) one (b) two

(c) one two three (d) None of above

46.

```
int count=0;
class obj
{
        public:
        obj( ){count++;}
        ~obj( ) {count--;}
};
void main( )
{       obj A,B,C,D,E;
        obj F;
        { obj g;
        }
return 0;
}
```

What is the value of "count" immediately after the return statement above is executed?

(a) 6 (b) 5

(c) 0 (d) 1

47.

```
char sing [ ]="Macarena";
void main ( )
{       char sing[ ]= "Los";
        {       char sing[ ]= "Del";
                {       char sing [ ]= "Rio";
```

Answers : **39.** (b) **40.** (a) **41.** (c) **42.** (a) **43.** (d) **44.** (b) **45.** (d) **46.** (c)

```
cout<sing;   }}      }
```

What will be the output?

(a) Error (b) Macaren

(c) Los Rio (d) Rio

48. ***1. Contents of object can change even if there is a const reference to it***

2. Contents of object cannot change if there is a const reference to its

3. It is necessary to initialize the object if there is a const reference to its

4. It is not necessary to initialize the reference in declaration

From above statements what is correct:

(a) 1 & 3 are true (b) 2 & 4 are false

(c) 1 & 4 are true (d) 1 & 4 are false

49. ***01100011 + 10011100 =***

(a) 0256 (b) 256

(c) 0xFF (d) all of the above

50. ***What is true about main ( )***

(a) returns 0 implicitly (b) returns 1 implicitly

(c) returns 1 explicitly (d) need not return anything

51. ***main( )***

```
{       int i=0,j=0,k=0,result;
        result = (i++ && j++ && ++k);
        cout < "result=" <result;
        cout< "i=" <i;
        cout < "j="<j;
        cout <"k="<k;
```

(a) result = 1 i=1 j=1 k=1 (b) result = 1 i=1 j=0 k=1

(c) result =0 i=1 j=0 k=0 (d) result=0 I=1 j=1 k=0

52. ***class mumbai***

```
{ int bhai ;
        public : mumbai( ) { bhai =10 ;}
        mumbai & mul ( mumbai daud ,mumbai gawali)
            { mumbai police;
                police.bhai *= daud.bhai*gawali.bhai;
                return police;
```

```
        }
        void display ( ) { cout < bhai; }
};
void main ( )
{ mumbai gang1,gang2,gang3;
        gang3.mul(gang1,gang2);
        gang3.display( );
}
```

(a) 100 (b) 1000
(c) 10 (d) none of the above

53. #include

```
g.h
 void main ( )
 { int i =strlen("Blue")+strlen("People")/
                strlen("Red")-strlen("Green");
     cout < i ;
 }
```

(a) 0 (b) 1
(c) 2 (d) none of these

54. ***#define ABS(A) (a) ? - (a) : (a)***

```
#define GTR(b) (b)9 ? (1) : (0)
int answer = GTR(ABS(10-20));
```

After the above code is compiled and executed, what will be the value of "answer"?

(a) 0 (b) 1
(c) -1 (d) Error

55.

```
class X
{ public: int x;
        static void f(int z);
};
void X::f(int y) {x=y;}
```

What is the error in the sample code above?

(a) The static member function f( ) accesses the non-static x.
(b) The class X does not have any private members.

Answers : **47.** (d) **48.** (c) **49.** (b) **50.** (a),(b) **51.** (c) **52.** (c) **53.** (a) **54.** (b)

(c) The static member function f( ) accesses the non-static z.

(d) The member function f( ) must return a value.

56.
```
void main ( )
    {   const int b[10] = {10,20,30,40,50,60,70,80,90,100};
        for( i = 0  i  ;i++)
         b[i] += 5;
        cout <b[5];
    }
```

(a) 50 (b) 65

(c) 60606060656565656565 (d) compilation error

57.
```
void main( )
   { int a[ ] = { 10, 20 ,30 ,40 ,50}; j,*p;
      for( p = a+4 j=0 ; j4 ; j++)  cout < *p[k];
   }
```

(a) 10203040 (b) 5040302010

(c) syntax error (d) 40302010

58.
```
class thak
{ int i =1;
      public:
            void milao(int i)
            { int j =1;
                  i=++i - --j/ ++j - --i;
                  cout<i;
            }
};
void main( )
{
      thak t1;
      t1.milao(1);
}
```

(a) 0 (b) Error

(c) 1 (d) Garbage value

59.
```
void main ( )
  {
      char j = l ;
while (j 255)  printf ("%d", j++);
```

```
}
```

(a) 1 ....255 (b) All the ascii char from 1 255

(c) Indefinite loop (d) 1....254

60.
```
void main ( )
    { for (int i = 1 ;i+++;)    cout <I;
    }
```

(a) compilation error (b) 2 32767

(c) indefinite loop (d) none of the above

61.
```
class odyssy
        {  int a;
        public :
odyssy(int a)  { a = a; cout < "para odyssy ";}
};
class vip : public odyssy
 {  int a;
        public :
            vip(int a)  { a = a; cout < "para vip ";}
             vip ( ) { cout < "vip const "; }
};
void main ( ) { vip ob(10); }
```

(a) para vip

(b) para odyssy.para vip

(c) para odyssy.para vip .vip const

(d) compilation error

62.
```
void main( )
        {     cout.setf(ios::hex||ios::scientific);
                cout < "Hi" < 100 < endl;
        }
```

What is the output of above code?

(a) Hi 100 (b) 123.12 Hi 100

(c) 12.13e+01Hi 100 (d) 1.2312e+02Hi 64

63.
```
        class animal {};
        class pet{};
        class Name{};
```

Answers : **55.** (a) **56.** (d) **57.** (c) **58.** (b) **59.** (c) **60.** (a) **61.** (d) **62.** (a)

```
        class dog : public pet{};
        class string {};
        class petdogs : public dog, public animal
        {       protected:
        string Name;
        };
petdogs lassie;
```

What is the order of constructor invocation when "lassie" is created?

(a) pet( ), dog( ), animal( ), string( ), Name( ), and petdogs( )

(b) pet( ), dog( ), animal( ), string( ) and petdogs( )

(c) petdogs( ), pet( ), dog( ), animal( ) and String( )

(d) Error

64. ***const int size=18;String *tbl2=new string [size];***

```
        cout < sizeof(*tbl2);
```

What will be the sample code above do when it is executed?

(a) 4 (b) 2

(c) 16 (d) 18

65. ***class Animal***

```
        {       public:
                        Animal( ):type("Animal") {};
                        virtual  Animal( ) {};
                        virtual void showType( )=0;
                        virtual int getWeight( ) {return weight;};
                private:
                        int weight;
                        std:: string type;
        };
        class Dog:public Animal
        {       public:
                        Dog( ):type("Dog"){}
                        ~Dog( ){};
                private:
                        std::string type;
        };
```

Referring to the sample code above, what needs to be done to create an instance of Dog?

(a) Dog needs to add a copy constructor which takes type Animal and returns type Dog.

(b) An overloaded assignment operator needs to be added to animal.

(c) Dog needs to override showType and getWeight.

(d) None of the above

66. *Shallow copy is*

(a) Member wise copying of objects

(b) A substitute for the operator

(c) Same kind like deep copy

(d) Used in constructor

67. *Which member functions of a class cannot modify its object attributes*

(a) Friend functions
(b) Private member functions
(c) Constant member functions
(d) Static member functions

68. *What is most appropriate, for getting success if condition is (a && b)*

(a) a and b both can be false
(b) a and b both can be true
(c) a or b or both can be true
(d) a or b or both can be false

69. *Which of the following is/are false?*

(a) Inheritance is deriving new class from an existing class

(b) In an inheritance , all data and function members of base class are derived by derived class

(c) We can specify which data and function members of base class will be inherited by derived class

(d) We can add new functions to derived class without recompiling the base class

70. *class compiler*

```
    { protected : int data ;
        void accesss(int a ) { logo = a; cout< logo; output( ); }
    private : int logo ;
        void output ( ) { data = 20 ; cout <data ; }
    };
    class linker:protected compiler
    { public:void getlogo( ) { data =100; access(100);}
    };
```

Answers :

63. (b) **64.** (c) **65.** (c) **66.** (a)
67. (c) **68.** (b) **69.** (b)

```
void main ( ) { linker ob; ob.getlogo( ); }
```

(a) compilation error
(b) 20100
(c) 10020
(d) linker error

71.
```
class india
      {   int a;
      public : india ( ) { a = 10 ; cout < a; }
               india(int  d) { a = d ; cout<a;}
               ~india( ) { cout <"pakistan "; };
               friend ~ india( ) { cout <"china"; };
   };
   void main ( ) { india ob,ob1(100);  }
```

(a) 10100 pakistan pakistan
(b) 0100 pakistan
(c) 10100 china pakistan
(d) compilation error

72.
```
class Class
      {   int a;
      public :
               inline Class ( ) { a =10 ;cout <a; }
      };
inline void main ( ) { Class ob;}
```

(a) compilation error
(b) linker error
(c) 10
(d) late binding

Answers : **70.** (c) **71.** (a) **72.** (c)

CHAPTER 12

ELEMENTS OF PROBABILITY

1. ***Let A and B be two events such that $P(A) = 0.3$ and $P(A \cup B) = 0.8$. If A and B are independent events, then $P(B)$ equals to :***

(a) 5/6 (b) 4/7

(c) 5/8 (d) 5/7

2. ***A bag contains 6 red and 3 white balls. 4 balls are drawn out one by one and not replaced. The probability that they are alternatively of different colaurs :***

(a) 5/84 (b) 1/144

(c) 5/42 (d) 1/12

3. ***If $P(A) = 0.5$, $P(B) = 0.3$, $P(AB) = 0.2$, the probability in various cases will be :***

(i) A occurs but not B :

(a) 0.3 (b) 0.35

(c) 0.5 (d) 0.15

(ii) At least one of A and B occurs :

(a) 0.65 (b) 0.60

(c) 0.70 (d) 0.55

(iii) Neither of A and B accurs :

(a) 0.4 (b) 0.35

(c) 0.15 (d) 0.30

4. ***A drawer contains 50 bolts and 150 nuts. Half of the bolts and half of the nuts are rusted. If one item is chosen at random, then probability that it is rusted or a bolt is :***

(a) 1/8 (b) 2/8

(c) 7/8 (d) 5/8

5. ***In a race, the odds in favour of horses A, B, C, D are 1 : 3, 1 : 4, 1 : 5 and 1 : 6 respectively. The prabability that one of them wins the race will be :***

Answers : **1.*** (d) **2.*** (c) **3.** (i)* (a), (ii)* (b), (iii)* (a) **4.*** (d)

(a) $\frac{319}{420}$ (b) $\frac{139}{420}$

(c) $\frac{12}{319}$ (d) $\frac{439}{520}$

6. ***If P (A) = $\frac{3}{4}$, P (B) = $\frac{1}{2}$, P (A – B) = $\frac{3}{8}$, the probability that exactly one of A and B occurs is :***

(a) $\frac{1}{3}$ (b) $\frac{2}{3}$

(c) $\frac{1}{2}$ (d) $\frac{3}{4}$

7. ***Find the chance of throwing at least an ace in a single throw of 2 dice :***

(a) $\frac{11}{36}$ (b) $\frac{8}{36}$

(c) $\frac{1}{4}$ (d) $\frac{10}{36}$

8. ***Two integers are selected at random from integers 1 to 11. If the sum is even, then the probability that both the numbers are odd is :***

(a) $\frac{2}{5}$ (b) $\frac{3}{5}$

(c) $\left(\frac{4}{5}\right)$ (d) $\frac{11}{15}$

9. ***Consider a random experiment in which a coin is tossed and if the coin shows head it is tossed again but if it shows a tail then a die is tossed. If 8 possible out comes are equally likely, then the probability that the die shows a number greater than four if it is known that the first throw of the coins results in a tail :***

(a) $\frac{7}{8}$ (b) $\frac{1}{3}$

(c) $\frac{2}{3}$ (d) $\frac{5}{9}$

10. ***An unbaised coin is tossed. If the result is a head, a pair of unbaised dice is rolled and the sum of the numbers obtained is noted. If the result is a tail, a card from a well shuffled pack of 11 cards numbered 2, 3, 4, ... 12, is picked and the number on the card is noted. What is the chances that the noted number is either 7 or 8 ?***

(a) $\frac{193}{792}$ (b) $\frac{139}{792}$

(c) $\frac{293}{792}$ (d) $\frac{329}{792}$

11. ***A man is known to speak truth 3 out of 4 times. He throws a die and reports that it is a six. The probability that it is actually a six :***

(a) $\frac{2}{3}$ (b) $\frac{5}{8}$

(c) $\frac{3}{8}$ (d) $\frac{7}{8}$

12. ***In a test, an examinee either guesses or copies or knows the answer to a multiple choice question with 4 choices. The probability that he makes a guess is*** $\frac{1}{3}$ ***and the probability that he copies the answer is*** $\frac{1}{6}$. ***The probobility that his answer is correct, given that he copied it, is*** $\frac{1}{8}$. ***Then the probability that he knew the answer to the question, given that he correctly answered it is :***

(a) $\frac{11}{25}$ (b) $\frac{12}{29}$

(c) $\frac{19}{29}$ (d) $\frac{24}{29}$

13. ***A man takes a step forward with probability 2/5 and backwards with probability 3/5. Find the probability that at the end of eleven steps he is just one step away from the starting point :***

(a) $462\ (0.24)^5$ (b) $462\ (0.40)^2$

(c) $264\ (0.18)^5$ (d) $462\ (0.24)^3$

14. ***One mapping is selected from all the mappings of the set*** $A = \{1, 2, 3, ..., n\}$ ***into itself. The probability that it is injective mapping :***

(a) $\frac{1}{n^n}$ (b) $\frac{n^2}{n^n}$

(c) $\frac{2^n}{n^n}$ (d) $\frac{n!}{n^n}$

Answers :

5.* (a)	**6.*** (c)	**7.*** (a)	**8.*** (b)	**9.*** (b)
10.* (a)	**11.*** (c)	**12.*** (d)	**13.*** (a)	**14.** (d)

15. ***Items produced by a certain process, each may have one or both of two types of defects, A and B. It is known that 22% if the items have type A defects and 12% have type B defects. Further 8% have both type of defects. The probability that a randomly selected item will be defective is :***

(a) 0.24 (b) 0.25
(c) 0.26 (d) 0.27

16. ***A six faced die is so biased that it is twice as likely to show an even number as an odd number, When it is thrown. The probability that the sum of two numbers is even is***

(a) $\frac{4}{9}$ (b) $\frac{8}{9}$
(c) $\frac{5}{9}$ (d) $\frac{7}{9}$

17. ***Two persons A and B throw a die alternatively till one of them gets a "THREE" and wins the game. The probability of winning of A is :***

(a) $\frac{6}{11}$ (b) $\frac{8}{11}$
(c) $\frac{7}{11}$ (d) $\frac{9}{11}$

18. ***A player tosses a fair die. If a prime number occurs he wins that number of rupees, but if a non-prime number occurs he loses that number of rupees. The expected gain of the player will be :***

(a) $-\frac{1}{6}$ (b) $\frac{2}{5}$
(c) $\frac{1}{2}$ (d) $-\frac{1}{3}$

19. ***A and B take turns in throwing two dice, the first to throw 10 being awarded the prize. If A has to first throw, chance of winning is :***

(a) $\frac{12}{23}$ (b) $\frac{21}{23}$
(c) $\frac{13}{23}$ (d) $\frac{14}{23}$

20. ***A makes a bet with B of 5s to 2s that in a single throw with two dice he will throw seven before B throws four, Each has a pair of dice and they throw simultaneously until one of them wins, equal throws being disregarded. Then B's expectation will be :***

(a) d (b) $2d$

(c) $3d$ (d) $4d$

21. ***If 6n tickets numbered 0, 1, 2, ... (2n – 1) are placed in a bag and three are drawn out, the chance that the sum of the numbers on them is equal to 6n :***

(a) $\frac{3n}{(6n-1)(6n-2)}$ (b) $\frac{3n}{(6n+1)(6n-2)}$

(c) $\frac{3n}{(3n+1)(6n+2)}$ (d) $\frac{3n}{(3n-1)(6n+2)}$

22. ***A bag contains a coin of value M, and a number of other coins whose aggregate value is m. A person draws one at a time till he draws the coin M; the value of his expectation :***

(a) $M+\frac{m}{2}$ (b) $M-\frac{m}{2}$

(c) $M+m$ (d) $M-m$

23. ***There are n letters and n addressed envelopes. If the letters are placed randomly, then the probability that all the letters are not placed in the right envelops :***

(a) $\frac{1}{n!}$ (b) $1-n!$

(c) $1-\frac{1}{n!}$ (d) $\frac{1}{n!}-1$

24. ***For any two events A and B which is true ?***

(a) $P(\overline{A}\cap\overline{B}) = 1 + P(A\cap B) + P(A) + P(B)$

(b) $P(\overline{A}\cap\overline{B}) \le 1 - P(A) - P(B)$

(c) $P(\overline{A}\cap\overline{B}) \ge P(A) + P(B) - 1$

(d) $P(A\cap B) \le P(A) + P(B)$

25. ***A can hit a target 4 times in 5 shots; B 3 times in 4 shots, C twice in three shots. They fire a volley, the chance that at least two shot hit :***

(a) $\frac{5}{6}$ (b) $\frac{1}{2}$

(c) $\frac{2}{15}$ (d) $\frac{2}{5}$

26. ***In a college 25% students in mathematics, 15% students in physics and 10% students in physics and mathematics both are failed. A***

Answers : **15.*** (c) **16.*** (c) **17.*** (a) **18.*** (a) **19.*** (a) **20.*** (d)
21. (a) **22.*** (c) **23.*** (c) **24.** (d) **25.*** (a)

student is selected at random, then the chance of his failure in physics if he was failed in mathematics :

(a) $\frac{2}{3}$ (b) $\frac{2}{5}$

(c) $\frac{3}{10}$ (d) $\frac{3}{4}$

27. ***The probability that a 50 years old man will be alive at 60 is 0.83 and probability that a 45 year old woman will be alive at 55 is 0.87, then the chance that a man who is 50 and women who is 45 will be alive 10 years hence***

(a) 0.7221 (b) 0.2771

(c) 0.7321 (d) 0.7231

28. ***If p is the chance that an odd number of aces turn up when n ordinary dice are thrown, then the value of p is :***

(a) $\frac{1}{2}\left[\left(\frac{2}{3}\right)^n + 1\right]$ (b) $\frac{1}{2}\left[1 - \left(\frac{2}{3}\right)^n\right]$

(c) $\frac{1}{2}\left[\left(\frac{2}{3}\right)^n - 1\right]$ (d) $\frac{1}{2}\left[1 + \left(\frac{2}{3}\right)^n\right]$

29. ***An event A can be explained by a set of exhaustive and mutually exclusive hypothesis $B_1, B_2, \ldots B_n$. Given, a priori probabilities $P(B_1), P(B_2) \ldots P(B_n)$. Corresponding to a total absence of knowledge regarding the occurrence of A. Then the posterior probability $P(B_i/A)$ is given by :***

(a) $\frac{P(B_i)\,P(A/B_i)}{\sum_{i=1}^{n} P(B_i)\,P(A/B_i)}$ (b) $\frac{P(A)\,P(A/B_i)}{\sum_{i=1}^{n} P(A)\,P(A/B_i)}$

(c) $\frac{P(B_i)\,P(B_i/A)}{\sum_{i=1}^{n} P(B_i)\,P(B_i/A)}$ (d) $\sum_{i=1}^{n} P(B_i)\,P(B_i/A)$

30. ***The expected value of the number of points that will be obtained in a single throw with an ordinary die :***

(a) $\frac{3}{2}$ (b) $\frac{5}{2}$

(c) $\frac{7}{2}$ (d) $\frac{9}{2}$

31. ***Let X be a discrete random variable with***

$$P(X = j) = C \cdot \left(\frac{1}{2}\right)^j \quad j = 1, 2, \ldots$$

Then the value of C is :

(a) 1 (b) $\frac{1}{2}$

(c) 2 (d) $\frac{3}{2}$

32. ***A bag contains 9 balls which are numbered 1 to 9. Three balls are drawn without replacement from this; the expectation of the sum of the numbers on these balls :***

(a) 5 (b) 15

(c) 3 (d) 9

33. ***A box contains a white and b black balls; c balls are drawn. The expectation of the number of white balls drawn is :***

(a) $\frac{cb}{a+b}$ (b) $\frac{c}{a+b}$

(c) $\frac{ca}{a+b}$ (d) $\frac{c^2}{a+b}$

34. ***Mathematical expectation of a random experiment is :***

(a) finite (b) infinite

(c) a & b both (d) None of these

35. ***The expected value of the product of points on n dice :***

(a) $\left(\frac{7}{2}\right)^n$ (b) $\frac{7}{2}n$

(c) $\left(\frac{2}{7}\right)^n$ (d) $\frac{2}{7}n$

36. ***A continuous random variable X has the probability density function $f(x) = 3x^2$, $0 \le x \le 1$, then the value of a if $P(X \le a) = P(X > a)$***

(a) $(1.05)^{1/3}$ (b) $(1.05)^{1/2}$

(c) $\left(\frac{1}{3}\right)^{1/2}$ (d) $\left(\frac{1}{2}\right)^{1/3}$

Answers : **26.*** (b) **27.*** (a) **28.*** (b) **29.*** (a) **30.*** (c) **31.*** (a) **32.*** (a) **33.*** (c) **34.** (c) **35.*** (a) **36.*** (d)

37. ***The constant C for the p.d.f.***

$$f(x) = \begin{cases} Cx^2 & 0 \le x \le 3 \\ 0 & \text{otherwise} \end{cases}$$

is :

(a) $\frac{1}{3}$ (b) $\frac{1}{9}$

(c) $\frac{1}{6}$ (d) $\frac{1}{8}$

38. ***The mean in the following p.d.f.***

$$f(x) = \begin{cases} \frac{(x-1)^3}{4}; & 1 \le x \le 3 \\ 0 & \text{otherwise} \end{cases}$$

(a) 1.62 (b) 2.60

(c) 3.65 (d) 2.58

39. ***The mode for the frequency curve*** $y = \frac{1}{2} \sin x, 0 \le x \le \pi$ ***is :***

(a) π (b) $\frac{\pi}{6}$

(c) $\frac{\pi}{3}$ (d) $\frac{\pi}{2}$

40. ***The moment generating function of the sum of two independent random variable is :***

(a) The sum of their m.g.f.

(b) The product of their m.g.f.

(c) The division of their m.g.f.

(d) None of these

41. ***Which of the followings is true ?***

(a) $\beta_1 = \frac{\mu_3^2}{\mu_2^2}$ (b) $\beta_2 = \frac{K_4}{K_2^2} - 3$

(c) $\beta_1 = \frac{\mu_3^2}{\mu_2^3}$ (d) $K_3 = \mu_3 + \mu_3'$

42. ***If the m.g.f. of a random variable X is*** $\left(\frac{1}{3} + \frac{2}{3} e^t\right)^5$***, then*** $P(x = 2)$ ***is :***

(a) $\frac{19}{241}$ (b) $\frac{91}{241}$

(c) $\frac{30}{243}$ (d) $\frac{40}{243}$

43. *For Poisson distribution, which of the following is true ?*

(a) $M = 7, \sigma^2 = 6$ (b) $M = 7, \sigma = 6$

(c) $M = 7, \sigma^2 = 7$ (d) $M = 7, \sigma = 7$

44. *In a Poisson distribution probability for x = 0 is 10% . Then mean :*

(a) 1.414 (b) 0.4771

(c) 1.4313 (d) 2.3026

45. *If $P(X = 2) = 9P(X = 4) + 90\,P(X = 6)$ in Poisson distribution, then $E(x)$:*

(a) 1 (b) 2

(c) 3 (d) $\pm 2i$

46. *A student takes on 18-question multiple choice exam; with four choices per question. Suppose one of the choices is obviously incorrect, and the student makes an "educated" guess of the remaining choices. The expected number E(x) of correct answers :*

(a) 5 (b) 6

(c) 7 (d) 8

47. *The batting average of a baseball player is 0.300. He comes to bat four times. Then the probability that he will get exactly two hits :*

(a) 0.1212 (b) 0.1323

(c) 0.4337 (d) 0.2646

48. *The probability that Poonia scores a three point basket ball shot is p = 0.4. He shots 5 times. Then the probability that he scores at least once :*

(a) 0.7599 (b) 0.6649

(c) 0.6799 (d) 0.6599

49. *A lottery with 500 tickets give one prize of $ 100, three prize of $ 50 each and five prizes of $ 25 each. If a ticket costs $ 1, then the expected value of game :*

(a) – 0.35 (b) 0.35

(c) – 0.25 (d) 0.25

50. *A player toses three fair coins. He wins $ 5 if three head occur, $ 3 if two head occur and $ 1 if only one head occur. On the other hand,*

Answers : **37.*** (b) **38.*** (b) **39.*** (d) **40.*** (b) **41.** (c) **42.*** (d) **43.*** (c) **44.*** (d) **45.*** (a) **46.*** (b) **47.*** (d) **48.*** (a) **49.** (c)

he loses $ 15 if three tails occur. Then the value of the game to the player :

(a) – 0.35 (b) 0.35

(c) – 0.25 (d) 0.25

51. ***A pair of fair dice is thrown. Let X denote the maximum of the two numbers which appears. The mean will be :***

(a) 0.25 (b) 0.35

(c) 0.45 (d) 0.55

52. ***A fair die is tossed. Let X denote twice the number appearing. Then mean will be :***

(a) 8 (b) 7

(c) 6 (d) 5

53. ***A linear Array EMPLOYEE has n elements. Suppose NAME appears randomly in the array, and there is a linear search to find the location K of NAME, i.e., to find K such that EMPLOYEE [K] = NAME. Let f (n) denote the number of comparisons in the linear search. The maximum value (worst case) of f (n) will be :***

(a) 1 (b) $n - 1$

(c) n (d) $n!$

54. ***A class of 30 students occupy a class room containing 5 rows of seats, with 8 seats in each row. If the students seat themselves at random, the probability that the sixth seat in the fifth row will be empty is :***

(a) $\frac{1}{5}$ (b) $\frac{1}{3}$

(c) $\frac{1}{4}$ (d) $\frac{2}{5}$

55. ***A box contains 2 black, 4 white and 3 red balls. One ball is drawn at random from the box and kept aside. From the remaining balls in the box, another ball is drawn at random and kept beside the first. This process is repeated till all the balls are drawn from the box. The probability that the balls drawn are in the sequence 2 black, 4 white, and 3 red is :***

(a) $\frac{1}{1260}$ (b) $\frac{17}{1260}$

(c) $\frac{12}{1260}$ (d) $\frac{13}{1260}$

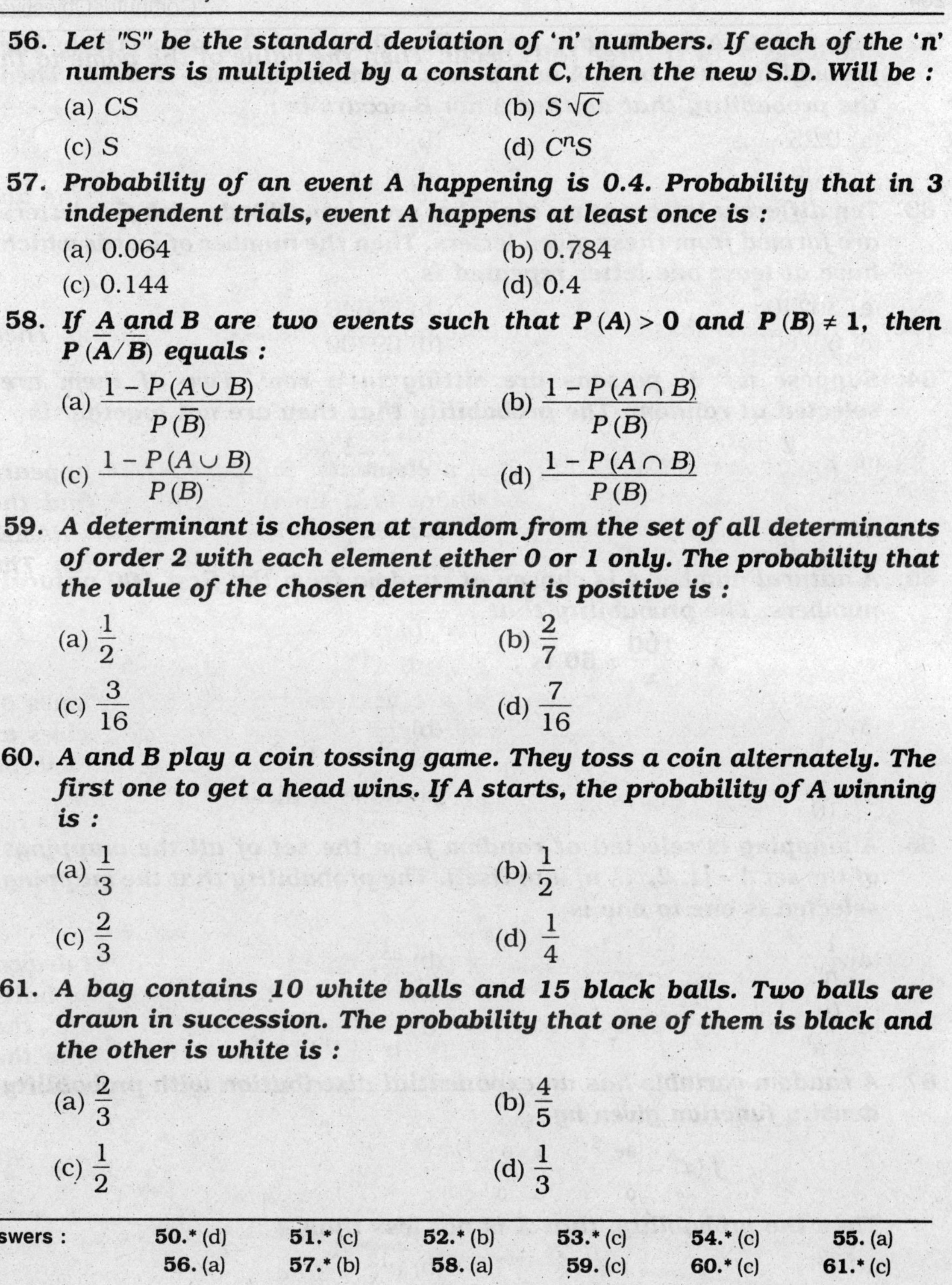

56. *Let "S" be the standard deviation of 'n' numbers. If each of the 'n' numbers is multiplied by a constant C, then the new S.D. Will be :*

(a) CS (b) $S\sqrt{C}$

(c) S (d) C^nS

57. *Probability of an event A happening is 0.4. Probability that in 3 independent trials, event A happens at least once is :*

(a) 0.064 (b) 0.784

(c) 0.144 (d) 0.4

58. *If A and B are two events such that $P(A) > 0$ and $P(B) \neq 1$, then $P(\bar{A}/\bar{B})$ equals :*

(a) $\dfrac{1 - P(A \cup B)}{P(\bar{B})}$ (b) $\dfrac{1 - P(A \cap B)}{P(\bar{B})}$

(c) $\dfrac{1 - P(A \cup B)}{P(B)}$ (d) $\dfrac{1 - P(A \cap B)}{P(B)}$

59. *A determinant is chosen at random from the set of all determinants of order 2 with each element either 0 or 1 only. The probability that the value of the chosen determinant is positive is :*

(a) $\dfrac{1}{2}$ (b) $\dfrac{2}{7}$

(c) $\dfrac{3}{16}$ (d) $\dfrac{7}{16}$

60. *A and B play a coin tossing game. They toss a coin alternately. The first one to get a head wins. If A starts, the probability of A winning is :*

(a) $\dfrac{1}{3}$ (b) $\dfrac{1}{2}$

(c) $\dfrac{2}{3}$ (d) $\dfrac{1}{4}$

61. *A bag contains 10 white balls and 15 black balls. Two balls are drawn in succession. The probability that one of them is black and the other is white is :*

(a) $\dfrac{2}{3}$ (b) $\dfrac{4}{5}$

(c) $\dfrac{1}{2}$ (d) $\dfrac{1}{3}$

Answers : **50.*** (d) **51.*** (c) **52.*** (b) **53.*** (c) **54.*** (c) **55.** (a)
56. (a) **57.*** (b) **58.** (a) **59.** (c) **60.*** (c) **61.*** (c)

62. *Two events A and B have probability 0.25 and 0.5 respectively The probability that both A and B occur simultaneously is 0.14. Then the probability that neither A nor B occurs is :*

(a) 0.25 (b) 0.75
(c) 0.39 (d) 0.11

63. *Ten different letters of an alphabet are given. Words with five letters are formed from these given letters. Then the number of words which have at least one letter repeated is :*

(a) 30240 (b) 60640
(c) 69760 (d) 69700

64. *Suppose n (≥ 3) persons are sitting in a row. Two of them are selected at random. The probability that they are not together is :*

(a) $1 - \frac{2}{n}$ (b) $1 - \frac{1}{n}$
(c) $1 + \frac{2}{n}$ (d) $1 + \frac{1}{n}$

65. *A natural number x is chosen at random from the first 100 natural numbers. The probability that*

$$x + \frac{100}{x} > 50 \text{ is :}$$

(a) $\frac{2}{10}$ (b) $\frac{11}{55}$
(c) $\frac{4}{10}$ (d) None of these

66. *A mapping is selected at random from the set of all the mappings of the set A = {1, 2, ..., n} into itself. The probability that the mapping selected is one to one is :*

(a) $\frac{1}{n}$ (b) $\frac{1}{n!}$
(c) $\frac{(n-1)!}{n^{n-1}}$ (d) $\frac{n!}{n^{(n+1)}!}$

67. *A random variable has an exponential distribution with probability density function given by*

$$f(x) = \begin{cases} 3e^{-3x} & x > 0 \\ 0 & x \leq 0 \end{cases}$$

Then the probability, that X is not less than 4 :

(a) e^2 (b) e^{12}

(c) e^{-12} (d) e^{-2}

68. *In question No. 67, the mean is :*

(a) $\frac{1}{2}$ (b) $\frac{1}{3}$

(c) $\frac{1}{9}$ (d) $\frac{1}{4}$

69. *In question No. 67, the variance is given by :*

(a) $\frac{1}{2}$ (b) $\frac{1}{3}$

(c) $\frac{1}{4}$ (d) $\frac{1}{9}$

70. *For exponential distribution, which of the following is true ?*

(a) Mean = Variance (b) Mean = S.D.

(c) $(\text{Mean})^2$ = S.D. (d) Mean = $\frac{1}{2}$ *S. D.*

71. *Let E_1 and E_2 are events in a probability space satisfying the following constraints*

***(i)* $P(E_1) = P(E_2)$**

***(ii)* $P(E_1 \cup E_2) = 1$**

(iii)* E_1 and E_2 *are independent

The prabability of the event E_1 is :

(a) 0 (b) $\frac{1}{4}$

(c) $\frac{1}{2}$ (d) 1

72. *Seven (distinct) car accidents occured in a week. What is the probability that they all occured on the same day ?*

(a) $\frac{1}{7^7}$ (b) $\frac{1}{7^6}$

(c) $\frac{1}{2^7}$ (d) $\frac{7}{2^7}$

73. *Supposse that the expectation of a random variable X is 5. Which of the following is true ?*

Answers : **62.*** (c) **63.** (c) **64.** (a) **65.** (d) **66.** (c) **67.*** (c)
68.* (b) **69.*** (d) **70.*** (b) **71.** (d) **72.*** (a)

(a) There is a sample point at which X has the value 5

(b) There is a sample point at which X has value greater than 5

(c) There is a sample point at which X has a value greater than or equal to 5

(d) None of the above.

74. ***Consider two events E_1 and E_2 such that probability of E_1, $P(E_1) = \frac{1}{2}$, probability of E_2, $P(E_2) = \frac{1}{3}$ and probability of E_1 and E_2, $P(E_1 \text{ and } E_2) = \frac{1}{5}$. Which of the following statements is/are true ?***

(a) $P(E_1 \text{ or } E_2) = \frac{2}{3}$

(b) Events E_1 and E_2 are independent

(c) Events E_1 and E_2 are not independent

(d) $P\left(\frac{E_1}{E_2}\right) = \frac{4}{5}$

75. ***Which of the following statements is/are false ?***

(a) For Poisson distribution, the mean is twice the variance

(b) In quening theory, if arrivals occur according to Poisson distribution, then the interarrival time is exponentially distributed

(c) The distribution of waiting time is independent of the service descipline used in selecting the waiting customers for service

(d) If the time between successive arrivals is exponential, then the time between the occurrences of every third arrival is also exponential

76. ***The point of inflexion of the normal curve are :***

(a) $m \pm \sigma$ (b) $m \pm 2\sigma$

(c) $m \pm 3\sigma$ (d) $m \pm \frac{2}{3}\sigma$

77. ***For the normal distribution what is the ratio between quartile deviation, mean deviation, and standard deviation ?***

(a) 1 : 2 : 3 (b) 4 : 5 : 9

(c) 10 : 12 : 15 (d) 8 : 11 : 14

78. ***How much % area of the normal curve lie in the region***

$$P[\mu - 3\sigma < X < \mu + 3\sigma] ?$$

(a) 68.26% (b) 95.44%

(c) 99.73% (d) 98.89%

79. ***Normal curve is :***

(a) Very flat

(b) Bell shaped symmetrical about mean

(c) Very peaked

(d) Smooth

80. ***From a pack of 52 cards an even number of cards is drawn. Then the probability that half of these carrds being red is :***

(a) 5,29,623

(b) $\dfrac{52\,!}{2^{51}-1}$

(c) $\dfrac{\dfrac{52\,!}{(26\,!)^2}-1}{2^{51}-1}$

(d) $\dfrac{152 \times (\lfloor 26)^2}{2^{51}-1}$

Answers : **73.** (c) **74.*** (c) **75.** (a) **76.** (a) **77.** (c) **78.** (c) **79.** (b) **80.** (c)

SOLUTIONS

1. Since $P(A \cup B) = P(A) + P(B) - P(A \cap B)$

$$= P(A) + P(B) - P(A) \cdot P(B)$$

{for independent $P(A \cap B) = P(A) \cdot P(B)$}

2. If red is drawn first, then

$$= \frac{6}{9} \times \frac{3}{8} \times \frac{5}{7} \times \frac{2}{6} \quad ...(1)$$

If white is drawn first, then

$$= \frac{3}{9} \times \frac{6}{8} \times \frac{2}{7} \times \frac{5}{6} \quad ...(2)$$

Required prabability = (1) + (2)

3. (i) $P(A) - P(AB)$

(ii) $P(A \cup B) = P(A) + P(B) - P(AB)$

(iii) 1 – (Probability that at least one of them accurs)

4. $P(A) = \frac{100}{200}$, $P(B) = \frac{50}{200}$, $P(AB) = \frac{25}{200}$

Required probability = $P(A \cup B)$

5. $P(A) = \frac{1}{4}$, $P(B) = \frac{1}{5}$, $P(C) = \frac{1}{6}$, $P(D) = \frac{1}{7}$

Required probability = $P(A \cup B \cup C \cup D)$

$$= P(A) + P(B) + P(C) + P(D)$$

(By addition theorem)

6. $P(A - B) = P(A) - P(A \cap B)$

and $P(B - A) = P(B) - P(A \cap B)$

Probability that exactly one of A and B occurs is

$$= P(A - B) + P(B - A)$$

7. $A = \{(1, 1), (1, 2), (1, 3), (1, 4), (1, 5), (1, 6), (2, 1), (3, 1), (4, 1), (5, 1), (6, 1)\}$

$n(A) = 11$

8. Let

A = Both the numbers chosen are odd.

B = The sum of the numbers chosen is even.

$$P(A) = \frac{^6C_2}{^{11}C_2}, \ P(B) = \frac{^6C_2 + {^5C_2}}{^{11}C_2}, \ P(AB) = \frac{^6C_2}{^{11}C_2}$$

$\therefore$ Required probability $= P(A/B) = \dfrac{P(A \cap B)}{P(B)}$

9. $S = \{(H, H), (H, T), (T, 1)\ (T, 2), (T, 3), (T, 4), (T, 5), (T, 6)\}$

Let A be the event that the die shows a number greater than 4 and B be the event that the first throw of the coin results in a tail. Then

$A = \{(T, 5), (T, 6)\}$

$B = \{(T, 1)\ (T, 2), (T, 3), (T, 4), (T, 5), (T, 6)\}$

Required probability $= P(A/B)$

10. E_1 = Coin shows a head.

E_2 = Coin shows a tail.

A = Noted numbers is 7 or 8.

$$P(E_1) = \frac{1}{2},\ P(E_2) = \frac{1}{2},\ P\left(A/E_1\right) = \frac{11}{36},\ P\left(A/E_2\right) = \frac{2}{11}$$

Required probability $= P(A)$

$= P(E_1)\,P(A/E_1) + P(E_2)\,P(A/E_2)$

11. E_1 = Six occurs.

E_2 = Six does not occur.

A = Man reports that it is a six

$P(E_1) = \dfrac{1}{6}$ $\qquad P(E_2) = \dfrac{5}{6}$

$P\left(A/E_1\right) = \dfrac{3}{4},$ $\qquad P\left(A/E_2\right) = \dfrac{1}{4}$

By Baye's theorem

$$P\left(E_1 A\right) = \frac{P(E_1)\,P(A/E_1)}{\sum_{e=1}^{2} P(E_i)\,P(A/E_i)}$$

12. E_1 – Examinee guesses the answer.

E_2 – Examinee copies the answer.

E_3 – Examinee knows the answer.

A – Examinee answers correctly.

$P(E_1) = \dfrac{1}{3},$ $\qquad P(E_2) = 16,$ $\qquad P(E_3) = \dfrac{1}{2}$

$P(A/E_1) = 1/4,$ $\qquad P(A/E_2) = 1/8,$ $\qquad P(A/E_3) = 1$

Required probability $= P(E_3/A)$

$$= \frac{A(E_3)\, P(A/E_3)}{\sum_{e=1}^{3} P(E_i)\, P(A/E_i)}$$

13. p-Probability that the man takes a step forward.

X = Number of steps taken in forward direction.

$n = 11,\ p = 0.4,\ q = 0.6$

Required probability $= P(X = 5) + P(X = 6)$

15. $P(A) = 0.22,\ P(B) = 0.12,\ P(AB) = 0.08$

Required probability $= P(A \cup B)$

16. p - probability that biased die shows an odd number.

$2p$ - probability that it shows an even number.

A - odd No. appears on both die.

B - even No. appears on both die.

$P(A \cup B) = P(A) + P(B)$ (By addition theorem)

17. $P(E) = \frac{1}{6}\quad P(\overline{E}) = \frac{5}{6}$

$P(F) = \frac{1}{6}\quad P(\overline{F}) = \frac{5}{6}$

$P(A \text{ wins}) = P(E) + P(\overline{E})\, P(\overline{F})\, P(E) + [P(\overline{E})]^2\, [P(\overline{F})]^2\, P(E) + \ldots$

18.

Outcomes on a die	:	1	2	3	4	5	6
Associated gain to outcomes (x_i)	:	-1	2	3	-4	5	-6
$f(x_i)$	:	$\frac{1}{6}$	$\frac{1}{6}$	$\frac{1}{6}$	$\frac{1}{6}$	$\frac{1}{6}$	$\frac{1}{6}$

19. $E = \{(4, 6), (6, 4), (5, 5)\}$

Probability of A winning

$$= \frac{3}{36} + \left(\frac{33}{36}\right)^2 \left(\frac{3}{36}\right) + \left(\frac{33}{36}\right)^4 \left(\frac{3}{36}\right) + \ldots$$

20. The chance of 7 throwing with two dice $= \frac{1}{6}$.

Similarly the chance of throwing 4 is $= \frac{1}{12}$.

Let x = B's chance of supposition.

$2x$ = A's chance of supposition.

A's chance + B's chance = 1

$$\Rightarrow \qquad x = \frac{1}{3}$$

$\therefore$ B's expectation $= \frac{1}{3}$ of $5s - \frac{2}{3}$ of $2s$

$$= \frac{1}{3} s$$

$$= 4d \quad (\because 1s = 12d)$$

22. Let the bag contains $(n + 1)$ coins in all, one is of value M and the other n coins are of aggregate value m. The expectation of first draw is

$$\frac{1}{n+1}(M + m)$$

Chance for the second draw $= 1 - \frac{1}{n+1}$

$$= \frac{n}{n+1}$$

and here it is certain that M coin and also $(n - 1)$ other coins each of which has an average value $\frac{m}{n}$, their total value is, therefore $= \frac{n-1}{n} m$

Total amount in the bag is now

$$= M + \frac{n-1}{n} m$$

Probability of success in second draw $= \frac{n}{n+1} \cdot \frac{1}{n}$

$\therefore$ Expectation in second draw

$$= \frac{n}{n+1} \cdot \frac{1}{n}\left[M + \frac{n-1}{n} m\right]$$

$$= \frac{1}{n+1}\left[M + \frac{n-1}{n} m\right]$$

Continuing, the expectation in $(n + 1)$ *i.e.*, last draw

$$= \frac{1}{n+1}(M + 0)$$

Adding, we get the result.

23. Total no. of placing n letters in n envelops $= n! = n(S)$

$\therefore$ Probability that all the letters are sent wrongly = 1 – prab. that all the letters sent in right envelops.

25. Required probability

$$= P(ABC) + P(\overline{A}BC) + P(A\overline{B}C) + P(AB\overline{C})$$

$$= \frac{2}{5} + \frac{1}{10} + \frac{2}{15} + \frac{1}{5} = \frac{5}{6}$$

26. $P(B/A) = \frac{P(A \cap B)}{P(A)} = \frac{\frac{1}{10}}{\frac{1}{4}} = \frac{2}{5}$

27. Probability that both will live 10 years hence

$$= \frac{83}{100} \times \frac{87}{100} = 0.7221$$

28. $p = {}^nC_1 \left(\frac{1}{6}\right)^1 \left(\frac{5}{6}\right)^{n-1} + {}^nC_3 \left(\frac{1}{6}\right)^3 \left(\frac{5}{6}\right)^{n-3} + \ldots$

29. Statement of Baye's theorem.

30. $$E(x) = p_1x_1 + p_2x_2 + \ldots + p_nx_n$$
$$= \frac{1}{6} \cdot 1 + \frac{1}{6} \cdot 2 + \ldots + \frac{1}{6} \cdot 6 = \frac{7}{2}$$

31. Because $\sum_{j=1}^{\infty} P(X = j) = 1$

$\Rightarrow$ $$C \cdot \sum_{j=1}^{\infty} \left(\frac{1}{2}\right)^j = 1$$

$\Rightarrow$ $C = 1$ (by G .P.)

32. $$E(S) = E(X_1) + E(X_2) + E(X_3)$$

But $E(X_i) = \frac{1}{9}[1 + 2 + 3 + 4 + \ldots + 9] = 5$

$\therefore$ $E(S) = 5 + 5 + 5 = 15$

33. Here

$$P(X_i = 1) = \frac{a}{a+b}, \; P(X_i = 0) = \frac{b}{a+b}$$

where $X_i = \begin{cases} 1 \text{ if drawn ball is white} \\ 0 \text{ if drawn ball is black} \end{cases}$

$\therefore$ $E(X_i) = 1 \cdot \frac{a}{a+b} + 0 \cdot \frac{b}{a+b} = \frac{a}{a+b}$

$\therefore$ $E(s) = \frac{a}{a+b} + \frac{a}{a+b} + \ldots + \frac{a}{a+b}$ (c times)

$$= \frac{ca}{a+b}$$

35. For every single dice

$$E(x_i) = \frac{7}{2}\ ;\ i = 1, 2, 3, \ldots, n.$$

Then $\quad E(x) = E(x_1\, x_2 \ldots x_n)$

$$= E(x_1) \cdot E(x_2) \ldots E(x_n)$$

36. We have

$$\int_{-\infty}^{\infty} f(x)\, dx = 0$$

$$\int_{-\infty}^{a} f(x)\, dx + \int_{a}^{\infty} f(x)\, dx = 1$$

$$P(X \le a) + P(X > a) = 1$$

$\Rightarrow \quad P(X \le a) = P(X > a) = \frac{1}{2}$ (By given cond.)

$\therefore \quad P(X \le a) = \left(\frac{1}{2}\right)^{1/3}$

37. $\quad \int_{-\infty}^{\infty} f(x)\, dx = 1$

$\Rightarrow \quad \int_{0}^{3} Cx^2\, dx = 1 \Rightarrow C = \frac{1}{9}$

38. $\quad \text{Mean} = E(x) = \int_{-\infty}^{\infty} x f(x)\, dx$

$$= 2.60$$

39. Total frequency $= \int_{0}^{\pi} \frac{1}{2} \sin x\, dx$

$$= 1$$

The mode is that value of x for which $\frac{dy}{dx} = 0$ and $\frac{d^2y}{dx^2} =$ Negative

$\therefore \quad x = \frac{\pi}{2}$

42. Let $\quad P(X = x) = {}^nC_x\, p^x q^{n-x},\ x = 0, 1, 2, \ldots n$

Then $Mo(t) = (q + pe^t)^n$

But $Mo(t) = \left(\frac{1}{3} + \frac{2}{3}e^t\right)^5$

$$\therefore \quad p = \frac{2}{3},\ q = \frac{1}{3},\ n = 5$$

$$P(X = x) = {}^5C_x \left(\frac{2}{3}\right)^x \left(\frac{1}{3}\right)^{5-x}$$

43. For Poisson distribution mean and variance are always equal.

44. Let m is the mean, then

$$P(X = x) = e^{-m} \cdot \frac{m^x}{x!}$$

$$\therefore \quad P(X = 0) = e^{-m}$$

$$\therefore \quad e^{-m} = 10\% = 0.1$$

$$\therefore \quad m = \log e^{10}$$

45. Let $P(X = x) = e^{-m} \cdot \frac{m^x}{x!}$, $x = 0, 1, 2, \ldots \infty$

Given $\quad P(X = 2) = 9\,P(X = 4) + 90\,P(X = 6)$

$$\frac{e^{-m} \cdot m^2}{2!} = 9e^{-m} \cdot \frac{m^4}{4!} + 90\,e^{-m} \cdot \frac{m^6}{6!}$$

$$\therefore \quad (m^2 + 4)(m - 1) = 0$$

$$\Rightarrow \quad m = 1 \text{ (acceptable)}$$

46. $n = 18,\ p = \frac{1}{3},\ q = \frac{2}{3}$

$$E(x) = np \text{ (In Binomial distribution)}$$

47. $n = 4,\ p = 0.300,\ q = 0.700$

$$P(X = 2) = {}^4C_2\,(.3)^2\,(.7)^2$$

48. $n = 5,\ p = 0.4,\ q = 0.6$

$$P(x \geq 1) = P(x = 1) + P(x = 2) + P(X = 3) + P(X = 4) + P(X = 5)$$

$$= 1 - P(X = 0)$$

$$= 1 - {}^5C_0\,(0.4)^0\,(0.6)^{5-0}$$

$$= 1 - (.6)^5$$

50. $S = \{(HHH), (HHT), (HTH), (THH), (HTT), (THT), (TTH), (TTT)\}$

$$E(x) = 5 \times \frac{1}{8} + 3 \times \frac{3}{8} + 1 \times \frac{3}{8} - 15 \times \frac{1}{8}$$

$$= 0.25$$

51. x_i : 1 2 3 4 5 6

$p(x_i)$	:	$\frac{1}{36}$	$\frac{3}{36}$	$\frac{5}{36}$	$\frac{7}{36}$	$\frac{9}{36}$	$\frac{11}{36}$

Mean $= E(x) = p \cdot x$

52. $S = \{1, 2, 3, 4, 5, 6\}$

Images of sample point are :

x_i	:	2	4	6	8	10	12
$p(x_i)$	:	$\frac{1}{6}$	$\frac{1}{6}$	$\frac{1}{6}$	$\frac{1}{6}$	$\frac{1}{6}$	$\frac{1}{6}$

Mean $= E(x) = p \cdot x$

53. If NAME appears at the end of the array, then $f(n) = n$.

54. Required probability $= \frac{{}^{39}P_{30}}{{}^{40}P_{30}}$.

57. Required probability

$$= 1 - P(0)$$
$$= 1 - (.6)^3 = 1 - .216 = 0.784$$

60. A may win in the first or second ... or nth toss. So, the required probability is

$$\left(\frac{1}{2}\right) + \left(\frac{1}{2}\right)^3 + \left(\frac{1}{2}\right)^5 + \ldots$$

61. The probability that the first ball drawn is white and the second black is

$$\frac{10}{25} \times \frac{15}{24} = \frac{1}{4}$$

The probability that the first ball drawn is black and the second white is

$$\frac{15}{25} \times \frac{10}{24} = \frac{1}{4}$$

Required probability $= \frac{1}{2}$

62. We have

$$P(\overline{A} \cap \overline{B}) = 1 - P(A \cup B)$$
$$= 1 - \{P(A) + P(B) - P(A \cap B)\}$$
$$= 1 - 0.61$$
$$= 0.39$$

67.

$$P(X \nless 4) = P(X \geq 4)$$
$$= \int_4^{\infty} 3e^{-3x}\, dx = e^{-12}$$

68. Mean $= E(x) = \int_0^\infty x \,.\, 3e^{-3x}\, dx$

$$= 3\int_0^\infty x e^{-3x}\, dx$$

$$= 3 \cdot \frac{\lceil 2}{3^2} = \frac{1}{3}$$

69. Variance $= E(X - E(x))^2$

$$= E(X^2) - (E(x))^2$$

$$= \int_0^\infty x^2 \,.\, 3e^{-3x}\, dx - \left(\frac{1}{3}\right)^2$$

$$= 3 \cdot \frac{\lceil 3}{3^3} - \frac{1}{9} = \frac{1}{9}$$

70. The exponential distribution is

$$f(x) = \begin{cases} \theta e^{-\theta x}, & x \geq 0,\ \theta > 0 \\ 0, & \text{otherwise} \end{cases}$$

$$\text{Mean} = E(x) = \int_{-\infty}^\infty x f(x)\, dx = \frac{1}{\theta}$$

$$\text{Variance} = E(X - E(X))^2 = \frac{1}{\theta^2}$$

74. $P(E_1 \text{ or } E_2) = P(E_1) + P(E_2) - P(E_1 \text{ and } E_2)$

$$= \frac{19}{30} \neq \frac{2}{3}$$

$$P(E_1 \text{ and } E_2) = \frac{1}{5} \neq P(E_1) * P(E_2)$$

$$P\left(\frac{E_1}{E_2}\right) = \frac{P(E_1 \cap E_2)}{P(E_2)} = \frac{3}{5} \neq \frac{4}{5}$$

■□■

CHAPTER 13

SET THEORY, HASSE DIAGRAM AND LATTICES

1. ***Let*** $A = \{x : 3x^2 - 7x - 6 = 0\}$

$B = \{x : 6x^2 - 5x - 6 = 0\}$

then $A \cap B$ ***will be :***

(a) $\left\{-\frac{2}{3}\right\}$ (b) $\left\{-\frac{2}{3}, 3\right\}$

(c) $\left\{-\frac{2}{3}, \frac{3}{2}\right\}$ (d) $\left\{3, \frac{3}{2}\right\}$

2. ***If a finite set S has n elements, then the power set of S has elements:***

(a) 2^{n+1} (b) 3^n

(c) 2^n (d) 2^{n-1}

3. ***If A, B and C are three sets, then*** $A - (B \cup C)$ ***is equal to :***

(a) $\{\phi\}$ (b) $(A - B) \cap (A - C)$

(c) $(A - B) \cup (A - C)$ (d) $(A - C)\ (A - B)$

4. ***If*** $A = \{-2, -1, 0, 1, 2\}$. ***If the function*** $f : A \to R$ ***be defined by the formula*** $f(x) = x^2 + 1$, ***then the range of f is :***

(a) {5, 2, 1} (b) {1, 2, 3, 4}

(c) {– 2, 2} (d) {0, 1, 2, 3, 4}

5. ***Suppose*** $A_1, A_2, \ldots A_{30}$ ***are thirty sets each having 5 elements and*** $B_1, B_2, \ldots B_n$ ***are n sets each having 3 elements. Let*** $\bigcup_{i=1}^{30} A_i = \bigcup_{j=1}^{n} B_j = S$ ***and each element of S belongs to exactly 10 of the*** A_i***'s and exactly 9 of the*** B_j***'s. Then n is equal to :***

(a) 45 (b) 15

(c) 5 (d) 3 .

Answers : **1.*** (a) **2.** (c) **3.** (b) **4.*** (a) **5.*** (a)

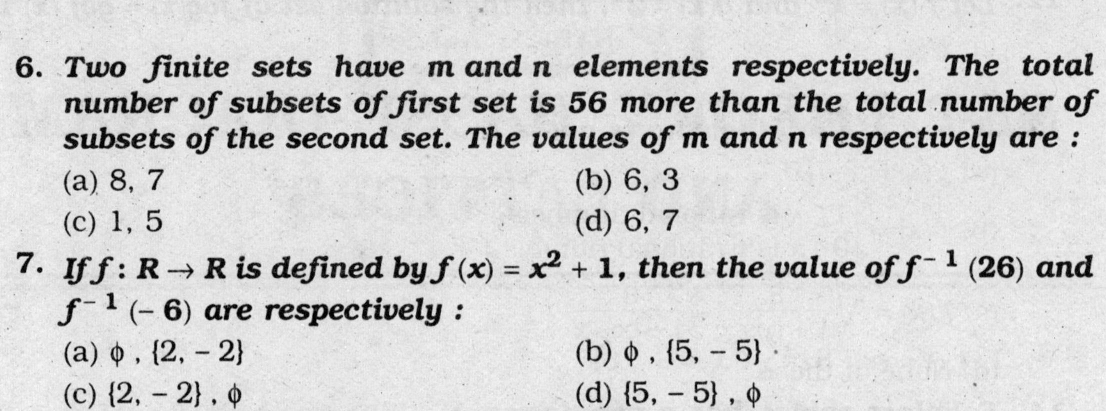

6. ***Two finite sets have m and n elements respectively. The total number of subsets of first set is 56 more than the total number of subsets of the second set. The values of m and n respectively are :***

(a) 8, 7 (b) 6, 3
(c) 1, 5 (d) 6, 7

7. ***If $f : R \to R$ is defined by $f(x) = x^2 + 1$, then the value of $f^{-1}(26)$ and $f^{-1}(-6)$ are respectively :***

(a) ϕ, $\{2, -2\}$ (b) ϕ, $\{5, -5\}$
(c) $\{2, -2\}$, ϕ (d) $\{5, -5\}$, ϕ

8. ***The functions f and g are given by $f(x) = (x)$, the fractional part of x and $g(x) = \frac{1}{2} \sin [x] \pi$, where [x] denotes the integral part of x, then range of gof is :***

(a) $[0, 1]$ (b) $\{-1, 1\}$
(c) $\{\phi\}$ (d) $[-1, 1]$

9. ***A and B two sets having 3 and 4 elements respectively and having 2 elements in common. The number of relations which can be defined from A to B is :***

(a) 2^5 (b) 2^{12}
(c) 2^{10} (d) $2^{12} - 1$

10. ***Which of the following relations is a function ?***

(a) $R = \{(x, y) : x^2 + y^2 \leq 9\}$ on R
(b) $A = \{1, 2, 3\}$, $B = \{1, 2, 3, 4, 5\}$ and $R = \{(x, y) : 5x + 2y$ is a prime number $\}$ on A
(c) $A = \{1, 2, 3, 4\}$ and $B = \{1, 2, 3, 4, 5, 6, 7\}$ and $R = \{(x, y) : y = x^2 - 3x + 3\}$ on A
(d) None of these

11. ***The relation R defined on the set $A = \{1, 2, 3, 4, 5\}$ by***

$$R = \{(x, y) : | x^2 - y^2 | < 16\}$$

is given by :

(a) $R_1 = \{(1, 1), (2, 1), (3, 1), (4, 1), (2, 3)\}$
(b) $R_2 = \{(2, 2), (3, 2), (4, 2), (2, 4)\}$
(c) $R_3 = \{(3, 3), (4, 3), (5, 4), (3, 4)\}$
(d) None of these

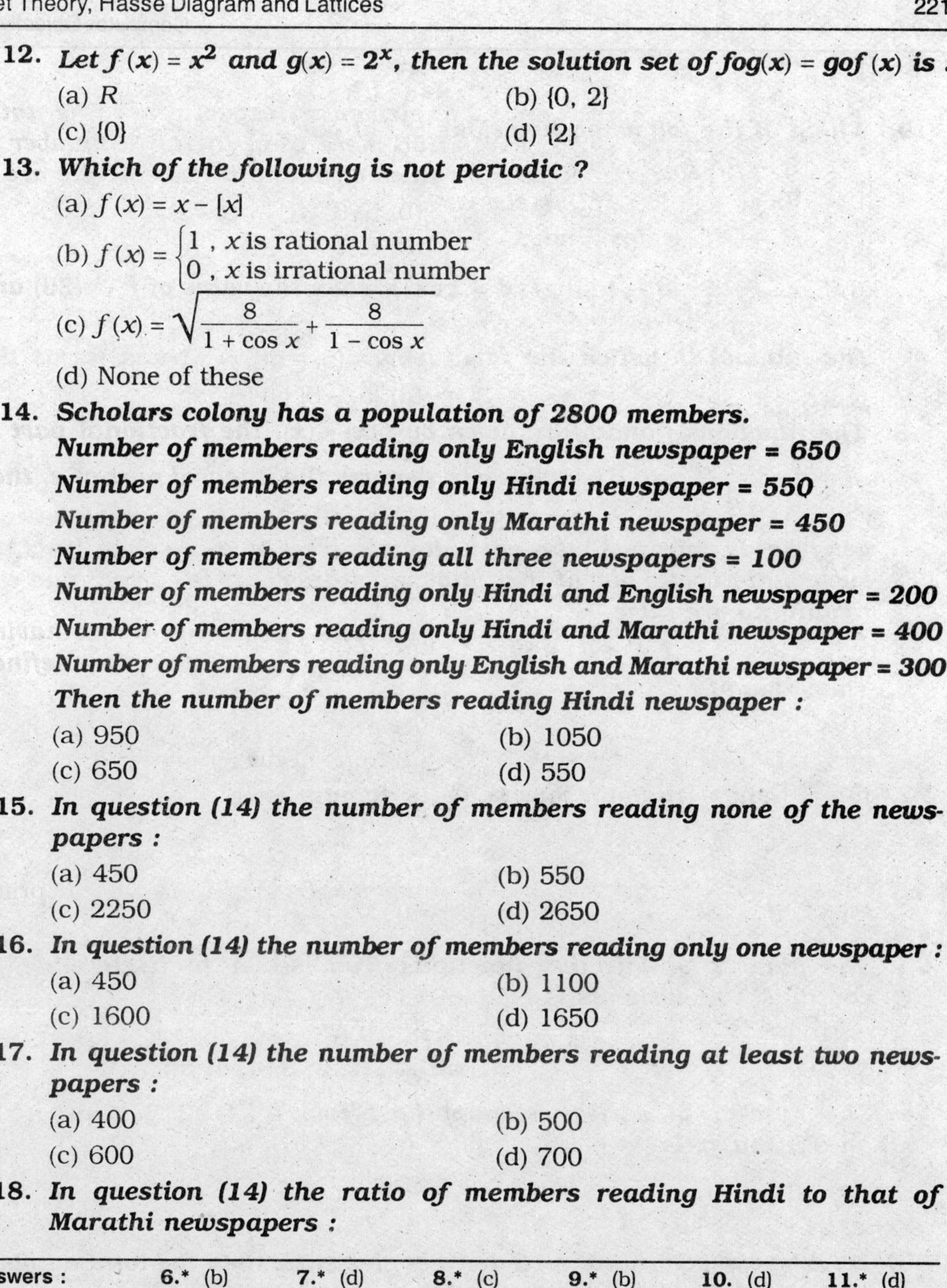

12. ***Let $f(x) = x^2$ and $g(x) = 2^x$, then the solution set of $fog(x) = gof(x)$ is :***

(a) R (b) $\{0, 2\}$

(c) $\{0\}$ (d) $\{2\}$

13. ***Which of the following is not periodic ?***

(a) $f(x) = x - [x]$

(b) $f(x) = \begin{cases} 1, & x \text{ is rational number} \\ 0, & x \text{ is irrational number} \end{cases}$

(c) $f(x) = \sqrt{\dfrac{8}{1 + \cos x} + \dfrac{8}{1 - \cos x}}$

(d) None of these

14. ***Scholars colony has a population of 2800 members.***
Number of members reading only English newspaper = 650
Number of members reading only Hindi newspaper = 550
Number of members reading only Marathi newspaper = 450
Number of members reading all three newspapers = 100
Number of members reading only Hindi and English newspaper = 200
Number of members reading only Hindi and Marathi newspaper = 400
Number of members reading only English and Marathi newspaper = 300
Then the number of members reading Hindi newspaper :

(a) 950 (b) 1050

(c) 650 (d) 550

15. ***In question (14) the number of members reading none of the newspapers :***

(a) 450 (b) 550

(c) 2250 (d) 2650

16. ***In question (14) the number of members reading only one newspaper :***

(a) 450 (b) 1100

(c) 1600 (d) 1650

17. ***In question (14) the number of members reading at least two newspapers :***

(a) 400 (b) 500

(c) 600 (d) 700

18. ***In question (14) the ratio of members reading Hindi to that of Marathi newspapers :***

Answers :

6.* (b)	**7.*** (d)	**8.*** (c)	**9.*** (b)	**10.** (d)	**11.*** (d)
12.* (b)	**13.*** (d)	**14.*** (b)	**15.*** (a)	**16.*** (d)	**17.*** (d)

(a) 1 : 1 (b) 2 : 1

(c) 1 : 2 (d) 1.5 : 1

19. *Which of the following functions is not one-one ?*

(a) $f: R \to R, f(x) = 2x + 5$

(b) $f: [0, \pi] \to [-1, 1], f(x) = \cos x$

(c) $f: R \to [-1, 1], f(x) = \sin x$

(d) $f: \left[-\frac{\pi}{2}, \frac{\pi}{2}\right] \to [-1, 1], f(x) = 2 \sin x + 3$

20. *The interval in which the function $y = \frac{x - 1}{x^2 - 3x + 3}$ trans forms the real line is :*

(a) $(0, \infty)$ (b) $\left[-\frac{1}{3}, 1\right]$

(c) $(-\infty, \infty)$ (d) $[0, 1]$

21. *Let f be an injective map with domain {x, y, z} and range {1, 2, 3} such that exactly one of the following statements is correct and the remaining are false*

$$f(x) = 1, f(y) \neq 1 \text{ and } f(z) \neq 2$$

The value of $f^{-1}(1)$ is :

(a) x (b) y

(c) z (d) None of these

22. *$f(x) = |\sin x|$ has an inverse if its domain is :*

(a) $\left[0, \frac{\pi}{2}\right]$ (b) $\left[-\frac{\pi}{4}, \frac{\pi}{4}\right]$

(c) $[0, \pi]$ (d) $\left[-\frac{\pi}{2}, \frac{\pi}{2}\right]$

23. *The number of bijective functions from set A to itself when A contains 106 elements is :*

(a) 106 (b) $(106)^2$

(c) (106) ! (d) 2^{106}

24. *The number of surjective mappings from $A = \{1, 2, 3, \ldots n\}, n \geq 2$ onto $B = \{a, b\}$ is :*

(a) $P(n, 2)$ (b) $2^n - 1$

(c) $2^n - 2$ (d) 2^n

25. *Let A be a set containing 10 distinct elements, then the total number of distinct functions from A to A is :*

(a) 10^{10} (b) $10^{10} - 1$
(c) 2^{10} (d) (10) !

26. ***Set A has 4 elements and set B has 5 elements. The number of injective mapping that can be defined from A to B is :***

(a) 144 (b) 24
(c) 120 (d) 64

27. ***Let R be a relation from a set A to another set B, than :***

(a) $R = A \cup B$ (b) $R \subseteq A \times B$
(c) $R = A \cap B$ (d) $R \subseteq B \times A$

28. ***If $R \subseteq A \times B$ and $S \subseteq B \times C$ be two relations, then $(SOR)^{-1}$ is :***

(a) $S_O R$ (b) $R_O S$
(c) $R_O^{-1} S^{-1}$ (d) $S_O^{-1} R^{-1}$

29. ***Let L be the set of all straight lines in the Euclidean plane. Two lines l_1 and l_2 are said to be related by the relation R if $l_1 \,||\, l_2$. Then the relation R is :***

(a) Reflexive (b) Symmetric
(c) Transitive (d) All the above

30. ***In order that a relation R defined on a non-empty set A is an equivalence relation, it is sufficient, if R is :***

(a) Reflexive (b) Transitive
(c) Symmetric (d) All the above

31. ***Let n be a fixed positive integer. Define a relation R on the set Z of integers by***

$_aR_b \Leftrightarrow n \mid a - b$. Then R is :

(a) Equivalence (b) Symmetric
(c) Transitive (d) All the above

32. ***Let $f : R \to R$ be given by $f(x) = (x + 1)^2 - 1, x \geq -1$, then the set S, such that $S = \{x : f(x) = f^{-1}(x)\}$***

(a) {0, – 1} (b) {0, 1}
(c) {1, 2} (d) {0, – 2}

33. ***If $f(x) = \cos(\log x)$, then***

$$f(x^2)\, f(y^2) - \frac{1}{2}\left[f\left(\frac{x^2}{y^2}\right) + f(x^2y^2) \right]$$ ***has the value :***

Answers : **18.*** (a) **19.*** (d) **20.*** (b) **21.*** (b) **22.*** (a) **23.*** (c) **24.*** (c) **25.** (a)
26.* (c) **27.** (b) **28.** (c) **29.** (d) **30.** (d) **31.** (d) **32.** (a)

(a) – 2 (b) – 1

(c) $\frac{1}{3}$ (d) None of these

34. *Which of the following functions is not invertible ?*

(a) $f: R \to R, f(x) = 4x + 5$ (b) $f: R^+ \to R^+, f(x) = \frac{1}{x^2}$

(c) $f: R \to R^+ \, U\{0\}$ (d) None of these

35. *0.15252525252 ... is equal to :*

(a) $\frac{52}{99}$ (b) $\frac{151}{990}$

(c) $\frac{51}{99}$ (d) None of the above

36. *The function $f(x) = \left| \frac{x}{x+1} \right|$ is :*

(a) Is less than 1, for all x

(b) Equals $1 - f\left(\frac{1}{x}\right)$

(c) Equals $f(-x)$

(d) None of the above

37. *The domain of the function log {log sin (x)} is :*

(a) $0 < x < \pi$ (b) Empty set

(c) $2n\pi < x < (2n+1)\pi, n \in N$ (d) None of the above

38. *Let R be a symmetric and transitive relation on a set A. Then :*

(a) R is reflexive and hence an equivalence relation

(b) R is reflexive and hence a partial order

(c) R is not reflexive and hence not an equivalence relation

(d) None of the above

39. *Given the relation R = {(1, 2), (2, 3)}. Then minimum number of ordered pairs that must be added to this set so that the enlarged relation is an equivalence relation :*

(a) 7 (b) 6

(c) 5 (d) 4

40. *Let A be a finite set of size 'n'. The number of elements in the power set of A × A is*

(a) 2^{2^n} (b) 2^{n^2}

(c) $(2^n)^2$ (d) $(2^2)^n$

41. *A relation R is defined in $N \times N$, such that $(a, b) R (c, d)$ iff $a + d = b + c$. The relation R is :*

(a) Reflexive but not transitive

(b) Reflexive and transitive but not symmetric

(c) An equivalence relation

(d) A partial order

42. *Let A and B be sets with cardinalities m and n respectively. The number of possible one-one mapping (injective) from A to B, when $m < n$ is :*

(a) m^n (b) ${}^mC_n$

(c) ${}^mP_2$ (d) ${}^nP_m$

43. *Let A and B be the sets with cardinality m and n respectively. If the number of possible functions that can be defined with domain A and co-domain B is exactly 10, then :*

(a) $m = n = 10$ (b) $m = n = 5$

(c) $m = 10, n = 1$ (d) $m = 1, n = 10$

44. *Let A = {1, 2, 3, 4}. Describe the ordered pairs in the relation determined by the Hasse diagram in the figure given below*

4
3
2
1

(a) {(1, 1), (2, 2), (3, 3), (4, 4), (1, 3), (1, 4), (2, 3), (2, 4), (3, 4)}

(b) {(1, 1), (2, 2), (3, 3), (4, 4), (1, 2), (1, 3), (1, 4), (2, 3), (2, 4), (3, 4)}

(c) Both *a* and *b*

(d) None of the above

45. *Determine the matrix of the partial order whose Hasse diagram is given by*

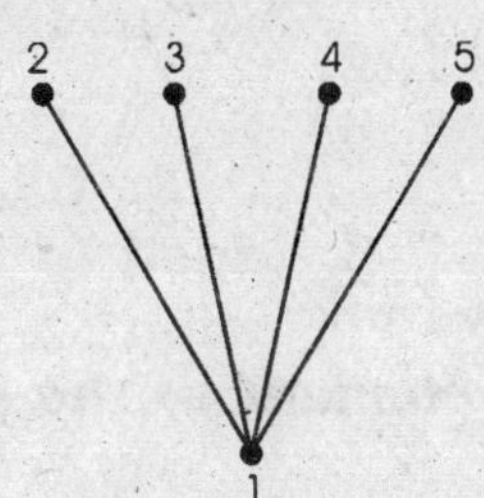

Answers :					
33. (d)	**34.** (c)	**35.*** (b)	**36.** (d)	**37.*** (b)	**38.*** (c)
39.* (a)	**40.*** (b)	**41.** (c)	**42.*** (d)	**43.*** (d)	**44.** (b)

(a) $\begin{bmatrix} 1 & 1 & 1 & 1 & 1 \\ 0 & 1 & 0 & 0 & 0 \\ 0 & 0 & 0 & 0 & 0 \\ 0 & 0 & 0 & 0 & 1 \\ 0 & 0 & 0 & 0 & 1 \end{bmatrix}$ (b) $\begin{bmatrix} 1 & 1 & 1 & 1 & 1 \\ 1 & 0 & 0 & 1 & 0 \\ 0 & 0 & 1 & 0 & 0 \\ 0 & 0 & 0 & 1 & 0 \\ 0 & 0 & 0 & 0 & 1 \end{bmatrix}$

(c) $\begin{bmatrix} 1 & 1 & 1 & 1 & 1 \\ 0 & 1 & 0 & 0 & 0 \\ 0 & 0 & 1 & 0 & 0 \\ 0 & 0 & 0 & 1 & 0 \\ 0 & 0 & 0 & 1 & 1 \end{bmatrix}$ (d) $\begin{bmatrix} 1 & 1 & 1 & 1 & 1 \\ 0 & 1 & 0 & 0 & 0 \\ 0 & 0 & 1 & 0 & 0 \\ 0 & 0 & 0 & 1 & 0 \\ 0 & 0 & 0 & 0 & 1 \end{bmatrix}$

46. *Determine the matrix of the partial order whose Hasse diagram is given below*

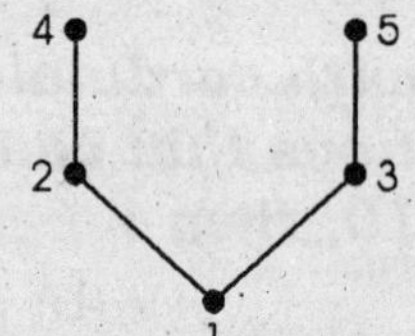

(a) $\begin{bmatrix} 1 & 1 & 1 & 1 & 1 \\ 0 & 1 & 0 & 0 & 0 \\ 0 & 1 & 0 & 0 & 1 \\ 1 & 0 & 0 & 1 & 0 \\ 0 & 0 & 0 & 1 & 1 \end{bmatrix}$ (b) $\begin{bmatrix} 1 & 1 & 1 & 1 & 1 \\ 0 & 1 & 0 & 1 & 0 \\ 0 & 0 & 1 & 0 & 1 \\ 0 & 0 & 0 & 1 & 0 \\ 0 & 0 & 0 & 0 & 1 \end{bmatrix}$

(c) $\begin{bmatrix} 1 & 1 & 1 & 1 & 1 \\ 1 & 0 & 1 & 0 & 0 \\ 0 & 0 & 0 & 1 & 0 \\ 0 & 0 & 1 & 0 & 0 \\ 0 & 0 & 1 & 1 & 1 \end{bmatrix}$ (d) None of these

47. *The greatest and least element of the poset are :*

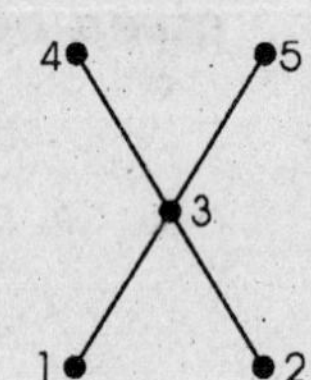

(a) greatest – 4, 5; least – 1, 2
(b) greatest – 3, 3; least – 1, 2
(c) greatest – 1, 4; least – 2, 5
(d) greatest – None, least–None

48. *The greatest and least element of the poset are :*

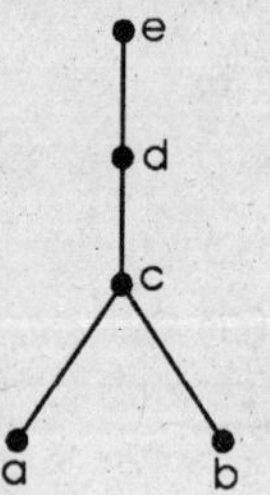

(a) greatest-a ; least-e
(b) greatest-e ; least-a, b
(c) greatest-e ; least-None
(d) greatest-a, e ; least- b, e

49. ***The greatest and least element of the poset are :***

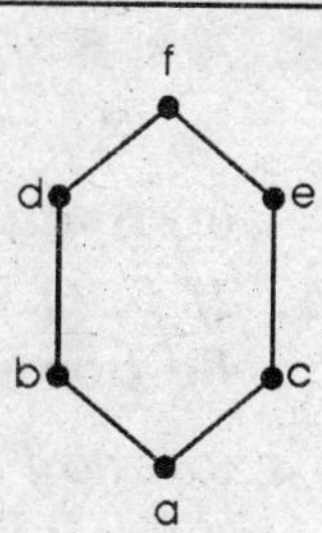

(a) greatest-a, f ; least-a, f
(b) greatest-None ; least-None
(c) greatest-f ; least-a
(d) greatest-a ; least-f

50. ***The maximal and minimal elements of the poset are :***

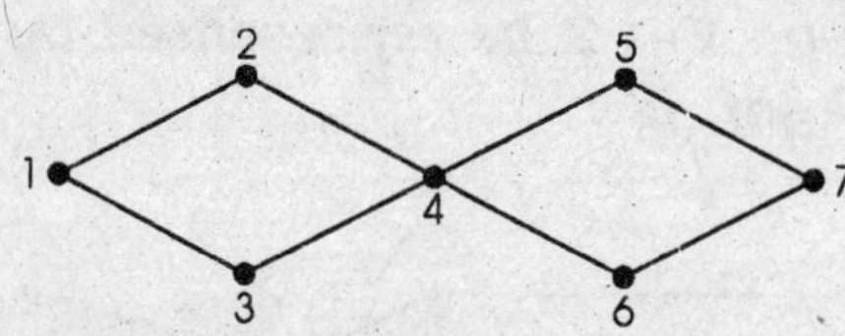

(a) Maximal- 2, 5 ; Minimal- 3, 6
(b) Maximal- 3, 6 ; Minimal- 2, 5
(c) Maximal- None ; Minimal- None
(d) Maximal- 2, 3 ; Minimal- 5, 6

51. ***Let A = {1, 2, 3, 4} and the matrix of relation R is :***

$$M_R = \begin{bmatrix} 1 & 0 & 0 & 1 \\ 0 & 1 & 1 & 0 \\ 0 & 1 & 1 & 0 \\ 1 & 0 & 0 & 1 \end{bmatrix}$$

Then the matrix of the transitive closure by using Warshall's algorithm :

(a) $\begin{bmatrix} 1 & 1 & 0 & 1 \\ 0 & 1 & 1 & 0 \\ 0 & 0 & 1 & 1 \\ 1 & 0 & 0 & 1 \end{bmatrix}$ (b) $\begin{bmatrix} 1 & 0 & 0 & 1 \\ 1 & 1 & 0 & 1 \\ 0 & 0 & 1 & 0 \\ 0 & 0 & 0 & 1 \end{bmatrix}$

(c) $\begin{bmatrix} 1 & 0 & 0 & 1 \\ 1 & 1 & 0 & 0 \\ 0 & 0 & 1 & 0 \\ 1 & 0 & 0 & 1 \end{bmatrix}$ (d) $\begin{bmatrix} 1 & 0 & 0 & 1 \\ 0 & 1 & 1 & 0 \\ 0 & 1 & 1 & 0 \\ 1 & 0 & 0 & 1 \end{bmatrix}$

52. ***For a constant function :***

(a) Domain contains only one element
(b) Range or co-domain contains only one element
(c) Domain and range contains only one element
(d) All of the above

Answers : **45.** (d) **46.** (d) **47.** (a) **48.** (c) **49.** (c) **50.** (a) **51.** (d) **52.*** (b)

53. $A \cup B = A \cap B$ ***iff :***

(a) A is empty set (b) B is empty set

(c) A and B both are empty sets (d) A and B are non-empty sets

54. ***If*** $f : Q \rightarrow Q$ ***such that*** $f(x) = 2x$ ***and*** $g : Q \rightarrow Q$ ***such that*** $g(x) = x + 2$ ***be two mappings, then which of the following is true ?***

(a) $(go\,f)^{-1} = f^{-1} og^{-1}$ (b) $(go\,f)^{-1} = g^{-1} of^{-1}$

(c) $(go\,f)^{-1} = gof$ (d) $(go\,f)^{-1} = fog$

55. ***Let*** $f : X \rightarrow Y$ ***and*** $g : Y \rightarrow Z$ ***be represented by the following diagram The value of the (gof) is :***

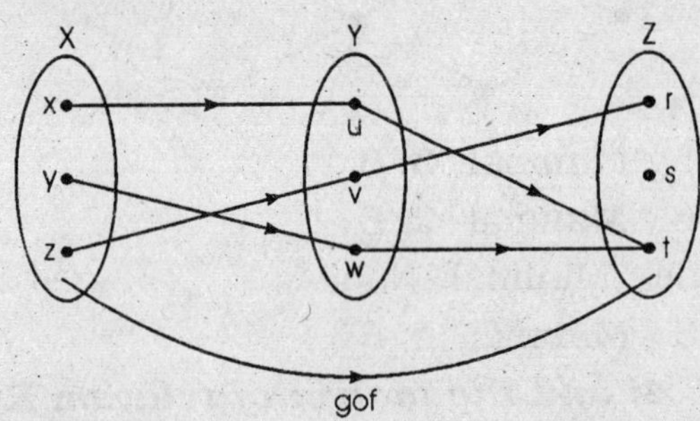

(a) {(x, s), (y, t), (z, r)} (b) {(x, t), (y, r), (z, s)}

(c) {(x, r), (y, s), (z, t)} (d) {(x, t), (y, t), (z, r)}

56. ***Consider a positive integer Z and set of all divisors of z, Dz . Then which of the followings are lattices ?***

(a)

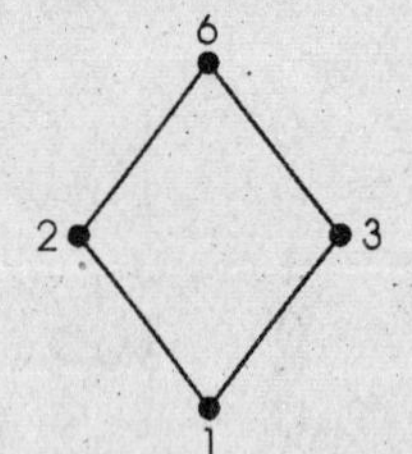

(b)

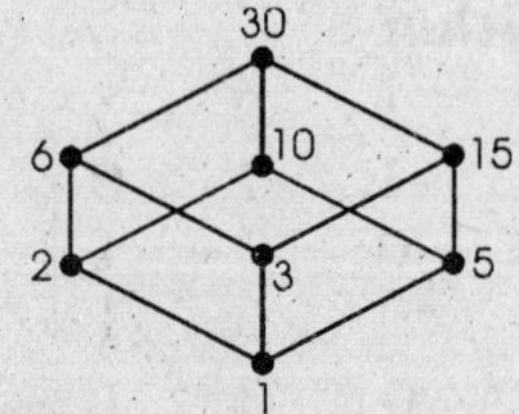

(c)

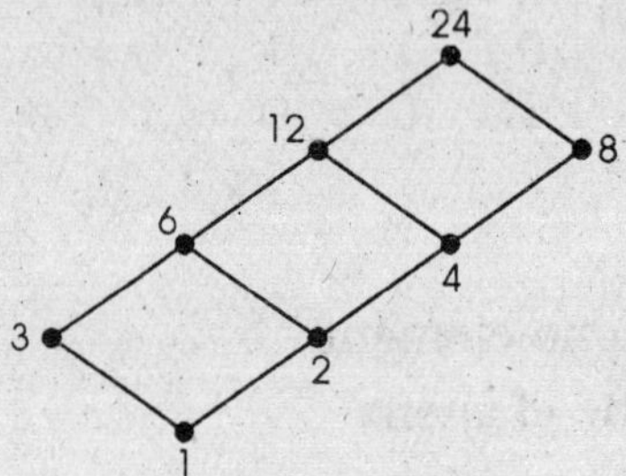

(d) All of the above

57. ***Two subsets X_1 and X_2 of the poset X = {a, b, c, d, e} shown in figure, such that X_1 and X_2 are lattices :***

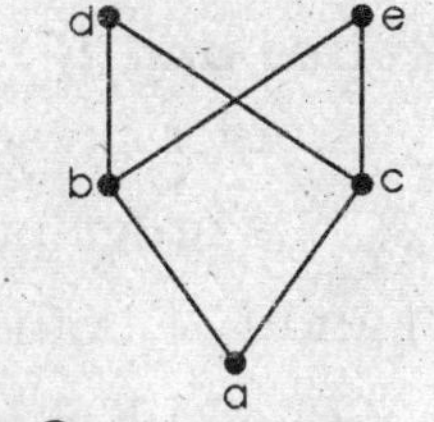

(a) {(a, b, d, e) , (a, b, c, e)}
(b) {(a, b, c, d) , (a, b, c, e)}
(c) {(b, c, d, e) , (a, b, c, d)}
(d) All the above

58. ***Which of the following posets are not lattices ?***

(a)
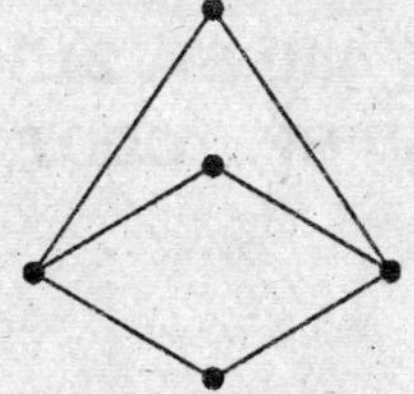

(b)
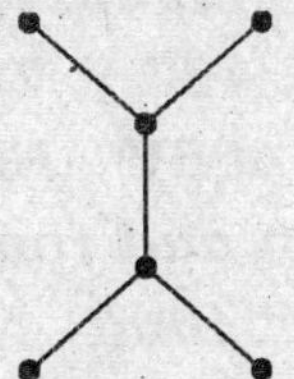

(c)
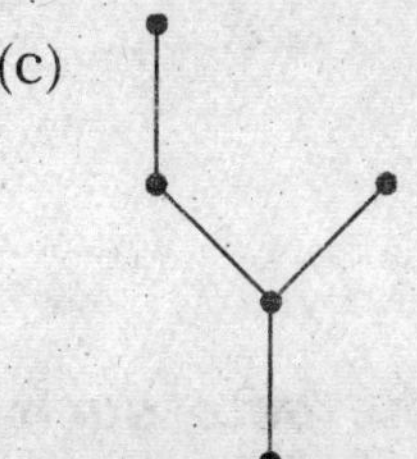

(d) a and c both

59. ***A poset (L, ≤) is a lattice iff***

(a) Poset has two upper and two lower bounds
(b) Every non-empty finite subset of *L* does not have a unique glb and lub.
(c) Every non-empty finite subset of *L* has glb and lub
(d) None of these

60. ***How many partitions can be exist in a set of four element ?***

(a) 15 (b) 7
(c) 31 (d) 52

61. ***The operations of meet (∧) and join (∨) on a lattice are :***

(a) Commutative (b) Associative
(c) Idempotent (d) All of the above

62. ***A lattice will be a chain if it has :***

(a) Two or fewer elements (b) Three or fewer elements
(c) Four or fewer elements (d) For any number of elements

Answers : **53.*** (c) **54.*** (a) **55.*** (d) **56.** (d) **57.*** (b)
58.* (d) **59.** (c) **60.** (a) **61.** (d) **62.** (a)

63. ***Two partially ordered sets (p, ≤) and (Q, ≤′) are called order-isomorphic if there exists a mapping $f : P \to Q$ which is bijective and if :***

(a) f is order-preserving

(b) f^{-1} is order-preserving

(c) f and f^{-1} both are order-preserving

(d) None of these

64. ***Let A = {CDOT, NTPC, BARC, NPIL, CPWD}***
B = { 750 C, 466 V, 786 SZ, PS 60, 525 SX, 450 SV, 215 X }
and R = {(NTPC, 466V), (NPIL, PS60), (CPWD, 450 SV), (CDOT, 215 X) }
then the domain and range of R is

(a) Domain {NTPC, BARC, NPIL, CPWD }
Range {466V, 786SZ, PS60, 450SV }

(b) Domain {NTPC, CDOT, NPIL, CPWD }
Range {466V, PS60, 450SV, 525SX }

(c) Domain {NTPC, NPIL, CPWD, CDOT }
Range {466V, PS60, 450SV, 215X }

(d) All of the above

65. ***Let S be an infinite set and $S_1, S_2, \ldots S_n$ be the sets such that $S_1 U S_2 U \ldots U S_n = S$. Then :***

(a) At least one of the sets S_i is a finite set

(b) At least one of the set S_i is an infinite set

(c) Not more than ane of the sets S_i should be finite

(d) Not more than ane of the sets S_i should be in finite

66. ***Consider the function $h : N \times N \to N$ so that $h(a, b) = (2a + 1) 2^b - 1$, where N = {1, 2, 3, 4, ... } is the set of natural numbers. Then h is :***

(a) Injective mapping
(b) Surjective mapping
(c) Bijective mapping
(d) None of these

67. ***Let R_1 and R_2 be regular sets defined over the alphabet Σ, then :***

(a) $R_1 \cap R_2$ is not regular
(b) $\Sigma^* - R_1$ is regular
(c) $R_1 \cup R_2$ is regular
(d) R_1^* is not regular

68. ***Let A and B sets with cardinalities m and n respectively. The number of one-one mapping (injections) from A to B, when m < n is :***

(a) m^n
(b) ${}^nP_m$

(c) ${}^{m}C_n$ (d) ${}^{m}P_n$

69. ***The less-than relation <, on real numbers is :***

(a) Not a partial ordering because it is not anti symmetric and not reflexive
(b) A partial ordering since it is asymmetric and reflexive
(c) A partial ordering since it is antisymmetric and reflexive
(d) Not a partial ordering because it is not asymmetric and not reflexive

70. ***The number of subset of {1, 2, 3, ... n} with odd cardinality is***

(a) 2^n (b) $2^n - 1$
(c) 2^{n-1} (d) $2^n - 2$

71. ***The relation $R = \{(x, y) \in N^2 : x \neq y\}$ satisfy :***

(a) Reflexivity (b) Symmetry
(c) Antisymmetry (d) Transitivity

72. ***Let R be a symmetric and transitive relation on a set A. Then :***

(a) R is reflexive and hence an equivalence relation
(b) R is reflexive and hence a poset
(c) R is not reflexive and hence not an equivalence relation
(d) None of these

73. ***Let A and B be sets and let A^C and B^C denote the compliments of the sets A and B. Then the set $(A - B) \cup (B - A) \cup (A \cap B)$ is equal to :***

(a) $A \cup B$ (b) $A^C \cup B^C$
(c) $A \cap B$ (d) $A^C \cap B^C$

74. ***Let X = {2, 3, 6, 12, 24}, let $\leq$ be the partial order defined by $X \leq Y$ if x divides y. Number of edges as in the Hasse diagram of $(X, \leq)$ is :***

(a) 3 (b) 4
(c) 9 (d) 7

75. ***Suppose X and Y are sets and $|x|$ and $|y|$ are their respective cardinalities. It is given that there are exactly 97 functions from X to Y. From this one can conclude that :***

(a) $|X| = 1, |Y| = 97$
(b) $|X| = 97, |Y| = 97$
(c) $|X| = 97, |Y| = 1$
(d) None of the above

Answers : **63.** (c) **64.** (c) **65.** (b) **66.** (a),(b) **67.** (b),(c) **68.*** (b) **69.** (a) **70.*** (c) **71.** (a) **72.** (d) **73.** (a) **74.*** (b) **75.*** (b)

76. ***Let R denote the set of real numbers. Let $f: R \times D \to R \times R$ be a bijective function defined by***

$f(x, y) = (x + y, x - y)$.

Then the inverse function of f is :

(a) $f^{-1}(x, y) = \left(\frac{1}{x+y}, \frac{1}{x-y}\right)$

(b) $f^{-1}(x, y) = \left(\frac{x+y}{2}, \frac{x-y}{2}\right)$

(c) $f^{-1}(x, y) = (x - y, x + y)$

(d) $f^{-1}(x, y) = \{2(x - y), 2(x + y)\}$

77. ***Let R be a non-empty relation on a collection of sets defined by $_A R_B$ iff $A \cap B = \phi$, then :***

(a) R is reflexive and transitive

(b) R is an equivalence relation

(c) R is symmetric and not transitive

(d) R is not reflexive and not symmetric

78. ***In the lattice defined by the Hasse diagram given in following figure, haw many compliments does the element e have ?***

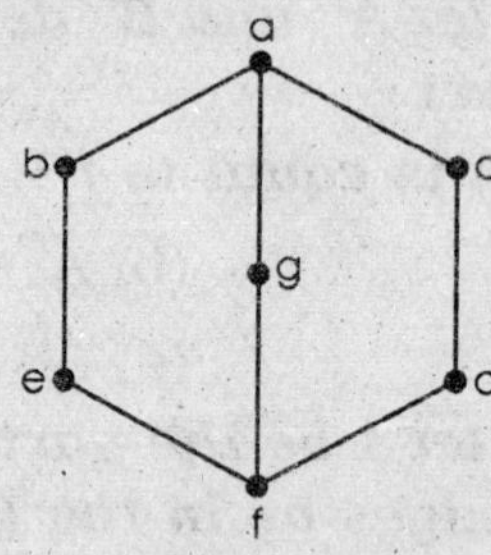

(a) 0 (b) 1

(c) 2 (d) 3

79. ***What is the maximum value of the function $f(x) = 2x^2 - 2x + 6$ in the interval [0, 2] is :***

(a) 2 (b) 6

(c) 12 (d) 10

80. ***The number of equivalence relations of the set {1, 2, 3, 4} is :***

(a) 15 (b) 4

(c) 16 (d) 24

81. ***A partial order $\leq$ is defined on the set $S = \{x, a_1, a_2 \ldots a_n, y\}$ as $x \leq a_i$ for all i and $a_i \leq y \ \forall i$, when $n \geq 1$. The number of total orders on the set S which contain the partial order $\leq$ is :***

(a) 1 (b) n

(c) $n + 2$ (d) $n\,!$

82. ***Which of the statement is false ?***

(a) Every finite sub set of a non-regular set is regular

(b) Every subset of a regular set is regular

(c) Every finite subset of a regular set is regular

(d) The intersection of two regular sets is regular

Answers : **76.*** (b),(c) **77.** (c) **78.*** (d) **79.** (d) **80.** (a) **81.** (d) **82.** (d)

SOLUTIONS

1. We have

$$3x^2 - 7x - 6 = 0 \quad \text{and} \quad 6x^2 - 5x - 6 = 0$$

$$(3x+2)(x-3) = 0 \qquad (3x+2)(2x-3) = 0$$

$$\Rightarrow \quad x = -\frac{2}{3}, 3 \qquad x = -\frac{2}{3}, \frac{3}{2}$$

i.e., $A = \left\{-\frac{2}{3}, 3\right\}$ $\quad B = \left\{-\frac{2}{3}, \frac{3}{2}\right\}$

$\therefore \quad A \cap B = \left\{-\frac{2}{3}\right\}$

2. Because, the total number of subsets in a set of n elements = 2^n.

4. Range are those elements, which are the images of domain elements.

5. $S = \bigcup_{i=1}^{30} A_i$, So $n(S) = \frac{1}{10}(5 \times 30) = 15$ (Because elements in the union S belongs to exactly 10 of the A_i's.

Again $S = \bigcup_{i=1}^{n} B_j$, $n(S) = \frac{1}{9}(3 \times n) = \frac{n}{3}$

Thus $\frac{n}{3} = 15 \Rightarrow n = 45$.

6. We have $2^m = 2^n + 56$

Which is satisfied when $m = 6$, $n = 3$.

7. For any subset $A \subseteq R$, we have $f^{-1}(A) = \{x \in R : f(x) \in A\}$

Thus, $f^{-1}(26) = \{x : f(x) \in 26\} = \{x : f(x) = 26\}$

$= \{x : x^2 + 1 = 26\} = \{5, -5\}$

and similarly $f^{-1}(-6) = \{x : x^2 + 1 = -6\} = \phi$.

8. $gof(x) = g\{f(x)\} = \frac{1}{2} \sin [(x)]\pi = 0 \ \forall\, x \in R$, and hence range of gof is $\{0\}$.

9. The number of elements in $A \times B$ is 12. Hence, the number of subsets of $A \times B$ is 2^{12}.

10. The relation in (a) contains {1, – 1} and {1, 1} so is not a function. Relation is (b) contains {1, 1} and {1, 3}, so it is not a function, and the relation R in (C) contains {1, 1} and {1, 2} so it is not a function.

11. All three sets R_1, R_2 and R_3 satisfy the criterion $|x^2 - y^2| < 16$, but exclude the pairs (1, 5), (5, 1), (2, 5) and (5, 2).

12. $fog(x) = f\{g(x)\} = f(2^x) = (2^x)^2 = 2^{2x}$, and

$$gof(x) = g\{f(x)\} = g(x^2) = 2^{x^2}$$

This $\Rightarrow \quad 2^{2x} = 2^{x^2}$

$\Rightarrow \quad 2x = x^2 \quad \Rightarrow \quad x = \{0, 2\}$.

13. All three (a), (b) and (c) are periodic with period 1, r and π respectively as

(a) $f(x + 1) = f(x)$

(b) $f(x + r) = f(x)$ for every rational r.

(c) $f(x) = \dfrac{4}{|\sin x|}$, and this $\Rightarrow f(x + \pi) = f(x)$

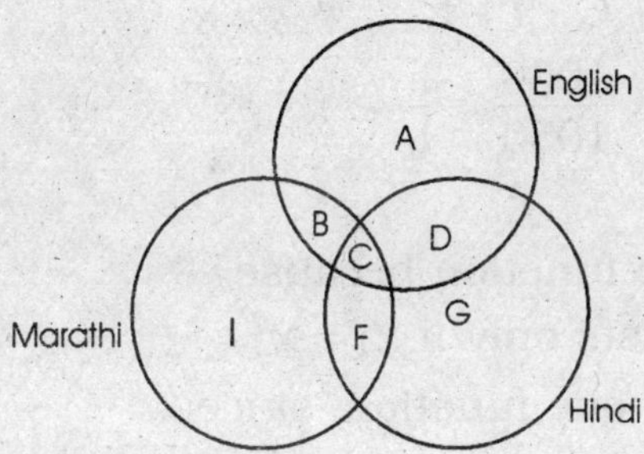

Solution for Questions (14—18)

$E \cap H \cap M = 100 = C$ ...(1)

$E \cap M = 200 = D + C$ ...(2)

$E \cap M = 300 = C + B$ ...(3)

$M \cap H = 400 = C + F$ ...(4)

Only English $= A = 600$ ...(5)

Only Hindi $= G = 550$ ...(6)

Only Marathi $= I = 450$ ...(7)

14. Number of members reading Hindi newspaper

$= C + D + F + G$

$= 200 + (400 - 100) + 550$

$= 200 + 300 + 550 = 1050$

15. Number of members reading None of the newspaper

$= 2800 -$ (Members reading at least one Newspaper)

$= 2800 - \{A + B + C + D + I + F + G\}$

$= 2800 - \{650 + (300 - 100) + 1050 + 450\}$

$= 2800 - 2350$

$= 450$

16. Number of members reading only one newspaper

$$= A + I + G$$
$$= 650 + 450 + 550$$
$$= 1650$$

17. Number of members reading at least two news paper = No. of members reading two newspaper + No. of members reading three newspaper

$$= B + C + D + F$$
$$= 200 + 100 + 100 + 300 = 700$$

18. Required Ratio $= \dfrac{C + D + F + G}{B + C + I + F}$

$$= \frac{1050}{1050} = \frac{1}{1}$$

$\therefore$ Ratio = 1 : 1

19. Here (a) is a one-one function because,

$2x_1 + 5 = 2x_2 + 5$ exists only if $x_1 = x_2$

similarly (b) is a one-one function, since

$\cos x_1 = \cos x_2$ iff $\sin \dfrac{x_1 - x_2}{2} = 0$ *i.e.*, $x_1 = x_2$

also (c) is one-one function. But (d) is not one-one as $f(\pi) = f(2\pi) = 0$.

20. Here, we have to find the range of $f(x)$ which is $\left[-\dfrac{1}{3}, 1\right]$

21. Here three cases arises

Case I — When $f(x) = 1$ is true :

In this case the remaining two statements are false.

$\therefore \quad f(y) = 1$ and $f(z) = 2$

This means x and y have same images. So $f(x)$ is not an injective mapping. Which is a contradiction. Hence $f(x) = 1$ is not true.

Case II — When $f(y) \neq 1$ is true :

Then remaining two are false, so

$f(x) \neq 1$ and $f(z) = 2$

This shows that x and y both are not mapped to 1, so they might associate to 3 or associate to 2 or one is mapped to 3 and other to 2. In all the three cases f cannot be an injective mapping.

So, $f(y) \neq 1$ is not true.

Case III — When $f(z) \neq 2$ is true :

Then the remaining will be false, so

$$f(x) \neq 1 \quad \text{and} \quad f(y) = 1$$

But f is an injective mapping. Thus, we have

$$f(y) = 1, f(z) = 3 \text{ and } f(x) = 2$$

Hence $f^{-1}(1) = y$.

22. $f(x) = |\sin x|$ has inverse if it is bijective. Clearly. $f(x) = |\sin x|$ is injective if its domain is $\left[0, \frac{\pi}{2}\right]$. Also $f(x)$ is surjective if its co-domain is $[0, 1]$. Hence $f(x) = |\sin x|$ is invertible if it is a function from $\left[0, \frac{\pi}{2}\right]$ to $[0, 1]$.

23. The total number of bijective functions from a set containing n elements to itself is $n!$. Hence required number = (106) !

24. The total number of mappings from A to B is 2^n of which two mappings $f(x) = a$ for all $1 \leq x \leq n$ and $g(x) = b$ for all $1 \leq x \leq n$ are not surjective. Thus the number of surjective mappings are $2^n - 2$.

26. The total number of injective mappings from a set A containing m elements to a set B containing n elements is equal to the total number of arrangements of n by taking m at a time

i.e., $P(n, m)$

i.e., in this case = $P(5, 4) = 120$.

32. First obtain inverse of $f(x)$. Let $f(x) = y$, then

$$f(x) = y \Rightarrow (x+1)^2 - 1 = y$$

$$\Rightarrow \quad x = -1 + \sqrt{y+1}$$

$$\therefore \quad f^{-1}(y) = -1 + \sqrt{y+1}$$

$$\Rightarrow \quad f^{-1}(x) = -1 + \sqrt{x+1}$$

Now $\quad f(x) = f^{-1}(x)$

$$\Rightarrow \quad (x+1)^2 - 1 = -1 + \sqrt{x^2+1}$$

$$\Rightarrow \quad x = 0 \text{ or } x = -1$$

Thus $S = \{x : f(x) = f^{-1}(x)\} = \{0, -1\}$

35. Let $x = 0.15252525252...$

$\Rightarrow 1000x - 10x = 151$

$$\Rightarrow \quad x = \frac{151}{990}.$$

37. $\log \sin(x) > 0 \Rightarrow \sin x > e^0 = 1$ which is impossible.

38. Let $_aR_b$. Since the relation is symmetric, $_bR_a$. Since transitivity holds good, aRb and bRa implies bRb and aRa. If R has to be an equivalence relation, it has to be reflexive *i.e.*, for any x belonging to A, xRx should be valid. Hence R need not be reflexive and so need not be an equivalence relation.

For example,

Let $A = \{1, 2, 3\}$ and $R = \{(1, 1), (1, 2), (2, 1), (2, 2)\}$

Here R is both symmetric and transitive but not reflexive as (3, 3) is missing.

39. Remaining ordered pairs are

$$\{(1, 1), (1, 3), (2, 1), (2, 2), (3, 1), (3, 2), (3, 3)\} \Rightarrow 7$$

40. The number of elements in the power set of a set with n elements is 2^n. The given set A has n elements. So, $A \times A$ will have n^2 elements. So, its power set will have 2^{n^2} elements.

42. The first element of A may be mapped to any one of the n elements of B. The second element to any one of the remaining $(n-1)$ elements. Continuing in this way, the mth element can be mapped to one of the remaining $(n-m+1)$ left out elements of B. So, we have

$$n \times (n-1) \times (n-2) \ldots (n - \overline{m-1}) = {}^nP_m \text{ ways.}$$

43. The total number of possible functions is n^m. If it is to be 10, then $n = 10$ and $m = 1$.

47. Because they do not have a unique answer.

52. Because for every element x, the image will always be a unique element *i.e.*,

$f(x) = a$ (constant function).

53. If any one (A or B) is empty, then union of both A and B will be the second set (B or A) and the intersection will be a null set,

i.e., $A \cup B \neq A \cap B$.

Hence this equality can be exist only if both A and B are empty sets.

54. Whatever is the mapping, the condition given in (a) is always true.

55. By the given diagram

$$(gof)(x) = g\{f(x)\} = g(u) = t$$
$$(gof)(y) = g\{f(y)\} = g(w) = t$$
$$(gof)(z) = g\{f(z)\} = g(v) = r$$

57. It is clear that the poset $X = \{a, b, c, d, e\}$ is not a lattice, because $g.l.b\,(d, e)$ is not unique, and sup $\{d, e\}$ does n't exist. But we know that any linearly ordered subset is a lattice. Hence the two subsets which are lattices are (a, b, c, d) and (a, b, c, e).

58. For a and c there does not exist a unique lower and upper bounds.

68. Let $A = \{1, 2, \ldots m\}$ and $B = \{1, 2, \ldots, m, m+1, \ldots n\}$ and $m < n$. If $f: A \to B$ is an injective mapping then $f(A) < B$ and $f(A)$ will have m elements in element set B. Hence f represent a subset of m elements in B. If

$$f(i) = i \text{ then } f(A) = \{1, 2, 3, \ldots m\} \subseteq B$$

Hence there is one-one correspondence between numbers is one-one mapping and all possible permutations (ordered sets) of subset B of n elements. Hence we have ${}^nP_m$ one-one mappings.

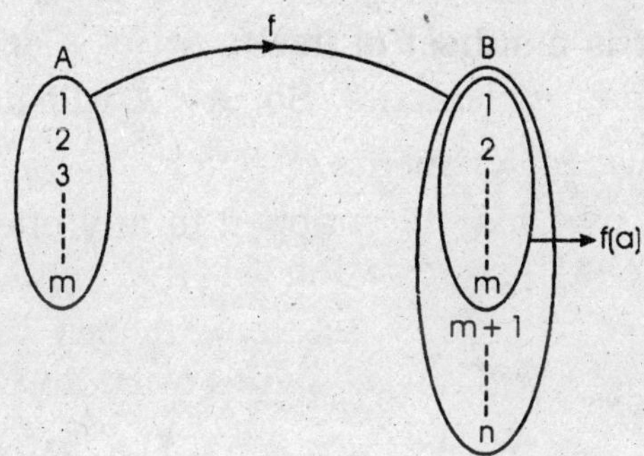

70. Let $S = \{1, 2, \ldots n\}$

then $P(S) = 2^n$, we get

$${}^nC_0 + {}^nC_1 + {}^nC_2 + \ldots + {}^nC_{n-1} + {}^nC_n = 2^n$$

Clearly ${}^nC_0 + {}^nC_2 + {}^nC_4 + \ldots$ gives number of subsets with even cardinality, and ${}^nC_1 + {}^nC_3 + {}^nC_5 + \ldots$ gives the number of subsets with odd cardinality.

Hence ${}^nC_0 + {}^nC_2 + {}^nC_4 + \ldots = {}^nC_1 + {}^nC_2 + {}^nC_3 + \ldots = 2^{n-1}$.

74. The Hasse diagram for the poset $(X, \leq)$ is

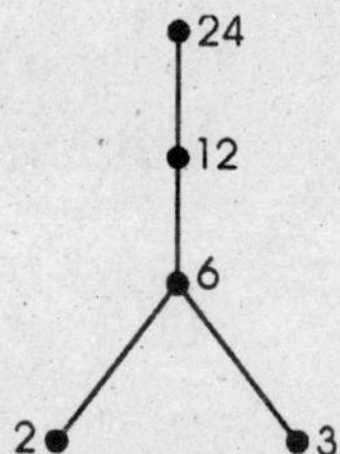

75. Because we can have only two types of functions

(i) one-one

(ii) many-one

79. It will have 3-compliments as follows :

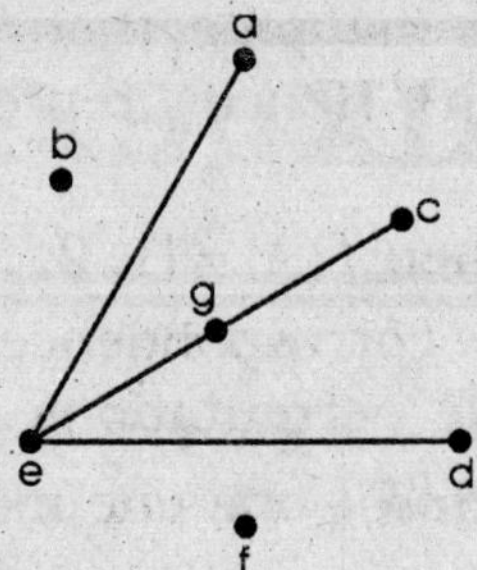

82. A non-regular set is a subset of itself.

■□■

CHAPTER 14

MATRIX ALGEBRA

1. ***The roots of the equation*** $\begin{vmatrix} x-1 & 1 & 1 \\ 1 & x-1 & 1 \\ 1 & 1 & x-1 \end{vmatrix} = 0$ ***are :***

(a) 1, 0 (b) – 1, 2

(c) 1, – 2 (d) – 1, 2

2. ***From the matrix equation AB = AC we can conclude B = C provided***

(a) A is singular (b) A is non-singular

(c) A is symmetric (d) A is square

3. ***If k is a scalar and A is an*** $n \times n$ ***square matrix. Then*** $|kA| =$

(a) $k\,|A|^n$ (b) $k\,|A|$

(c) $k^n\,|A^n|$ (d) $k^n\,|A|$

4. $\begin{vmatrix} x & 4 & y+z \\ y & 4 & z+x \\ z & 4 & x+y \end{vmatrix} = ?$

(a) 0 (b) $x + y + z$

(c) xyz (d) $d = x - 4$

5. ***Let a, b, c be positive real numbers. The following system of equations in x, y and z***

$$\frac{x^2}{a^2} + \frac{y^2}{b^2} - \frac{z^2}{c^2} = 1,\ \frac{x^2}{a^2} - \frac{y^2}{b^2} + \frac{z^2}{c^2} = 1,\ -\frac{x^2}{a^2} + \frac{y^2}{b^2} + \frac{z^2}{c^2} = 1$$ ***has :***

(a) No solution (b) Unique solution

(c) Infinitely many solutions (d) Finitely many solutions

6. ***If A and B are two matrices such that A + B and AB are both defined, then :***

(a) A and B are two matrices not necessarily of same order

(b) A and B are square matrices of same order

(c) Number of columns of A = number of rows of B

(d) None of these

Answers : **1.*** (b) **2.*** (b) **3.*** (d) **4.*** (a) **5.*** (b) **6.** (b)

7. ***If 1, ω, ω^2 are the cube roots of unity, then***

$$\Delta = \begin{vmatrix} 1 & \omega^n & \omega^{2n} \\ \omega^{2n} & 1 & \omega^n \\ \omega^n & \omega^{2n} & 1 \end{vmatrix} \text{ has the value :}$$

(a) 0 (b) ω

(c) ω^2 (d) – 1

8. ***If every element of a third order determinant of value Δ is multiplied by 5, then the value of new determinant is :***

(a) Δ (b) 5Δ

(c) 25Δ (d) 125Δ

9. ***In a third order determinant, each element of the first column consists of sum of two terms, each element of the second column consists of sum of three terms and each element of the third column consists of sum of four terms. Then it can be decomposed into n determinants, where n has the value :***

(a) 1 (b) 9

(c) 16 (d) 24

10. ***If the value of a third order determinant is 11, then the value of the square of the determinant formed by the cofactors will be :***

(a) 11 (b) 121

(c) 1331 (d) 14641

11. ***Consider the system of equations $a_1x + b_1y + c_1z = 0$, $a_2x + b_2y + c_2z = 0$, $a_3x + b_3y + c_3z = 0$ if***

$$\begin{vmatrix} a_1 & b_1 & c_1 \\ a_2 & b_2 & c_2 \\ a_3 & b_3 & c_3 \end{vmatrix} = 0,$$

then the system has :

(a) More than two solutions

(b) One trivial and one non-trivial solutions

(c) No solution

(d) Only trivial soluton (0, 0, 0)

12. $$\begin{vmatrix} \sin^2 x & \cos^2 x & 1 \\ \cos^2 x & \sin^2 x & 1 \\ -10 & 12 & 2 \end{vmatrix} = :$$

(a) 0 (b) $12 \cos^2 x - 10 \sin^2 x$

(c) $12 \sin^2 x - 10 \cos^2 x - 2$ (d) $10 \sin 2x$

13. ***If x, y, z are distinct and*** $\begin{vmatrix} x^k & x^{k+2} & x^{k+3} \\ y^k & y^{k+2} & y^{k+3} \\ z^k & z^{k+2} & z^{k+3} \end{vmatrix}$

$= (x-y)(y-z)(z-x)\left(\frac{1}{x}+\frac{1}{y}+\frac{1}{z}\right)$, ***then :***

(a) $k = -2$ (b) $k = -1$

(c) $k = 1$ (d) $k = 2$

14. ***If*** $\theta \in \mathbf{R}$, ***then***

$\Delta = \begin{vmatrix} 1 & \sin\theta & 1 \\ -\sin\theta & 1 & \sin\theta \\ -1 & -\sin\theta & 1 \end{vmatrix}$ ***lies in the interval :***

(a) [2, 3] (b) [2, 4]

(c) [– 1, 2] (d) [0, 4]

15. ***If*** $\Delta = \begin{vmatrix} x+1 & x+2 & x+a \\ x+2 & x+3 & x+b \\ x+3 & x+4 & x+c \end{vmatrix} = 0$, ***then a, b, c are in :***

(a) A.P. (b) G.P.

(c) H.P. (d) None of these

16. ***If*** $\omega\ (\neq 1)$ ***is a cube root of unity and***

$$\begin{vmatrix} x+1 & \omega & \omega^2 \\ \omega & x+\omega^2 & 1 \\ \omega^2 & 1 & x+\omega \end{vmatrix} = 0, \text{ then :}$$

(a) $x = 1$ (b) $x = 0$

(c) $x = \omega^2$ (d) None of these

17. ***If*** $U_n = \begin{vmatrix} n & 1 & 5 \\ n^2 & 2N+1 & 2N+1 \\ n^3 & 3N^2 & 3N+1 \end{vmatrix}$, ***then*** $\sum_{n=1}^{N} U_n$ ***is equal to :***

(a) $3\sum_{n=1}^{N} n^2$ (b) $2\sum_{n=1}^{N} n^2$

(c) $\frac{1}{2}\sum_{n=1}^{N} n^2$ (d) 0

18. ***If a, b, c are non-zero real numbers and***

$$\Delta = \begin{vmatrix} 1/a & a^2 & bc \\ 1/b & b^2 & ca \\ 1/c & c^2 & ab \end{vmatrix}, \text{ then :}$$

Answers :						
	7.* (a)	**8.*** (d)	**9.*** (d)	**10.** (b)	**11.** (a)	**12.*** (a)
	13.* (b)	**14.*** (b)	**15.*** (a)	**16.*** (b)	**17.*** (b)	

(a) Δ is independent of a, b, c (b) $-abc$

(c) $a^2b^2c^2$ (d) None of these

19. ***If*** $\Delta_r = \begin{vmatrix} 1 & r & 2^r \\ 2 & n & n^2 \\ n & \frac{1}{2}n(n+1) & 2^{n+1} \end{vmatrix}$***, then value of*** $\sum_{r=1}^{n} \Delta_r$ ***is***

(a) $-n$ (b) n

(c) $-2n$ (d) $3n^2$

20. ***If*** α, β, γ ***are the roots of*** $x^3 + px + q = 0$***, then value of***

$$\Delta = \begin{vmatrix} \alpha & \beta & \gamma \\ \beta & \gamma & \alpha \\ \gamma & \alpha & \beta \end{vmatrix}$$

is :

(a) 0 (b) $-p$

(c) $2q - p^2$ (d) None of these

21. ***If*** $i = \sqrt{-1}$***, then value of***

$$\Delta = \begin{vmatrix} a_1 + b_1 i & a_1 i - b_1 & c_1 \\ a_2 + b_2 i & a_2 i - b_2 & c_2 \\ a_3 + b_3 i & a_3 i - b_3 & c_3 \end{vmatrix}$$ ***is :***

(a) -1 (b) 2

(c) 0 (d) None of these

22. ***Let*** $\Delta = \begin{vmatrix} \frac{1 - a_1^3 b_1^3}{1 - a_1 b_1} & \frac{1 - a_1^3 b_2^3}{1 - a_1 b_2} & \frac{1 - a_1^3 b_3^3}{1 - a_1 b_3} \\ \frac{1 - a_2^3 b_1^3}{1 - a_2 b_1} & \frac{1 - a_2^3 b_2^3}{1 - a_2 b_2} & \frac{1 - a_2^3 b_3^3}{1 - a_2 b_3} \\ \frac{1 - a_3^3 b_1^3}{1 - a_3 b_1} & \frac{1 - a_3^3 b_2^3}{1 - a_3 b_2} & \frac{1 - a_3^3 b_3^3}{1 - a_3 b_3} \end{vmatrix}$

then :

(a) $\Delta = 0$ (b) Δ depends only on a_1, a_2, a_3

(c) Δ depends only on b_1, b_2, b_3 (d) Δ depends on $a_1, a_2, a_3, b_1, b_2, b_3$

23. ***Let*** $S_k = \alpha^k + \beta^k + \gamma^k$***, then***

$$\Delta = \begin{vmatrix} S_0 & S_1 & S_2 \\ S_1 & S_2 & S_3 \\ S_2 & S_3 & S_4 \end{vmatrix}$$ ***is equal to :***

(a) S_6 (b) $S_5 - S_3$
(c) $S_6 - S_4$ (d) None of these

24. ***If the system of equations***
$x + \lambda y + 2 = 0,\ \lambda x + y - 2 = 0,\ \lambda x + \lambda y + 3 = 0$
is consistent, then :

(a) $\lambda = \pm 1$ (b) $\lambda = \pm 2$
(c) $\lambda = 1, -2$ (d) $\lambda = -1, 2$

25. ***If the system of equations*** $-ax + y + z = 0,\ x - by + z = 0$ ***and*** $x + y - cz = 0\ (a, b, c \neq -1)$ ***has a non-trivial solution, then the value of***

$$\frac{1}{1+a} + \frac{1}{1+b} + \frac{1}{1+c} \text{ is :}$$

(a) -1 (b) 0
(c) 1 (d) -2

26. ***The system of linear equations*** $x + y - z = 6,\ x + 2y - 3z = 14$ ***and*** $2x + 5y - \lambda z = 9\ (\lambda \in \mathbf{R})$ ***has a unique solution if***

(a) $\lambda = 8$ (b) $\lambda \neq 8$
(c) $\lambda = 6$ (d) $\lambda \neq 6$

27. ***If*** $0 < \theta < \pi$ ***and the system of equations***

$$(\sin\theta)\, x + y + z = 0$$
$$x + (\cos\theta)\, y + z = 0$$
$$(\sin\theta)\, x + (\cos\theta)\, y + z = 0$$

has a non-trivial solution, then :

(a) $\theta = \pi/6$ (b) $\theta = \pi/4$
(c) $\theta = \pi/3$ (d) $\theta = \pi/2$

28. ***The system of equations***
$x + y + z = 4,\ x + ky + z = 3,\ x + 2ky + z = 4$
is consistent if :

(a) $k = 1/2$ (b) $k = 2$
(c) $k = -2$ (d) 1

29. ***If*** $a \neq b$, ***then the system of equations***
$ax + by + bz = 0,\ bx + ay + bz = 0,\ bx + by + az = 0$
will have a non-trivial solution if :

(a) $a + b = 0$ (b) $a + 2b = 0$

Answers : **18.*** (a) **19.*** (c) **20.*** (a) **21.*** (c) **22.** (d) **23.** (d)
24.* (a) **25.*** (c) **26.*** (b) **27.*** (d) **28.*** (a)

(c) $2a + b = 0$ (d) $a + 4b = 0$

30. ***Suppose $x \in R$ and $a_i, b_i, c_i \in R$ for $i = 1, 2, 3$. The determinant***

$$\begin{vmatrix} a_1 + b_1 x & a_1 x + b_1 & c_1 \\ a_2 + b_2 x & a_2 x + b_2 & c_2 \\ a_3 + b_3 x & a_3 x + b_3 & c_3 \end{vmatrix}$$

is equal to zero if :

(a) $x = 1$ (b) $x = -1$

(c) $\begin{vmatrix} a_1 & b_1 & c_1 \\ a_2 & b_2 & c_2 \\ a_3 & b_3 & c_3 \end{vmatrix} = 0$ (d) None of these

31. ***If $0 \le x \le 1$ and $f(x) = \begin{vmatrix} x & 1 & 1 \\ -1 & x & 1 \\ -1 & -1 & x \end{vmatrix}$, then :***

(a) Least value of $f(x)$ is 0

(b) Greatest value of $f(x)$ is 4

(c) $f(x)$ has a local maximum at $x = 2/3$

(d) $f(x)$ has a local minimum at $x = 1/3$

32. ***Let $f(x) = \begin{vmatrix} 2\cos x & 1 & 0 \\ 1 & 2\cos x & 1 \\ 0 & 1 & 2\cos x \end{vmatrix}$, then :***

(a) $\int_0^{\pi} f(x)\, dx = 0$ (b) Maximum value of $f(x)$ is 4

(c) $\lim_{x \to \pi/2} f(x) = 0$ (d) $f'(0) = 0$

33. ***All the elements of a determinant D are integers, and determinant Δ is formed by the cofactors of elements of corresponding determinant Δ; then :***

(a) $\Delta = D^2$

(b) $D = 0$ implies $\Delta = 0$

(c) If $D = 27$, then Δ is a perfect cube

(d) None of these

34. ***Let $f(x) = \begin{vmatrix} 2\sin x & \sin^2 x & 0 \\ 1 & 2\sin x & \sin^2 x \\ 0 & 1 & 2\sin x \end{vmatrix}$, then :***

(a) $f(x)$ is independent of x (b) $f'(\pi/2) = 0$

(c) $\int_{-\pi/2}^{\pi/2} f(x)\, dx = 0$

(d) Tangent to the curve $y = f(x)$ at $x = 0$ is $y = 0$

35. ***Let*** $\phi_1(x) = x + a_1$, $\phi_2(x) = x^2 + b_1 x + b_2$, ***and***

$$\Delta = \begin{vmatrix} 1 & 1 & 1 \\ \phi_1(x_1) & \phi_1(x_2) & \phi_1(x_3) \\ \phi_2(x_1) & \phi_2(x_2) & \phi_2(x_3) \end{vmatrix}, \text{ then :}$$

(a) Δ is independent of a_1 (b) Δ is independent of b_1 and b_2

(c) Δ is independent of x_1, x_2 and x_3 (d) None of these

36. ***Let*** $\Delta = \begin{vmatrix} 1 & x & x^2 \\ x^2 & 1 & x \\ x & x^2 & 1 \end{vmatrix}$, ***then***

(a) $1 - x^3$ is a factor of Δ (b) $(1 - x^3)^2$ is a factor of Δ

(c) $\Delta(x) = 0$ has 4 real roots (d) $\Delta'(1) = 0$

37. ***Let*** $\Delta = \begin{vmatrix} x^2 + 4x + 5 & x + 2 & 5 \\ 2x^2 + 6x + 10 & 2x + 3 & 10 \\ 4x^2 - 2x + 20 & 4x - 1 & 20 \end{vmatrix}$, ***then :***

(a) $y = \Delta$ represents a parabola passing through the origin

(b) $y = \Delta$ represents a straight line through the origin

(c) $\Delta = 0$ has two distinct real roots

(d) $\Delta = 0$ has exactly one real

38. ***Let*** $f(x) = \begin{vmatrix} 1/x & \log x & x^n \\ 1 & -1/n & (-1)^n \\ 1 & a & a^2 \end{vmatrix}$, ***then***

(a) $f^n(1)$ is independent of a

(b) $f^n(1)$ is independent of n

(c) $f^n(1)$ depends on a and n

(d) $y = a(x - f^n(1))$ represents a straight line through the origin

39. ***The determinant***

$$\Delta = \begin{vmatrix} a & b & a\alpha + b \\ b & c & b\alpha + c \\ a\alpha + b & b\alpha + c & 0 \end{vmatrix}$$

Answers : **29.*** (b) **30.*** (a),(b),(c) **31.*** (a),(b) **32.*** (a),(b),(c),(d) **33.*** (a),(b),(c) **34.*** (b),(c),(d) **35.*** (a),(b) **36.*** (a),(b),(c) **37.*** (b) **38.*** (a),(b),(c)

is equal to zero if :

(a) a, b, c are in A.P. (b) a, b, c are in G.P.

(c) a, b, c are in H.P. (d) α is a root of $ax^2 + 2bx + c = 0$

40. ***Let*** $\Delta = \begin{vmatrix} \sin(x+\alpha) & \cos(x+\alpha) & a + x\sin\alpha \\ \sin(x+\beta) & \cos(x+\beta) & b + x\sin\beta \\ \sin(x+\gamma) & \cos(x+\gamma) & c + x\sin\gamma \end{vmatrix}$***, Then :***

(a) Δ is independent of x

(b) $y = \Delta$ represents a straight line parallel to x-axis

(c) $f(x) = \Delta$ has a local maximum at $x = (\alpha + \beta + \gamma)/3$

(d) $f(x) = \Delta$ has a local minimum at $x = (\alpha + \beta + \gamma)/3$

41. ***If the capital letters denote the cofactor of the corresponding small letters in the determinant***

$\begin{vmatrix} \alpha_1 & \beta_1 & \gamma_1 \\ \alpha_2 & \beta_2 & \gamma_2 \\ \alpha_3 & \beta_3 & \gamma_3 \end{vmatrix}$ ***and if*** $\Delta_1 = \begin{vmatrix} A_1 & B_1 & C_1 \\ A_2 & B_2 & C_2 \\ A_3 & B_3 & C_3 \end{vmatrix}$ ***then*** Δ_1 ***is equal to :***

(a) Δ (b) Δ^2

(c) $\Delta + 1$ (d) Δ^3

42. ***If*** x ***is a real number in the following determinant such that***

$\begin{vmatrix} x+1 & x+2 & x+\alpha \\ x+2 & x+3 & x+\beta \\ x+3 & x+4 & x+\gamma \end{vmatrix}$ ***the*** α, β ***and*** γ ***are in :***

(a) Geometrical progression (b) Harmonic progression

(c) Arithmetic progression (d) None of the above

43. ***If*** λ ***is an eigen value of a matrix A, then it is a solution to :***

(a) $(A - \lambda I) = 0$ (b) det $| A - \lambda I | = 0$

(c) det $| A - I | = 0$ (d) det $| A - \lambda | = 0$

44. ***If*** $A = \begin{bmatrix} 5 & 0 \\ 0 & 5 \end{bmatrix}$ ***and*** $B = \begin{bmatrix} a & b \\ c & d \end{bmatrix}$***, then AB :***

(a) A (b) $5B$

(c) B^5 (d) $5A$

45. ***A matrix*** $A = [a_{ij}]$ ***is an upper triangular matrix if***

(a) It is a square matrix and $a_{ij} = 0, i < j$

(b) It is a square matrix and $a_{ij} = 0, i > j$

(c) It is not a square matrix and $a_{ij} = 0, i > j$

(d) It is not a square matrix and $a_{ij} = 0, i < j$

46. ***If*** $E(\theta) = \begin{bmatrix} \cos^2\theta & \cos\theta\sin\theta \\ \cos\theta\sin\theta & \sin^2\theta \end{bmatrix}$ ***and*** θ ***and*** ϕ ***differ by an odd multiple of*** $\pi/2$***, then*** $E(\theta)\,E(\phi)$ ***is a :***

(a) Null matrix (b) Unit matrix

(c) Diagonal matrix (d) None of these

47. ***If*** $A = \begin{bmatrix} \cos^2\alpha & \cos\alpha\sin\alpha \\ \cos\alpha\sin\alpha & \sin^2\alpha \end{bmatrix}$

and $B = \begin{bmatrix} \cos^2\beta & \cos\beta\sin\beta \\ \cos\beta\sin\beta & \sin^2\beta \end{bmatrix}$

are two matrices such that the product AB is the null matrix, then $\alpha - \beta$ ***is :***

(a) 0 (b) Multiple of π

(c) An odd multiple of $\pi/2$ (d) None of these

48. ***If A is a square matrix such that*** $AA^T = I = A^TA$***, then A is :***

(a) A symmetric matrix (b) A skew symmetric matrix

(c) A diagonal matrix (d) An orthogonal matrix

49. ***If*** $D = diag(d_1, d_2, d_3, \ldots, d_n)$***, where*** $d_i \neq 0$ ***for all*** $i = 1, 2, \ldots, n$***, then*** D^{-1} ***is equal to :***

(a) D (b) Diag $(d_1^{-1}\, d_2^{-1}, \ldots, d_n^{-1})$

(c) I_n (d) None of these

50. ***If A, B are two square matrices such that AB = A and BA = B, then :***

(a) A, B are idempotent (b) Only A is idempotent

(c) Only B is idempotent (d) None of these

51. ***The inverse of a diagonal matrix is***

(a) A symmetric matrix (b) A skew-symmetric matrix

(c) A diagonal matrix (d) None of these

52. ***If A is a symmetric matrix and*** $n \in N$***, then*** A^n ***is :***

(a) Symmetric (b) Skew-symmetric

(c) A diagonal matrix (d) None of these

53. ***If A is a skew-symmetric matrix and n is a positive integer, then*** A^n ***is :***

(a) A symmetric matrix (b) Skew-symmetric matrix

(c) Diagonal matrix (d) None of these

Answers : **39.*** (b),(d) **40.** (a),(b) **41.** (b) **42.** (c) **43.** (b) **44.** (b) **45.** (b) **46.*** (a) **47.** (c) **48.** (d) **49.** (b) **50.*** (a) **51.** (c) **52.*** (a) **53.*** (d)

54. ***If A is a skew-symmetric matrix and n is an even positive integer then A^n is :***

(a) A symmetric matrix (b) A skew-symmetric matrix

(c) A diagonal matrix (d) None of these

55. ***If A, B are symmetric matrices of the same order then AB − BA is***

(a) Symmetric matrix (b) Skew-symmetric matrix

(c) Null matrix (d) Unit matrix

56. ***If the product AB = 0, then we can conclude :***

(a) $A = 0$ or $B = 0$ (b) $A = 0$ or $B = 0$

(c) $A \neq 0$ or $B \neq 0$ (d) None of these

57. ***If*** $A = \begin{bmatrix} \cos\alpha & -\sin\alpha \\ \sin\alpha & \cos\alpha \end{bmatrix}$ ***then*** $A' + A = I_2$ ***if***

(a) $\alpha = n\pi$ (b) $\alpha = (2n+1)\pi/2$

(c) $\alpha = 2n\pi + \pi/3$ (d) None of these

58. ***If*** $A = \begin{bmatrix} 1 & 2 & x \\ 0 & 1 & 0 \\ 0 & 0 & 1 \end{bmatrix}$ ***and*** $B = \begin{bmatrix} 1 & -2 & y \\ 0 & 1 & 0 \\ 0 & 0 & 1 \end{bmatrix}$ ***and*** $AB = I_3$, ***then*** $x + y$ ***equals :***

(a) 0 (b) − 1

(c) 2 (d) None of these

59. ***The system of equations***

$x + y + z = 5$, $x + 2y + 3z = 9$, $x + 3y + \lambda z = \mu$ ***has a unique solution if :***

(a) $\lambda = 5, \mu = 13$ (b) $\lambda \neq 5$

(c) $\lambda = 5, \mu \neq 13$ (d) $\mu \neq 13$

60. ***The system of equations in question 59 has no solution if :***

(a) $\lambda = 5, \mu = 13$ (b) $\lambda = 5$

(c) $\lambda = 5, \mu \neq 13$ (d) $\mu = 13$

61. ***The system of equations in Question 59 has infinite number of solution if :***

(a) $\lambda = 5, \mu = 13$ (b) $\lambda \neq 5$

(c) $\lambda = 5, \mu \neq 13$ (d) None of these

62. ***If AB = A and BA = B, then :***

(a) $A^2B = A^2$ (b) $B^2A = B$

(c) $ABA = A$ (d) $BAB = B$

63. ***D is a 3 × 3 diagonal matrix. Which of the following statements is not true?***

(a) $D' = D$

(b) $AD = DA$ for each matrix of order 3×3

(c) D^{-1} if exists is a scalar matrix

(d) None of these

64. *If* $A = \begin{pmatrix} 1 & a \\ 0 & 1 \end{pmatrix}$ ***then*** $\lim_{n \to \infty} \frac{1}{n} A^n$ ***is :***

(a) $\begin{pmatrix} 0 & a \\ 0 & 0 \end{pmatrix}$ (b) $\begin{pmatrix} 0 & 0 \\ 0 & 0 \end{pmatrix}$

(c) $\begin{pmatrix} 0 & 1 \\ 0 & 0 \end{pmatrix}$ (d) Does not exist

65. *Let* $A = \begin{bmatrix} 1 & 0 \\ 1 & 1 \end{bmatrix}$ ***then :***

(a) $A^{-n} = \begin{bmatrix} 1 & 0 \\ -n & 1 \end{bmatrix} \forall n \in N.$ (b) $\lim_{n \to \infty} \frac{1}{n} A^{-n} = \begin{bmatrix} 0 & 0 \\ -1 & 0 \end{bmatrix}$.

(c) $\lim_{n \to \infty} \frac{1}{n^2} A^{-n} = \begin{bmatrix} 0 & 0 \\ 0 & 0 \end{bmatrix}$ (d) None of these

66. *Let A, B and C be 2 × 2 matrices with entries from the set of real numbers. Define * as follows :*

$A * B = \frac{1}{2}(AB + BA)$, ***then :***

(a) $A * B = B * A$ (b) $A * A = A^2$

(c) $A * (B + C) = A * B + A * C$ (d) $A * I = A$

67. *Which of the following is correct ?*

(a) Determinant is a square matrix

(b) Determinant is a number associated to a matrix

(c) Determinant is a number associated to a square matrix

(d) None of these

68. *If A is an orthogonal matrix then :*

(a) $|A| = 0$ (b) $|A| = \pm 1$

(c) $|A| = \pm 2$ (d) None of these

69. *Which of the following ?*

(i) Adjoint of a symmetric matrix is symmetric

(ii) Adjoint of a unit matrix is a unit matrix

(iii) $A(adj\ A) = (adj\ A)\ A = |A|\ I$

Answers : **54.** (a) **55.*** (b) **56.** (d) **57.*** (c) **58.*** (a) **59.*** (b) **60.** (c) **61.** (a) **62.*** (a),(b),(c),(d) **63.*** (a),(c) **64.*** (a) **65.** (a),(b) **66.** (a),(b),(c),(d) **67.** (c)

(iv) Adjoint of a diagonal matrix is a diagonal matrix, is/are incorrect

(a) (i) (b) (ii)
(c) (iii) and (iv) (d) None of these

70. If $A = [a_{ij}]_{m \times n}$ is a matrix of rank r, then :

(a) $r = \min(m, n)$ (b) $r < \min(m, n)$
(c) $r \le \min(m, n)$ (d) None of these

71. If A is a matrix such that there exists a square submatrix of order r which is non-singular and every square submatrix of order r + 1 or more is singular, then :

(a) rank $(A) = r + 1$ (b) rank $(A) = r$
(c) rank $(A) > r$ (d) rank $(A) \ge r + 1$

72. If A is a non-zero column matrix of order $m \times 1$ and B is a non-zero row matrix of order $1 \times n$ then rank of AB equals :

(a) m (b) n
(c) 1 (d) None of these

73. Let A be a non-singular square matrix. Then |adj A| is equal to

(a) $|A|^n$ (b) $|A|^{n-1}$
(c) $|A|^{n-2}$ (d) None of these

74. Which of the following statements is not correct

(a) $(AB)' = A'B'$ (b) $(A')' = A$
(c) $(A + B)' = A' + B'$ (d) $(kA)' = kA'$ (k is a scalar)

75. If $A = \begin{pmatrix} \cos\theta & \sin\theta \\ -\sin\theta & \cos\theta \end{pmatrix}$, then $\lim_{n \to \infty} \frac{1}{n} A^n$ is

(a) A zero matrix (b) An identity matrix
(c) $\begin{pmatrix} 0 & 1 \\ -1 & 0 \end{pmatrix}$ (d) None of these

76. The trace $T_r(A)$ of a 3×3 matrix $A = (a_{ij})$ is defined by the relation $T_r(A) = a_{11} + a_{22} + a_{33}$ (i.e., $T_r(A)$ is sum of the main diagonal elements). Which of the following statements cannot hold ?

(a) $T_r(kA) = kT_r(A)$ (k is a scalar) (b) $T_r(A + B) = T_r(A) + T_r(B)$
(c) $T_r(I_3) = 3$ (d) $T_r(A^2) = T_r(A)^2$

77. What is wrong in the following computation ?

$$\begin{bmatrix} 1 & 0.01 \\ 1 & 1 \end{bmatrix}^n = \left\{\begin{bmatrix} 1 & 0 \\ 1 & 1 \end{bmatrix} + 10^{-2}\begin{bmatrix} 0 & 1 \\ 0 & 0 \end{bmatrix}\right\}^n$$

$$= \begin{bmatrix} 1 & 0 \\ 1 & 1 \end{bmatrix}^n + n \times 10^{-2} \begin{bmatrix} 1 & 0 \\ 1 & 1 \end{bmatrix}^{n-1} \begin{bmatrix} 0 & 1 \\ 0 & 0 \end{bmatrix},$$

since $\begin{bmatrix} 0 & 1 \\ 0 & 0 \end{bmatrix}^k = \begin{bmatrix} 0 & 0 \\ 0 & 0 \end{bmatrix}$ ***for*** $k \geq 2$ **:**

(a) $\begin{bmatrix} 0 & 1 \\ 0 & 0 \end{bmatrix}^k = \begin{bmatrix} 0 & 0 \\ 0 & 0 \end{bmatrix}$ for $k \geq 2$ is not true

(b) Computation of second term on R.H.S. is not valid

(c) First term should be calculated completely

(d) None of these

78. ***If*** $A = \begin{bmatrix} 1 & -5 & 7 \\ 0 & 7 & 9 \\ 11 & 8 & 9 \end{bmatrix}$, ***then trace of matrix A is :***

(a) 17 (b) 25

(c) 3 (d) 12

79. ***If*** $A = \begin{bmatrix} 1 & 1 \\ 1 & 1 \end{bmatrix}$ ***and*** $n \in N$, ***then*** A^n ***is equal to :***

(a) $2^n A$ (b) $2^{n-1} A$

(c) $n A$ (d) None of these

80. ***If*** $A = [a_{ij}]$ ***is a scalar matrix, then trace of A is***

(a) $\sum_i \sum_j a_{ij}$ (b) $\sum_i a_{ij}$

(c) $\sum_j a_{ij}$ (d) $\sum_i a_{ii}$

81. ***If A and B are matrices such that AB and A + B both are defined, then :***

(a) A and B can be any two matrices

(b) A and B are square matrices not necessarily of the same order

(c) A, B are square matrices of the same order

(d) number of columns of A is same as the number of rows of B

82. ***If A is an invertible matrix, then which of the following is correct ?***

(a) A^{-1} is multivalued (b) A^{-1} is singular

(c) $(A^{-1})^T \neq (A^T)^{-1}$ (d) $|A| \neq 0$

83. ***A square matrix A with elements from the set of real numbers is said to be orthogonal if*** $A' = A^{-1}$. ***If A is an orthogonal matrix, then :***

(a) A' is orthogonal (b) A^{-1} is orthogonal

Answers : **68.*** (b) **69.** (d) **70.** (c) **71.** (b) **72.** (c) **73.** (b) **74.** (a) **75.** (a) **76.** (a),(d) **77.** (d) **78.*** (a) **79.*** (b) **80.*** (d) **81.** (c) **82.** (d)

(c) $Adj . A = A'$ (d) $|A^{-1}| = 1$

84. ***If A is a square matrix of order 2 × 2 such that $A^2 = 0$, then :***

(a) $A = \begin{bmatrix} \alpha & \beta \\ \gamma & -\alpha \end{bmatrix}$ where α, β, γ are numbers such that $\alpha^2 + \beta\gamma = 0$

(b) $A = \begin{bmatrix} \alpha & \beta \\ \beta & -\alpha \end{bmatrix}$ with $\alpha = \pm \beta$

(c) $A = \begin{bmatrix} \alpha & -\alpha \\ -\beta & \beta \end{bmatrix}$ with $\alpha^2 + \beta^2 = 1$

(d) None of these

85. ***Let*** $A = \begin{bmatrix} x+\lambda & x & x \\ x & x+\lambda & x \\ x & x & x+\lambda \end{bmatrix}$, ***then A^{-1} exists if :***

(a) $x \neq 0$ (b) $\lambda \neq 0$

(c) $3x + \lambda \neq 0, \lambda \neq 0$ (d) $x \neq 0, \lambda \neq 0$

86. ***Suppose $a_1, a_2, \ldots$ real numbers, with $a_1 \neq 0$. If $a_1, a_2, a_3, \ldots$ are in A.P. then***

(a) $A = \begin{bmatrix} a_1 & a_2 & a_3 \\ a_4 & a_5 & a_6 \\ a_5 & a_6 & a_7 \end{bmatrix}$ is singular

(b) The system of equations $a_1x + a_2y + a_3z = 0$, $a_4x + a_5y + a_6z = 0$, $a_7x + a_8y + a_9z = 0$ has infinite number of solutions

(c) $B = \begin{bmatrix} a_1 & ia_2 \\ ia_2 & a_1 \end{bmatrix}$ is non singular

(d) None of these

87. ***If*** $X = \begin{bmatrix} 3 & -4 \\ 1 & -1 \end{bmatrix}$, ***the value of X^n is :***

(a) $\begin{bmatrix} 3n & -4n \\ n & -n \end{bmatrix}$ (b) $\begin{bmatrix} 2+n & 5-n \\ n & -n \end{bmatrix}$

(c) $\begin{bmatrix} 3^n & (-4)^n \\ 1^n & (-1)^n \end{bmatrix}$ (d) None of these

88. ***Let a, b, c be positive real numbers. The following system of equations in x, y and z***

$$\frac{x^2}{a^2} + \frac{y^2}{b^2} - \frac{z^2}{c^2} = 1, \ \frac{x^2}{a^2} - \frac{y^2}{b^2} + \frac{z^2}{c^2} = 1, \ -\frac{x^2}{a^2} - \frac{y^2}{b^2} + \frac{z^2}{c^2} = 1 \text{ has :}$$

(a) No solution (b) Unique solution

(c) Infinitely many solutions (d) Finitely many solutions

89. ***The system of linear equations $x + y + z = 2$, $2x + y - z = 3$, $3x + 2y + kz = 4$ has a unique solution if :***

(a) $k \neq 0$ (b) $-1 < k < 1$

(c) $-2 < k < 2$ (d) $k = 0$

90. ***The rank of the following $(n + 1) \times (n + 1)$ matrix, where a is a real number is***

$$\begin{vmatrix} 1 & a & a^2 & \dots & a^n \\ 1 & a & a^2 & \dots & a^n \\ \dots & \dots & \dots & \dots & \dots \\ \dots & \dots & \dots & \dots & \dots \\ 1 & a & a^2 & \dots & a^n \end{vmatrix} :$$

(a) 1 (b) 2

(c) n (d) Depends on a

91. ***The determinant of a matrix has 5040 terms (in the unsimplified from). The order of the matrix is :***

(a) 5 (b) 6

(c) 7 (d) 8

92. ***Choose the incorrect statements :***

(a) The determinant of a matrix equals the sum of its eigen values

(b) Every matrix satisfies its own characteristic equation

(c) The sum of the principal diagonal elements is equal to the sum of all its eigen values

(d) If a row of a matrix is same as one of its columns, its determinant value is 0

93. ***A is a square matrix of order 'n' and its determinant value is 9. If all the elements are multiplied by 2, its determinant value becomes 2. Then n is***

(a) 2 (b) 3

(c) 4 (d) 5

94. ***Which of the following elementary operations may effect the rank of a matrix ?***

(a) Scalar multiplication

(b) Adding two rows

(c) Adding a row with the scalar multiple of another row

(d) None of the above

Answers : **83.** (a),(b) **84.** (a) **85.** (b),(c) **86.** (a),(b),(c) **87.** (d) **88.** (b) **89.*** (a) **90.*** (a) **91.*** (c) **92.*** (a),(d) **93.*** (d) **94.** (d)

95. ***Let A and B be two $n \times n$ real symmetric matrices then :***

(a) $AA' = 1$ (b) $AB = BA$

(c) $A = A^{-1}$ (d) $(AB)^1 = BA$

96. ***In a compact single dimensional array representation for lower triangular matrices of sine $n \times n$, non zero elements of each row are stored one after the other, starting from the first raw. The index of the $(\hat{i}, j)$th element of the lower triangular matrix in this new representation is***

(a) $\hat{i} + \frac{j}{2}$ (b) $\hat{i} + j - 1$

(c) $j + \frac{\hat{i}(i-1)}{2}$ (d) $\hat{i} + \frac{j(j-1)}{2}$

97. ***A is a 2×2 matrix with eigen values 2 and − 3. The eigen values of the matrix A^2 are :***

(a) Can't be determined from the given data

(b) 2 and− 3

(c) 4 and 9

(d) 4 and − 9

98. ***If the determinant of an $n \times n$ matrix A is zero, then***

(a) rank of A is n

(b) Rank of A is $(n - 2)$

(c) A has at least one zero eigen value

(d) The system of equations $AX = 0$ has only the trivial solution

99. ***If A and B are two complex matrices such that***

$$A = \begin{bmatrix} 0 & 1 & 0 & 0 \\ 0 & 0 & 1 & 0 \\ 0 & 0 & 0 & 1 \\ 1 & 0 & 0 & 0 \end{bmatrix}, \quad B = \begin{bmatrix} i & 0 & 0 & 0 \\ 0 & -1 & 0 & 0 \\ 0 & 0 & -i & 0 \\ 0 & 2 & 0 & 1 \end{bmatrix}$$

and $C = AB - iBA$, then which is true ?

(a) $C + C^2 + C^3 = 0$ (b) $C + C^2 - C^3 = 0$

(c) $C - C^2 + C^3 = 0$ (d) $C - C^2 - C^3 = 0$

100. ***For what value of α, the following matrix is invertible ?***

$$\begin{bmatrix} 0 & 1 & \alpha \\ 1 & \alpha & 0 \\ \alpha & 0 & 1 \end{bmatrix}$$

(a) $\alpha \neq 0, \pm 1$ (b) $\alpha \neq 0, \pm i$

(c) $\alpha = 0, \pm 1$ (d) $\alpha = 0, \pm i$

101. ***For similarity of matrices, which of the following is true ?***

(a) They are reflexive, symmetric and transitive

(b) They are reflexive, assymetric and transitive

(c) They forms an equivalence relation

(d) They forms a poset

102. ***The matrix*** $\begin{bmatrix} \cos\theta & \sin\theta \\ -\sin\theta & \cos\theta \end{bmatrix}$ ***is a :***

(a) Scalor matrix (b) Diagonal matrix

(c) Nilpotent matrix (d) Idempotent matrix

103. ***Suppose f (x) is a function satisfying the following conditions :***

(a) $f(0) = 2$, $f(1) = 1$

(b) $f(x)$ has a maximum value at $x = \frac{5}{2}$ and

(c) for all x, $f(x)$ $\begin{vmatrix} 2ax & aax-1 & 2ax+b+1 \\ b & b+1 & -1 \\ 2(ax=b) & 2ax+2b+1 & 2ax+b \end{vmatrix}$

where a and b are constant. Then the value of a and b are

(a) $\frac{1}{4}, -\frac{1}{4}$ (b) $\frac{1}{4}, -\frac{5}{4}$

(c) $\frac{1}{4}, -\frac{5}{4}$ (d) $\frac{1}{4}, \frac{7}{4}$

104. ***If*** $A = \begin{bmatrix} 1 & 0 \\ 1/2 & 1 \end{bmatrix}$, ***then*** A^{50} ***is :***

(a) $\begin{bmatrix} 1 & 0 \\ 0 & 50 \end{bmatrix}$ (b) $\begin{bmatrix} 1 & 0 \\ 50 & 1 \end{bmatrix}$

(c) $\begin{bmatrix} 1 & 25 \\ 0 & 1 \end{bmatrix}$ (d) None of these

105. ***Matrix has a value. This statement :***

(a) is always true (b) depends upon the matrics

(c) is false (d) None of the these

106. ***If every minor of order r of a matrix A is zero, then rank of A is***

(a) greater than r (b) equal to r

(c) less than or equal to r (d) less than r

107. ***If two eigen values of*** $\begin{bmatrix} 8 & -6 & 2 \\ -6 & 7 & -4 \\ 2 & -4 & 3 \end{bmatrix}$

Answers : **95.** (d) **96.** (c) **97.*** (c) **98.*** (c) **99.** (c) **100.** (b)
101. (a),(c) **102.** (b) **103.*** (c) **104.*** (d) **105.** (c) **106.** (d)

are 3 and 15,. then the third eigen value is—

(a) 0 (b) 7

(c) 3 (d) 8

108. ***If rank (A) = 2, rank (B) = 3, then rank (AB) is—***

(a) 2 (b) 3

(c) 6 (d) 5

109. ***Every Hermition matrix can be written as A + iB, where A is real and ..... and B is real and .....***

(a) symmetric, sew symmetric (b) skew symmetric, symmetric

(c) Hermition, sew hermition (d) skew Hermition, Hermition

110. ***The sum and product of the eigen values of *** are***

(a) 6, 8 (b) 8, 6

(c) 6, 5 (d) 5, 6

Answers : **107.*** (a) **108.*** (a) **109.** (a) **110.*** (c)

SOLUTIONS

1. By $C_1 \to C_1 + C_2 + C_3$

$$\begin{vmatrix} x+1 & 1 & 1 \\ x+1 & x-1 & 1 \\ x+1 & 1 & x-1 \end{vmatrix} = 0$$

$$\Rightarrow \qquad (x+1)(x-2)^2 = 0$$

$$\Rightarrow \qquad x = -1, 2.$$

2. $|A| \neq 0 \Rightarrow A^{-1}$ Exist.

$\Rightarrow$ A is non singular

Because $AB = AC \Rightarrow A^{-1}(AB) = A^{-1}(AC)$

$\Rightarrow$ $B = C$

3. Since k is common for each raw of $|kA|$ and n rows are there, so $|kA| = k^n |A|$.

4. By $C_1 \to C_1 + C_3$, then take common $(x + y + z)$ and 4 from C_1 and C_2 respectively, we get two columns are same of determinant.

5. Let $\frac{x^2}{a^2} = X$, $\frac{y^2}{b^2} = Y$ and $\frac{z^2}{c^2} = Z$, then we have the system of equations

$$\begin{aligned} X + Y - Z &= 1 \\ X - Y + Z &= 1 \Rightarrow AX = B \\ -X + Y + Z &= 1 \end{aligned}$$

where,
$$A = \begin{bmatrix} 1 & 1 & -1 \\ 1 & -1 & 1 \\ -1 & 1 & 1 \end{bmatrix}$$

But $|A| \neq 0$, so the rank $(A) = 3$ and hence the system have a unique solution.

7. $\because$ $\omega^3 = 1$ and $1 + \omega + \omega^2 = 0$.

8. $\because$ $|kA|_{n \times n} = k^n |A|_{n \times n}$.

9. $n = 2 \times 3 \times 4 = 24$.

12. Apply $C_1 \to C_1 + C_2$.

13. We have

$$x^k y^k z^k \begin{vmatrix} 1 & x^2 & x^3 \\ 1 & y^2 & y^3 \\ 1 & z^2 & z^3 \end{vmatrix} = \frac{(x-y)(y-z)(z-x)(xy+yz+zx)}{xyz}$$

$$\Rightarrow \quad x^{k+1}y^{k+1}z^{k+1}\begin{vmatrix} 1 & x^2 & x^3 \\ 1 & y^2 & y^3 \\ 1 & z^2 & z^3 \end{vmatrix} = (x-y)(y-z)(z-x)(xy+yz+zx)$$

Here degree of $\Delta = 5$

Thus degree of L.H.S. $= 3k + 3 + 5 = 3k + 8$

Also degree of R.H.S. $= 5$

$\therefore \quad 3k + 8 = 5 \Rightarrow k = -1$

14. By applying $C_2 \to C_2 - \sin\theta\, C_1$ and $C_3 \to C_3 - C_1$

$$\Delta = \begin{vmatrix} 1 & \theta & 0 \\ -\sin\theta & 1+\sin^2\theta & 2\sin\theta \\ -1 & 0 & 2 \end{vmatrix} = 2(1 + \sin^2\theta)$$

But $\sin^2\theta \in [0, 1]$

$1 + \sin^2\theta \in [1, 2]$

$2 + 2\sin^2\theta \in [2, 4] \Rightarrow \Delta \in [2, 4]$.

15. Apply $R_3 \to R_3 + R_2 - 2R_2$ and $R_2 \to R_2 - R_1$

We have $\Delta = \begin{vmatrix} x+1 & x+2 & x+a \\ 1 & 1 & b-a \\ 0 & 0 & a+c-2b \end{vmatrix} = 0$

$\Rightarrow \quad a + c - 2b = 0$

$\Rightarrow \quad a, b, c$ are in A.P.

16. Apply $C_1 \to C_1 + C_2 + C_3$, we get

$$\Delta = x^3 = 0 \Rightarrow x = 0.$$

17. We have

$$\Delta = \sum_{n=1}^{N} U_n = \begin{vmatrix} \sum_{x=1}^{N} n & 1 & 5 \\ \sum_{x=1}^{N} n^2 & 2N+1 & 2N+1 \\ \sum_{x=1}^{N} n^3 & 3N^2 & 3N+1 \end{vmatrix}$$

$$= \frac{N(N+1)}{12}\begin{vmatrix} 6 & 1 & 5 \\ 2(2N+1) & 2N+1 & 2N+1 \\ 3N(N+1) & 3N^2 & 3N+1 \end{vmatrix}$$

$$= \frac{1}{3} N(N+1)(2N+1)$$

$$= 2 \sum_{n=1}^{N} n^2.$$

18. Multiply R_1 by a, R_2 by b and R_3 by c, we get

$$\Delta = \begin{vmatrix} 1 & a^3 & abc \\ 1 & b^3 & abc \\ 1 & c^3 & abc \end{vmatrix} = 0$$

$\Rightarrow$ Δ is in dependent of a, b, c.

19. $\Sigma 1 = n, \; \Sigma r = \frac{n(n+1)}{2}, \; \Sigma 2^r = 2^{n+1} - 2.$

20. Apply $C_1 \to C_1 + C_2 + C_3$, we get

$$\Delta = \begin{vmatrix} \alpha+\beta+\gamma & \beta & \gamma \\ \alpha+\beta+\gamma & \gamma & \alpha \\ \alpha+\beta+\gamma & \alpha & \beta \end{vmatrix} = \begin{vmatrix} 0 & \beta & \gamma \\ 0 & \gamma & \alpha \\ 0 & \alpha & \beta \end{vmatrix} = 0$$

$\because$ By the eq^n $\alpha + \beta + \gamma = \frac{0}{1} = 0.$

21. Multiplying C_1 by $\hat{i}$, we get

$$\Delta = -\hat{i} \begin{vmatrix} a_1\hat{i} - b_1 & a_1\hat{i} - b_1 & c_1 \\ a_2\hat{i} - b_2 & a_2\hat{i} - b_2 & c_2 \\ a_3\hat{i} - b_3 & a_3\hat{i} - b_3 & c_3 \end{vmatrix}$$

$$= -\hat{i} \times 0 = 0 \qquad [\because C_1 \text{ and } C_2 \text{ are identical}]$$

24. The system will be consistent if

$$\Delta = \begin{vmatrix} 1 & \lambda & 2 \\ \lambda & 1 & -2 \\ \lambda & \lambda & 3 \end{vmatrix} = 0$$

$\Rightarrow$ $3(1 - \lambda^2) = 0$

$\Rightarrow$ $\lambda = \pm 1.$

25. For the system of equations to have zero solution, we must have

$$\Delta = \begin{vmatrix} -a & 1 & 1 \\ 1 & -b & 1 \\ 1 & 1 & -c \end{vmatrix} = 0$$

Apply $C_3 \to C_3 - C_2$ and $C_2 \to C_2 - C_1$, we get

$$\Delta = \begin{vmatrix} -a & 1+a & 0 \\ 1 & -(1+b) & 1+b \\ 1 & 0 & -(1+c) \end{vmatrix}$$

$$= -a(1+b)(1+c) + (1+a)(1+c) + (1+a)(1+b) = 0$$

Dividing through out by $(1 + a)(1 + b)(1 + c)$, we get

$$-\frac{a}{1+a} + \frac{1}{1+b} + \frac{1}{1+C} = 0$$

By adding 1, we get

$$\Rightarrow \quad \frac{1}{1+a} + \frac{1}{1+b} + \frac{1}{1+C} = 1.$$

26. System have a unique solution, if $\Delta \neq 0$

Now $\Delta = \begin{vmatrix} 1 & 1 & -1 \\ 1 & 2 & -3 \\ 2 & 5 & -\lambda \end{vmatrix} = -\lambda + 8$

If $\quad \Delta \neq 0 \Rightarrow \lambda \neq 8.$

27. For the system have a non-trivial solution if

$$\begin{vmatrix} \sin\theta & 1 & 1 \\ 1 & \cos\theta & 1 \\ \sin\theta & \cos\theta & 1 \end{vmatrix} = 0$$

$$\Rightarrow \quad (1 - \sin\theta)(1 - \cos\theta) = 0$$

As $0 < \theta < \pi$, $\cos\theta \neq 1$

This $\Rightarrow 1 - \sin\theta = 0 \Rightarrow \sin\theta = 1 \Rightarrow \theta = \frac{\pi}{2}.$

28. Subtracting (2) from (3), we get

$$ky = 1$$

$$\Rightarrow \quad x + z = 2$$

and $\quad$ hence $y = 2 \Rightarrow k = \frac{1}{2}.$

29. The system will have a non-trivial solution if $\Delta = 0$

$\Rightarrow \quad (a + 2b)(a - b)^2 = 0$

As $\quad a \neq b$, this $\Rightarrow a + 2b = 0.$

30. We have

$$\Delta = \begin{vmatrix} a_1 & a_1x + b_1 & c_1 \\ a_2 & a_2x + b_2 & c_2 \\ a_3 & a_3x + b_3 & c_3 \end{vmatrix} + x \begin{vmatrix} b_1 & a_1x + b_1 & c_1 \\ b_2 & a_2x + b_2 & c_2 \\ b_3 & a_3x + b_3 & c_3 \end{vmatrix}$$

$$= \Delta_1 + x\Delta_2$$

Now for Δ_1, by applying $C_2 \to C_2 - xC_1$, we get

$$\Delta_1 = \begin{vmatrix} a_1 & b_1 & c_1 \\ a_2 & b_2 & c_2 \\ a_3 & b_3 & c_3 \end{vmatrix}$$

and for Δ_2, apply $C_2 \to C_2 - xC_1$, we get

$$\Delta_2 = \begin{vmatrix} b_1 & xa_1 & c_1 \\ b_2 & xa_2 & c_2 \\ b_3 & xa_3 & c_3 \end{vmatrix} = -x\Delta_1$$

$\therefore \quad \Delta = \Delta_1 - x^2\Delta_1 = (1 - x^2)\,\Delta_1$

But $\quad \Delta = 0 \Rightarrow \quad x = \pm 1$ or $\Delta_1 = 0$.

31. We get

$$f(x) = \begin{vmatrix} x & 1 & 1 \\ -1 & x & 1 \\ -1 & -1 & x \end{vmatrix} = x^3 + 3x$$

Now $\quad f'(x) = 3x^2 + 3 = 3\,(x^2 + 1) > 0$ for $0 < x < 1$

$\therefore \quad f(x)$ is increasing on $[0, 1]$

$\therefore \quad$ Least value of $f(x)$ at $x = 0 = 0$

Greatest value of $f(x)$ at $x = 1 = 4$.

32. Expanding along C, we get $f(x) = 2\,[\cos x + \cos 3x]$

Now $\displaystyle\int_0^{\pi} f(x)\,dx = \left[\frac{2}{3}\sin 3x + \sin x\right]_0^{\pi} = 0$

Maximum value at $x = 0$ is 4.

Now $\displaystyle\lim_{x \to \pi/2} f(x) = 0$ and $f'(0) = 0$.

33. a and b both are true from the given theory. Also for $D = 27$, we get

$$\Delta = 27^2 = (3^3)^2 = 9^3$$

which is a perfect cube.

34. We get $f(x) = 4\sin^3 x$

$$f'(x) = 12\sin^2 x \cos x$$

Here $f'\left(\frac{\pi}{2}\right) = 0$

Also the equation of the tangent to $y = f(x)$, we get

$$y - \sin^3 0 = 0\,(x - 0)$$

$\Rightarrow \quad y = 0$

Because $f(x)$ is an odd function, therefore

$$\int_{-\pi/2}^{\pi/2} f(x)\, dx = 0.$$

35. By appling the equations in the determinant, we get

$$\Delta = (x_1 - x_2)(x_2 - x_3)(x_3 - x_1)$$

36. By solving, we get

$$\Delta = \begin{vmatrix} 1 & x & x^2 \\ x^2 & 1 & x \\ x & x^2 & 1 \end{vmatrix} = (1 - x^3)^2$$

Hence $(1 - x^3)$ and $(1 - x^3)^2$ are the factor of Δ

Now by putting $\Delta = 0$, we get just two real roots

Now $\Delta'(x) = 2(1 - x^3)(-3x^2)$

$\Rightarrow \quad \Delta'(1) = 0.$

37. After solving, we get

$$\Delta = 0$$

$\Rightarrow$ It represents x – *axis*.

38. Given $f(x) = \begin{vmatrix} 1/x & \log x & x^n \\ 1 & -1/n & (-1)^n \\ 1 & a & a^2 \end{vmatrix}$.

$$\Rightarrow \quad f^n(x) = \begin{vmatrix} \dfrac{(-1)^n n!}{x^{n+1}} & \dfrac{(-1)^{n-1}(n-1)!}{x^n} & n! \\ 1 & -\dfrac{1}{n} & (-1)^n \\ 1 & a & a^2 \end{vmatrix}$$

Now put $x = 1$ and $(-1)^n n!$ common, we get

$f^n(1) = 0$

Also $y = a\{x - f^n(1)\} = ax$ represents a straight line through the origin.

39. By expanding, we get

$$\Delta = (b^2 - ac)(a\alpha^2 + 2b\alpha + c)$$

$\Rightarrow \quad$ putting $\Delta = 0$, we get

$(b^2 - ac)(a\alpha^2 + 2b\alpha + c) = 0$

$\Rightarrow \quad b^2 - ac = 0 \Rightarrow a, b, c$ are in G.P.

or α is a root of $ax^2 + 2bx + c = 0$.

46. We have

$$E(\theta) \,.\, E(\phi) = \begin{bmatrix} \cos^2\theta & \cos\theta\sin\theta \\ \cos\theta\sin\theta & \sin^2\theta \end{bmatrix}\begin{bmatrix} \cos^2\phi & \cos\phi\sin\phi \\ \cos\phi\sin\phi & \sin^2\phi \end{bmatrix}$$

$$= \begin{bmatrix} \cos\theta\cos\phi\cos(2n+1)\frac{\pi}{2} & \cos\phi\cos\phi\cos(2n=1)\frac{\pi}{2} \\ \cos\phi\sin\theta\cos(2n+1)\frac{\pi}{2} & \sin\theta\sin\phi\cos(2n+1)\frac{\pi}{2} \end{bmatrix}$$

$$= \begin{bmatrix} 0 & 0 \\ 0 & 0 \end{bmatrix}\left[\because\ \theta - \phi = (2n+1)\frac{\pi}{2} \text{ is given}\right]$$

= Null matrix.

50. We have $AB = A$ and $BA = B$

Now $AB = A \Rightarrow (AB)\,A = A\,.\,A$

$\Rightarrow$ $A\,(BA) = A^2$

$\Rightarrow$ $AB = A^2$

$\Rightarrow$ $A = A^2$

and $BA = B \Rightarrow (BA)\,B = B\,.\,B = B^2$

$\Rightarrow$ $.\,B\,(AB) = B^2$

$\Rightarrow$ $BA = B^2$

$\Rightarrow$ $B = B^2$

$\therefore$ A and B both are idempotent matrices.

52. Since A is symmetric so, $A^T = A$

Now $(A^n)^T = (A^T)^n = A^n$

So A^n also symmetric.

53. Because A^n is skew-symmetric, we have

$$A^T = -A \Rightarrow (A^T)^n = (-A)^n = (-1)^n A^n$$

$\Rightarrow$ $(A^n)^T = (\ 1)^n A^n$

$\therefore$ $(A^n)^T = \begin{cases} A^n \text{ if } n \text{ is even} \\ -A^n \text{ if } n \text{ is odd.} \end{cases}$

55. We have

$$\begin{aligned}(AB - BA)^T &= (AB)^T - (BA)^T \\ &= B^TA^T - A^TB^T \\ &= BA - AB \\ &= -(AB - BA)\end{aligned}$$

$\therefore$ $(AB - BA)$ is skew-symmetrc matrix.

57. $A' + A = \begin{bmatrix} \cos\alpha & \sin\alpha \\ -\sin\alpha & \cos\alpha \end{bmatrix} + \begin{bmatrix} \cos\alpha & -\sin\alpha \\ \sin\alpha & \cos\alpha \end{bmatrix}$

$$= \begin{bmatrix} 2\cos\alpha & 0 \\ 0 & 2\cos\alpha \end{bmatrix}.$$

$\because \quad A' + A = I_2 \Rightarrow 2\cos\alpha = 1$

$\Rightarrow \quad \cos\alpha = \frac{1}{2}$

$\Rightarrow \quad \alpha = 2n\pi + \frac{\pi}{3}$

where $n \in I$.

58. We have

$$I_3 = AB = \begin{bmatrix} 1 & 2 & x \\ 0 & 1 & 0 \\ 0 & 0 & 1 \end{bmatrix} \begin{bmatrix} 1 & -2 & y \\ 0 & 1 & 0 \\ 0 & 0 & 1 \end{bmatrix}$$

$$= \begin{bmatrix} 1 & 0 & x+y \\ 0 & 1 & 0 \\ 0 & 0 & 1 \end{bmatrix}$$

$\Rightarrow \quad x + y = 0.$

59. The system have a unique solution if

$$\begin{vmatrix} 1 & 1 & 1 \\ 1 & 2 & 3 \\ 1 & 3 & \lambda \end{vmatrix} \neq 0 \Rightarrow \lambda \neq 5.$$

62. We have

$$AB = A \Rightarrow A(AB) = (A.A) \Rightarrow A^2B = A^2$$

$$BA = B \Rightarrow B(BA) = (B.B) \Rightarrow B^2A = B^2$$

$$ABA = A(BA) = A.B = A$$

and $BAB = B(AB) = BA = B.$

63. Let $D = \begin{bmatrix} d_1 & 0 & 0 \\ 0 & d_2 & 0 \\ 0 & 0 & d_3 \end{bmatrix} \Rightarrow D' = D$

Also $AD \neq DA$

If $d_1 d_2 d_3 \neq 0 \Rightarrow D^{-1} = \begin{bmatrix} d_1^{-1} & 0 & 0 \\ 0 & d_2^{-1} & 0 \\ 0 & 0 & d_3^{-1} \end{bmatrix}.$

64. We have

$$A^n = \begin{bmatrix} 1 & na \\ 0 & 1 \end{bmatrix} \forall n \geq 1$$

$$\therefore \lim_{n\to\infty} \frac{1}{n} A^n = \lim_{n\to\infty} \begin{bmatrix} 1/n & a \\ 0 & 1/n \end{bmatrix} = \begin{bmatrix} 0 & a \\ 0 & 0 \end{bmatrix}.$$

68. Because A is orthogonal, so we have

$$AA^T = I = A^T A$$

$$\Rightarrow \quad |AA^T| = |I| = |A^T A|$$

$$\Rightarrow \quad |A| . |A^T| = D = |A^T| . |A|$$

$$\Rightarrow \quad |A|^2 = 1 \Rightarrow |A| = I1$$

75. We have $A = \begin{bmatrix} \cos\theta & \sin\theta \\ -\sin\theta & \cos\theta \end{bmatrix}$

$$\Rightarrow \quad A^n = \begin{bmatrix} \cos n\theta & \sin n\theta \\ -\sin n\theta & \cos n\theta \end{bmatrix}$$

$$\Rightarrow \quad \frac{1}{n} A^n = \begin{bmatrix} \frac{\cos n\theta}{n} & \frac{\sin n\theta}{n} \\ \frac{-\sin n\theta}{n} & \frac{\cos n\theta}{n} \end{bmatrix}$$

$$\therefore \lim_{n\to\infty} \frac{1}{n} A^n = \begin{pmatrix} 0 & 0 \\ 0 & 0 \end{pmatrix} = \text{zero matrix.}$$

78. We know that if $A = [a_{ij}]$ is a square matrix of order $n \times n$, then

$$\text{trace } (A) = \sum_{e=1}^{n} a_{ii}$$

$$\therefore \text{ if } \quad A = \begin{bmatrix} 1 & -5 & 7 \\ 0 & 7 & 9 \\ 11 & 8 & 9 \end{bmatrix} \Rightarrow tr\,(A) = 1 + 7 + 9 = 17.$$

79. It is given that

$$A = \begin{bmatrix} 1 & 1 \\ 1 & 1 \end{bmatrix}$$

$$\therefore \quad A^2 = \begin{bmatrix} 1 & 1 \\ 1 & 1 \end{bmatrix} \begin{bmatrix} 1 & 1 \\ 1 & 1 \end{bmatrix} = \begin{bmatrix} 2 & 2 \\ 2 & 2 \end{bmatrix} = 2A = 2'A$$

$$\therefore \quad A^n = 2^{n-1} A.$$

80. Trace can be defined as the sum of all the diagonal elements.

89. The given system of equation has a unique solution if

$$|A| \neq 0$$

$$\Rightarrow \quad \begin{vmatrix} 1 & 1 & 1 \\ 2 & 1 & -1 \\ 3 & 2 & k \end{vmatrix} \neq 0 \Rightarrow k \neq 0.$$

90. The rank of a matrix of order $n \times n$ is said to be n if the determinant value of at least 1 submatrix of order $n \times n$ is not 0, and all $(n+1) \times (n+1)$ is zero. So, the rank of the matrix is 1, as the submatrix of order 2×2 has 0 determinant.

91. Let us consider a matrix of order $n \times n$. To find the determinant of the matrix, we have to multiply each element of the first row, with its co-factor. The co-factor is the determinant value of a $(n-1) \times (n-1)$ matrix. So the total number of terms in the determinant value of a $n \times n$ matrix is

$$\begin{aligned} T_n &= n \times T_{n-1} \\ &= n \times (n-1) \times T_{n-2} \\ &= n \times (n-1) \times (n-2) \times \ldots \\ &= n! \end{aligned}$$

Here $\quad n! = 5040 \Rightarrow n = 7.$

92. The value of the determinant is equal to the product of the eigen values

93. We have, $|kA| = k^n |A|$

$$|2A| = 2^n |A|$$

$$288 = 2^n \times 9$$

$$\Rightarrow \quad 2^n = 32 = 2^5 \Rightarrow n = 5.$$

95. For symmetric matrices , we have $A^1 = A$, then

$$(AB)' = B' A' = BA$$

{$\because$ A and B both are symmetric matrices}.

97. If $\lambda_1, \lambda_2 \ldots \lambda_n$ are the eigen values of matrix A and order $n \times n$, the the eigen values of A^m will be $\lambda_1^m, \lambda_2^m, \ldots \lambda_n^m$.

98. Eigen value A satisfies the equation $|A - \lambda I| = 0$. Put $m = 0$, we get $|A| = 0$, which is given. So $m = 0$ is an eigen value.

103. We have

$$f'(x) = 2ax + b$$

As f has a maximum at $x = \frac{5}{2}$, $f'\left(\frac{5}{2}\right) = 0$, then

$$5a + b = 0 \quad \ldots(1)$$

Integrating $f'(x)_1$, we get

$$f(x) = ax^2 + bx + c$$

As $\quad f(0) = 2 \Rightarrow c = 0$

and $\quad f(1) = 1 \Rightarrow a + b = -1 \quad \ldots(2)$

Solving we get the result.

104. We have $A^2 = \begin{bmatrix} 1 & 0 \\ 1/2 & 1 \end{bmatrix}\begin{bmatrix} 1 & 0 \\ 1/2 & 1 \end{bmatrix} = \begin{bmatrix} 1 & 0 \\ 2(1/2) & 1 \end{bmatrix}$

$$A^4 = \begin{bmatrix} 1 & 0 \\ 1 & 1 \end{bmatrix}\begin{bmatrix} 1 & 0 \\ 1 & 1 \end{bmatrix} = \begin{bmatrix} 1 & 0 \\ 2 & 1 \end{bmatrix}$$

$$A^n = \begin{bmatrix} 1 & 0 \\ 2(n/2) & 1 \end{bmatrix}$$

$\therefore \; A^{50} = \begin{bmatrix} 1 & 0 \\ 25 & 1 \end{bmatrix}$.

107. Sum of eigen values = Sum of principal diagonal elements ***

108. $r = Min\,(A, B)$

$= Min\,(2, 3)$

$= 2$

110. Sum of eigen values = Sum of diagonal elements.

Product of eigen values = $|A|$

■□■

CHAPTER 15

COMBINATORICS

1. *How many 4-digit numbers can be formed using the digits 2, 3, 5, 6, 8 and 9 if repetitions are allowed ?*

(a) 6^4 (b) $6^4 - C(6, 4)$

(c) $C(6, 4)$ (d) $P(6, 4) - C(6, 4)$

2. *In the above problem if repetitions are not allowed :*

(a) $6 \times 5 \times 4 \times 3$ (b) $5 \times 4 \times 3 \times 2$

(c) $6 \times 6 \times 6 \times 6$ (d) None of these

3. *The possible telephone numbers are when there are seven digits, the first two of which are between 2 and 9 inclusive, the third digit between 1 and 9 inclusive, and each of the remaining may be between 0 and 9 inclusive :*

(a) 10^7 (b) $9 \times 9 \times 8 \times 10^4$

(c) $8 \times 8 \times 9 \times 10^4$ (d) $10 \times 9 \times 8 \times 7 \times 10^3$

4. *Suppose that a state's licence plates consist of three letters following by three digits. Then the number of plates manufactured when repetition are allowed are :*

(a) $26^3 \times 9 \times 10^2$ (b) $26^3 \times 10^3$

(c) $26 \times 25 \times 24 \times 10^3$ (d) $26^3 \times 10 \times 9 \times 8$

5. *The number of integers between 1 and 10^4 contains exactly one 8 and one 9 are :*

(a) $4 \times 3 \times 8 \times 7$ (b) $4 \times 3 \times 2 \times 8$

(c) $4^2 \times 3^2 \times 8^2$ (d) $4 \times 3 \times 8^2$

6. *The 5-letter words can be formed when the first and last letters are vowels and the middle letters are consonants :*

(a) $21^2 \,.\, 26^3$ (b) $5^2 \,.\, 26^3$

(c) $5^2 \,.\, 21^3$ (d) $21^2 \,.\, 21^3$

7. *The 5-letter words can be formed if vowels can only appear (if at all) at the first or last letters :*

(a) $26^2 \,.\, 21^3 + 21^5$

(b) $2.5.21^4$

(c) $26^2 . 21^3 + 21^5 + 2.5.24^4 + 5^2 . 21^3$

(d) $26^2 . 21^3 + 21^5 + 2.5.21^4 + 5^2 . 21^3$

8. ***There are five different roads from city A to city B, three different roads from city B to city C and three different roads to go directly from A to C. Then the total ways are there to go from A to C via B :***

(a) 10 (b) 15

(c) 21 (d) 24

9. ***In the above problem total ways are there from A to C altogether :***

(a) 12 (b) 15

(c) 18 (d) 21

10. ***In the question 8, total ways are there from A to C and back again to A that visit B both going and coming :***

(a) 15 (b) 150

(c) 225 (d) 270

11. ***In the Q.8, total number of ways are there from A to C via B and return directly from C to A :***

(a) 30 (b) 45

(c) 60 (d) 75

12. ***A newborn child can be given 1, 2 or 3 names. In how many ways can a child be named if we can choose from 300 names (and no name can be repeated) ?***

(a) 300^3

(b) $300 + 300 \times 299 + 300 \times 299 \times 298$

(c) $300^3 - 300 \times 299 \times 298$

(d) None of these

13. ***A shoe store has 30 styles of shoe. If each style is available in 12 different lengths, 4 different width and 6 different colors, then total number of shoes must be kept in stock :***

(a) $4 \times 6 \times 8 \times 10$ (b) $12 \times 16 \times 30 \times 6$

(c) $30 \times 25 \times 20 \times 15$ (d) $30 \times 12 \times 4 \times 6$

14. ***A tire store carries 10 different sizes of tires, each in both tube and tubeless variety, each with either nylon, rayon cord, or steel-belted, and each with white side walls or plain black. Then total number of tires does the store have :***

Answers : **1.*** (a) **2.*** (a) **3.*** (c) **4.*** (b) **5.*** (c) **6.*** (d) **7.** (d)
8.* (b) **9.*** (c) **10.*** (c) **11.*** (b) **12.*** (b) **13.** (d)

(a) 600 (b) 120
(c) 1920 (d) 36

15. ***The number of ways in which 5 children can ride a toboggan if 1 of the 3 children must drive :***

(a) $3 \times 4!$ (b) $3! \times 4$
(c) $3! \times 4!$ (d) None of these

16. ***A farmer buys 3 cows, 8 pigs and 12 chickens from a man who has 9 cows, 25 pigs and 100 chickens. Then the total choices does the farmer have :***

(a) $C(100, 12) \times C(9, 3)$ (b) $C(25, 8) \times C(9, 3)$
(c) $C(9, 3) \times C(25, 8) \times C(100, 12)$ (d) None of these

17. ***A collection of 100 light bulbs contains 8 defective ones. Then the number of ways in which the sample of 10 bulbs be selected so that either the sample contains 6 good ones and 4 defective one or 5 good ones and 5 defective ones :***

(a) $C(92, 6) \times C(8, 4)$
(b) $C(92, 5) \times C(8, 5)$
(c) $C(92, 5) \times C(92, 6) + C(8, 4) \times C(8, 6)$
(d) $C(92, 6) \times C(8, 4) + C(92, 5) \times C(8, 5)$

18. ***A committee is to be chosen from a set of 9 women and 5 men. Then the number of ways are there to form the committee if the committee has any number of people but equal numbers of women and men :***

(a) 2000 (b) 2001
(c) 2002 (d) 2003

19. ***A man has 15 close friends of whom 6 are women. Then the total number of ways can he invite 3 or more of his friends if he wants the same number of men (including himself) and women :***

(a) 1927 (b) 2052
(c) 2993 (d) None of these

20. ***Dean of B.I.T. Meerut has a pool of 10 chemists, 7 psychologists and 3 statisticians from which to form a committee. Then the total number of ways in which a 5 member committee can be formed so that the number of chemists is greater than or equal to the number of psychologists and the number of psychologists is greater than or equal to the number of statisticians :***

(a) 15,504 (b) 16,504
(c) 17,504 (d) 9597

21. ***Total number of ways in which 9-letter words can be formed that contain 3, 4 or 5 vowels (No repetition allowing) :***

(a) 650, 370 (b) 650, 270

(c) 650, 170 (d) 650, 070

22. ***In how many ways a 5-card poker hands have 4 aces ?***

(a) 40 (b) 44

(c) 48 (d) 27, 885

23. ***In how many ways a 5-card poker hands have a spade flush ?***

(a) $C(13, 5)$ (b) $C(26, 5)$

(c) $C(39, 5)$ (d) $C(52, 5)$

24. ***In how many ways a 5-card poker hands have an ace high spade flush ?***

(a) $C(9, 4)$ (b) $C(10, 4)$

(c) $C(11, 4)$ (d) $C(12, 4)$

25. ***The total number of ways can 30 distinguishable books be distributed among 3 people A, B and C so that A and B together receive exactly twice as many books as C :***

(a) $C(30, 30) \times 2^{10}$ (b) $C(30, 10) \times 20$

(c) $C(30, 10) \times 2^{20}$ (d) $C(30, 10) \times 20^2$

26. ***A teacher wishes to given an examination with 10 questions. Then the total number of ways can the test be given a total of 30 points if each question is to be worth 2 or more points :***

(a) $C(30, 20)$ (b) $C(30, 10)$

(c) $C(19, 10)$ (d) $2 \times C(19, 10)$

27. ***Six distinct symbols are transmitted through a communication channel. A total of 12 blanks are to be inserted between the symbols with at least two blanks between every pair of symbols. In how many ways can the symbols and blanks be arranged ?***

(a) $P(6, 6) \times C(6, 2)$ (b) $P(6, 6) \times C(6, 6)$

(c) $C(6, 2)$ (d) $P(6, 6)$

28. ***The total number of ways are there to arrange a deck of 52 cards with no adject hearts :***

(a) $C(52, 13)$ (b) $C(52, 13) \times 13! \times 39!$

(c) $C(40, 26) \times 13! \times 13!$ (d) $C(40, 13) \times 13! \times 39!$

Answers : **14.*** (b) **15.** (a) **16.** (c) **17.*** (d) **18.*** (b) **19.*** (d) **20.*** (d) **21.*** (a) **22.*** (c) **23.** (a) **24.** (d) **25.** (c) **26.** (c) **27.** (a) **28.** (d)

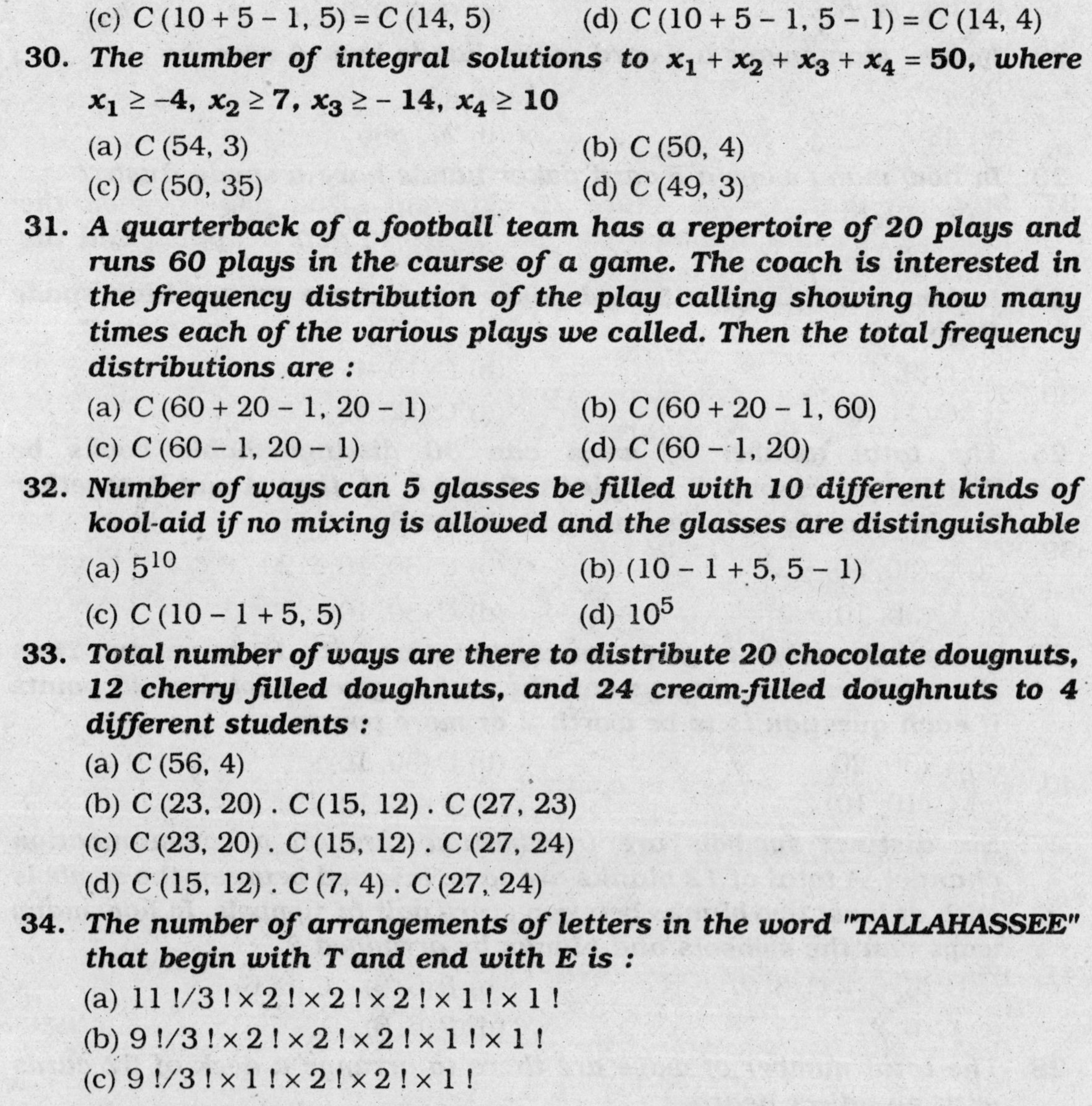

29. ***The total number of non-negative integral solutions to*** $x_1 + x_2 + x_3 + x_4 + x_5 = 10$ **:**

(a) $C(10 - 1, 5) = C(9, 5)$ (b) $C(10 - 1, 5 - 1) = C(9, 4)$

(c) $C(10 + 5 - 1, 5) = C(14, 5)$ (d) $C(10 + 5 - 1, 5 - 1) = C(14, 4)$

30. ***The number of integral solutions to*** $x_1 + x_2 + x_3 + x_4 = 50$, ***where*** $x_1 \geq -4$, $x_2 \geq 7$, $x_3 \geq -14$, $x_4 \geq 10$

(a) $C(54, 3)$ (b) $C(50, 4)$

(c) $C(50, 35)$ (d) $C(49, 3)$

31. ***A quarterback of a football team has a repertoire of 20 plays and runs 60 plays in the caurse of a game. The coach is interested in the frequency distribution of the play calling showing how many times each of the various plays we called. Then the total frequency distributions are :***

(a) $C(60 + 20 - 1, 20 - 1)$ (b) $C(60 + 20 - 1, 60)$

(c) $C(60 - 1, 20 - 1)$ (d) $C(60 - 1, 20)$

32. ***Number of ways can 5 glasses be filled with 10 different kinds of kool-aid if no mixing is allowed and the glasses are distinguishable***

(a) 5^{10} (b) $(10 - 1 + 5, 5 - 1)$

(c) $C(10 - 1 + 5, 5)$ (d) 10^5

33. ***Total number of ways are there to distribute 20 chocolate dougnuts, 12 cherry filled doughnuts, and 24 cream-filled doughnuts to 4 different students :***

(a) $C(56, 4)$

(b) $C(23, 20) . C(15, 12) . C(27, 23)$

(c) $C(23, 20) . C(15, 12) . C(27, 24)$

(d) $C(15, 12) . C(7, 4) . C(27, 24)$

34. ***The number of arrangements of letters in the word "TALLAHASSEE" that begin with T and end with E is :***

(a) $11!/3! \times 2! \times 2! \times 2! \times 1! \times 1!$

(b) $9!/3! \times 2! \times 2! \times 2! \times 1! \times 1!$

(c) $9!/3! \times 1! \times 2! \times 2! \times 1!$

(d) $11!/3! \times 1! \times 2! \times 2! \times 1!$

35. ***How many arrangements are there of (of letters) 7 . a, 5 . c, 1 . h, 7 . i, 9 . n, 5 . t :***

(a) $P(34; 7, 5, 1, 7, 9, 5)$ (b) $P(13; 7, 5, 1) \times P(21; 7, 9, 5)$

(c) $P(34; 7, 5, 1, 9)$ (d) None of these

36. ***Suppose that U.P. Technical university has a residence hall that has 5 single rooms, 5 double rooms, and 3 rooms for 3 students each. Then the total number of ways can 24 students be assigned to the 13 rooms :***

(a) $P(24; 5, 10, 9)$

(b) $P(13; 1, 1, 1, 1, 1, 2, 2, 2, 2, 2)$

(c) $P(24; 13)$

(d) $P(24; 1, 1, 1, 1, 1, 2, 2, 2, 2, 2, 3, 3, 3)$

37. ***Suppose that 3 boys share 15 different sized apples, then the number of ways in which the youngest boy gets 7 apples and the other two boys get 4 each :***

(a) $P(15; 5, 4, 3)$ (b) $P(15; 3, 3, 3)$

(c) $P(15; 5, 5, 5)$ (d) $P(15; 7, 4, 4)$

38. ***The total number in which 12 white pawns and 12 black pawns be placed on the black squares of an 8 × 8 chess board :***

(a) $P(32; 12, 10, 8)$ (b) $P(32; 12, 8, 12)$

(c) $P(32; 12, 8, 8)$ (d) $P(32; 12, 12, 12)$

39. ***The total number of bridge deals are there in which North and South get all the spades :***

(a) $C(39, 13) \times C(39, 13) \times C(26, 13)$

(b) $C(39, 13) \times C(26, 13) \times C(26, 13)$

(c) $C(39, 13) \times C(26, 13) \times C(13, 13)$

(d) $C(52, 13) \times C(39, 13) \times C(26, 13)$

40. ***If there are six periods in each working day of a institute, then the total number of ways can one arrange 5 subjects such that each subjects is allowed at least one period :***

(a) 3000 (b) 3600

(c) 4200 (d) 4900

41. ***When a group photograph is taken, all the seven teachers should be in the first row and all the twenty students should be in the second row. If the two corners of the second row are reserved for the two tallest students, interchangeable only between them, if the middle seat of the front raw is reserved for the principal, then the total number of arrangements are possible :***

(a) $P(18, 18) \times 1440$ (b) $(18)! \times 1210$

(c) $(18)! \times 11440$ (d) $(17)! \times 1210$

Answers : **29.** (d) **30.** (a) **31.** (b) **32.** (d) **33.** (c) **34.** (c) **35.** (a) **36.** (d) **37.** (d) **38.** (b) **39.** (b) **40.** (b) **41.** (a)

42 Suppose that a department contains 10 men and 15 women. Then total number of ways are there to form a committee with 6 members if it must have the same number of men and women :

(a) 53,600 (b) 52,600

(c) 51,600 (d) 54,600

43. A professor mathematics writes 40 true/false questions. Of the statement in these questions, 17 are true. If the questions can be positioned in any order, then the total possible answers keys are :

(a) $2^{17} + 2^{23}$ (b) 2^{40}

(c) 40^2 (d) None of these

44. How many bit strings contain exactly eight 0's and ten 1's if every 0 must be followed by a_1 :

(a) 18 (b) 27

(c) 36 (d) 45

45. How many bit strings of length 10 contains at least three 1's and at least three 0's ?

(a) 912 (b) 913

(c) 914 (d) 915

46. One hundred tickets, numbered 1, 2, 3, ... 99, 100 are sold to 100 different people for a drawing. Four different prizes are awarded, including a grand prize (a trip to Kullu-Manali). Then the total numbner of ways are to award the prizes if the grand prize winner is a person holding ticket 19, 47, 73 or 97 :

(a) 1, 764, 376 (b) 2, 764, 366

(c) 3, 764, 376 (d) 4, 764, 376

47. In the above problem total number of ways if the people holding the tickets 19 and 47 both win prizes :

(a) 214, 172 (b) 114, 172

(c) 214, 072 (d) 114, 072

48. If a group contains n men and n women. How many ways are there to arrange these people in a row if the men and women alternate ?

(a) $n! \times n!$ (b) $2 \times (n-1)!$

(c) $2 \times (n!)^2$ (d) $n! \times (n-1)!$

49. A club has 25 members. Then the total number of ways in which we can select a president, vicepresident, secretary and treasurer of the club :

(a) 303, 600 (b) 403, 600

(c) 600, 303 (d) 600, 403

50. ***Suppose that in B.I.T. Meerut, the number of bacteria doubles every hour, then the recurrence relation for the number of bacteria after n hour have elapsed is :***

(a) $a_n = a_{n-1} + a_{n-2}$ (b) $a_n = a_{n-1}$

(c) $a_n = 2a_{n-1}$ (d) $a_n = 3a_{n-1}$

51. ***In the above problem, if there are 100 bacteria initially, then the number of bacteria at the end of 10 hours :***

(a) 72900 (b) 204800

(c) 51200 (d) 102400

52. ***A factory makes custom sports cars at an increasing rate. In the first month only one car is made, in the second month two cars are made, and so on, with n cars mode in the nth month. Then the recurrence relation for the number of cars produced in the first n months :***

(a) $a_n = n + a_{n-1}, a_0 = 0$ (b) $a_n = a_{n-1} + a_{n-2}, a_0 = 0, a_1 = 1$

(c) $a_n = (a_{n-1})^2, a_0 = 0$ (d) $a_n = 2n + a_{n-1}, a_0 = 0$

53. ***In the above question what will be the explicit formula for the number of cars :***

(a) $a_n = n(n-1)(n-2)$ (b) $a_n = \frac{n(n+1)(2n+1)}{6}$

(c) $a_n = 2n + n^2$ (d) $a_n = \frac{n(n+1)}{2}$

54. ***The recurrence relation for the number of bit strings of length n that contain a pair of consecutive 0's :***

(a) $a_n = a_{n-1} + a_{n-2}\ ;\ n \geq 2$

(b) $a_n = 2a_{n-1} + 2^{n-2}\ ;\ n \geq 1$

(c) $a_{n-1} = 2a_{n-1} + a_{n-2} + 2^{n-2}\ ;\ n \geq 2$

(d) $a_n = a_{n-1} + a_{n-2} + 2^{n-2}\ ;\ n \geq 2$

55. ***The recurrence relation for the number of bit strings of length n that do not contain three consecutive 0's :***

(a) $a_n = a_{n-1} + a_{n-2} + 2^{n-2}\ ;\ n \geq 2$

(b) $a_n = a_{n-1} + a_{n-2} + 2^{n-2} + 3^{n-3}\ ;\ n \geq 2$

Answers : **42.*** (d) **43.** (b) **44.** (d) **45.** (a) **46.** (c) **47.** (d) **48.** (c) **49.** (a) **50.** (c) **51.** (d) **52.** (a) **53.** (d) **54.** (a)

(c) $a_n = a_{n-1} + a_{n-2} + a_{n-3}$; $n \geq 3$

(d) None of these

56. ***The recurrence relation for the number of ways to climb n stairs if the person climbing the stairs can take one stair or two stairs at a time :***

(a) $a_n = a_{n-1} + a_{n-2}$; $n \geq 2$

(b) $a_n = a_{n-1} + a_{n-2} + 2^{n-2}$; $n \geq 2$

(c) $a_n = n + a_{n-1}$; $n \geq 1$

(d) $a_n = a_{n-1} + 2a_{n-2}$; $n \geq 2$

57. ***The recurrence relation for the number of ternary strings that do not contain two consecutive 0's :***

(a) $a_n = a_{n-1} + 2a_{n-2}$; $n \geq 2$ (b) $a_n = 2a_{n-1} + a_{n-2}$; $n \geq 2$

(c) $a_n = 2a_{n-1} + 2a_{n-2}$; $n \geq 2$ (d) None of these

58 ***The recurrence relation for the number of ternary strings that do not contain two consecutive 0's or two consecutive 1's :***

(a) $a_n = a_{n-1} + 2a_{n-2}$; $n \geq 2$ (b) $a_n = 2a_{n-1} + 2a_{n-2}$; $n \geq 2$

(c) $a_n = 2a_{n-1} + a_{n-2}$; $n \geq 2$ (d) None of these

59. ***The recurrence relation for the number of ternary strings that do not contain consecutive symbols which are the same :***

(a) $a_n = a_{n-1} + a_{n-2}$; $n \geq 2$ (b) $a_n = 2a_{n-1}$; $n \geq 2$

(c) $a_n = 3a_{n-1}$; $n \geq 2$ (d) $a_n = a_{n-1} + 2^{n-1}$; $n \geq 2$

60. ***The recurrence relation for the number of ways to lay out a walkway with slate tiles if the tiles are red, green, or gray, so that no two red tiles are adjecent and tiles of the same colour are considered indistinguishable***

(a) $a_n = 2a_{n-1} + a_{n-2}$; $n \geq 2$ (b) $a_n = a_{n-1} + 2a_{n-2}$; $n \geq 2$

(c) $a_n = 2a_{n-1} + 2a_{n-2}$; $n \geq 2$ (d) None of these

61. ***The recurrence relation for the number of regions into which three dimensional space is divided into by n planes if every three of the planes meet in one point, but no four of the planes go through the same point :***

(a) $a_n = 2a_{n-1} + a_{n-2} + \frac{n(n+1)(n+2)}{6}$

(b) $a_n = a_{n-1} + a_{n-1} + 2^{n-3}$

(c) $a_n = a_{n-1} + \frac{(n^2 - n + 2)}{2}$

(d) $a_n = n + a_{n-1} + a_{n-2}$

62. ***The solution of the recurrence relation***
$\boldsymbol{a_n = 6a_{n-1} - 11a_{n-2} + 6a_{n-3}\ ;\ a_0 = 2,\ a_1 = 5,\ a_2 = 15}$
is given by :

(a) $a_n = 1 - 2^n + 3^n$
(b) $a_n = 1 - 2^n + 2.3^n$
(c) $a_n = 1 + 2^n + 3^n$
(d) $a_n = 1 + 2^n + 2.3^n$

63. ***The solution to the recurrence relation***
$\boldsymbol{a_n = -3a_{n-1} - 3a_{n-2} - a_{n-3}\ ;\ a_0 = 1,\ a_1 = -2,\ a_2 = -1}$
is given by :

(a) $a_n = (1 + 3n - 2n^2)(-1)^n$
(b) $a_n = (1 + 3n - n^2)(-1)^n$
(c) $a_n = (1 - 3n + n^2)(-1)^n$
(d) $a_n = (1 - 3n - 2n^2)(-1)^n$

64. ***The solution to the recurrence relation***
$\boldsymbol{a_n = 3a_{n-1} + 2n\ ;\ a_1 = 3}$ ***is :***

(a) $a_n = n + \frac{3}{2} + \left(\frac{11}{6}\right)2^n$
(b) $a_n = n + \frac{3}{2} - \left(\frac{11}{6}\right)3^n$
(c) $a_n = n + \frac{3}{2} + \left(\frac{11}{6}\right)2^n$
(d) $a_n = -n - \frac{3}{2} + \left(\frac{11}{6}\right)3^n$

65. ***Let a_n be the sum of the first n positive integers, so that***

$$\boldsymbol{a_n = \sum_{k=1}^{n} k\ ;\ a_1 = 1}$$

then the solution to a_n is :

(a) $a_n = n(n+1)$
(b) $a_n = n(n+1)(2n+1)$
(c) $a_n = \frac{n(n+1)(2n+1)}{6}$
(d) $a_n = \frac{n(n+1)}{2}$

66. ***All solutions to the recurrence relation***
$\boldsymbol{a_n = 5a_{n-1} - 6a_{n-2} + 2^n + 3n}$ ***is given by :***

(a) $a_n = \alpha \,.\, 2^n + \beta \,.\, 3^n - n \,.\, 2^{n+1} + \frac{3n}{2} + \frac{21}{4}$

(b) $a_n = \alpha \,.\, 3^n + \beta \,.\, 2^n + n \,.\, 2^{n+1} + \frac{3n}{2} + \frac{21}{4}$

Answers :

55. (c)	**56.** (a)	**57.** (c)	**58.** (c)	**59.** (b)	**60.** (c)
61. (c)	**62.** (b)	**63.** (a)	**64.** (d)	**65.** (d)	

(c) $a_n = \alpha \,.\, 2^n + \beta \,.\, 3^n - \frac{n^2}{4} + \frac{1}{8}$

(d) None of these

67. ***Total number of comparisons are needed for a binary search in a set of 64 elements :***

(a) 7 (b) 14

(c) 21 (d) 16

68. ***Suppose that*** $f(n) = f\left(\frac{n}{3}\right) + 1$ ***when n is divisible by 3 and*** $f(1) = 1$***, then*** $f(729)$ ***is :***

(a) 7 (b) 14

(c) 21 (d) 16

69. ***Suppose that*** $f(n) = f\left(\frac{n}{5}\right) + 3n^2$ ***when n is divisible by 5 and*** $f(1) = 4$***, then*** $f(3125)$ ***is :***

(a) 30, 517, 579 (b) 30, 517, 479

(c) 30, 517, 379 (d) 30, 517, 279

70. ***Suppose that*** $f(n) = f\left(\frac{n}{2}\right) + 1$***, and*** $n = 2^k$ ***with*** $f(1) = 1$***. Then the size of f if f is an increasing function :***

(a) $O(\log n)$ (b) $O(\log 3^n)$

(c) $O(n^{\log 3^2})$ (d) none of these

71. ***Suppose that*** $f(x) = 5 \,.\, f\left(\frac{n}{4}\right) + 6n$ ***and*** $n = 4^k$ ***with*** $f(1) = 1$***. Then the size of f if f is an increasing function :***

(a) $O(\log n)$ (b) $O({}_n \log 5^4)$

(c) $O({}_n \log 3^2)$ (d) $O({}_n \log 4^5)$

72. ***The integral solutions are of*** $x_1 + x_2 + x_3 + x_4 = 20$ ***if*** $1 \le x_1 \le 6$***,*** $1 < x_2 \le 7$***,*** $1 \le x_3 \le 8$***, and*** $1 \le x_4 \le 9$ ***:***

(a) 217 (b) 225

(c) 296 (d) 196

73. ***Suppose we repeatedly bet Rs 1 on the toss of a coin; heads you win, tails I win. Each of us has a probability of*** $\frac{1}{2}$ ***of winning on each flip of the coin. Suppose, further, that you have Rs 100 and I have Rs***

200 to begin with. Let a_n be the probability that you win all Rs 300 when you have n rupees. Then the recurrence relation for a_n is :

(a) $a_n = a_{n-1} + a_{n+1}$; $n \geq 2$

(b) $a_n = 2a_{n-1} + a_{n+1}$; $n \geq 2$

(c) $a_n = a_{n-1} + 2a_{n+1}$; $n \geq 2$

(d) $a_n = \frac{1}{2} a_{n-1} + \frac{1}{2} a_{n+1}$; $n \geq 2$

74. ***Let a_0, a_1, a_2 be the lucas sequence i.e., $a_n = a_{n-1} + a_{n-2}$; $n \geq 2$ and $a_0 = 2$, $a_1 = 1$, then the value of $a_0 + a_1 + a_2 + ... + a_n$ is :***

(a) $a_{n+1} - 1$

(b) $a_{n+2} - 1$

(c) $a_{n+1} + a_{n+2}$

(d) $a_{n-1} + a_{n+1}$

75. ***The values of C_1 and C_2 such that the recursion $a_n + C_1 a_{n-1} + C_2 a_{n-2} = 0$ has the characteristic roots $1 \pm \sqrt{-1}$:***

(a) $C_1 = 2$ $C_2 = 2$

(b) $C_1 = 2$ $C_2 = -2$

(c) $C_1 = -2$ $C_2 = -2$

(d) $C_1 = -2$ $C_2 = 2$

76. ***The solution to the recursion $a_{n+1} = \sqrt{5}\, a_n$ and $a_0 = 2$ is :***

(a) $2(5)^n$, $n \geq 0$

(b) $2(5)^{-n}$, $n \geq 0$

(c) $2(5)^{n/2}$, $n \geq 0$

(d) $2(5)^{-n/2}$, $n \geq 0$

77. ***The generating function to the sequence 1, − 1, 1, − 1, ,1, − 1, ... is :***

(a) $(1 + z)^{-1}$

(b) $(1 + 2z)^{-1}$

(c) $(1 - z)^{-1}$

(d) $(1 - 2z)^{-1}$

78. ***The generating function to the sequence 1, 2, 4, 8, 16, 32, ... is :***

(a) $(1 + z)^{-1}$

(b) $(1 + 2z)^{-1}$

(c) $(1 - z)^{-1}$

(d) $(1 - 2z)^{-1}$

79. ***If the generating function of a sequence $a_0, a_1, a_2, ...$ is given by $A(z) = \dfrac{2}{1 - 4z^2}$, then a_n is :***

(a) $-2^n - (-2)^n$

(b) $2^n + (-2)^n$

(c) $2^n - (-2)^n$

(d) $-2^n + (-2)^n$

80. ***The generating function of $(n + 1)\, a_n$ is :***

(a) $(1 - az)^{-1}$

(b) $(1 + az)^{-1}$

(c) $(1 - az)^{-2}$

(d) $(1 + az)^{-2}$

Answers : **66.** (b) **67.** (b) **68.** (a) **69.** (a) **70.** (a) **71.** (d) **72** (a) **73.** (a) **74.** (b) **75.** (d) **76.** (c) **77.** (a) **78.** (d) **79.** (b) **80.** (c)

81. ***The generating function for bna^n is :***

(a) $abz\,(1 - az)^{-1}$ (b) $abz\,(1 + az)^{-1}$

(c) $abz\,(1 - az)^{-2}$ (d) $abz\,(1 + az)^{-2}$

82. ***The generating function for ^kC_n is :***

(a) $(1 + z)^k$ (b) $(1 - z)^{-k}$

(c) $(1 - z)^k$ (d) $(1 + z)^{-k}$

83. ***Coefficient of x^{23} in $(1 + x^5 + x^9)^{10}$ is :***

(a) 10 !/5 ! 4 ! (b) 10 !/8 !

(c) 10 !/2 ! 7 ! (d) (10) !/3 ! 6 !

84. ***The generating function for a_r i.e., the number of ways of distributing r similar balls in 7 boxes numbered 1, 2, 3, ... where the 2nd, 3rd, 4th and 5th boxes are non-empty :***

(a) $(1 + x + \ldots)^3(x + x^2 + \ldots)^4$ (b) $(1 + x + \ldots)^{-3}(1 + x^2 + x^4 + \ldots)^{-4}$

(c) $(1 + x + \ldots)^3(1 + x^2 + x^4 + \ldots)^{-4}$ (d) $(1 + x + x^2 + \ldots)^{-3}(x + x^2 + \ldots)^4$

85. ***The generating function for the sequence $A = \sum_{r=0}^{\infty} a_r$ where***

$$a_r = \begin{cases} 1 & \text{if } 0 \le r \le 2 \\ 3 & \text{if } 3 \le r \le 5 \\ 0 & \text{if } r \ge 6 \end{cases}$$

is :

(a) $1 + x + x^2 + 3x^3 + 3x^4 + 3x^5$

(b) $1 - x + x^2 - 3x^3 + 3x^4 - 3x^5 + \ldots$

(c) $-1 - x - x^2 - 3x^3 - 3x^4 - 3x^5 \ldots$

(d) $1 + x + x^2 + 3x^3 + 3x^4 + 3x^5 + 6x^6 + 6x^7 + \ldots$

86. ***How many ways are there to place an order for 12 chocolate sundaes if there are 5 types of sundaes, and at most 4 sundaes of one type are allowed ?***

(a) $C(16, 9) + C(5, 2)\,C(11, 8) - C(5, 3)\,C(6, 3)$

(b) $C(16, 12) + C(5, 1)\,C(11, 7) + C(5, 2)\,C(6, 2)$

(c) $C(16, 12) + C(5, 1)\,C(11, 7) - C(5, 2)\,C(6, 2)$

(d) $C(16, 12) - C(5, 1)\,C(11, 7) + C(5, 2)\,C(6, 2)$

87. ***In which function the coefficient of x^{12} is $(-2)^{12}\,C(19, 12)$?***

(a) $(1 + 2x)^{-19}$ (b) $(1 - 4x)^{19}$

(c) $(1 - x)^{19}$ (d) $(1 - 2x)^{19}$

88. ***In haw many ways 10 identical balloons can be given to four children if each child receives at least two balloons ?***

(a) 5 (b) 10

(c) 15 (d) 20

89. ***The prabability when four number from 1 to 100, inclusive are picked at random with no repetitions allowed, either all are odd, all are divisible by 3, or all are divisible by 5 :***

(a) 4972/71,295 (b) 9472/71,295

(c) 4729/71,295 (d) 9274/71,295

90. ***The total number of solutions of the equation***

$$x_1 + x_2 + x_3 = 11$$

have, where x_1, x_2, x_3 are non-negative integers, with $x_1 \leq 3$, $x_2 \leq 4$ and $x_3 \leq 6$:

(a) 6 (b) 8

(c) 10 (d) 12

91. ***The total number of elements are in the union of four sets if the sets have 50, 60, 70 and 80 elements, respectively, each pair of the sets has 5 elements in common, each triple of the sets has one common element, and no element is in all four sets :***

(a) 234 (b) 432

(c) 423 (d) 243

92. ***The total number of permutations of the 10 digits either begin with the three digits 987, contain the digit 45 in the fifth and sixth positions, or end with the 3 digits 123 :***

(a) 50, 183 (b) 50, 831

(c) 50, 318 (d) 50, 138

93. ***Total number of bit strings of length eight do not contain six consecutive 0's :***

(a) 248 (b) 284

(c) 348 (d) 384

94. ***The total number of ways can the digits 0, 1, 2, 3, 4, 5, 6, 7, 8, 9 be arranged so that no even digit is in its original position :***

(a) 2,170,880 (b) 2,170,780

(c) 2,170,680 (d) 2,170,580

Answers : **81.** (c) **82.** (a) **83.** (c) **84.** (a) **85.** (a) **86.** (d) **87.** (d) **88.** (b) **89.** (a) **90.** (a) **91.** (a) **92.** (d) **93.** (a) **94.** (c)

95. ***A group of 10 people begin a chain letter with each person sending the letter to 4 other people. Each of these people sends the letter to 4 additional people. Then the recurrence relation for the number of letters sent at the nth stage of this chain letter if no person ever receives more than one letter :***

(a) $a_n = a_{n-1}$; $n \geq 1$, $a_1 = 40$ (b) $a_n = 2a_{n-1}$; $n \geq 1$, $a_1 = 40$

(c) $a_n = 3a_{n-1}$; $n \geq 1$, $a_1 = 40$ (d) $a_n = 4a_{n-1}$; $n \geq 1$, $a_1 = 40$

96. ***A machine that inserts letters into envelops goes haywire and inserts letters randomly into envelops. Then the probability that in a group of 100 letters exactly 1 letter is put into the correct envelop :***

(a) D 100/(100) ! (b) C (100, 2)/(100) !

(c) 0 (d) 100 D 99/(100) !

97. ***The total number of positive integral solutions are there to the equation***

$$x_1 + x_2 + x_3 = 20$$

with $2 < x_1 < 6$, $6 < x_2 < 10$ ***and*** $0 < x_3 < 5$ **:**

(a) 0 (b) 1

(c) 2 (d) 3

98. ***A class is composed of 2 brother and 6 other guys. In haw many ways can all the boys be seated at a round table so that the two brothers are not seated together ?***

(a) 2050 (b) 3600

(c) 2600 (d) 3000

99. ***The sum of all numbers greater than 10,000 formed by using the digits 0, 2, 4, 6, 8 no digit being repeated in any number is :***

(a) 5199960 (b) 2742790

(c) 2449002 (d) 8411420

100. ***For a game in which 2 partners oppose 2 other partners, six men are available. If every possible pair must play against every other pair, the number of games to be played is :***

(a) 42 (b) 45

(c) 48 (d) 90

101. ***At any time, the total number of persons on earth who have shaken hands an odd number of times has to be :***

(a) an even number (b) an odd number

(c) a prime number (d) a perfect square

102. ***Six x's have to placed in the squares in the adjacent figure such that each row contains at least one x. This can be done in :***

(a) 26 ways

(b) 110 ways

(c) 180 ways

(d) 210 ways

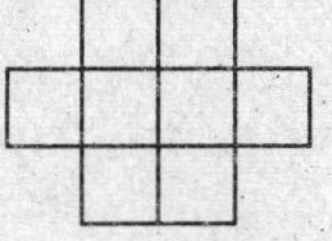

103. ***Ten different letters are given five letter words are formed from these given letters. The number of words which have at least one letter repeated is***

(a) 92,182 (b) 69,760

(c) 29,160 (d) 87,882

104. ***The number of permutations of 'n' different things taken not more than 'r' at a time, with repetitions being allowed is :***

(a) $\left(\dfrac{n^r - 1}{n - 1}\right)$ (b) $\dfrac{(n^r - r)}{(n - 1)\,!}$

(c) $\dfrac{n\,(n^r - 1)}{(n - 1)}$ (d) $\dfrac{(n^r - 1)}{n\,!}$

Answers :

95. (a)	**96.** (a)	**97.** (a)	**98.*** (b)	**99.*** (a)
100.* (b)	**101.*** (a)	**102.*** (a)	**103.*** (b)	**104.*** (c)

SOLUTIONS

1. By the principle of multiplication $= 6 \times 6 \times 6 \times 6 = 6^4$

2. Because repetitions are not allowed, therefore one time we can use all the 6 digits, second time we can use only 5 digits, ... so on. Hence by the principle of multiplication $= 6 \times 5 \times 4 \times 3$

3. For first two number there are 8 possibilities and for 3rd total 9 possibilities, while for the remaining there are 10 possibilities.

Hence by principle of multiplication $= 8 \times 8 \times 9 \times 10 \times 10 \times 10 \times 10$.

4. By the principle of multiplication $= 26 \times 26 \times 26 \times 10 \times 10 \times 10$ because repetition is allowed.

5. Because between 1 and 10,000 we have at most 4 digits in which only one 8 and one 9 are there, so, there will be 4 ways for 8 and then 3 ways to 9 and remaining 8 digits can take the other two places.

Hence total ways $= 4 \times 3 \times 8 \times 8$.

6. We know that total vowels are 5 and consonents are 21, there- fore total ways for a 5 letter word

$$= 5 \times 21 \times 21 \times 21 \times 5$$

$$= 5^2 \times 21^3$$

8. Total ways from A to $B = 5$

Total ways from B to $C = 3$

Hence by principle of multiplication $= 5 \times 3$.

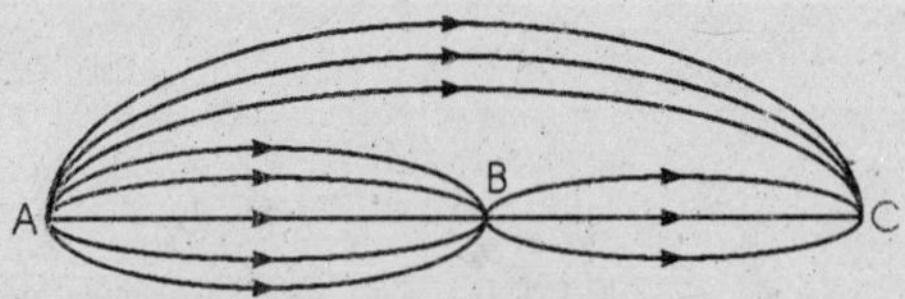

9. In this total ways from A to C via $B = 15$

But there are 3 ways also from A to C directly, hence total ways altogether $= 15 + 3 = 18$ ways.

10. Total ways from A to C via $B = 15$

Similarly ways from C to A via $B = 15$

$\therefore$ Total ways (Going and Coming) $= 15 \times 15 = 225$.

11. Total ways from A to C via $B = 15$

Total ways from C to A directly $= 3$

$\therefore$ Total number of ways = $15 \times 3 = 45$ ways

12. If to the Newborn child given one name then the total number of ways = 300

If given two names (No name repeated) = 300×299

If three name given (No name repeated) = $300 \times 299 \times 298$

$\therefore$ By the principle of addition total no. of ways

$$= 300 + 300 \times 299 + 300 \times 299 \times 298$$

14. In terms of sizes total ways = 10

In terms of variety total ways = 2

In terms of quality total ways = 3

In terms of color total ways = 2

Hence by the principle of nultiplication = $10 \times 2 \times 3 \times 2$.

17. Because total good bulbs = 92

Total defective bulbs = 80

Hence by principle of addition and multiplication we have the total no. of ways

$$= C(92, 6) \times C(8, 4) + C(92, 5) \times C(8, 5)$$

18. Because men and women should be equal, therefore the selection will be as (1, 1), (2, 2), (3, 3), (4, 4), (15, 5)

Hence total ways

$$= C(9, 1)\, C(5, 1) + C(9, 2)\, C(5, 2) + C(9, 3)\, C(5, 3) + C(9, 4)\, C(5, 4) + C(9, 5)\, C(5, 5)$$

19. Total ways are

$$= (9, 1)\, C(6, 2) + C(9, 2)\, C(6, 3) + C(9, 3)\, C(6, 4) + C(9, 4)\, C(6, 5) + C(9, 5)\, C(6, 6)$$

20. Total number of ways

$$= C(10, 5) + C(10, 4)\, C(7, 1) + C(10, 3)\, C(7, 2) + C(10, 3)\, C(7, 1)\, C(13, 1) + C(10, 2)\, C(7, 2)\, C(3, 1)$$

21. When No repetition is allowed, then total number of ways

$$= C(5, 3)\, C(21, 6) + C(5, 4)\, C(21, 5) + C(5, 5)\, C(21, 4)$$

22. The total number of non-negative integral solutions to $x_1 + x_2 + \ldots + x_n = m$ is given by

$$C(m + n - 1, n)$$

42. Total ways are

$$C(10, 3) \times C(15, 3)$$

98. The required value is, number of arrangements with out repetition

$$(8-1)!-(7-1)!\,2!=6!\times(7-2)$$

99. Including 0 occupying the most significant position, the sum will be

$$24\,(2+4+6+8)\,(10{,}000+1000+100+10+1)=24\times 20\times 11111 \quad ...(1)$$

Out of these, 0 occupies the most significant place in 4 ! numbers. Sum of these will be

$$\frac{4\,!}{4}\,(2+4+6+8)\,(1000+100+10+1)=6\times 20\times 1111 \quad ...(2)$$

Required sum = (1) – (2).

100. It is $\frac{{}^6C_2 \times {}^4C_2}{2} = 45.$

101. Because two persons will shaken hand one time and the next every person will be added continuously *i.e.*, if there are n persons, so total hands shaken will be $(n-1)$ and therefore if $(n-1)$ is odd, so n will be even.

102. There are 8 available squares and we have to select 6, this can be done in $C(8, 6) = 28$ ways. This includes two possibilities which should be ignored. One with top row empty and second one is with bottom row empty. So required possibilities = 28 – 2 = 26 ways.

103. $10^5 - {}^{10}P_5 = 69{,}760.$

104. Here we have to arrange 1 or 2 or 3 or ... or r at a time. Therefore number of ways of arranging 1 at a time is n

number of ways of arranging 2 at a time is n^2

number of ways of arranging 3 at a time is n^3

....

....

number of ways of arranging r at a time is n^r

∴ Total number of ways = $n + n^2 + ... + n^r$

■□■

CHAPTER 16

NUMERICAL ANALYSIS

1. ***In Numerical analysis, accuracy means***
   (a) The number of significant figures representing a quantity
   (b) The spread in repeated readings of an instrument in measuring a particular physical quantity
   (c) The proximity of an approximate number or measurement to the true value it is supposed to represent
   (d) All of the above
2. ***Which of the following remains about an ill-Conditioned system of equations are true?***
   (a) Small change in coefficient will result in large change in solution
   (b) A wide range of solutions can approximately satisfy the equations
   (c) If slope of two lines are almost same, they make up an ill- conditioned system of equations
   (d) None of these
3. ***Consider the equation $x^7 - 2x^5 + 7x^4 + x^3 - 9 = 0$. The number of imaginary roots will be atleast***
   (a) 1 (b) 2
   (c) 3 (d) 4
4. ***The advantages of partial pivoting in the solution of a system of equations are***
   (a) ill-conditioned system can be handled efficiently
   (b) division by zero can be avoided
   (c) round-off errors can be minimized
   (d) All of the above
5. ***The number of real roots of the equation***

   $$|x|^2 - 3|x| + 2 = 0 \text{ is}$$

   (a) 4 (b) 3
   (c) 2 (d) 1
6. $-20\sqrt{-20\sqrt{-20\sqrt{\ldots\infty}}}$ ***equal to***

Answers : **1.** (c) **2.** (a),(b),(c) **3.*** (b) **4.** (d) **5.** (a)

(a) -1
(b) -2
(c) -3
(d) -4

7. ***If $|x - 1| + |x - 2| + |x - 3| \geq 6$, then which of the following is true***
(a) $x \leq 0$ or $x \geq 4$
(b) $x \leq 3$
(c) $x \geq 1$
(d) $1 \leq x \leq 3$

8. ***The error in using Simpson's rule is of order***
(a) h
(b) h^2
(c) h^3
(d) h^4

9. ***The iteration formula to find the square root of a positive real number b, using Newton-Raphson method***
(a) $x_{K+1} = \frac{3(x_K + b)}{2x_K}$
(b) $x_{K+1} = x_K - \frac{2x_K}{x_K^2 + b}$
(c) $x_{K+1} = \frac{x_K^2 + b)}{2x_K}$
(d) None of the above

10. ***If f(a) and f(b) are of the same sign, then f(x) = 0***
(a) has either no root or odd number of roots between a and b
(b) has either no root or even number of roots between a and b
(c) must have atleast one root between a and b
(d) has odd number of roots between a and b

11. ***Any polynomial of even degree in which the last term is negative and the coefficient of the highest power is positive, has at least***
(a) 2 positive roots
(b) 2 positive and 1 negative root
(c) 2 negative roots
(d) 1 positive and 1 negative

12. ***If $\log_5 10 = \log_7 x . \log_n m$, then the values of x, m, n are***
(a) 6, 3, 1
(b) 7, 4, 2
(c) -3, 2, 1
(d) 10, 7, 5

13. ***The equation $x^5 + x^3 - 8x - 5 = 0$ has***
(a) exactly 3 real roots and 2 complex roots
(b) no complex root
(c) no real root
(d) exactly 2 real and 3 complex roots

14. ***When the polynomial f(x) is divided by $(x - \alpha)(x - \beta)$, $\alpha \neq \beta$, then the remainder is given by***
(a) $\frac{(x-\beta) f(\alpha) - (x-\alpha) f(\beta)}{\alpha - \beta}$
(b) $\frac{f(\alpha) - f(\beta)}{\alpha - \beta}$

(c) $\dfrac{(x-\alpha)\,f(\beta)-(x-\beta)\,f(\alpha)}{\alpha-\beta}$ (d) $\dfrac{(x-\alpha)\,f(\beta)\,f(\beta)+(x-\beta)\,(f\alpha)}{\alpha-\beta}$

15. ***What is the value of log 0***

(a) ∞ (b) $-\infty$

(c) undefined (d) depends on the base

16. ***If a_1 - a_2,.....a_n are the roots of the equation $x^n + nax - b = 0$, then $(a_1 - a_2)(a_1 - a_3).....(a_1 - a_n)$ equals to***

(a) $n(a+a_1^{n-1})$ (b) $\dfrac{(a+a_1^{n-1})}{n}$

(c) $n(a-a_1^{n-1})$ (d) $\dfrac{(a-a_1^{n-1})}{n}$

17. ***Let us consider a function y = f(x) which have a root in [a, b]. Then to obtion an accuracy ε, how many interations, we required if the process is repeated n times***

(a) $\dfrac{(b-a)^n}{2}\le\varepsilon$ (b) $\dfrac{(b-a)}{2^n}\ge\varepsilon$

(c) $\dfrac{(b-a)}{2^n}\le\varepsilon$ (d) $\dfrac{(b-a)^n}{2}\ge\varepsilon$

18. ***Which of the following methods gives the least error when e^x is integrated from 0 to 0.4?***

(a) Trapezoidal rule with the internal width as 0.2

(b) trapezoidal rule with the interval width as 0.1

(c) Simpson's 1/3 rule with the interval width as 0.1

(d) Simpson's 1/3 rule with the interval width as 0.2

19. ***In the expansion $1-\dfrac{x^2}{2!}+\dfrac{x^4}{4!}\ldots+(-1)^n\dfrac{x^{2n}}{2!}+\ldots$ for 5 digit accuracy, if $|x|<\dfrac{\pi}{2}$ the number of terms in the series that should be considered is***

(a) 5 (b) 6

(c) 7 (d) 8

20. ***If one has to obtain the roots of $x^2 - 2x + \log 2 = 0$ to four decimal places, log 2 should be given to the accuracy of approximately***

(a) 8×10^{-5} (b) 7×10^{-5}

(c) 8×10^{6} (d) 7×10^{-6}

Answers : **6.** (d) **7.** (a) **8.** (d) **9.*** (b) **10.*** (b) **11.*** (d) **12.*** (d) **13.*** (d) **14.*** (a) **15.** (d) **16.*** (c) **17.** (b) **18.** (c) **19.*** (c) **20.*** (a)

21. *Newton-Rapson method*

(a) is not efficient to obtain multiple roots

(b) have a slow rate of convergence

(c) should not be preferred if there is a point of inflextion in the vicnity of the root

(d) should not be preferred if the graph of the curve is almost parallel to the x axis, in the vicinity of the root

(e) All of the above

22. *If a function y = f(x) has an inverse function, then f(x) cannot be*

(a) symmertric about x-axis (b) symmetric about y-axis

(c) an odd function (d) an even function

23. *Trapezoidal rule gives the exact solution when the curve is*

(a) concave towards the base line (b) convex towards the base line

(c) a straight line (d) All of the above

24. *In the bisection method for finding the roots of an equation, the approximate relative error is always*

(a) greater than the relative error (b) equal to the relative error

(c) less than the relative error (d) none of these

25. *Backward Euler's method (Modified Euler's Method) for solving the differential equation dy / dx = f(x, y) is specified by*

(a) $y_{n+1} = y_n + h f(x_n, y_n)$ (b) $y_{n-1} = y_{n-1} + 2h f(x_n, y_n)$

(c) $y_{n+1} = y_n + h f(x_{n+1}, y_{n+1})$ (d) $y_{n+1} = (1 + h) f(x_{n+1}, y_{n+1})$

26. *The method(s) of interpolation is (are)*

(a) the graphical method (b) the method of least squares

(c) the method of finite differences (d) All of the above

27. *The process of estimating the value of y (dependent variable) for any value of x (the independent variable) with in the given limits (or interval) is called*

(a) Interpolation (b) Extrapolation

(c) Fore casting (d) All of the above

28. *If $u_1 = 1$, $u_2 = 8$, $u_3 = 27$, $u_4 = 4$, $u_5 = 125$, $u_6 = 216$, $u_7 = 343$, then u_8*

(a) 625 (b) 349

(c) 512 (d) 486

29. *If E = 1 + Δ, then the 8th term of the series 1, 1, 3, 7, 13, ...*

(a) 21 (b) 23

(c) 19 (d) 25

30. *Data collection about each and every item in the populatino is called*

(a) sample survey (b) pilot survey

(c) census survey (d) primary data

31. *A function f(x) will be a cubic spline if*

(a) f(x) is a linear polynomial outside the internal (x_0, x_n)

(b) f(x) is a Cubic polynomial in each of the subintervals

(c) $f(x)$ and $f'(x)$ are continuous at each point

(d) All of the above

32. *Which of the following are true*

(a) Interpolation is the technique of estimating the value of a function for any intermediate value of the independent variable

(b) Extra polation is the process of estimating the value of the function out side the given range

(c) The study of Interpolation is based on the calculus of finite differences

(d) Newton's backward interpolation formula is used for interpolating the values of y near the starting of tabulated values

33. *Which of the following(s) is/are false for the choice of an interpolation formula*

(a) to find a tabulated value near the beginning of the table, use Newton's forward formula

(b) to find a tabulated value near the end of the table, use Newton's backward formula

(c) To find a tabulated value near the centre of the table, use either stirling's or Bessel's or Everett's formula

(d) None of the above

34. *Which of the following method(s) have the greatest rate of convergence*

(a) Newton Raphson method (b) Regula-Falsi method

(c) Bisection Method (d) All of the above

35. *What is the order of the rate of convergence of Newton Raphson method*

(a) Linear (b) quadratic

(c) Cubic (d) Biquadratic

36. *What is the order of the Generalised Newton's formula for determining a multiple root*

Answers : **21.** (e) **22.** (b),(d) **23.** (c) **24.** (a) **25.** (a) **26.** (d) **27.** (a) **28.** (c) **29.** (a) **30.** (c) **31.** (d) **32.*** (d) **33.** (d) **34.*** (a) **35.*** (b)

(a) Linear (b) quadratic
(c) Cubic (d) Biquadratic

37. ***In which of these method(s) we have no requirement of any prior information about the roots***

(a) Newton Raphson method (b) Bisection method
(c) Mullter's method (d) Graffer's root squaring method

38. ***If the roots are real and distinct, then which of the following is the most suitable***

(a) Newtion Raphson method (b) Muller's method
(c) Horner's method (d) Graeffer's root squaring method

39. ***Find the number of students who obtained less than 45 marks, from the following data :***

Marks	***30—40***	***40—50***	***50—60***	***60—70***	***70—80***
No. of students	***31***	***42***	***51***	***35***	***31***

(a) 45 (b) 75
(c) 105 (d) 52

40. ***The root of*** x^3–2x–5=0 ***correct to three decimal places by using Newton-Raphson method is***

(a) 2.0946 (b) 0.2713
(c) 1.7321 (d) 0.7011

41. ***The real root of*** e^x ***= cot x correct of four significant figures by interative method is***

(a) 0.5314 (b) 0.7011
(c) 1.7321 (d) 2.7132

42. ***The general term of the series 3, 9, 20, 28, 65,..... is***

(a) $\frac{1}{2}(x+1)$ (b) $\frac{1}{6}(2x+3)(2x+1)$
(c) $\frac{1}{6}(2x^2+3x+2)$ (d) $\frac{1}{6}(2x^3+3x^2+13x)$

43. ***The 7th term of the series 3, 9, 20, 38, 65,..... is***

(a) 154 (b) 165
(c) 175 (d) 184

44. ***The real root of sin x = 10 (x - 1) correct to four significant figures by iterative method, is***

(a) 3.1927 (b) 2.7932

(c) 1.6071 (d) 1.088

45. ***The solution of $x^2 + y = 11$***

$$y^2 + x = 7$$

system of nonlinear equations, are by Newton's method

(a) + 1.9266, - 1.8533 (b) 3.584428, = 1.848127

(c) 0.58273, 3.27278 (d) None of the above

46. ***The root of sin x = 1 - x correct of three decimal places by using Newton-Raphson method is***

(a) 0.7011 (b) 0.2713

(c) 0.1312 (d) 0.5110

47. ***The population of a town in decimal census were as under :***

Year	*1921*	*1931*	*1941*	*1951*	*1961*
Population (in thousands)	*46*	*66*	*81*	*93*	*101*

Estimate the population for the year 1955.

(a) 96.66 thousand (b) 99.67 thousand

(c) 94.73 thousand (d) 95.69 thousand

48. ***Given $u_2 = 110$, $u_1 = 108$, $u_0 = 105$, $u_{-1} = 110$, find $u_{1/2}$ by Gauss's forward formula.***

(a) 107 (b) 108

(c) 104 (d) 106

49. ***Given $u_{14} = 3.4707$, $u_{18} = 2.8143$, $u_{22} = 2.1069$, $u_{26} = 1.3431$ and $u_{30} = 0.5153$, find u_{23} by Gauss's forward formula.***

(a) 1.7128 (b) 1.8273

(c) 1.9284 (d) 1.9158

50. ***Given that $a = 10.00 \pm 0.05$***

$$b = 0.0356 \pm 0.0002$$

$$c = 15300 \pm 100$$

$$d = 62000 \pm 500$$

Find the maximum value of the absolute error in a + b + c + d.

(a) 1000.05 (b) 600.05

(c) 738.07 (d) None of the above

51. ***The root of $x^3 - 18 = 0$ correct to three decimal places by method of the false position is***

Answers : **36.** (b) **37.** (d) **38.** (d) **39.** (d) **40.** (a) **41.** (c) **42.** (d) **43.** (a) **44.** (d) **45.** (b) **46.** (d) **47.** (a) **48.** (d) **49.** (d) **50.** (b)

(a) 2.6207 (b) 2.7065

(c) 1.7963 (d) None of the above

52. ***The root of $x^3 + x^2 + x + 7 = 0$ correct to three decimal places by method of false position is***

(a) 2.7065 (b) - 2.1049

(c) 1.7963 (d) None of the above

53. ***Given $u_1 = 5225$, $u_6 = 4316$, $u_{11} = 3236$, $u_{16} = 1926$. Find u_{21}***

(a) 3937 (b) 3538

(c) 3327 (d) 306

54. ***The real root of cos x = 3x - 1 correct to four significant figures by iterative method is***

(a) 0.7073 (b) 0.6071

(c) 0.1275 (d) 0.6566

55. ***The value of $\sqrt{102} - \sqrt{101}$ correct to four significant figures is***

(a) 0.04963 (b) 0.01729

(c) 0.1273 (d) None of the above

56. ***The finite difference method of interpolation was originated by***

(a) Thomson Jacob (b) Athanasios Paoulis

(c) Sri Issac Newton (d) J. P. Tremblay

57. ***The finite difference method of interpolation gives best possible estimates on the basis of***

(a) the variables y whose value is to be estimated is a function of the other variable x

(b) the function can be expressed in a polynomial form

(c) the changes in the values of y are also supposed to be uniform without the sudden downward or upward trends

(d) All of the above

58. ***If $u_x = \frac{1}{x^2 + 5x + 6}$. Find u_{10}***

(a) $-\frac{1}{(1 + x)(x + 4)}$ (b) $\frac{-2}{(x + 1)(x + 2)(x + 3)}$

(c) $\frac{-2}{(x + 2)(x + 3)(x + 4)}$ (d) None of the above

59. ***Find u_0 given that $u_0 = -3$, $u_1 = 6$, $u_2 = 8$, $u_3 = 12$; third differences being constant***

(a) 57 (b) 120

(c) 126 (d) None of the above

60. ***By using the relation E = 1 + Δ find the first term of the series whose second term and the subsequent term are 8, 3, 0, -1, 0, ...***

(a) 17 (b) 9

(c) 15 (d) None of the above

61. ***If u_x is a rational integral function of x of degree n, then nth difference of this polynomial is constant and the (n + 1)th and higher differences are***

(a) one (b) zero

(c) infinite (d) None of the above

62. ***By extending the difference table on either side find u_0 and u_8 being given that***

$u_1 = 4$, $u_2 = 8$, $u_3 = 14$, $u_4 = 22$, $u_5 = 32$, $u_6 = 44$ and $u_7 = 58$

(a) $u_0 = 2$, $u_8 = 74$ (b) $u_0 = 2$ $u_8 = 78$

(c) $u_0 = 4$ $u_8 = 80$ (d) None of the above

63. ***Find the polynomial of 4th degree from the following data***

$u_0 = 1$, $u_1 = 1$, $u_2 = 11$, $u_3 = 61$, $u_4 = 205$, $u_5 = 521$

(a) $u_x = 1 - x + x^2 + x^3 + x^4$ (b) $u_x = 1 + x - x^2 + x^3 - x^4$

(c) $u_x = 1 - 2x + 3x^2 - 4x^3 + 5x^4$ (d) None of the above

64. ***The population of a country is as given below. Estimate the population for the year 1925.***

Year t :	***1891***	***1901***	***1911***	***1921***	***1931***
Population (000) u_t :	***46***	***66***	***81***	***93***	***101***

(a) 96.8368 (b) 92.7329

(c) 99.3117 (d) None of the above

65. ***Find the number of students who obtain less than 45 marks, from the following data :***

Marks :	**30-40**	**40-50**	**50-60**	**60-70**	**70-80**
No. of students :	**31**	**42**	**51**	**35**	**31**

(a) 62 (b) 53

(c) 48 (d) None of the above

66. ***Find the missing data :***

x = 0 1 2 3 4

Answers : **51.** (a) **52.** (b) **53.** (d) **54.** (b) **55.** (a) **56.** (c) **57.** (d) **58.** (c) **59.** (c) **60.** (c) **61.** (b) **62.** (a) **63.** (a) **64.** (a) **65.** (c)

$u_x =$ 580 556 520 — 385

(a) 400 (b) 410

(c) 465 (d) None of the above

67. *Find the above value of A and B in the following table :*

$x = 0$	0.1	0.2	0.3	0.4	0.5	0.6
$u_x = 0.135$	A	0.111	0.10	B	0.082	0.074

(a) A = 0.128, B = 0.098 (b) A = 0.123, B = 0.090

(c) A = 0.131, B = 0.089 (d) None of the above

68. *Using $u_x = (a + \Delta)^x u_0$. Find u_9 given that*

$u_0 = 1, u_1 = 11, u_2 = 21, u_3 = 28, u_4 = 29$

(a) 20 (b) - 17

(c) - 161 (d) None of the above

69. *The Lagrange's Interpolation Formula is*

(a) $$u_x = \frac{(x-b)(x-c)\ldots(x-j)(x-k)}{(a-b)(a-c)\ldots(a-j)(a-k)} u_a + \frac{(x-a)(x-c)\ldots(x-j)(x-k)}{(b-a)(b-c)\ldots(b-j)(b-k)} u_b + \frac{(x-a)(x-b)\ldots(x-j)(x-k)}{(c-a)(c-b)\ldots(c-j)(c-k)} u_c \ldots + \frac{(x-a)(x-b)\ldots(x-j)}{(k-a)(k-b)\ldots(k-j)} u_k$$

(b) $$u_x = \frac{u_a}{(x-a)(x-b)\ldots} + \frac{u_b}{(a-x)(a-b)\ldots} + \ldots$$

(c) $$u_x = \frac{(x-a)(x-b)\ldots(x-j)(x-k)}{(a-b)(a-c)\ldots(a-j)(a-k)} u_a + \frac{(x-b)(x-c)\ldots(x-j)(x-k)}{(b-a)(b-c)\ldots(b-j)(b-k)} u_b + \frac{(x-c)(x-b)\ldots(x-j)(x-k)}{(c-a)(c-b)\ldots(c-j)(c-k)} u_c \ldots + \frac{(x-a)(x-b)\ldots(x-k)}{(k-a)(k-b)\ldots(k-j)} u_k$$

(d) None of the above

70. *Find the third divided difference with arguments 2, 4, 9, 10 of the function $f(x) = x^3 - 2x$.*

(a) 1 (b) 2

(c) 3 (d) None of the above

71. *If $u_{35.0} = 1175$, $u_{35.5} = 1280$, $u_{39.5} = 2180$, $u_{40.5} = 2420$. Obtain u by using Newton's divided difference formula.*

(a) 2300 (b) 2400

(c) 2350 (d) 2372

72. *By menas of Lagrange's formula find the value of u_1, given $u_0 = 0.4$, $u_2 = 0.128$, $u_3 = 0.224$, $u_4 = 0.376$.*

(a) 1.73 (b) 0.342

(c) 0.287 (d) 0.162

73. *From the following data :*

Income :	*Below 500*	*500-1000*	*1000-2000*	*2000-3000*
No. of Persons :	*600*	*4250*	*3600*	*1500*

Income :	*3000-4000*
No. of Persons :	*650*

Estimate the number of persons having incomes between 1000 and 1500.

(a) 2000 (b) 2760

(c) 3637 (d) 2320

74. *Which of the following is "Gauss's Forward Formula"?*

(a) $u_x = u_0 + {}^xC_1\,\Delta u_0 + {}^xC_2\,\Delta^2 u_{-1} + {}^{x+1}C_3\Delta^3 u_{-1} + {}^{x+1}C_4\Delta^4 u_{-2} + \ldots + \ldots$

(b) $u_x = u_0 + {}^xC_1\,\Delta u_{-1} + {}^{x+1}C_2\,\Delta^2 u_{-1} + {}^{x+1}C_3\Delta^3 u_{-2} + {}^{x+2}C_4\Delta^4 u_{-2} + {}^{x+2}C_5\Delta^5 u_{-3} + \ldots$

(c) $u_x = u_0 + {}^xC_1\,\frac{1}{2}(\Delta u_0 + \Delta u_{-1}) + \frac{1}{2}({}^xC_2 + {}^{x-1}C_3\,\Delta^2 u_{-1} + {}^{x+1}C_3 \cdot \frac{1}{2}(\Delta^3 u_{-1} + \Delta^3 u_{-2}){}^{x+1}C_4\Delta^4 u_{-2} + \frac{1}{2}({}^{x+1}C_4 + {}^{x+2}C_2)\Delta^4 u_{-2} + \ldots$

(d) None of the above

75. *Which of the following is "Stirling's Formula"?*

(a) $u_x = u_0 + {}^xC_1\,\Delta u_0 + {}^xC_1\,\Delta^2 u_{-1} + {}^{x+1}C_3\Delta^3 u_{-1} + {}^{x+1}C_4\Delta^4 u_{-2} + \ldots + \ldots$

(b) $u_x = u_0 + {}^xC_1\,\Delta u_{-1} + {}^{x+1}C_2\,\Delta^2 u_{-1} + {}^{x+1}C_3\Delta^3 u_{-2} + {}^{x+2}C_4\Delta^4 u_{-2} + {}^{x+2}C_5\Delta^5 u_{-3} + \ldots$

(c) $u_x = u_0 + {}^xC_1\,\frac{1}{2}(\Delta u_0 + \Delta u_{-1}) + \frac{1}{2}({}^xC_2 + {}^{x-1}C_3)\,\Delta^2 u_{-1} + {}^{x+1}C_3 \cdot \frac{1}{2}(\Delta^3 u_{-1} + \Delta^3 u_{-2}) + \frac{1}{2}({}^{x+1}C_4 + {}^{x+2}C_2)\Delta^4 u_{-2} + \ldots$

(d) None of the above

Answers :

66. (c)	**67.** (b)	**68.** (c)	**69.** (a)	**70.** (a)
71. (a)	**72.** (d)	**73.** (d)	**74.** (a)	**75.** (c)

76. *Which of the following is "Gauss's Backward Formula"?*

(a) $u_x = u_0 + {}^xC_1\ \Delta\ u_0 + {}^xC_2\ \Delta^2\ u_{-1} + {}^{x+1}C_3\Delta^3\ u_{-1} + {}^{x+1}C_4\Delta^4\ u_{-2} + \ldots + \ldots$

(b) $u_x = u_0 + {}^xC_1\ \Delta\ u_{-1} + {}^{x+1}C_2\ \Delta^2\ u_{-1} + {}^{x+1}C_3\Delta^3\ u_{-2} + {}^{x+2}C_4\Delta^4\ u_{-2} + {}^{x+2}C_5\Delta^5\ u_{-3} + \ldots$

(c) $u_x = u_0 + {}^xC_1\ \frac{1}{2}\ (\Delta\ u_0 + \Delta u_{-1}) + \frac{1}{2}\ ({}^xC_2 + {}^{x-1}\ C_3)\ \Delta^2\ u_{-1} + {}^{x+1}C_3 \cdot \frac{1}{2}\ (\Delta^3\ u_{-1} + \Delta^3 u_{-2}) + \frac{1}{2}\ ({}^{x+1}C_4 + {}^{x+2}C_2)\Delta^4\ u_{-2} + \ldots$

(d) None of the above

77. *The Newton-Raphson method is to be used to find the root of the equation f(x) = 0 where x_0 is the initial approximation and f is the derivative of f. The method converges*

(a) Always

(b) only if $f(x_0) < 0$

(c) only if f is polynomial

(d) None of the above

78. *Which of the following statements applies to the bisection method used for finding roots of functions*

(a) converges with in a few iterations

(b) guranted to work for all continuous functions

(c) is faster than the Newton Raphson method.

(d) requires that there is no error in determining the sign of the function

79. *The Newton-Raphson method is used to find the root of the eqation $x^2 - 2 = 0$. If the iteration is started from -1, the iterations will*

(a) Converges to -1

(b) Converges to $-\sqrt{2}$

(c) Converges to $\sqrt{2}$

(d) Not converge

80. *Using the forward Euler method to solve*
$y''(\pm) = f(t)$, y107 = 0, $y'(0) = 0$ with a step size of h, we obtian the following values of y in the first four iterations

(a) 0, $hf(0)$, $h\{f(0) + f(h)\}$ and $h\{f(0) + f(h) + f(2h)\}$

(b) 0, 0, $h^2f(0)$ and $2h^2\ f(0) + f(h)$

(c) 0, 0, $h^2\ f(0)$ and $3h^2f(0)$

(d) 0, 0, $hf(0) + h^2f(0)$ and $hf(0)\ h^2f(0) + hf(h)$

81. *Newton-Raphson iteration method formula for finding $3\sqrt{c}$ where $c > 0$ is*

(a) $x_{n+1} = \frac{2x_n^3 + 3\sqrt{c}}{3x_n^2}$ (b) $x_{n+1} = \frac{2x_n^3 - 3\sqrt{c}}{3x_n^2}$

(c) $x_{n+1} = \frac{2x_n^3 + c}{3x_n^2}$ (d) $x_{n+1} = \frac{2x_n^3 - c}{3x_n^2}$

82. ***The order of convergence in Newton-Raphson method is***

(a) 2 (b) 3

(c) 0 (d) None of these

83. ***As soon as a new value of a variable is found by iteration, it is used immediately in the following equations, this method is called***

(a) Gauss-Jordan method (b) Gauss-Seidal method

(c) Jacobi's method (d) Relaxation method

84. ***Which one of the following is correct***

(a) $\Delta x^n = nx^{n-1}$ (b) $\Delta x^{(n)} = nx^{(n-1)}$

(c) $\Delta^x e^x = e^x$ (d) $\Delta \cos x = - \sin x$

85. ***The relation between, operators E and D is***

(a) $D = e^{hE}$ (b) $hD = \log (1 + E)$

(c) $E = \log (1 + D)$ (d) $E = e^{hD}$

Answers :	**76.** (b)	**77.** (d)	**78.** (b)	**79.** (b)	**80.** (d)
	81. (b)	**82.** (a)	**83.** (b)	**84.** (b)	**85.** (d)

SOLUTIONS

3. By descarte's rule of signs, the number of positive real root can not be more then the number of changes of sign in f(x), in this case 3, as there are 3 change of signs in f(x). The number of negtive roots cannot be more than the number of change of signs in f(-x) i.e. 2 in this case. So, altogether it cannot have more than 5 real root. So it must have (7 - 5) = 2 at least imaginary roots.

9. The required formula is $x_{K+1} = x_K + \frac{f(x_K)}{f'(x_K)}$.

Here $x = \sqrt{b}$ i.e. $x^2 - b = 0$. Taking $f(x) = x^2 - b$, we get the required answer.

10. Consider the graph for $f(x) = 0$ from the graph, it is clear that if f(a) and f(b) are of same sign, then it will cut the x-axis either 0 or even number of times. So, it will have as many roots as the number of times it is cutting the x-axis.

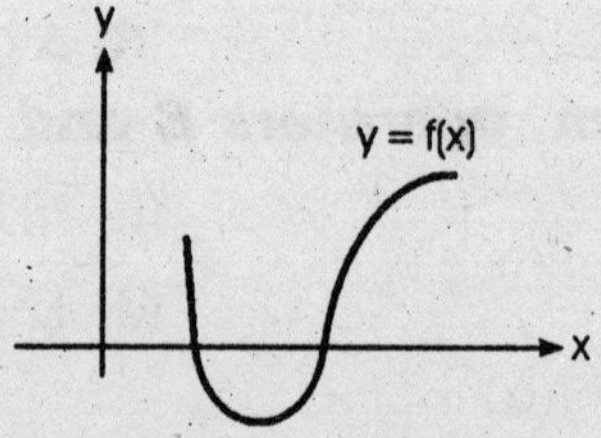

11. $f(-\infty)$ and $f(\infty)$ both are positive, but $f(0)$) is negative. So it should have at least 1 root between $(-\infty, 0)$ and at least one root between $(0, \infty)$.

13. f(x) has one change of sign and f(-x) has two changes of sign, so it must have 3 real and 2 complex root.

14. After solving we will get the remainder is a first degree polynomial. Let it be $Mx + N$. So $f(x) = (x - \alpha)(x - \beta)Q + (mx + N)$ {Q is quotient} putting $x = \alpha\ \beta$, we get two equation, by solijng we get the result.

16. Because $a_1, a_2, \ldots a_n$ are the roots of the given polynonial, therefore

$$x^n + nax - b = (a - a_1)(x - a_2)\ldots\ldots(x - a_n)$$

Differentiating both sides and put $x = a_1$, we get the result.

18. Since the number of subintervals wil be greater than the others and simpson's is more accurate than the trapezoidal.

19. To ensure 5 digit accuracy, the error term $\frac{x^{2n+2}}{(2n+2)!}$ should be less than $\frac{1}{2} \times 10^{-n}$ solving, we get $n = 7$.

20. We have $x = \dfrac{-b \pm \sqrt{b^2 - 4ac}}{2a}$

Differentiating, we get $dx = \dfrac{dC}{\sqrt{b^2 - 4ac}}$

for dx to b less than 5×10^{-5}, de must be to the accuracy of approximately 8×10^{-5}. It can be cheered by putting $b = -1$, $a = 1$ and $c = \log 2$.

32. Newton backward interpolation is used for those values of y which are near the end of the tabulated values.

34. Rate of convergence—Bisection < Regula-Falsi < Newton-Raphson.

35. Suppose rot differs by a small quantity ε_n.

Then $x_n = \alpha + \varepsilon_n$ and $x_{n+1} = \alpha + \varepsilon_{n+1}$

$$\therefore \quad x_{n+1} = x_n - \frac{f(x_n)}{f'(x_n)}$$

$$\alpha + \varepsilon_{n+1} = \alpha + \varepsilon_n - \frac{f(\alpha + \varepsilon_n)}{f'(x + \varepsilon_n)}$$

$$\Rightarrow \quad \varepsilon_{n+1} = \varepsilon_n - \frac{f(\alpha + \varepsilon_n)}{f'(\alpha + \varepsilon_n)}$$

$$= \varepsilon_n - \frac{f(\alpha) + \varepsilon f'(\alpha) + \frac{1}{2!}\varepsilon_n^2 f''(\alpha)}{f'(\alpha) + \varepsilon f''(\alpha)}$$

But $\quad f(\alpha) = 0$

$$= \varepsilon - \frac{\varepsilon f'(\alpha) + \frac{1}{2}\varepsilon_n^2 f''(\alpha) + \ldots}{f'(\alpha) + \varepsilon_n f''(\alpha) + \ldots}$$

$$= \frac{\varepsilon_n^2 f''(\alpha)}{2f'(\alpha) + \varepsilon_n f''(\alpha)} = \frac{\varepsilon_n^2}{2} \times \frac{f''(\alpha)}{f'(\alpha)}$$

= quadraic order

77. The method converges only if f is continuous.

78. It converges after many number of iterations and the rate of convergence is les than the Newton Raphson method, so, it is slower. It have some error in determining the sign of the function.

79. Because $x^2 - 2 = 0 \Rightarrow x = \pm\sqrt{2}$

and $x = -\sqrt{2}$ is nearer to −1.

■ □ ■

CHAPTER 17

GRAPH THEORY

1. ***The number of vertices of odd degree in a graph is :***
   (a) Always even (b) Sometimes even sometimes odd
   (c) Always odd (d) Neither even nor odd
2. ***A graph in which all vertices are of equal degree is :***
   (a) Regular graph (b) Simple graph
   (c) Complete graph (d) Bipartite graph
3. ***Which of the following is not correct ?***
   (a) Every graph is its own subgraph
   (b) A subgraph of a subgraph of graph G is a subgraph of graph G
   (c) A single edge in G together with its end vertices is a subgraph of graph G
   (d) Two subgraphs g_1 and g_2 of a graph G are said to be edge disjoint if g_1 and g_2 have an edge in common
4. ***A ...... graph is a directed graph with the property that no edge connects a vertex to itself, and between any two vertices there is at most one edge :***
   (a) Complete or round robin, (b) Single elimination
   (c) Tournament (d) Regular
5. ***A ..... tournament graph is a tournament graph with the property that between any two distinct vertices there is exactly one edge :***
   (a) Complete or round-robin (b) Single-elimination
   (c) Tournament (d) Regular
6. ***A simple graph (i.e., a graph without self loops and parallel edges) with n vertices and k-components can have at most ... edges :***
   (a) $\frac{n(n-k)}{2}$ (b) $\frac{(n-k)(n-k-1)}{2}$
   (c) $\frac{(n-k)(n-k+1)}{2}$ (d) $\frac{(n+k)(n+k-1)}{2}$
7. ***A graph G can be decomposed into two subgraphs g_1 and g_2 if***

   $g_1 \cup g_2 = G$

and $g_1 \cap g_2$ = a null graph.

In decomposition, isolated vertices are disregarded. Let a graph containing m edges $\{e_1, e_2, \ldots e_m\}$, then in how many ways can this be decomposed in different ways into pairs of subgraphs g_1 and g_2 ?

(a) 2^m (b) 2^{m-1}

(c) $2^{m-1} - 1$ (d) $2^{m-1} - 2m$

8. ***The length of a Hamiltonian path (if it exist) in a connected graph of n-vertices is :***

(a) $n - 1$ (b) $\frac{n-1}{2}$

(c) $\frac{n(n-1)}{2}$ (d) $\frac{n(n+1)}{2}$

9. ***A simple graph in which there exists an edge between every pair of vertices is called a complete graph. Then the degree of every vertex and total number of edges in a complete graph G of n vertices is :***

(a) $n, n - 1$ (b) $n - 1, \frac{n(n-1)}{2}$

(c) $\frac{n(n-1)}{2}, n - 1$ (d) $n - 1, \frac{(n-1)}{2}$

10. ***The edge-disjoint Hamiltonian circuits in a complete graph with n-vertices, if n is an odd number ≥ 3, are :***

(a) $n - 1$ (b) $\frac{n(n-1)}{2}$

(c) $\frac{n-1}{2}$ (d) n

11. ***Total number of different (not edge disjoint) Hamiltonian circuits in a complete graph of n-vertices are :***

(a) $(n-1)!$ (b) $\frac{n(n-1)}{2}$

(c) $\frac{(n-1)!}{2}$ (d) $n!$

12. ***How many maximum edges excluding self loops, does a simple undirected graph of eight vertices have ?***

(a) 7 (b) 28

(c) 8 (d) 14

Answers :

1.* (a)	**2.** (a)	**3.*** (d)	**4.** (c)	**5.** (a)	**6.** (c)
7. (c)	**8.** (a)	**9.** (b)	**10.** (c)	**11.** (c)	**12.** (b)

13. *How many edges does a complete tournament graph with n vertices have ?*

(a) n (b) $n-1$

(c) $\frac{n-1}{2}$ (d) $\frac{n(n-1)}{2}$

14. *The chromatic number of the following graphs are :*

(a) 2, 3

(b) 3, 3

(c) 3, 4

(d) 3, 2

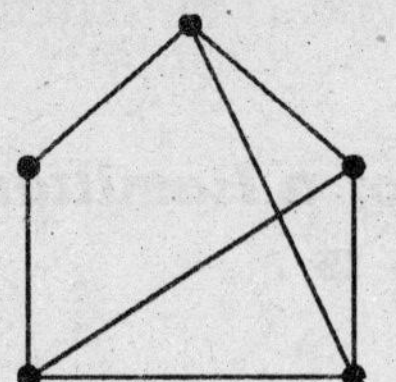

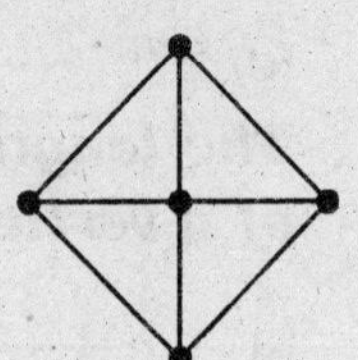

15. *Find the relation determined by the diagraph :*

(a) $R = \{(1, 2), (2, 3), (3, 4), (5, 4)\}$

(b) $R = \{(1, 2), (2, 2), (2, 3), (3, 4), (4, 4), (5, 1), (5, 4)\}$

(c) $R = \{(2, 2), (4, 4)\}$

(d) None of these

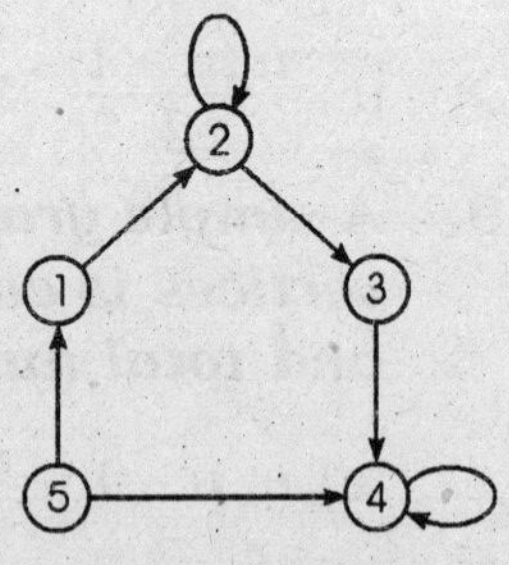

16. *Find the In-degree and the out-degree of each vertex for the digraph :*

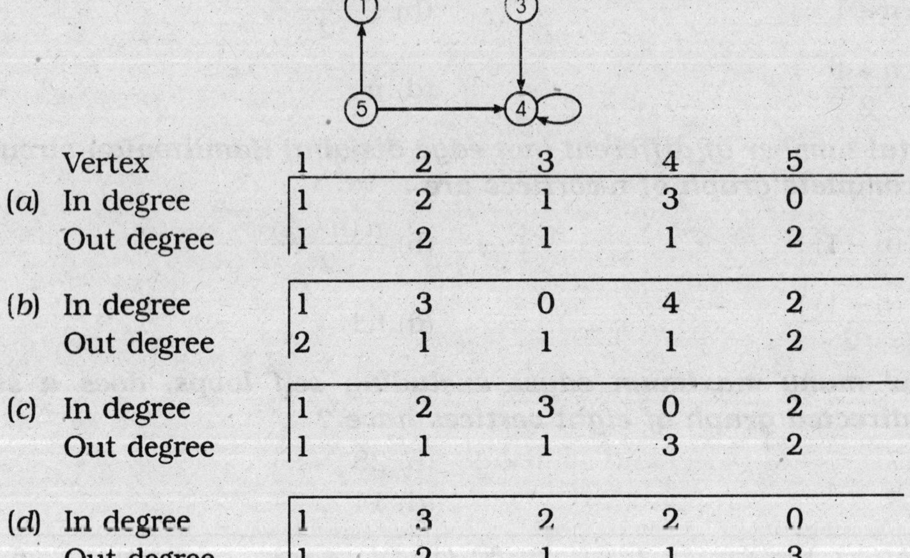

	Vertex	1	2	3	4	5
(*a*)	In degree	1	2	1	3	0
	Out degree	1	2	1	1	2
(*b*)	In degree	1	3	0	4	2
	Out degree	2	1	1	1	2
(*c*)	In degree	1	2	3	0	2
	Out degree	1	1	1	3	2
(*d*)	In degree	1	3	2	2	0
	Out degree	1	2	1	1	3

17. ***Consider the following arrays***

VERT = [1, 2, 6, 4]

TAIL = [1, 2, 2, 4, 4, 3, 4, 1]

HEAD = [2, 2, 3, 3, 4, 4, 1, 3]

NEXT = [8, 3, 0, 5, 7, 0, 0, 0]

These describe a relation R on the set A = {1, 2, 3, 4}. The digraph of R is :

(a) 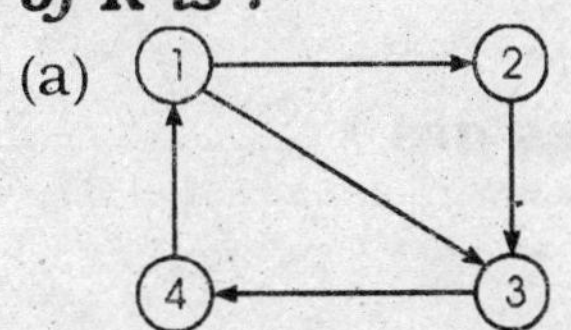

(b) 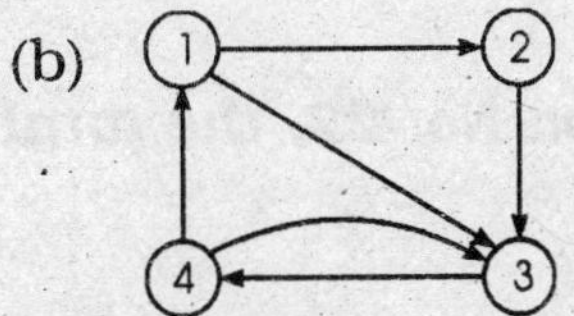

(c) 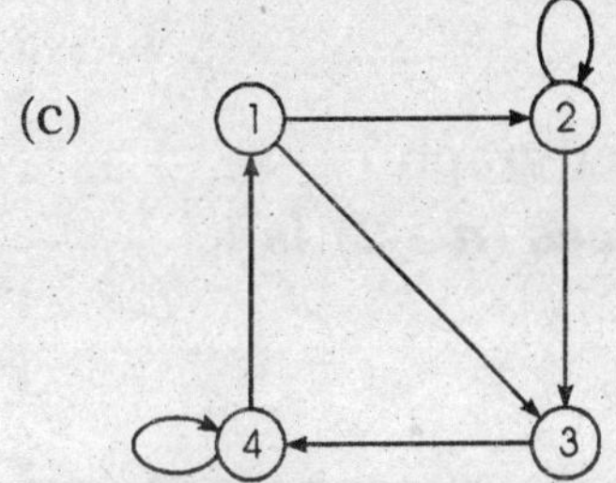

(d) None of these

18. ***The longest path (if exist) in a graph is :***

(a) Eulerian path (b) Hamiltonian path

(c) Fundamental path (d) Rooted path

19. ***A tree with n vertices have :***

(a) n edges (b) $(n-1)$ edges

(c) $\frac{n(n-1)}{2}$ edges (d) $\frac{n-1}{2}$ edges

20. ***For a tree, which of the following is not true ?***

(a) G is connected and is circuit less

(b) G is connected and has $(n-1)$ edges

(c) G is circuitless and has $(n-1)$ edges

(d) G is maximally connected graph

21. ***The number of vertices n in a binary tree is :***

(a) Always even

(b) Always odd

(c) Sometimes even and sometimes odd

(d) Neither even nor odd

Answers : **13.** (d) **14.** (b) **15.** (b) **16.** (a) **17.** (d) **18.** (b) **19.** (b) **20.** (d) **21.*** (b)

22. ***Let us consider structural isomers of the saturated hydrocarbons (paraffin series) C_k H_{2k+2} and we used a connected graph to represent the C_kH_{2k+2} molecule. Here a carbon atom was represented by a vertex of degree four and a hydrogen atom by a vertex of degree one (pendant vertices). Then total number of vertices in such a graph is :***

(a) $2k + 2$ (b) $3k + 2$
(c) $3k + 1$ (d) $3k - 1$

23. ***In question No. 22, the total number of edges are :***

(a) $3k + 1$ (b) $3k - 1$
(c) $2k + 2$ (d) $3k + 2$

24. ***In question No. 22 the graph obtained is :***

(a) Bipartite graph (b) Tree
(c) Eulerian graph (d) Planer graph

25. ***The number of labelled trees with n-vertices ($n \geq 2$) is :***

(a) 2^{n-1} (b) 2^{n-2}
(c) n^{n-1} (d) n^{n-2}

26. ***With respect to any of its spanning trees, a connected graph of n-vertices and e edges, has :***

(a) n chords and $(n - 1)$ tree branches
(b) $(n - 1)$ tree branches and $(e - n + 2)$ chords
(c) $(n - 1)$ tree branches and $(e - n + 1)$ chords
(d) $(e - n + 1)$ branches and $(n - 1)$ chords

27. ***Every cutset in a non-separable graph with more than two vertices contains :***

(a) Two edges (b) At least two edges
(c) One edge (d) At least one edge

28. ***Which of the following is false ?***

(a) Vertex connectivity $\leq$ edge connectivity $\leq \frac{2e}{n}$

(b) Vertex connectivity $\leq \frac{2e}{n}$

(c) Maximum vertex connectivity possible $= \frac{2e}{n}$

(d) Maximum edge connectivity $= e - n + 1$

29. ***If g_1 and g_2 are two 1-isomorphic graphs, then :***

(a) Rank of g_1 = Rank of g_2 (b) Nullity of g_1 = nullity of g_2

(c) Rank of g_1 = nullity of g_2 (d) nullity of g_1 = Rank of g_2

30. ***Two graphs with equal rank and with equal number of edges must have :***

(a) Same number of vertices (b) Same height

(c) Same nullity (d) Same edge connectivity

31. ***A drawing of a geometric representation of a graph on any surface such that no edge intersect is a :***

(a) Planar graph (b) Dual graph

(c) Circuit (d) Embedding

32. ***A complete graph of 5 vertices is a :***

(a) Planar graph (b) Non-planar graph

(c) Dual graph (d) Traceable graph

33. ***In the Kuratowski's two graphs K_5 and $K_{3,\ 3}$ if we remove one edge or a vertex, then the obtained graphs will be :***

(a) Planar graphs (b) Non-planar graphs

(c) Regular graphs (d) Traceable graphs

34. ***The two graphs of Kuratowski's are :***

(a) Planer graphs (b) Non-planar graphs

(c) Regular graphs (d) Complete graphs

35. ***How many regions a connected planar graph with n vertices and e edges have :***

(a) $e - n$ (b) $e - n + 1$

(c) $e - n + 2$ (d) $e - n - 1$

36. ***In any simple, connected planar graph with f-regions, n vertices and e edges ($e > 2$), which of the following must hold ?***

(a) $f \geq e - n + 2$ (b) $e \geq \frac{3f}{2}$

(c) $e \geq 3n - 6$ (d) $f = e - n - 2$

37. ***If in a planar graph of n vertices, we add k ($\leq n$) self loops to the n vertices, then the obtained graph will be :***

(a) Regular graph (b) Complete graph

(c) Planar graph (d) Non-planar graph

Answers : **22.** (b) **23.** (a) **24.*** (b) **25.** (d) **26.** (c) **27.** (b) **28.** (d) **29.** (a),(b)
30. (c) **31.** (d) **32.** (b) **33.** (a) **34.** (a) **35.** (c) **36.** (b) **37.** (c)

38. ***If every region of a simple planar graph (with n vertices and e edges) embedded in a plane is bounded by k edges, then :***

(a) $e = n - k + 1$ (b) $e = \frac{k(n-1)}{k-1}$

(c) $e = \frac{k(n-2)}{k-2}$ (d) $e = \frac{k(n-1)}{k-2}$

39. ***The two graphs shown in following figures are :***

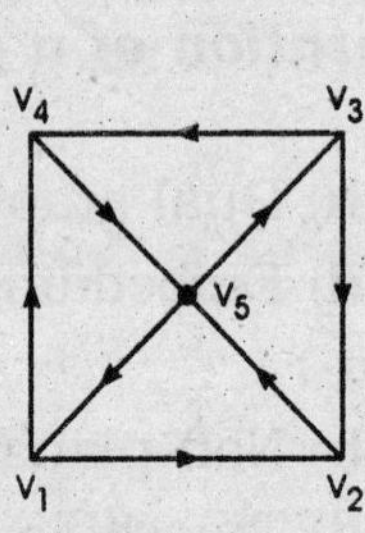

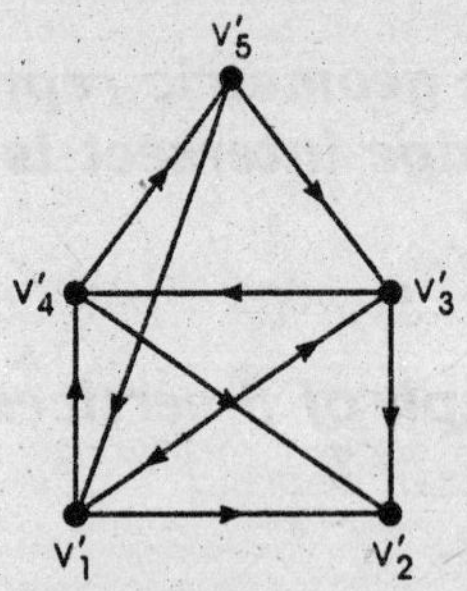

(a) Complete graphs (b) Planar graphs

(c) Regular graphs (d) Isomorphic graphs

40. ***In the graph shown in figure below, the depth-first spanning tree edges are marked with a "T".***

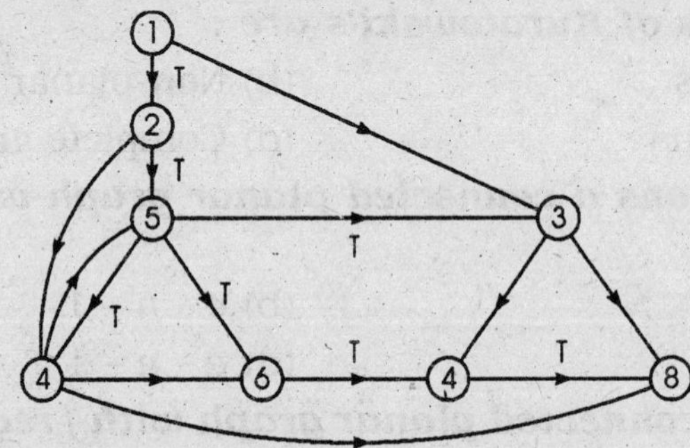

Then the forward edges are :

(a) 4 (b) 8

(c) 1 (d) None of these

41. ***In question No (40) the backward edges are :***

(a) 1 (b) 2

(c) 4 (d) 8

42. ***In question No. (40) the cross edges are :***

(a) 2 (b) 3

(c) 4 (d) None of these

43. *Which of the following graphs are planar ?*

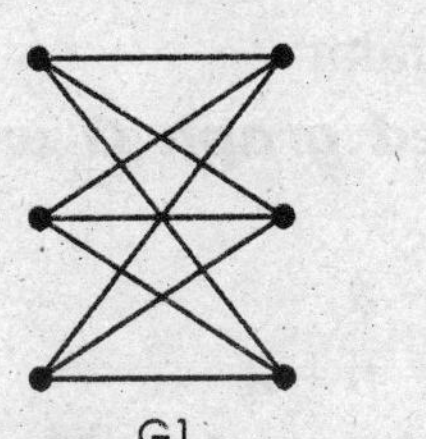

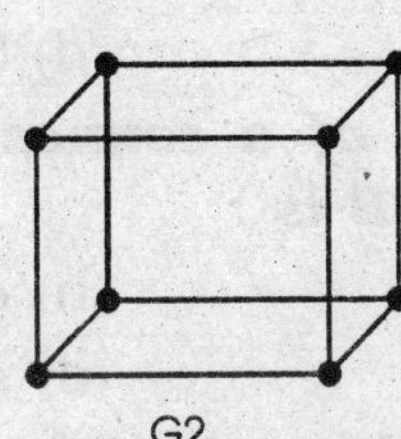

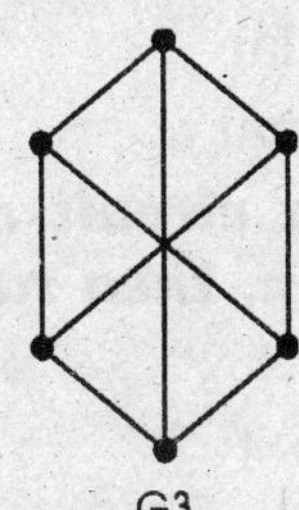

(a) G_1 and G_2 (b) G_1 and G_3

(c) G_2 (d) G_1

44. *The number of rooted binary trees with n-nodes is*

(A) equal to the number of ways of multiplying $(n + 1)$ matrices.

(B) equal to the number of ways of arranging n out of $2n$ distinct elements.

(C) equal to $\frac{1}{(n+1)}\binom{2n}{n}$

(D) equal to n !

(a) A, B (b) B, C

(c) A, C (d) B, D

45. *A graph is planar if and only if :*

(a) It does not contain subgraphs homeomorphic to K_5 and $K_{3,\,3}$.

(b) It does not contain subgraphs isomorphic to K_5 or $K_{3,\,3}$.

(c) It does not contain subgraphs isomorphic to K_5 and $K_{3,\,3}$.

(d) It does not contain subgraphs homeomorphic to K_5 or $K_{3,\,3}$.

46. *The total number of distinct bases possible in a cut-set subspace is :*

(a) $\prod_{i=0}^{r-1} \frac{1}{r!}(2^r - 2^i)$ (b) $\prod_{i=0}^{r-1} \frac{1}{(r-1)!}(2^r - 2^i)$

(c) $\prod_{i=0}^{r-1} \frac{1}{r!}(2^r + 2^i)$ (d) $\prod_{i=0}^{r-1} \frac{1}{(r-1)!}(2^r + 2^i)$

47. *If A (G) is an incidence matrix of a connected graph G with n vertices, then the rank of A (G) is :*

(a) n (b) $n - 1$

(c) $n(n-1)/2$ (d) $\frac{n+1}{2}$

Answers : **38.** (c) **39.*** (d) **40.** (c) **41.** (c) **42.** (c) **43.*** (c) **44.** (c) **45.*** (d) **46.** (a) **47.** (b)

48. The reduced incidence matrix of a tree is

(a) Singular (b) Non-singular

(c) Diagonal (d) Scalar

49. If B is a circuit matrix of a connected graph G with edge e and vertices n, then rank of B is :

(a) $n - e$ (b) $e - n$

(c) $e - n + 1$ (d) $e - n + 2$

50. The total number of fundamental circuits and fundamental cut sets with respect to T in the following spanning tree of rank 5 and nullity 4 :

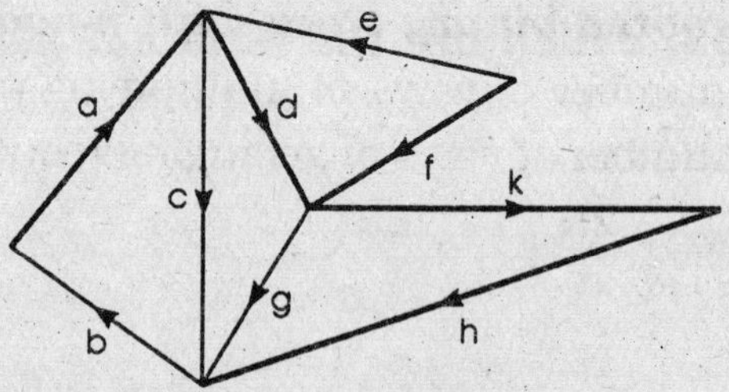

(a) 3, 4 (b) 6, 3

(c) 4, 5 (d) 3, 5

51. What is the preorder for the following tree T corresponding to the algebraic expression

$$\mathbf{E = (x + 3y)^4 (a - 2b)}$$

(a) $* \uparrow - x * 3y\ 4 + a2 * b$

(b) $\uparrow * - x * 3y\ 4 + a2 * b$

(c) $* \uparrow + x * 3y\ 4 - a2 * b$

(d) $\uparrow * + x * 3y\ 4 - a2 * b$

52. The preorder and in order traversals of a binary tree T yield the following sequence of nodes :

Preorder : G, B, Q, A, C, K, F, P, D, E, R, H

In order : Q, B, K, C, F, A, G, P, E, D, H, R

Which diagram suits the above data

(a)

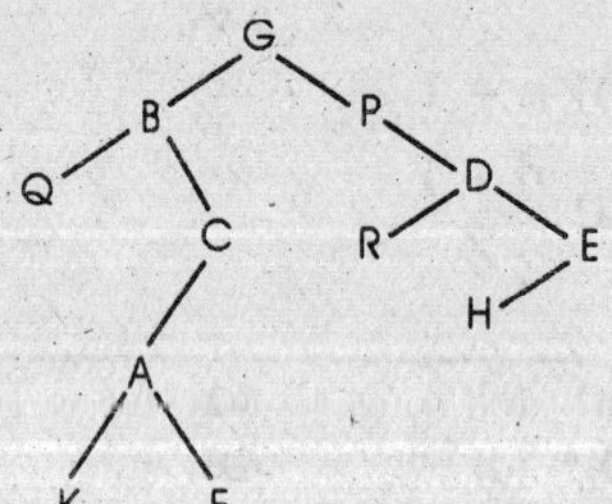

(b)

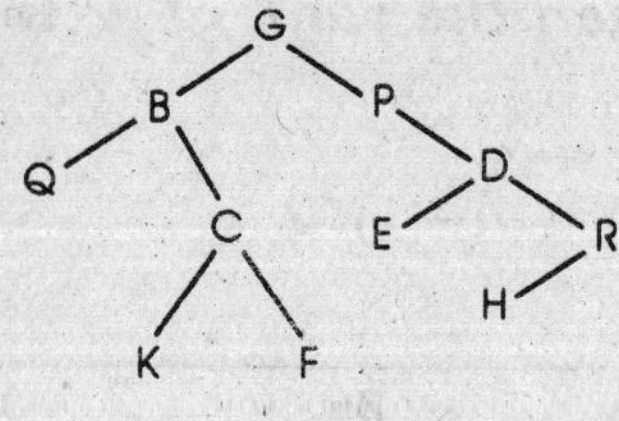

(c)

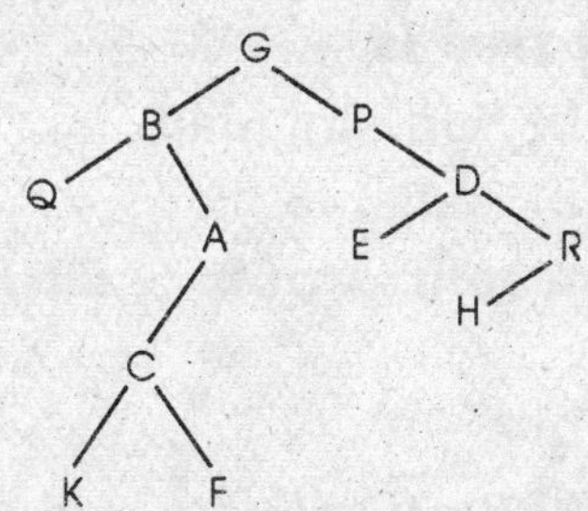

(d) None of these

53. ***In question No. 52 what is the depth of T ?***

(a) 2 (b) 3

(c) 5 (d) 4

54. ***In question No. 52, which are the terminal nodes ?***

(a) G, K, F, R, H (b) Q, K, F, E, H

(c) Q, K, F, E, R (d) Q, C, K, F, H

55. ***What is the preorder for the following binary tree ?***

(a) ABDEHPQSCFKRL

(b) DBPHQKFLSEARC

(c) DPSQHEBRKLCFA

(d) DBPHQSEACRKFL

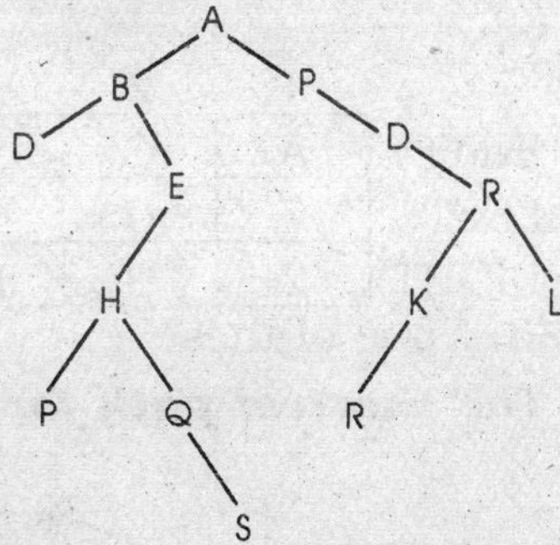

56. ***In question No. 55 what is the Inorder ?***

(a) ABDEHPQSCFKRL (b) DBPHQKFLSEARC

(c) DPSQHEBRKLCFA (d) DBPHQSEACRKFL

57. ***What is the post order for the given binary tree in question No. 55 ?***

(a) ABDEHPQSCFKRL (b) DBPHQKFLSEARC

(c) DPSQHEBRKLCFA (d) DBPHQSEACRKFL

58. ***Consider the binary tree in the following figure. Assume the nodes of T are stored in a linear array INFO with 10 lacations as follows:***
INFO [1] = A, INFO [2] = C, INFO [3] = E, INFO [4] = G,
INFO [7] = B, INFO [8] = D, INFO [9] = F, INFO [10] = H,
What is the linked representation of T in memory ?

Answers : **48.** (b) **49.** (c) **50.** (c) **51.** (c) **52.** (c)
53.* (d) **54.** (b) **55.** (a) **56.** (d) **57.** (c)

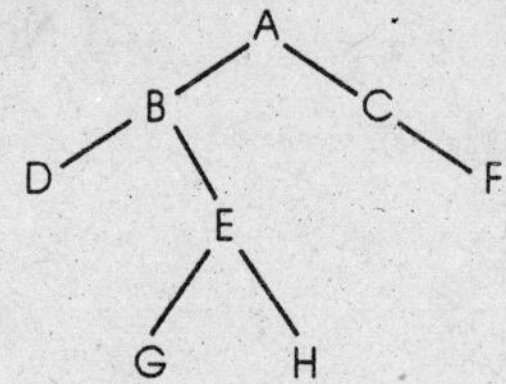

(a)

	1	2	3	4	5	6	7	8	9	10
INFO	A	C	E	G			B	D	F	H
LEFT	7	0	9	10			2	0	0	0
RIGHT	28	8	4	0			3	0	0	0

(b)

	1	2	3	4	5	6	7	8	9	10
INFO	A	C	E	G			B	D	F	H
LEFT	7	0	4	0			0	0	8	0
RIGHT	2	9	10	0			0	0	3	0

(c)

	1	2	3	4	5	6	7	8	9	10
INFO	A	C	E	G			B	D	F	H
LEFT	7	0	4	0			8	0	0	0
RIGHT	2	9	10	0			3	0	0	0

(d) None of these

59. ***The shortest path for the following digraph***

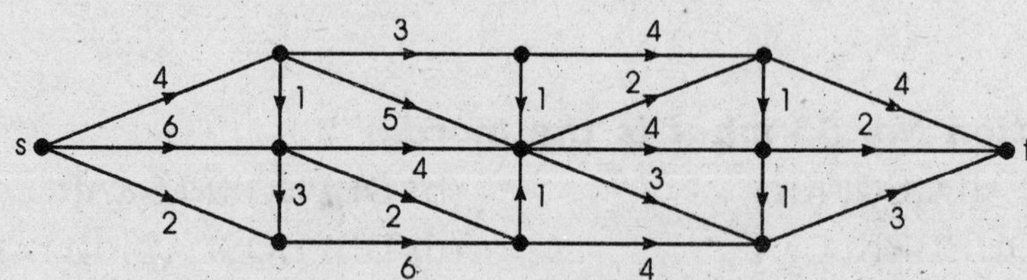

(a) *s*, 2, 3, 2, 1, 2, 1, 2, *t*
(b) *s*, 2, 6, 1, 2, 1, 2, *t*
(c) *s*, 4, 1, 2, 1, 2, 1, 1, 3, *t*
(d) *s*, 4, 1, 2, 1, 2, 1, 2, *t*

60. ***Suppose a graph G is presented by the following table***
G = [A : B, C ; B : C, D ; C : C ; D : B ; E : ϕ]
then for G which is true ?

(a) Weakly connected
(b) Strongly connected
(c) Unilaterally connected

(d) None of these

61. ***Which is true for the following given graph ?***

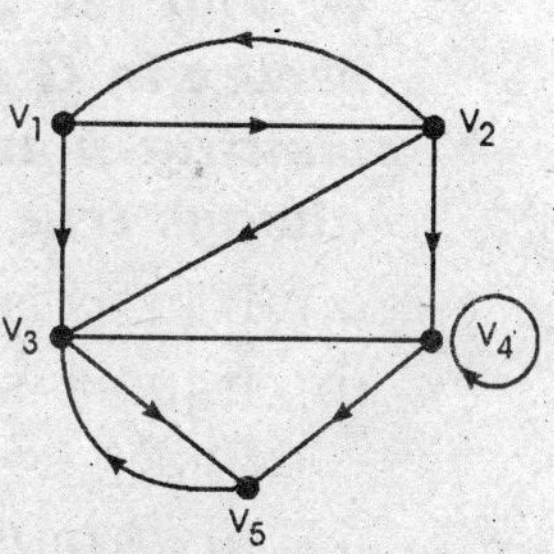

(a) Weakly connected
(b) Strongly connected
(c) Unilaterally connected
(d) None of these

62. ***The following addressess are in random order***
2.1.1, 3.1, 2.1, 1, 2.2.1.2, 0, 3.2, 2.2, 1.1, 2, 3.1.1, 2.2.1, 3, 2.2.1.1
The addressess in the lexicographic will be :

(a) 0, 1, 1.1, 2, 2.1, 2.1.1, 2.2, 2.2.1, 2.2.1.1, 2.2.1.2, 3, 3.1, 3.1.1, 3.2
(b) 3.2, 3.1.1, 3.1, 3, 2.2.1.2, 2.2.1.1, 2.2.1, 2.2, 2.1.1, 2.1, 2, 1.1, 1, 0
(c) Both a and b
(d) None of these

63. ***Find the set of vertices (V) and set of edges (E) for the graph G = {V, E, γ} given in the figure below :***

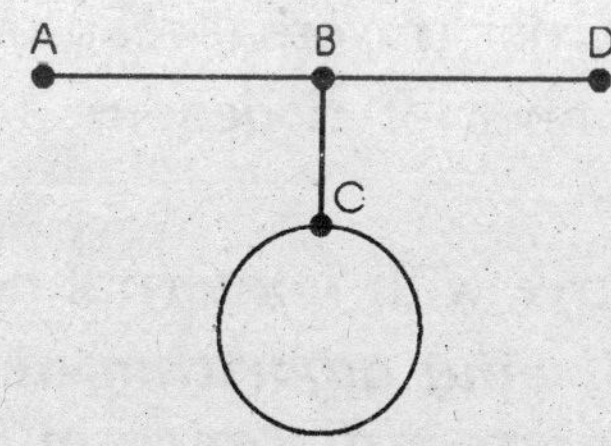

(a) $V = \{A, B, C, D\}$, $E = \{(A, B), (A, D), (B, C), (C, C)\}$
(b) $V = \{A, B, C, D\}$, $E = \{(A, B), (B, D), (B, C), (C, C)\}$
(c) $V = \{A, B, C, D\}$, $E = \{(A, B), (B, D), (C, D), (C, C)\}$
(d) None of these

64. ***Let G be an undirected connected graph with distinct edge weights. Let e_{max} be the edge with maximum Weight and e_{min} the edge with minimum weight. Which of the following statement is false ?***

(a) Every minimum spanning tree of G must contain e_{min}
(b) If e_{max} is in a minimum spanning tree, then its removal must disconnect G
(c) No minimum spanning tree contains e_{max}
(d) G has a unique minimum spanning tree

Answers :

58. (c)	**59.** (d)	**60.** (d)	**61.** (c)
62. (a)	**63.** (b)	**64.** (c)	

65. *Let G be an undirected graph. Consider a depth-first traversal of G, and let T be the resulting depth-first search tree. Let u be the vertex in G and let v be the first new (unvisited) vertex visited after visiting u in the traversal. Which of the following statements is always true ?*

(a) If $\{u, v\}$ is not an edge in G, then u is a leaf in T

(b) If $\{u, v\}$ is not an edge in G, then u and v must have the same parent in T

(c) $\{u, v\}$ must be an edge in G, and v is a descendant of u in T

(d) $\{u, v\}$ must be an edge in G, and u is a descendant of v in T

66. *A complete n-ary tree is one in which every node has 0 or n sons. If x is the number of internal nodes of a complete n-ary tree, the number of leaves in it is given by :*

(a) $x(n-1)+1$ (b) $xn-1$

(c) $xn+1$ (d) $x(n+1)$

67. *Which of the statements is false ?*

(a) A tree with n nodes has $(n-1)$ edges

(b) A labelled rooted binary tree can be uniquely constructed given its post-order and preorder traversal results

(c) The maximum number of nodes in a binary tree of height h is $(2^{h+1}-1)$

(d) A complete binary tree with n internal nodes has $(n+1)$ leaves

68. *Which one of the following algorithm design techniques is used in finding all pairs of shortest distance in a graph :*

(a) Dynamic programming (b) Backtracking

(c) Greedy (d) Divide and conquer

69. *Let G be a graph with 100 vertices numbered 1, 2, 3, ... 100. Two vertices i and j are adjacent if*

$$|\hat{i}-\hat{j}| = 8 \text{ or } |\hat{i}-\hat{j}| = 12$$

the number of connected components in G is :

(a) 4 (b) 8

(c) 12 (d) 25

70. *Consider a graph whose vertices are points in the plane with integer co-ordinates (x, y) such that $1 \le x \le n$ and $1 \le y \le n$, where $n \ge 2$ is an integer. Two vertices (x_1, y_1) and (x_2, y_2) are adjacent iff $|x_1 - x_2| \le 1$ and $|y_1 - y_1| \le 1$. The weight of an edge $\{(x_1, y_1), (x_2, y_2)\}$ is $\sqrt{(x_1 - x_2)^2 + (y_1 - y_2)^2}$.*

Then the weight of a minimum weight spanning tree in this graph is :

(a) n (b) $n(n-1)$

(c) $(n-1)(n-2)$ (d) $(n+1)(n-1)$

71. ***The weight of maximum weight spanning tree of the graph obtained in question No. 70, is***

(a) $\sqrt{2}\,[(n+1)(n+2)-1]+1$

(b) $\sqrt{2}\,[(n+1)(n-1)-1]+1$

(c) $\sqrt{2}\,[n(n+1)-1]+1$

(d) $\sqrt{2}\,[(n+1)(n-1)+1]-1$

72. ***In the balanced binary tree given below, how many nodes will become unbalanced when a node is inserted as a child of the node "g" ?***

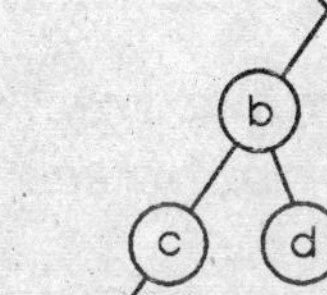

(a) 1

(b) 2

(c) 3

(d) 4

73. ***A binary tree T has n leaf nodes. The number of nodes of degree 2 in T is :***

(a) $\log_2 n$ (b) $(n-1)$

(c) n (d) 2^n

74. ***The minimum number of edges in a connected cycle graph on n-vertices is :***

(a) n (b) $n-1$

(c) $n+1$ (d) $\frac{n(n-1)}{2}$

75. ***Consider the complete Bi-partite graph $K_{m,n}$. Then the diameter of $K_{m,n}$ is :***

(a) 1 (b) 2

(c) $m-n$ (d) $n-m$

76. ***Consider the following tree. If the first order traversal gives ab – cd * + then the label of the nodes 1, 2, 3, ... will be :***

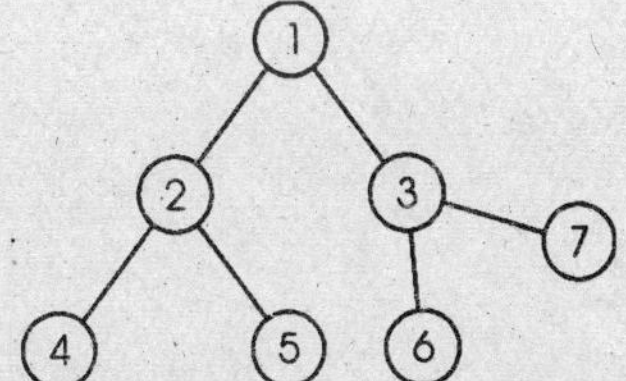

(a) +, –, *, a, b, c, d

(b) a, –, b, +, c, *, d

Answers :

65. (a)	**66.** (a)	**67.*** (d)	**68.** (a)	**69.** (a)	**70.** (d)
71. (b)	**72.** (c)	**73.** (b)	**74.** (a)	**75.*** (b).	

(c) $a, b, c, d, +, -, *$

(d) $-, a, b, +, *, c, d$

77. Consider the following tree

If this tree is used for sorting, then a new number 8 should be placed as the :

(a) Left child of node labelled 30

(b) Right child of node labelled 30

(c) Right child of node labelled 5

(d) Left child of node labelled 10

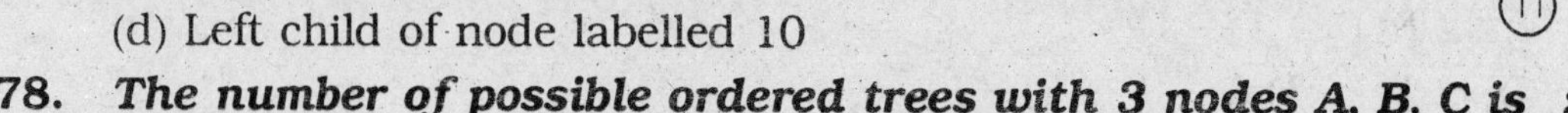

78. The number of possible ordered trees with 3 nodes A, B, C is :

(a) 6 (b) 10

(c) 12 (d) 16

79. A binary tree in which every non-leaf node has non-empty left and right subtrees is called a strictly binary tree. Such a tree with 10 leaves :

(a) Can't have more than 19 Nodes

(b) Has exactly 19 Nodes

(c) Has exactly 17 Nodes

(d) Can't have more than 17 Nodes

80. Which of the following algorithm solves all the pair shortest path problem ?

(a) Dijkstra's algorithm (b) F loyd's algorithm

(c) Prim's algorithm (d) Warshall's algorithm

81. Consider the graph given below. The ecentricity of node labelled 5 is :

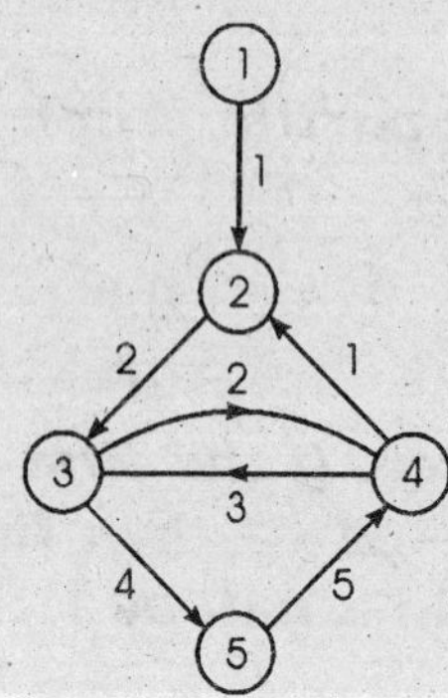

(a) 5 (b) 6

(c) 7 (d) 8

82. *In question No. 81, the centre of the graph is :*

(a) 4 (b) 2

(c) 3 (d) 4

83. *The order of the binary search algorithm is :*

(a) n (b) $n-1$

(c) $n \log n$ (d) $\log n$

84. *Let A be a 3×3, adjacency matrix corresponding to a given graph of three nodes labelled 1, 2, 3. If entry (1, 3) in M^3 is 2, then the graph is :*

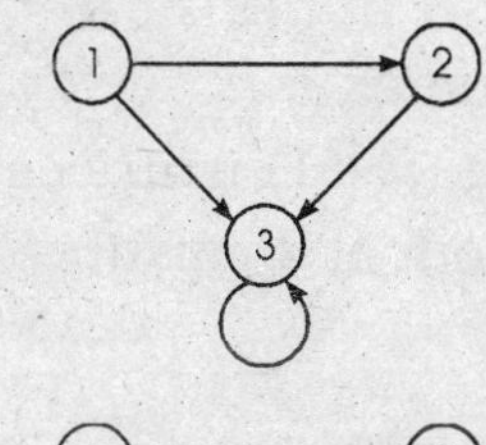

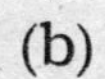

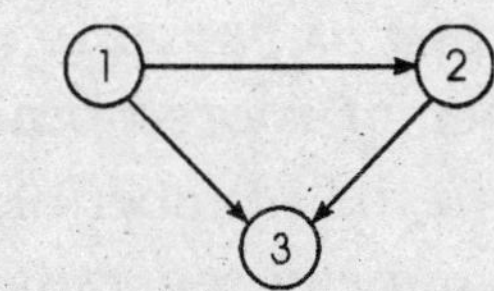

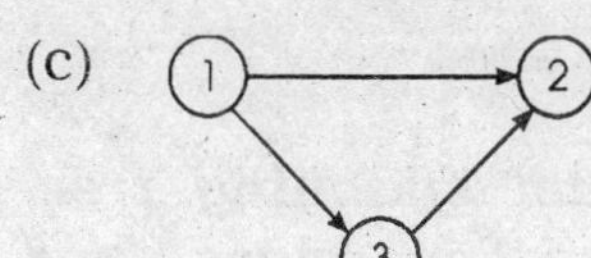

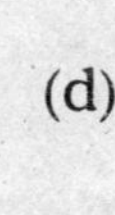

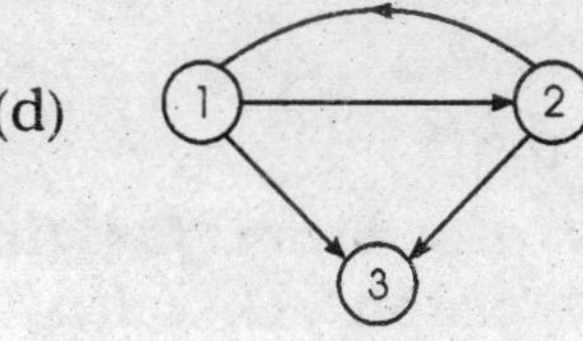

85. *Which of the following abstract data types can be used to represent a many to many relation ?*

(a) Tree (b) Queue

(c) Graph (d) Plex (Networking of fibre)

86. *Consider the following graphs*

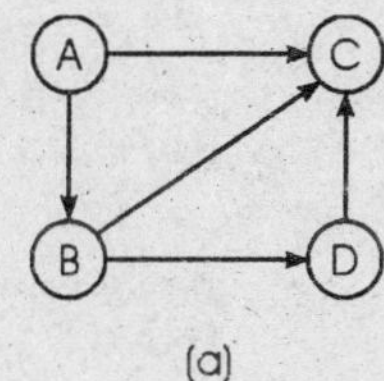

(a)

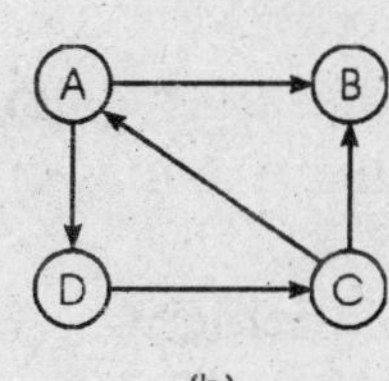

(b)

In fig (a) which is a valid topological sorting ?

(a) ABCD (b) BACD

(c) BADC (d) ABDC

87. *In fig. (b) which is a valid strong component ?*

(a) ACD (b) ABD

(c) BCD (d) ABC

Answers : **76.*** (a) **77.*** (d) **78.*** (c) **79.*** (b) **80.*** (b) **81.*** (c)
82.* (d) **83.*** (d) **84.*** (a) **85.** (c),(d) **86.*** (d) **87.*** (d)

88. ***The minimum number of colors needed to colour a graph of*** **$(n > 3)$** ***vertices and 2 edge is :***

(a) 1 (b) 2

(c) 3 (d) 4

89. ***A 3-ary tree is a tree in which every internal node has exactly 3 children. The number of leaf nodes in such a tree with six internal nodes will be :***

(a) 10 (b) 17

(c) 23 (d) 13

90. ***The number of rooted binary trees with n nodes is :***

(a) Equal to the number of ways of multiplying $(n + 1)$ matrices

(b) Equal to the number of ways of arranging n out of $2n$ distinct elements

(c) Equal to $\frac{1}{(n+1)}\binom{2n}{n}$

(d) Equal to $n\,!$

91. ***Kruskal's algorithm for finding a minimum spanning tree of a weighted graph G with n vertices and m edges has the time-complexity of :***

(a) $O(n^2)$ (b) $O(m, n)$

(c) $O(m \log n)$ (d) $O(m^2)$

92. ***Match the followings :***

(A)	The number of distinct binary trees with n nodes	(P)	$\frac{n\,!}{2}$
(B)	The number of binary strings of length $2n$ with an equal number of 0's and 1's	(Q)	${}^{3n}C_n$
(C)	The number of element permutations of n objects	(R)	${}^{2n}C_n$
(D)	The number of binary strings of length $6n$. which are palindromes with $2n$ 0's	(S)	$\frac{1}{n+1}\binom{2n}{n}$

(a) $A \to S, B \to P, C \to Q, D \to R$

(b) $A \to Q, B \to R, C \to P, D \to S$

(c) $A \to S, B \to R, C \to P, D \to Q$

(d) $A \to S, B \to Q, C \to P, D \to R$

93. The maximum number of edges in a planar graph with n vertices is :

(a) $n-1$ (b) n

(c) $2n+1$ (d) $3n-6$

94. The number of edges are there in a forest with p-components having n vertices in all :

(a) $3n-6$ (b) $p-n$

(c) $n-p$ (d) $2n-3p$

95. A non-planar graph with minimum number of vertices has :

(a) 9 edges, 6 vertices (b) 9 edges, 5 vertices

(c) 10 edges, 5 vertices (d) 10 edges, 6 vertices

96. The number of distinct simple graphs with upto three nodes is :

(a) 15 (b) 10

(c) 7 (d) 9

97. The number of edges in a regular graph of degree d and n vertices is :

(a) nd (b) $n+d$

(c) $\frac{nd}{2}$ (d) $\frac{n+d}{2}$

98. A binary tree T has n leaf nodes. The number of nodes of degree 2 in T is :

(a) $\log_2 n$ (b) 2^n

(c) n (d) $n-1$

99. The minimum number of edges in a connected cyclic graph on n-vertices is :

(a) n (b) $n+1$

(c) $n-1$ (d) $\frac{n(n-1)}{2}$

100. Consider the graph given below

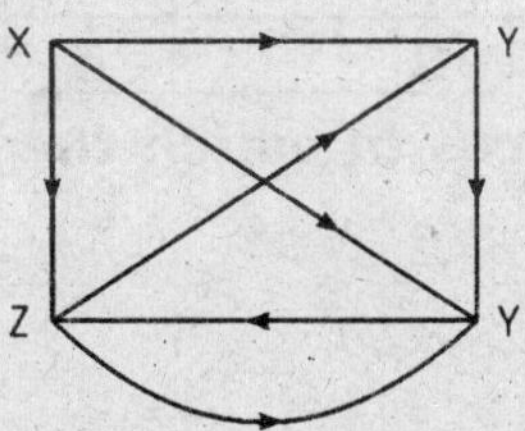

Answers : **88.** (b) **89.** (d) **90.** (a),(c) **91.** (c) **92.** (c) **93.** (d) **94.*** (c) **95.** (c) **96.** (c) **97.*** (c) **98.** (d) **99.*** (a)

Suppose the vertices are stored in memory in an array DATA as follows :

DATA : x, y, z, w

Then what is true about G —

(a) G is unilaterally Connected

(b) (x, y, z, w) is a spanning path

(c) G is strongly connected

(d) G is a multigraph

101. ***In Questoin 100, what is the path matrix—***

(a) $\begin{bmatrix} 1 & 0 & 1 & 1 \\ 1 & 1 & 1 & 1 \\ 1 & 0 & 0 & 1 \\ 0 & 1 & 1 & 1 \end{bmatrix}$ (b) $\begin{bmatrix} 0 & 0 & 0 & 0 \\ 1 & 1 & 1 & 1 \\ 1 & 0 & 0 & 1 \\ 1 & 1 & 1 & 1 \end{bmatrix}$

(c) $\begin{bmatrix} 0 & 1 & 1 & 1 \\ 0 & 1 & 1 & 1 \\ 0 & 1 & 1 & 1 \\ 0 & 1 & 1 & 1 \end{bmatrix}$ (d) $\begin{bmatrix} 0 & 1 & 1 & 1 \\ 0 & 1 & 1 & 1 \\ 1 & 1 & 1 & 0 \\ 1 & 1 & 1 & 0 \end{bmatrix}$

102. ***A weighted graph G with six vertices A, B, C, ...F, is stored in memory using a linked representation with a vertex file and an edge file as vertex file***

START [3]

	1	2	3	4	5	6	7	8
VERTEX	D		B	F	A		C	E
NEXT-V	7		1	5	0		8	4
PTR	9		3	0	6		10	1

Edge File	1	2	3	4	5	6	7	8	9	10
BEG-V	8	5	3		5	5	3		1	7
END-V	1	4	7		3	1	1		8	8
NEXT-E	0	5	7		0	2	0		0	0
NEIGHT	3	4	2		6	3	1		2	5

Then the order of vertices in which they appear

(a) B, A, C, E, D, F

(b) B, D, C, E, A, F

(c) B, D, C, E, F, A

(d) B, D, E, C, F, A

Answers : **100.** (a), (b) **101.** (c) **102.*** (c)

SOLUTIONS

1. By handshaking lemma, the vertices of odd degree in a graph is always even.

3. Two (or more) subgraphs g_1 and g_2 of a graph G are said to be edge disjoint if g_1 and g_2 do not have any edges in common.

21. Because, there is exactly one vertex of even degree, and the remaining $(n - 1)$ vertices are of odd degrees. But number of vertices of odd degree is even, so $(n - 1)$ is even. Hence n is odd.

24. Since the graph is connected and the number of edges is one less than the number of vertices. So, it is a tree.

39. Because number of vertices are same and number of edges are equal and there is a one to one correspondence between vertices and edges hence are isomorphic to each other.

43. Clearly G_1 is $K_{3,\,3}$ a non-planar graph, G_3 is also $K_{(3,\,3)}$ drawn in different form, hence both are non-planar. Also both are non-planar fundamental graph. Only G_2 is planar because

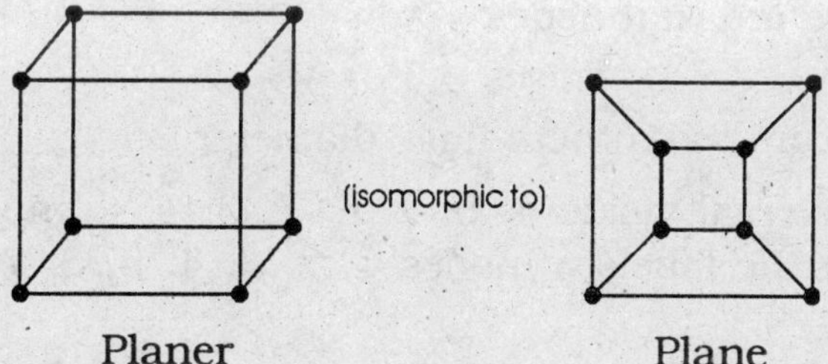

Planer Plane

Also by Kuratowski theorem G is non-planar iff it has a subgraph K_5 or $K_{3,\,3}$.

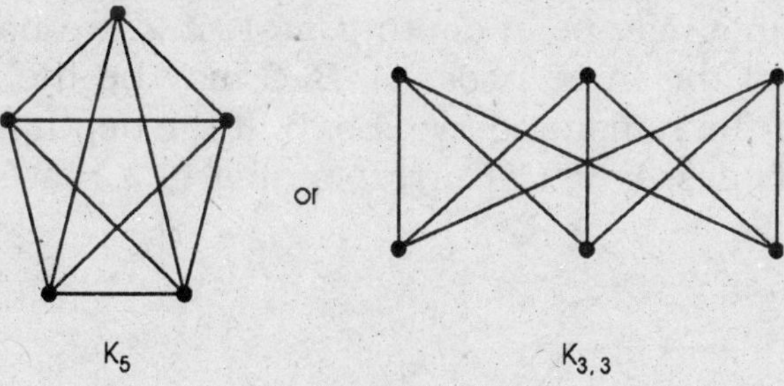

and G3 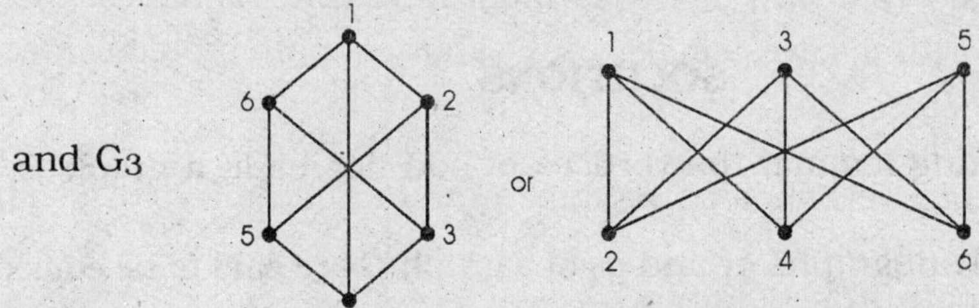

45. By Kurtoviskis theorem, G is a non-planar iff it has a subgraph K_5 or $K_{3,3}$.

53. d = depth = length of terminal node from root.

= $GBACK = GBACF = GPDRH$.

67. Consider the complete binary tree

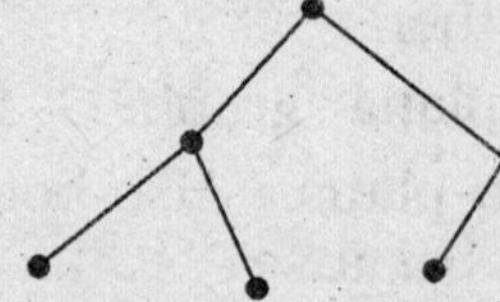

Here internal nodes = 3

leaves = 3

75. Dia $(K_{1,1}) = 1$ and all others have diameter 2.

76. Post-order traversal yields 4, 5, 2, 6, 7, 3, 1. Comparing with a, b, –, c, d, *, +, we get the labels of nodes 1, 2, 3, 4, 5, 6, 7 as +, –, *, a, b, c, d, respectively.

77. If it is to be used for sorting, label of left child should be less than the label of the current node. so, coming down the tree, we get left child of node labelled 10 as the correct slot for 8.

78. It is 12. The tree may be of depth 2 or 1. If 2, we have 6 possible trees. Because one of the three nodes A, B, C may be the root. The next level may be one of the remaining two. So, 6. If the depth is 2, the root may be one of the 3 nodes A, B, C. Corresponding to a root say A, two trees are possible as this.

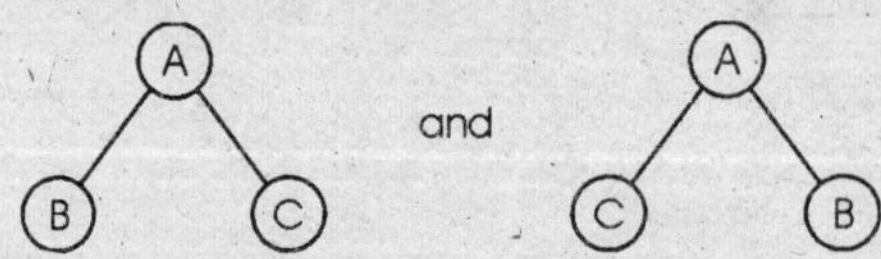

So, 6 possibilities. So, altogether 12 possible trees.

79. A strictly binary tree with 'n' leaves must have $(2n - 1)$ nodes.

80. Dijkstra's algorithm solves single source shortest path problem. Warshall's algorithm find transitive closure of a given path. Prim's algorithm constructs a minimum cost spanning tree for a given weighted graph.

81. Ecentricity of a given node is the maximum of minimum path from other nodes to the given node.

Cost of min. path from 1 to 5 = 7

Cost of min. path from 2 to 5 = 6

Cost of min. path from 3 to 5 = 4

Cost of min. path from 4 to 5 = 7

Since the maximum is 7, so the ecentricity of node 5 is 7.

82. Ecentricity of node 1 = ∞

Ecentricity of node 2 = 6

Ecentricity of node 3 = 8

Ecentricity of node 4 = 5

Ecentricity of node 5 = 7

Centre of the graph is the node with minimum ecentricity. so, the centre of the graph is node no. 4.

83. Let there be n items to searched. After the first search the list is divided into 2 *i.e.*, each of length $\left(\frac{n}{2}\right)$. After the next search, 2 lists, each of length $\frac{n}{4}$ and so on. The successive division has to stop when the length of list becomes 1. Let it be happen after r steps, so

$$\frac{n}{2^r} = 1$$

$$\Rightarrow \qquad n = 2^r$$

$$\Rightarrow \qquad r = \log_2 (n)$$

84. If the (1, 3) entry in M^3 is 2, it means there are 2 paths of length 3, connecting node 1 and 3.

86. In topological sorting we list out all the nodes in such a way that when ever there is an edge connecting i and j, i should precede j in the listing.

87. In strong component of a given graph is the maximal set of vertices such that for any two vertices i, j in the set, there is a path connecting i to j.

94. Let T be the forest with p-components C_1, C_2, ... C_p. Let e_i and n_i be the number of edges and vertices in the component C_i. Since each component is a tree.

$$e_1 = n_1 - 1$$
$$e_2 = n_2 - 1$$
$$\ldots\ldots\ldots\ldots\ldots$$
$$e_p = n_p - 1$$

Adding we get the result.

98. A graph is said to be *K*-regular if degree of all the vertices are of degree *K*.

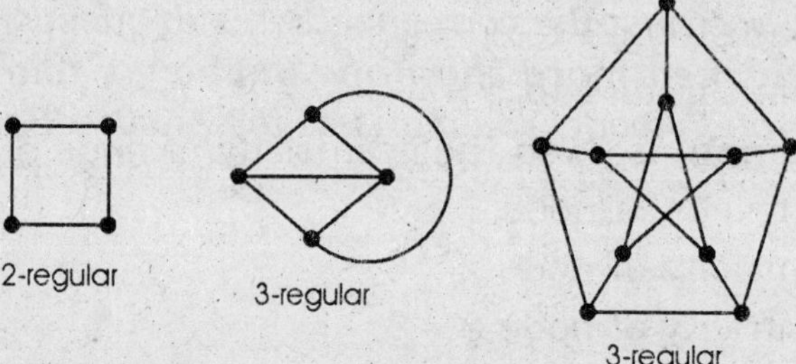

But we know that sum of degree of all the vertices is twice the number of edges. Let *G* is *d*-regular,

then $$\sum_{V = V(G)} d(v) = 2e$$

$\Rightarrow$ $d + d + \ldots\ n \text{ times} = 2e$

$\Rightarrow$ $e = \dfrac{nd}{2}$

99. Any connected acyclic graph is a tree having $(n - 1)$ edges. Hence, the minimum number of edges in a connected cyclic graph is $(n - 1) + 1 = n$. By adding an edge to a tree we get a minimal connected cyclic graph.

102. Since START = 3, the list begins with the vertex B. Then NEXT-V tells us to go to 1(D), then 7(C), then 8(E), then 4(F), and then 5(A); that is B, D, C, E, F, A.

■□■

2002

CS : Computer Science and Engineering

Section A

(75 marks)

CS1. *This question consists of TWENTY FIVE sub-questions, 1.1 to 1.25, of ONE mark each. For each of sub-questions, four alternativs, A, B, C, and D are provided. Choose the most appropriate alternative and darken its bubble on the OBJECTIVE RESPONSE SHEET (ORS) against the corresponding sub-question number using a soft HB pencil.* ***Do not darken more than one bubble*** *for any sub-question. Do not use the ORS for any rough work. You may use the Answer Boo (last few pages) for any rough work.*

1.1 ***The rank of the matrix*** $\begin{bmatrix} 1 & 1 \\ 0 & 0 \end{bmatrix}$ ***is***

(a) 4 (b) 2

(c) 1 (d) 0

1.2 ***The trapezoidal rule for intergration give exact result when the integrand is a polynominal of degree***

(a) 0 but not 1 (b) 1 but not 0

(c) 0 or 1 (d) 2

1.3 ***The solution to the recurrence equation***

$$T(2^k) = 3T(2^{k-1}) + 1,\ T(1) = 1 \text{ is;}$$

(a) 2^k (b) $(3^{k+1} - 1)/2$

(c) $3 \log_2 k$ (d) $2 \log_3 k$

1.4 ***The minimum numbers of colours required to colour the vertices of a cycle with n nodes in such a way that no two adjacent nodes havethe same colour is :***

(a) 2 (b) 3

(c) 4 (d) $n - 2 \mid n/2 \mid + 2$

1.5 ***In the worst case, the number of comparisons needed to search a singly linkedlist of length n fora given element is***

(a) $\log_2 n$ (b) $n/2$

(c) $\log_2 n - 1$ (d) n

1.6 ***Which of the following is true?***

(a) The set of all rational negative numbers forms a group under

Answers : **1.1.** (c) **1.2.** (b) **1.3.** (d) **1.4.** (d) **1.5.** (d)

multiplication.

(b) The set of all non-singular matrices forms a group under multiplication.

(c) The set of all matrices forms a group under multiplication.

(d) Both B and C are true.

1.7 ***The language accepted by a Pushdown Automaton in which the stack is limited to 10 items is best described as***

(a) Context Free (b) Regular

(c) Deterministic Context Free (d) Recursive

1.8 ***"If X then Y unless Z" is represented by which of the following formulas in propositional logic? ('—' is negation, "^" is conjunction and "→" is implication)***

(a) $(X \wedge - Z) \rightarrow Y$ (b) $(X \wedge Y) \rightarrow - Z$

(c) $(X \rightarrow (Y \wedge - Z)$ (d) $(X \rightarrow Y) \wedge - Z$

1.9 ***A device employing INTER line for device interrupt puts the CALL instruction on the data bus while***

(a) $\overline{\text{INTA}}$ is active (b) HOLD is active

(c) READ is active (d) None of the above

1.10 ***n 8085 which of the following modifies the program counter?***

(a) Only PCHL instruction (b) Only ADD instructions

(c) Only JMP and CALL instructions (d) All instructions

1.11 ***In serial data transmission, every byte of datais paddedwith a '0' in the beginning and one or two '1's at the end of byte because***

(a) Receiver isto be synchronized for byte reception

(b) Receiver recovers lost '0's and '1's from these padded bits

(c) Padded bits are useful in parity computation

(d) None of the above.

1.12 ***Minimum sum of product expression for f(w, x, y, z) shown in Karnaugh-map below is***

Yz \ Wx	00	01	11	10
00	0	1	1	0
01	x	0	0	1
11	x	0	0	1
10	0	1	1	x

(a) $xz = y'z$ (b) $xz' + zx'$

(c) $x'y + zx'$ (d) None of the above

1.13 ***Which of the following is not a form of memory?***

(a) instruction cache (b) instruction register

(c) instruction opcode (d) translation lookaside buffer

1.14 ***The decimal value 0.25***

(a) is equivalent to the binary value 0.1

(b) is equivalent to the binary value 0.01

(c) is equivalent to the binary value 0.00111.....

(d) cannot be represented precisely in binary

1.15 ***The 2's complement representation of the decimal value -15 is***

(a) 1111 (b) 11111

(c) 111111 (d) 100001

1.16 ***Sign extension is a step in***

(a) floating point multiplication

(b) signed 16bit interger addition

(c) arithmetic left shift

(d) converting asigned integer from one size to another

1.17 ***In the C languge***

(a) At most one activation record exists between the current activation record and the activation record for the aim

(b) The number of activation records between the current activation record and the activation record for the main depends on the actual function calling sequence.

(c) The visibility of global variables depends on the actual function calling sequence.

(d) Recursion requires the activation record for the recursive function to be saved on a different stack before the recursive function can be called.

1.18 ***The results returned by functions under value-result and reference parameter passing conventions***

(a) Do not differ

(b) Differ in the presence of loops

(c) Differ in all cases

(d) May differ in the presence of exceptions

1.19 ***Relation R with an associated set of functional dependencies, R, is decomposed into BCNF. The redundancy (arising out of functional dependencies) in the resulting set of relations is***

Answers : **1.6.** (c) **1.7.** (c) **1.8.** (a) **1.9.** (a) **1.10.** (c) **1.11.** (a) **1.12.** (b) **1.13.** (c) **1.14.** (b) **1.15.** (d) **1.16.** (d) **1.17.** (d) **1.18.** (b)

(a) Zero

(b) More than zero but less than that of an equivalent 3NF decomposition

(c) Proportional to the sizeof F^+

(d) Indeterminate

1.20 *With regard to the expressive power of the formal relation query languages, which of the following statements is true?*

(a) Reltional algebra is more powerful than relational calculus

(b) Relational algebra has the same power as relational calculus

(c) Relational algebra has the same power as safe relational calculus

(d) None of the above

1.21. *In 2's complement addition, overflow*

(a) is flagged whenever there is carry from sign bit addition

(b) cannot occur when a positive value is added to a negative value

(c) is flagged when the carries from sign bit and previous bit match

(d) None of the above

1.22 *Which of the following scheduling algorithmsis non- preemptive?*

(a) Round Robin

(b) Fist-In First-Out

(c) Multilevel Queue Scheduling

(d) Multilevel Queue Scheduling with Feedback

1.23 *The optimal page replacement algorithm will selectthe page that*

(a) Has not been used for the longest time in the past

(b) Will not be used for the longest time in the future

(c) Has been used least numberof times

(d) Has been used most number of times

1.24 *In the absolute addressing mode*

(a) the operand is inside the instruction

(b) the addressof the operand is inside the instruction

(c) the register containing the address of the operand is specified inside the instruction

(d) the location of the operand is implicit

1.25 *Maximum number of edges in a n-node undirected graph without self loops is*

(a) n^2 (b) $n(n-1)/2$

(c) $n-1$ (d) $(n+1)(n)/2$

Answers : **1.19.** (c) **1.20.** (b) **1.21.** (a) **1.22.** (b) **1.23.** (b) **1.24.** (b) **1.25.** (b)

CS2. This question consists of TWENTY FIVE sub-questions 2.1 to 2.25, of TWO marks each. For each of sub-questions, four alternativs, A, B, C, and D are provided. Choose the most appropriate alternative and darken its bubble on the OBJECTIVE RESPONSE SHEET (ORS) against the corresponding sub-question number using a soft HB pencil. Do not darken more than one bubble for any sub-question. Do not use the ORS for any rough work. You may use the Answer Boo (last few pages) for any rough work.

2.1 Consider the following logic circuit whose inputs are functions $f_1, f_2\ f_3$ and output is f.

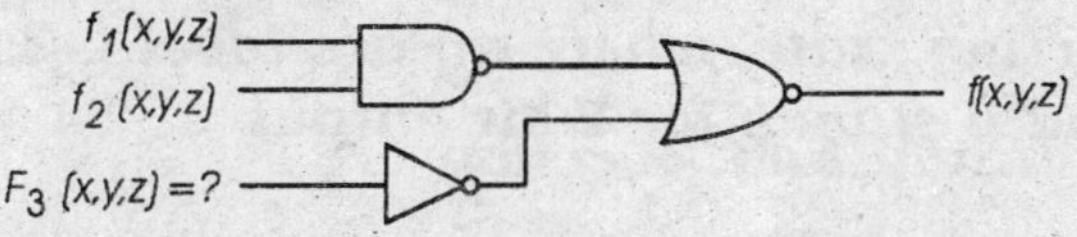

Given that

$f_1(x, y, z) = \Sigma\ (0, 1, 3, 5)$,

$f_2(x, y, z) = \Sigma\ (6, 7)$, and

$f(x, y, z) = \Sigma\ (1, 4, 5)$

(a) $\Sigma\ (1, 4, 5)$ (b) $\Sigma\ (6, 7)$

(c) $\Sigma\ (0, 1, 3, 5)$ (d) None of the above

2.2 Consider the following multiplexor where 10, 11, 12, 13, are four data input lines selected by two address line combinations A1 A0 = 00, 01, 10, 11 repsectively and f is the output of the multiplexor. EN is the Enable input.

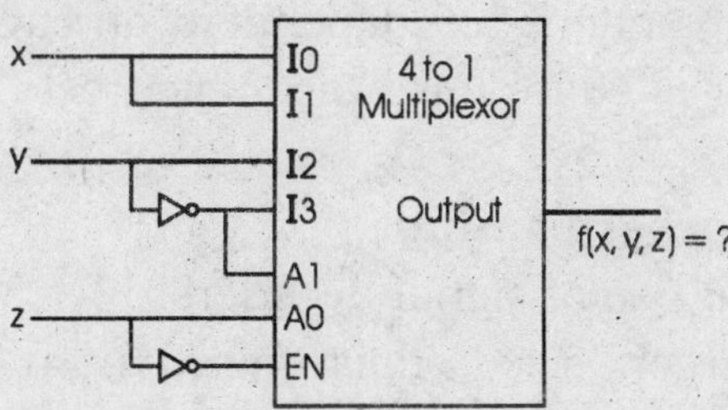

The function $f(x, y, z)$ implemented by the above circuit is

(a) xyz' (b) $xy + z$

(c) $x + y$ (d) None of the above

2.3 Let $f(A,B) = A' + B$. Simplified expression for function $f(f(x + y, y), z)$ is

(a) $x' + z$ (b) xyz

(c) $xy' + z$ (d) None of the above

Answers : 2.1. (2.2. (2.3. (

2.4 ***What are the states of the Auxillary Carry (AC) and Carry Flag (CY) after executing the following 8085 program?***

MVI H, 5DH

MVI L, 6BH

MOV A,H

ADD L

(a) AC = 0 and CY = 0 (b) AC = 1 and CY = 1

(c) AC = 1 and CY = 0 (d) AC = 0 and CY = 0

2.5 ***The Finite state machine described by the following state diagram with A as starting state, where an arc label is x/y and x stands for 1-bit input and y stands for 2-bit output***

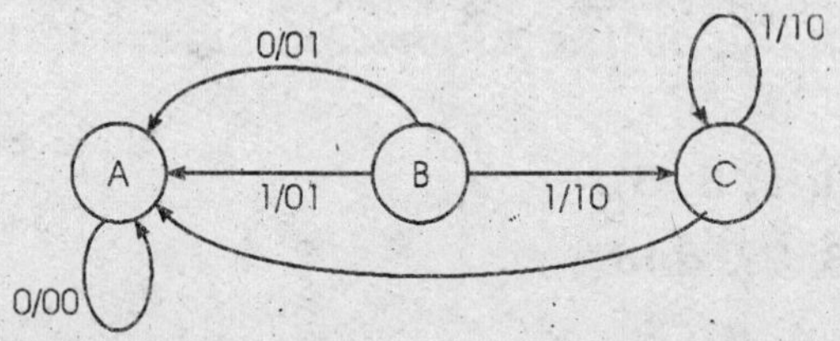

(a) Outputs the sum of the present and theprevious bits of the input

(b) Outputs 01 whenever the input sequence contains 11

(c) Outputs 00 whenever the input sequence contains 10

(d) None of the above

2.6 ***The performance of a pipelined processor suffers if***

(a) the pipeline stages have different delays

(b) consecutive instructions are dependent on each other

(c) the pipeline stages share hardware resources

(d) all of the above

2.7 ***Horizontal microprogramming***

(a) does not require use of signal decoders

(b) results in larger sized microinstructions than vertical microprogramming

(c) uses one bit for each control signal

(d) all of the above

2.8 ***Consider the following declaration of a two-dimensional array in C:***

char a[100][100];

Assuming that the main memory is byte-addressable and that the array is stored starting from memory address 0, the address of a[40][50]is

(a) 4040 (b) 4050

(c) 5040 (d) 5050

2.9 ***The number of leaf nodes in a rooted tree of n nodes, with each node having 0 or 3 children is :***

(a) $n/2$ (b) $(n - 1)/3$

(c) $(n - 1)/2$ (d) $(2n + 1)/3$

2.10 ***Consider the following algorithm for searching for a given number x in an unsorted array A[1.....n] having n distinct values :***

1. Choose an i uniformly at random from 1.....n;

2. If A[i] = x then Stop else Goto 1;

Assuming that x is present in A, what is the expected number of comparisons made by the algorithm before it terminates?

(a) n (b) $n - 1$

(c) $2n$ (d) $n/2$

2.11 ***The running time of the following algorithm***

Procedure A(n)

If 2 <= 2 return (1) else return $(A(\mid \sqrt{v} \mid))$

is best described by

(a) $O(n)$ (b) $O(\log n)$

(c) $O(\log \log n)$ (d) $O(1)$

2.12 ***A weight-balanced tree is a binary tree in which for each node, the number of nodes in the left subtree isatleasthalf and atmost twice the number of nodes in the right subtree. The maximum possible height (number of nodes on the path from the root to the furthest leaf) of such a tree on n nodes isbest described by which of the following?***

(a) $\log_2 n$ (b) $\log_{4/3} n$

(c) $\log_3 n$ (d) $\log_{3/2} n$

2.13 ***The smallest finite automaton which accepts the language***

{x | length of x is divisible by 3} has

(a) 2 states (b) 3 states

(c) 4 states (d) 5 states

2.14 ***Which of the following is true?***

(a) The complement of a recursive language is recursive

Answers : **2.4.** (c) **2.5.** (a) **2.6.** (d) **2.7.** (b) **2.8.** (b) **2.9.** (d) **2.10.** (a) **2.11.** (c) **2.12.** (d) **2.13.** (b)

(b) The complement of a recursively enumerable language is recursively enumerable

(c) The complement of a recursive language is either recursive or recursively enumerable

(d) The complement of a context-free language is context-free

2.15 ***The Newton-Raphson iteration $X_{n+1} = (X_n/2) + 3/(2X_n)$ can be used to solve the equation***

(a) $X^2 = 3$ (b) $X^3 = 3$

(c) $X^2 = 2$ (d) $X^3 = 2$

2.16 ***Four air coins are tossed simultaneously. The probability that at least one head and one tail turn up is***

(a) 1/16 (b) 1/8

(c) 7/8 (d) 15/16

2.17 ***The binary relation S = ϕ (empty set) on set A = {1, 2, 3} is***

(a) Neither reflexive nor symmertric

(b) Symmertric and reflexive

(c) Transitive and reflexive

(d) Transitive and symmetric

2.18 ***The C languageis***

(a) A context free language

(b) A context sensitive language

(c) A regular language

(d) Parsable fully only by a Turning machine

2.19 ***To evaluate an expression without any embedded function calls***

(a) One stac is enough

(b) Two stacs are needed

(c) As many stacks as the height of the expression tree are needed

(d) A Turning machine is needed in the general case

2.20 ***Dynamic linking can cause security concerns because***

(a) Security is dynamic

(b) The path for searchingdynamic libraries is not nown till runtime

(c) Linking is insecure

(d) Cryptographic procedures are not available for dynamic linking

2.21 ***Which combination of the following features will suffice to characterize an OS as a multiprogrammed OS? (a) More than one program may be loaded into mainmemory at the same time for***

execution. (b) If a program waits for certain events such as I/O, another programis immediately scheduledfor execution. (c) If the execution of a program terminate, another program is immediately scheduled for execution.

(a) a (b) a and b

(c) a and c (d) a, b and c

2.22 ***In the index allocation scheme of blocks of a file, the maximum possible size of the file depends on***

(a) the size of the blocs, and the size of the address of the blocks

(b) the number of blocks used for the index, and the size of the blocks

(c) the size of the blocs, the number of blocks used for the index, and the size of the address of the blocks

(d) None of the above

2.23 ***A B^+ -tree index is to be built on the Name attribute of the relation STUDENT. Assume that all student names are of length 8 bytes, disk blocks are of size 512 bytes, and index pointers are of size 4 bytes. Given this scenario, what would be the best choice of the degree (i.e. the number of pointers per node) ofthe B^+ - tree?***

(a) 16 (b) 42

(c) 43 (d) 44

2.24 ***Relation R is decomposed using a set of functional dependencies, F, and relation S is decomposed using another setoffunctional dependencies, G. One decomposition is definitely BCNF, the other is definitely 3NF but it is not nown which is which. To make a guaranteed identification, which one of the following tests should be used on the decompositions? (Assume that the closures of F and G are available).***

(a) Dependency-preservation (b) Lossless-join

(c) BCNF definition (d) 3NF definition

2.25 ***From the following instance of a relation schema R (A, B, C), we can conclude that :***

A	B	C
1	1	1
1	1	0
2	3	2
2	3	2

Answers : **2.15.** (a) **2.16.** (c) **2.17.** (b) **2.18.** (a) **2.19.** (a)
2.20. (b) **2.21.** (d) **2.22.** (c) **2.23.** (a) **2.24.** (a)

(a) A functionally determines B and B functionally determines C

(b) A functionally determines b and B does not functionally determine C

(c) B does not functionally determine C

(d) A does not functionally determine B and B does not functionally determine C

Answers : 2.25. (a)

GATE-2003

COMPUTER SCIENCE & ENGINEERING

Time Allowed : 3 Hours ***Maximum Marks : 150***

Read the following instructions carefully

1. This question paper contains 90 objective questions. Q. 1-30 carry one mark each and Q. 31-90 carry two marks each.

2. Answer all the questions.

3. Questions must be answered on special machine gradable **O**bjective **R**esponse **S**heet **(ORS)** by drakening the appropriate bubble (marked A, B, C, D) using HB pencil against the question number on the left hand side of the **ORS**. Each question has only one correct answer. In case you wish to change an answer, erase the old answer completely using a good soft eraser.

4. There will be **NEGATIVE** marking. For each wrong answer **0.25** mark from Q. 1-30 and **0.5** mark from Q. 31-90 will be deducted. More than one answer marked against a question will be deemed as an incorrect response and will be negatively marked.

5. Write your registration number, name of the Centre at the specified locations on the right half of the **ORS.**

6. Using HB pencil, draken the appropriate bubble under each digit of your registration number.

7. Using HB pencil, draken the appropriate bubble under the letters corresponding to your paper code.

8. No charts or tables are provided in the examination hall.

9. Use the blank pages given at the end of the question paper for rough work.

10. Choose the **closest** numerical answer among the choices given.

11. This question paper contains 28 pages. Please report if there is any discrepancy.

Q. 1—30 CARRY ONE MARK EACH

1. ***The regular expression 0* (10*)* denotes the same set as***
   (a) (1*0)*1*
   (b) 0 + (0 + 10)*
   (c) (0 + 1)* (10(0 + 1)*
   (d) none of the above

2. ***Nobody knows yet if*** P = NP. ***Consider the language L defined as follows :***

$$\mathbf{L} = \begin{cases} \mathbf{(0+1)^* \text{ if } P = NP} \\ \mathbf{\phi \text{ otherwise}} \end{cases}$$

   Which of the following statements is true ?
   (a) L is recursive
   (b) L is recursively enumerable but not recursive
   (c) L is not recursively enumerable
   (d) Whether L is recursive or not will be known after we find out if P = NP

3. ***Ram and Shyam have been asked to show that a certain problem*** Π ***is NP-complete. Ram shows a polynomial time reduction from the 3-SAT problem to*** Π, ***and Shyam shows a polynomial time reduction from*** Π ***to 3-SAT. Which of the following can be inferred from these reductions ?***
   (a) Π is NP-hard but not NP-complete
   (b) Π is in NP, but is not NP-complete
   (c) Π is NP-complete
   (d) Π is neither NP-hard, nor in NP

4. ***Consider an array multiplier for multiplying two*** n ***bit numbers. If each gate in the circuit has a unit delay, the total delay of the multiplier is***
   (a) $\Theta(1)$
   (b) $\Theta(\log n)$
   (c) $\Theta(n)$
   (d) $\Theta(n^2)$

5. ***For a pipelined CPU with a single ALU, consider the following situations***
   I. ***The j + 1-st instruction uses the result of the j-th instruction as an operand***
   II. ***The execution of a conditional jump instruction***

III. The j-th and j + 1-st instructions require the ALU at the same time

Which of the above can cause a hazard ?

(a) I and II only
(b) II and III only
(c) III only
(d) All the three

6. ***n couples are invited to a party with the condition that every husband should be accompanied by his wife. However, a wife need not be accompanied by her husband. The number of different gatherings possible at the party is***

(a) $\binom{2n}{n} * 2^n$
(b) 3^n
(c) $\frac{(2n)!}{2^n}$
(d) $\binom{2n}{n}$

7. ***Let A be a sequence of 8 distinct integers sorted in ascending order. How many distinct pairs of sequences, B and C are there such that (i) each is sorted in ascending order, (ii) B has 5 and C has 3 elements, and (iii) the result of merging B and C gives A ?***

(a) 2
(b) 30
(c) 56
(d) 256

8. ***Let P(E) denote the probability of the event E. Given P(A) = 1, P(B) = 1/2, the values of P(A\B) and P(B\A) respectively are***

(a) 1/4, 1/2
(b) 1/2, 1/4
(c) 1/2, 1
(d) 1, 1/2

9. ***Assuming the following C variable declaration***

int*A[10], B[10][10];

Of the following expressions

I. A[2]
II. A[2][3]
III. B[1]
IV. B[2][3]

which will not give compile-time errors if used as left hand sides of assignment statements in a C program ?

(a) I, II and IV only
(b) II, III and IV only
(c) II and IV only
(d) IV only

10. ***Consider the following C function.***

```
float f, (float x, int y) {
float p, s; int i;
```

Answers :

1.* (d)	**2.** (d)	**3.** (c)	**4.*** (d)	**5.** (d)
6. (a)	**7.** (d)	**8.*** (d)	**9.** (d)	

```
for (s = 1, p = 1; i = 1; i < y; i++) {
            p* = x/i;
            s+ = p;
      }
   return s;
}
```

For large values of y, the return value of the function f best approximates

(a) X^y (b) e^x

(c) ln (1 + x) (d) X^x

11. ***Consider the following SQL query***

select distinct a_1, a_2, ..., a_n

from r_1, r_2, ..., r_m

where P

For an arbitrary predicate P, this query is equivalent to which of the following relational algebra expressions ?

(a) $\Pi_{a_1, a_2, \ldots a_n} \sigma_p (r_1 \times r_2 \times \ldots \times r_m)$

(b) $\Pi_{a_1, a_2, \ldots a_n} \sigma_p (r_1 ** r_2 ** \ldots ** r_m)$

(c) $\Pi_{a_1, a_2, \ldots a_n} \sigma_p (r_1 \cup r_2 \cup \ldots \cup r_m)$

(d) $\Pi_{a_1, a_2, \ldots a_n} \sigma_p (r_1 \cap r_2 \cap \ldots \cap r_m)$

12. ***Which of the following scenarios may lead to an irrecoverable error in a database system?***

(a) A transaction writes a data item after it is read by an uncommitted transaction

(b) A transaction reads a data item after it is read by an uncommitted transaction

(c) A transaction reads a data item after it is written by a committed transaction

(d) A transaction reads a data item after it is written by an uncommitted transaction

13. ***Which of the following functionalities must be implemented by a transport protocol over and above the network protocol ?***

(a) Recovery from packet losses

(b) Detection of duplicate packets

(c) Packet delivery in the correct order

(d) End to end connectivity

14. *Which of the following assertions is FALSE about the Internet Protocol (IP) ?*

(a) It is possible for a computer to have multiple IP addresses

(b) IP packets from the same source to the same destination can take different routes in the network

(c) IP ensures that a packet is discarded if it is unable to reach its destination within a given number of hops

(d) The packet source cannot set the route of an outgoing packet; the route is determined only by the routing tables in the routers on the way

15. *In a system with 32 bit virtual addresses and 1 KB page size, use of one-level page tables for virtual to physical address translation is not practical because of*

(a) the large amount of internal fragmentation

(b) the large amount of external fragmentation

(c) the large memory overhead in maintaining page tables

(d) the large computation overhead in the translation process

16. *Assuming all numbers are in 2's complement representation, which of the following numbers is divisible by 11111011?*

(a) 11100111 (b) 11100100

(c) 11010111 (d) 11011011

17. *Let G be an arbitrary graph with n nodes and k components. If a vertex is removed from G, the number of components in the resultant graph must necessarily lie between*

(a) k and n (b) $k-1$ and $k+1$

(c) $k-1$ and $n+1$ (d) $k+1$ and $n-k$

18. *Consider the set $\sum^*$ of all strings over the alphabet $\sum = \{0, 1\}$. $\sum^*$ with the concatenation operator for strings*

(a) does not from a group

(b) forms a non-commutative group

(c) does not have a right identity element

(d) forms a group if the empty string is removed from $\sum^*$

Answers : **10.*** (c) **11.** (a) **12.** (d) **13.** (d) **14.** (a) **15.*** (a) **16.*** (a) **17.** (d) **18.*** (d)

19. ***Let T(n) be the number of different binary search trees on n distinct elements.***

Then $T(n) = \sum_{k=1}^{n} T(k-1)\,T(x)$ ***where x is***

(a) $n - k + 1$ (b) $n - k$

(c) $n - k - 1$ (d) $n - k - 2$

20. ***If the strings of a language L can be effectively enumerated in lexicographic (i.e., alphabetic) order, which of the following statements is true?***

(a) L is necessarily finite

(b) L is regular but not necessarily finite

(c) L is context free but not necessarily regular

(d) L is recursive but not necessarily context free

21. ***Which of the following suffices to convert an arbitrary CFG to an LL(1) grammar?***

(a) Removing left recursion alone

(b) Factoring the grammar alone

(c) Removing left recursion and factoring the grammar

(d) None of the above

22. ***Assume that the SLR parser for a grammar G has*** n_1 ***states and the LALR parser for G has*** n_2 ***states. The relationship between*** n_1 ***and*** n_2 ***is***

(a) n_1 is necessarily less than n_2 (b) n_1 is necessarily equal to n_2

(c) n_1 is necessary greater than n_2 (d) none of the above

23. ***In a bottom-up evaluation of a syntax directed definition, inherited attributes can***

(a) always be evaluated

(b) be evaluated only if the definition is L-attributed

(c) be evaluated only if the definition has synthesized attributes

(d) never be evaluated

24. ***Suppose the numbers 7, 5, 1, 8, 3, 6, 0, 9, 4, 2 are inserted in that order into an initially empty binary search tree. The binary search tree uses the usual ordering on natural numbers. What is the in-order traversal sequence of the resultant tree ?***

(a) 7510324689 (b) 0243165987

(c) 0123456789 (d) 9864230157

25. *Using a larger block size in a fixed block size file system leads to*

(a) better disk throughput but poorer disk space utilization

(b) better disk throughout and better disk space utilization

(c) poorer disk throughput but better disk space utilization

(d) poorer disk throughput and poorer disk space utilization

26. *Which of the following statements is FALSE ?*

(a) In statically typed language, each variable in a program has a fixed type

(b) In un-typed languages, values do not have any types

(c) In dynamically typed languages, variables have no types

(d) In all statically typed languages, each variable in a program is associated with values of only a single type during the execution of the program

27. *In a heap with n elements with the smallest element at the root, the 7th smallest element can be found in time*

(a) $\Theta(n \log n)$ (b) $\Theta(n)$

(c) $\Theta(\log n)$ (d) $\Theta(1)$

28. *The usual $\Theta(n^2)$ implementation of Insertion Sort to sort an array uses linear search to identify the position where an element is to be inserted into the already sorted part of the array. If, instead, we use binary search to identify the position, the worst case running time will*

(a) reamin $\Theta(n^2)$ (b) become $\Theta(n (\log n)^2)$

(c) become $\Theta(n \log n)$ (d) become $\Theta(n)$

29. *Consider the following graph*

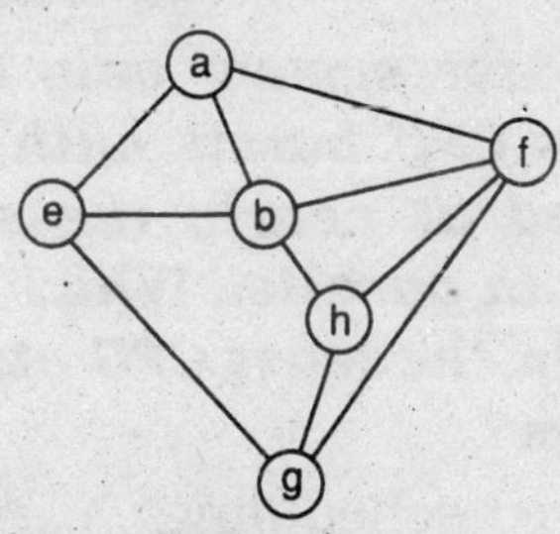

Among the following sequences

I. a b e g h f ***II. a b f e h g***

Answers : **19.*** (a) **20.** (a) **21.** (c) **22.** (b) **23.** (c) **24.*** (b) **25.** (d) **26.** (a) **27.** (c) **28.** (c)

III. a b f h g e ***IV. a f g h b e***

which are depth first traversal of the above graph ?

(a) I, II and IV only (b) I and IV only

(c) II, III and IV only (d) I, III and IV only

30. ***Consider the following three claims***

I. $(n + k)^m = \Theta(n^m)$, ***where k and m are constants***

II. $2^{n+1} = O(2^n)$

III. $2^{2n+1} = O(2^n)$

Which of these claims are correct ?

(a) I and II (b) I and III

(c) II and III (d) I, II and III

Q. 31—90 CARRY TWO MARKS EACH

31. ***Suppose a process has only the following pages in its virtual address space: two contiguous code pages starting at virtual address 0 × 00000000, two contiguous data pages starting at virtual address 0 × 00400000, and a stack page starting at virtual address 0 × FFFFF000. The amount of memory required for storing the page tables of this process is:***

(a) 8 KB (b) 12 KB

(c) 16 KB (d) 20 KB

32. ***Assuming that no page faults occur, the average time taken to access a virtual address is approximately (to the nearest 0.5 ns):***

(a) 1.5 ns (b) 2 ns

(c) 3 ns (d) 4 ns

33. ***A uni-processor computer system only has two processes, both of which alternate 10ms CPU bursts with 90ms I/O bursts. Both the processes were created at nearly the same time. The I/O of both processes can proceed in parallel. Which of the following scheduling strategies will result in the least CPU utilization (over a long period of time) for this system?***

(a) First come first served scheduling

(b) Shortest remaining time first scheduling

(c) Static priority scheduling with different priorities for the two processes

(d) Round robin scheduling with a time quantum of 5 ms

34. *Which of the following is NOT an advantage of using shared, dynamically linked libraries as opposed to using statically linked libraries ?*

(a) Smaller sizes of executable files

(b) Lesser overall page fault rate in the system

(c) Faster program startup

(d) Existing programs need not be re-linked to take advantage of newer versions of libraries

35. *Consider the following class definitions in a hypothetical Object Oriented language that supports inheritance and uses dynamic binding. The language should not be assumed to be either Java or C++, though the syntax is similar.*

```
Class P {                          Class Q subclass of P {
          void f (int i) {          void f (inf i, {
                print (i);                print (2*i);
          }                         }
}                                  }
```

Now consider the following program fragment:

```
Px = new Q();
Qy = new Q ();
Pz = new Q();
x.f(1); ((p)y).f(1);z.f(1);
```

Here ((P) y) denotes a typecast of y to P. The output produced by executing the above program fragment will be:

(1) 121 (b) 211

(c) 212 (d) 222

THE FOLLOWING INFORMATION PERTAINS TO Q. 36—37

The following program fragment is written in a programming language that allows variables and does not allow nested declarations of functions.

```
global int i = 100, j = 5;
void P(x) {
          int i = 10;
```

Answers : **29.** (d) **30.*** (a) **31.** (b) **32.*** (b)
33.* (a) **34.** (d) **35.*** (d)

```
        print (x + 10);
        i = 200;
        j = 20;
        print (x);
    }
    main ( ) {P(i + j);}
```

36. ***If the programming language uses dynamic scoping and call by name parameter passing mechanism, the values printed by the above program are :***

(a) 115, 220 (b) 25, 220
(c) 25, 15 (d) 115, 105

37. ***If the programming language uses static scoping and call by need parameter passing mechanism, the values printed by the above program are:***

(a) 115, 220 (b) 25, 220
(c) 25, 15 (d) 115, 105

38. ***The following resolution rule is used in logic programming: Derive clause* $(P \vee Q)$ *from clauses* $(P \vee R)$, $(Q \vee \neg R)$**

Which of the following statements related to this rule is FALSE?

(a) $((P \vee R) \wedge (Q \vee \neg R)) \Rightarrow (P \vee Q))$ is logically valid
(b) $(P \vee Q) \Rightarrow ((P \vee R) \wedge (Q \vee \neg R))$ is logically valid
(c) $(P \vee Q)$ is satisfible if and only if $(P \vee R) \wedge (Q \vee \neg R)$ is satisfiable
(d) $(P \vee Q) \Rightarrow$ FALSE if and only if both P and Q are unsatisfable

39. ***Consider the following logic program P***

$$A(x) \leftarrow B(x, y), C(y) \leftarrow B(x, x)$$

Which of the following first order sentences is equivalent to P?

(a) $(\forall x) [\exists y) [B(x, y) \wedge C(y)] \Rightarrow A(x)] \wedge \neg (\exists x) [B(xx)]$
(b) $(\forall x) [(\forall y) [B(x, y) \wedge C(y)] \Rightarrow A(x)] \wedge \neg (\exists x) [B(xx)]$
(c) $(\forall x) [\exists y) [B(x, y) \wedge C(y)] \Rightarrow A(x)] \vee \neg (\exists x) [B(xx)]$
(d) $(\forall x) [(\forall y) [B(x, y) \wedge C(y)] \Rightarrow A(x) \wedge (\exists x) [B(xx)]$

40. ***Let G = (V, E) be a directed graph with n vertices. A path from*** v_i ***to*** v_j ***in G is sequence of vertices*** $(v_i, v_{i+1}, \ldots v_j)$ ***such that*** $(v_k, v_{k+1}) \in E$ ***for all k in i through*** $j - 1$. ***A simple path is a path in which no vertex appears more than once.***

Let A be an $n \times n$ ***array initialized as follow***

$$A[j, k] = \begin{cases} 1 \text{ if } (j, k) \in E \\ 0 \text{ otherwise} \end{cases}$$

Consider the following algorithm.

for* i = 1 *to n

for* j = 1 *to n

for* k = 1 *to n

A [j, k] = max (A[j, k] (A[j, i] + A[i, k]);

Which of the following statements is necessarily true for all j and k after terminal of the above algorithm ?

(a) $A[j, k] \leq n$

(b) If $A[j, j] \geq n-1$, then G has Hamiltonian cycle

(c) If there exists a path from j to k, $A[j, k]$ contains the longest path from j to k

(d) If there exists a path from j to k, every simple path from j to k cotntain most $A[j, k]$ edges

41. ***Consider the syntax directed definition shown below:***

S → *id* : = E {gen (*id*.place = E.place;);}

E → E_1 + E_2 {*t* = newtemp ( );

***gen* (*t* = E_1. place + E_2.place;);**

E.place = *t*}

E → *id* {E.place = *id*.place;}

Here, gen is a function that generates the output code, and newtemp is a function that returns the name of a new temporary variable on every call. Assume that t_i's are the temporary variable names generated by newtemp.

For the statement 'X: = Y + Z', the 3-address code sequence generated by this definition is:

(a) X = Y + Z

(b) t_1 = Y + Z; X t_1

(c) t_1 = Y; t_2 = t_1 + Z; X = t_2

(d) t_1 = Y; t_2 = Z; t_3 = t_1 + t_2; X = t_3

42. ***Consider the translation scheme shown below:***

S → TR

S → + T {print ('+'); }R | ε

T → num {print (num.val);}

Here num is a token that represents an integer and num.val

Answers : **36.*** (a) **37.*** (d) **38.** (b) **39.** (c) **40.** (d) **41.*** (c)

represents the corresponding integer value. For an input string '9 + 5 + 2', this translation scheme will print:

(a) 9 + 5 + 2
(b) 9 5 + 2 +
(c) 9 5 2 ++
(d) ++ 9 5 2

43. ***Consider the grammar shown below:***

S → C C

S → c C | d

The grammar is :

(a) LL (1)
(b) SLR (1) but not LL (1)
(c) LALR (1) but not SLR (1)
(d) LR (1) but not LALR (1)

44. ***Consider the grammar shown below:***

S → *i* E *t* S S′ | *a*

S′ → *e* S | ε

E → *b*

In the predictive parse table. M, of this grammar, the entries M[S′, e] and M[S′, $] respectively are:

(a) {S′ → *e* S} and {S′ → ε}
(b) {S′ → *e* S} and { }
(c) {S′ → ε} and {S′ → ε}
(d) {S′ → *e* S, S′ → ε} and {S′ → ε}

45. ***Consider the NFA M shown below:***

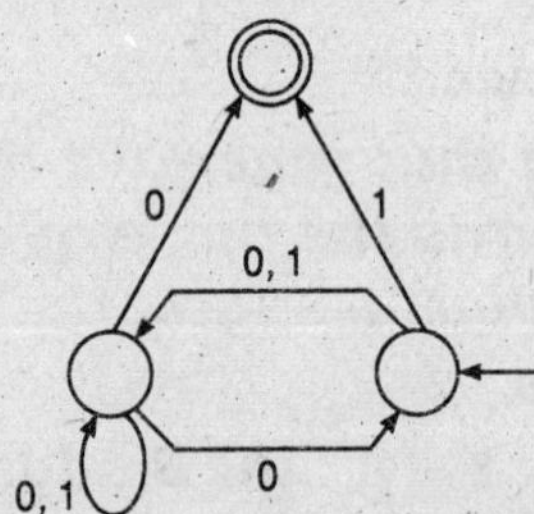

Let the language accepted by M be L. Let L_1 be the language accepted by the NFA M_1, obtained by changing the accepting state of M to a non-accepting state and by changing the non-accepting state of M to accepting states. Which of the following statemets is true?

(a) $L_1 = \{0, 1\}^* - L$
(b) $L_1 = \{0, 1\}^*$
(c) $L_1 \subseteq L$
(d) $L_1 = L$

46. ***Define languages L_0 and L_1 as follows:***

$L_0 = \{ < M, w, 0 > \mid$ **M *halts on w*** $\}$

$L_0 = \{< M, w, 1 > \mid$ **M *does not halts on w*** $\}$

Here < M, u, i > is a triplet, whose first component M is an encoding of a Turing Machine, second component, w, is a string and third component, i, is a bit.

Let L= $L_0 \cup L_1$. Which of the following is true?

(a) L is recursively enumerable, but $\overline{L}$ is not

(b) $\overline{L}$ is recursively enumerable, but L is not

(c) Both L and $\overline{L}$ are recursive

(d) Neither L nor $\overline{L}$ is recursively enumerable

47. ***A single tape Turing Machine M has two states q_0 and q_1, of which q_0 is the starting state. The tape alphabet of M is {0, 1, B } and its input alphabet is {0, 1}. The symbol B is the blank symbol used to indicate end of an input string. The transition function of M is described in the following table***

	0	1	B
q_0	q_1, 1, R	q_1, 1, R	Halt
q_1	q_1, 1, R	q_0, 1, L	q_0, B, L

The table is interpreted as illustrated below. The entry (q_1, 1, R) in row q_0 and column 1 signifies that if M is in state q_0 and reads 1 on the current tape square, then it writes 1 on the same tape square, moves its tape head one position to the right and transitions to state q_1. Which of the following statements is true about M?

(a) M does not halt on any string in $(0 + 1)^+$

(b) M does not halt on any string in $(00 + 1)^*$

(c) M halts on all string ending in a 0

(d) M halts on all string ending in a 1

48. ***Consider two languages L_1 and L_2 each on the alphabet Σ. Let $f: \Sigma \rightarrow \Sigma$ be a polynomial time computable bijection such that $(\forall x)$ [$x \in L_1$ iff $f(x) \in L_2$]. Further, let f^{-1} be also polynomial time computable.***

Which of the following CANNOT be true?

(a) $L_1 \in P$ and L_2 is finite

(b) $L_1 \in NP$ and $L_2 \in P$

(c) L_1 is undecidable and L_2 is decidable

(d) L_1 is recursively enumerable and L_2 is recursive

Answers : **42.*** (d) **43.** (d) **44.*** (a) **45.*** (c) **46.** (a) **47.** (d) **48.** (c)

49. ***Let G = ({S}, {a, b} R, S) be a context free grammer where the rule set R is***

$$S \rightarrow a S b \mid S S \mid \varepsilon$$

Which of the following statements is true?

(a) G is not ambiguous

(b) There exist $x, y \in L(G)$ such that $xy \notin L(G)$

(c) There is a deterministic pushdown automation that accepts L(G)

(d) We can find a deterministic finite state automation that accepts L(G)

50. ***Consider the following deterministic finite state automation M.***

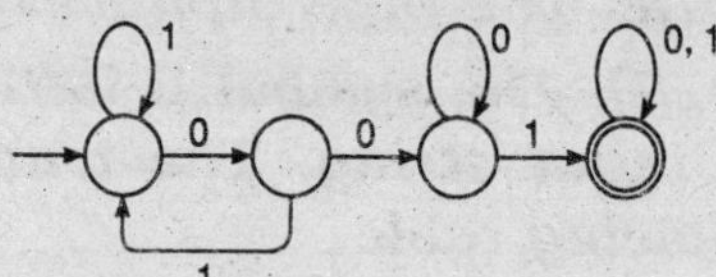

Let S denote the set of seven bit binary strings in which the first, the fourth, and the last bits are 1. The number of strings in S that are accepted by M is:

(a) 1 (b) 5

(c) 7 (d) 8

51. ***A graph G = (V, E) satisfies |E| ≤ |V| – 6. The min-degree of G is defined as*** $\min_{v \in V}$ **{degree (v)}.**

Therefore, min-degree of G cannot be:

(a) 3 (b) 4

(c) 5 (d) 6

52. ***Let Σ = (a, b, c, d, e) be an alphabet. We define an encoding scheme as follows:***

$g(a) = 3,\ g(b) = 5,\ g(c) = 7,\ g(d) = 9,\ g(e) = 11$

Let p_i denote the i-th prime number ($p_1 = 2$)

For a non-empty string $s = a_1 \ldots a_n$, where each $a_i \in \Sigma$, define

$f(s) = \prod_{i=1}^{n} P_i^{g(a_i)}$. ***For a non-empty sequence <$s_1 \ldots s_n$> of strings from***

Σ^+, ***define*** $h(<s_1 \ldots s_n>) = \prod_{i=1}^{n} P_i^{f(s_i)}$

Which of the following numbers is the encoding, h of a non-empty sequence of strings ?

(a) $2^7\ 3^7\ 5^7$ (b) $2^8\ 3^8\ 5^8$

(c) $2^9\ 3^9\ 5^9$

(d) $2^{10}\ 5^{10}\ 7^{10}$

53. ***Consider the set {a, b, c} with binary operators + and × defined as follows:***

+	a	b	c
a	b	a	c
b	a	b	c
c	a	c	b

×	a	b	c
a	a	b	c
b	b	c	a
c	c	c	b

For example, $a + c = c$, $c + a = a$, $c \times b = c$ and $b \times c = a$. Given the following set of equations:

$$(a \times x) + (a \times y) = c$$
$$(b \times x) + (c \times y) = c$$

the number of solution(s) (i.e., pair(s) (x, y) that satisfy the equation) is

(a) 0

(b) 1

(c) 2

(d) 3

54. ***Let $f : A \rightarrow B$ be an injective (one-to-one) function. Define $g : 2^A \rightarrow 2^B$ as :***

$g(C) = \{f(x) \mid x \in C\}$, for all subsets C of A.

Define $h : 2^B \rightarrow 2^A$ as: $h(D) = \{x \mid x \in A, f(x) \in D\}$, for all subsets D of B.

Which of the following statements is always true?

(a) $g(h(D)) \subseteq D$

(b) $g(h(D)) \geq D$

(c) $g(h(D)) \cap D = \phi$

(d) $g(h(D)) \cap (B - D) \neq \phi$

55. ***How many perfect matchings are there in a complete graph of 6 vertices?***

(a) 15

(b) 24

(c) 30

(d) 60

56. ***Consider the following recurrence relation***

$$T(1) = 1$$

$$T(n + 1) = T(n) + \lfloor \sqrt{n+1} \rfloor \text{ for all } n \geq 1$$

The value of $T(m^2)$ for $m \geq 1$ is

(a) $\frac{m}{6}(21m - 39) + 4$

(b) $\frac{m}{6}(4m^2 - 3m + 5)$

(c) $\frac{m}{2}(3m^{5/2} - 11m + 20) - 5$

(d) $\frac{m}{6}(5m^3 - 34m^2 + 137m - 104) + \frac{5}{6}$

Answers : **49.*** (d) **50.*** (a) **51.*** (c) **52.*** (b) **53.*** (d) **54.*** (d) **55.*** (a) **56.*** (b)

57. ***m identical balls are to be placed in n distinct bags. You are given that $m > kn_y$ where k is a natural number > 1. In how many ways can the balls be placed in the bags if each bag must contain at least k balls?***

(a) $\binom{m-k}{n-1}$ (b) $\binom{m-kn+n-1}{n-1}$

(c) $\binom{m-1}{n-k}$ (d) $\binom{m-kn+n+k-2}{n-k}$

58. ***Consider the following formula a and its two interpretations I_1 and I_2***

$a : (\forall\ x)\ [Px \Leftrightarrow (\forall\ y)\ [Qxy \Leftrightarrow \neg\ Q_{yy}]] \Rightarrow (\forall x)\ [\neg Px]$

I_1 : Domain : the set of natural numbers

Px ≡ 'x is a prime number'

Qxy ≡ 'y divides x'

I_2 : same as I_1 except that Px = 'x is a composite number.'

Which of the following statements is true?

(a) I_1 satisfies α, I_2 does not (b) I_2 satisfies α, I_1 does not

(c) Neither I_1 and nor I_2 satisfies α. (d) Both I_1 and I_2 satisfy α

59. ***Which of the following is a valid first order formula? (Here α and β are first order formulae with x as their only free variable)***

(a) $((\forall x)\ [\alpha] \Rightarrow (\forall x)\ [\beta]) \Rightarrow ((\forall x)\ [a \Rightarrow \beta]$

(b) $(\forall x)\ [\alpha] \Rightarrow (\exists x)\ [a \wedge \beta]$

(c) $((\forall x)\ [\alpha \vee \beta] \Rightarrow (\exists x)\ [\alpha]) \Rightarrow (\forall x)\ [\alpha]$

(d) $(\forall x)\ [\alpha \Rightarrow \beta] \Rightarrow ((\forall x)\ [\alpha] \Rightarrow (\forall x)\ [\beta])$

60. ***Let (S, ≤) be a partial order with two minimal elements a and b and a maximum element c. Let P : S → {True, False} be a predicate defined on S. Suppose that P(a) = True, P(b) = False and P(x) ⇒ P(y) for all x, y ∈ S satisfying x ≤ y, where ⇒ stands for logical implication. Which of the following statements CANNOT be true?***

(a) P(x) = True for all $x \in$ S such that $x \neq b$

(b) P(x) = False or all $x \in$ S such that $x \neq a$ and $x \neq c$

(c) P(x) = False for all $x \in$ S such that $b \leq x$ and $x \neq c$

(d) P(x) = False for all $x \in$ S such that $a \leq x$ and $b \leq x$

61. ***Consider the function f defined below:***

struct item {

```
int data;
struct item * next;
};
int, f (struct item *p) {
return ((p = = NULL) || (p - > next = = NULL) ||
((p - > data < = p - > next - > data) & &f) p - > next)));
}
```

For a given linked list p, the function f returns 1 if and only if:

(a) the list is empty or has exactly one element

(b) the elements in the list are stored in non-decreasing order of data value

(c) the elements in the list are sorted in non-increasing order of data value

(d) not all elements in the list have the same data value

62. ***Consider the C program shown below:***

```
# include < stdio.h>
# define print (x) print f("%d", x)
int x;
void Q (int z) {
z + = x; print (z);
}
void p (int * y) {
int x = *y + 2;
Q(x); *y = x - 1;
print (x)
}
main (void) {
x = 5;
P(&x);
print (x);
}
```

The output of this program is:

(a) 12 7 6

(b) 22 12 11

(c) 14 6 6

(d) 7 6 6

Answers : **57.*** (b) **58.*** (a) **59.*** (d) **60.*** (c) **61.** (d) **62.*** (a)

63. ***In the following C program fragment, j, k, n and Two Log_n are integer variables, and A is an array of integers. The variable n is initialized to an integer ≥ 3, and Two Log_n is initialized to the value of*** $2^* \lceil \log_2(n) \rceil$

```
for (k = 3; k < = n; k++)
A [k] = 0;
for (k = 2; k < = Two Log_n; k++)
for (j = k + 1; j < = n; j++)
A[ j ] = A[ j ] || (j%k);
for (j = 3; j < = n; j++)
if (!A[ j ]) printf("%d", j);
```

The set of numbers printed by this program fragment is:

(a) $\{m \mid m \le n, (\exists i)\ [m = i!]\}$

(b) $\{m \mid m \le n, (\exists i)\ [m = i^2]\}$

(c) $\{m \mid m \le n,\ m$ is prime$\}$

(d) { }

64. ***Consider three data items D1, D2 and D3 and the following execution schedule of transactions T1, T2 and T3. In the diagram, R(D) and W(D) denote the actions reading and writing the data item D respectively.***

time ↓	T1	T2	T3
		R (D3);	
		R (D2);	
		W (D2);	
			R (D2);
			R (D3);
	R (D1);		
	W (D1);		
			W (D2);
			W (D3);
		R (D1);	
	R (D2);		
	W (D2);		
		W (D1);	

(a) The schedule is serializable as T2; T3; T1

(b) The schedule is serializable as T2; T1; T3

(c) The schedule is serializable as T3; T2; T1

(d) The schedule is not serializable

65. ***Consider the set of relations shown below and the SQL query that follows:***

Students : (Roll_number, Name, Date_of_birth)

Courses : (Course_number, Course_name, Instructor)

Grades : (Roll_number, Course_number, Grade)

select distinct Name

from Students, Courses, Grades

where students. Roll_number = Grades.

Roll_number

and Courses. Instructor = Korth

and Courses. Course_number = Grades.

Course_number and Grades.grade = A

Which of the following sets is computed by the above query ?

(a) Names of students who have got an A grade in all courses taught by Korth

(b) Names of students who have got an A grade in all courses

(c) Name of students who have got an A grade in at least one of the courses taught by Korth

(d) None of the above

66. ***Consider the following functional dependencies in a database:***

Date_of_Birth → Age

Age → Eligibility

Name → Roll_number

Roll_number → Name

Course_number → Course_name

Course_number → Instructor

(Roll_number; Course_number) → Grade

The relation (Roll_number, Name, Date_of_birth, Age) is:

(a) in second normal form but not in third normal form

(b) in third normal form but not in BCNF

(c) in BCNF

(d) in none of the above

Answers : **63.** (b) **64.** (c) **65.** (c) **66.*** (a)

67. ***Host A is sending data to host B over a full duplex link. A and B are using the sliding window protocol for flow control. The send and receive window sizes are 5 packets each. Data packets (sent only from A to B) are all 1000 bytes long and the transmission time for such a packet is 50 μs. Acknowledgement packets(sent only from B to A) are very small and require negligible transmission time. The propagation delay over the link is 200 μs. What is the maximum achievable throughput in this communication ?***

(a) 7.69×10^6 bps

(b) 11.11×10^6 bps

(c) 12.33×10^6 bps

(d) 15.00×10^6 bps

68. ***A 2 km long broadcast LAN has 10^7 bps bandwidth and uses CSMA/CD. The signal travels along the wire at 2×10^8 m/s. What is the minimum packet size that can be used this network ?***

(a) 50 bytes (b) 100 bytes

(c) 200 bytes (d) None of the above

69. ***The subnet mask for a particular network is 252.255.31.0. Which of the following pairs of IP addresses could belong to this network?***

(a) 172.57.88.62 and 172.56.87.233

(b) 10.35.28.2 and 10.35.29.4

(c) 191.203.31.87 and 191.234.31.88

(d) 128.8.129.43 and 128.8.161.55

THE FOLLOWING INFORMATION PERTAINS TO Q.70—71

Suppose we want to synchronize two concurrent processes P and Q using binary semaphores S and T. The code for the processes P and Q is shown below.

```
Process P:                    Process Q:
    while (1) {                   while (1) {
    W:
        print '0';                print '1'
        print '0';                print '1'
        X:                        Z:
    }                         }
```

Synchronization statements can be inserted only at points W, X, Y and Z.

70. ***Which of the following will ensure that the output string never contains a substring of the from 0.1"0 or 10"1 where n is odd?***

(a) P(s) at W, V(S) at X, P(T) at Y, V(T) at Z, S and T initially 1

(b) P(S) at W, V(T) at X, P(T) at Y, V(S) at Z, S and T initially 1

(c) P(S) at W, V(S) at X, P(S) at Y, V(S) at Z, S initially 1

(d) V(S) at W, V(T) at X, P(S) at Y, P(T) at Z, S and T initially 1

71. ***Which of the following will always lead to an output starting with '001100110011'?***

(a) P(S) at W, V(S) at X, P(T) at Y, V(T) at Z, S and T initially 1

(b) P(S) at W, V(T) at X, P(t) at Y, V(S) at Z, S initially 1, and T initially 0

(c) P(S) at W, V(T) at X, P(T) at Y, V(S) at Z, S and T initially 1

(d) P(S) at W, V(S) at X, P(T) at Y, V(T) at Z, S initially 1 and T initially 0

72. ***The following are the starting and ending times of activities A, B, C, D, E, F, G and H respectively in chronological order: "a_s b_s a_s a_e d_s a_e e_c f_s b_e d_e g_s e_e f_e h_s g_e h_e" Here, x_s denotes the starting time and x_e denotes the ending time of activity X. W need to schedule the activities in a set of rooms available to us. An activity can be scheduled in a room only if the room is reserved for the activity for its entire duration. What is the minimum number of rooms required?***

(a) 3 (b) 4

(c) 5 (d) 6

73. ***What is the weight of a minimum spanning tree of the following graph?***

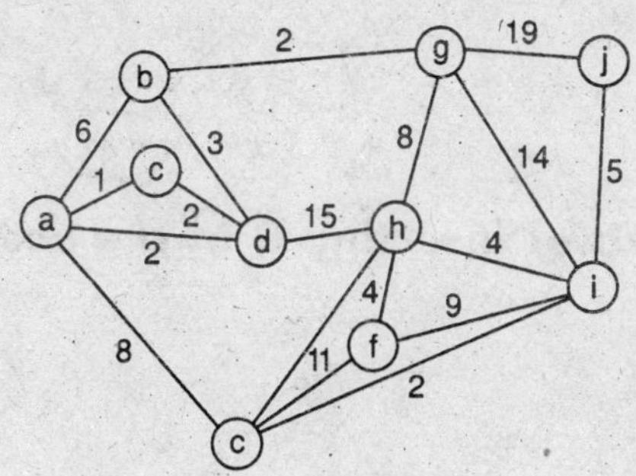

(a) 29 (b) 31

(c) 38 (d) 41

Answers : **67.*** (b) **68.*** (d) **69.** (c) **70.** (c) **71.** (a) **72.** (b) **73.*** (b)

74. ***Let G = (V, E) be an undirected graph with a subgraph $G_1 = (V_1, E_1)$. Weights are assigned to edges of G as follows:***

$$w(e) = \begin{cases} 0 \text{ if } e \in E_1 \\ 1 \text{ otherwise} \end{cases}$$

A single-source shortest path algorithm is executed on the weighted graph (V, E, w) with an arbitrary vertex v_1 of V_1 as the source. Which of the following can always be inferred from the path costs computed?

(a) The number of edges in the shortest paths from v_1 to all vertices of G

(b) G_1 is connected

(c) V_1 forms a clique in G

(d) G_1 is a tree

75. ***The cube root of a natural number n is defined as the largest natural number m such that $m^2 \leq n$. The complexity of computing the cube root of n (n is represented in binary notation) is:***

(a) $O(n)$ but not $O(n^{0.5})$

(b) $O(n^{0.5})$ but not $O((\log n)^k)$ for any constant $k > O$

(c) $O((\log n)^k)$ for some constant $k > O$, but not $O((\log \log n)^m)$ for any constant $m > O$

(d) $O((\log \log n)^k)$ for some constant $k > 0.5$, but not $O((\log \log n)^{0.5})$

76. ***Consider the following 2-3-4 tree (i.e., B-tree with a minmum degree of two) in which each data item is a letter. The usual alphabetical ordering of letters is used in constructing the tree***

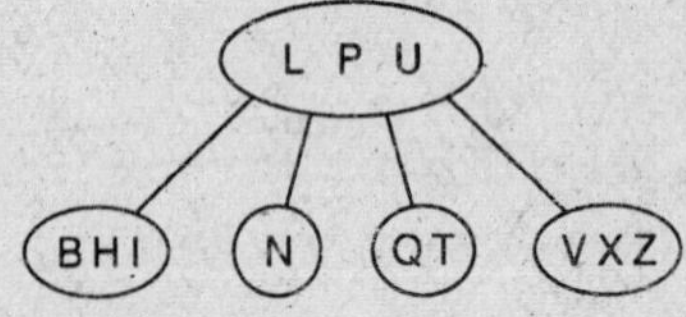

What is the result of inserting G in the above tree?

(a)

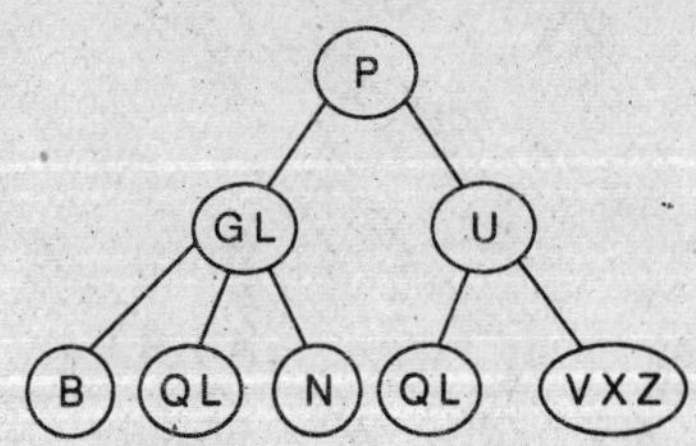

(b)

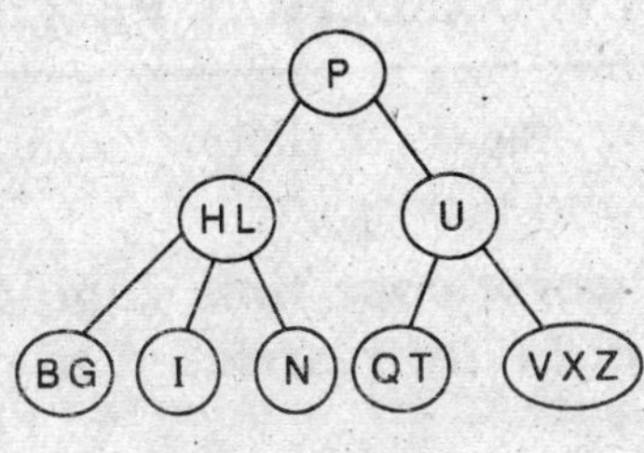

(c)

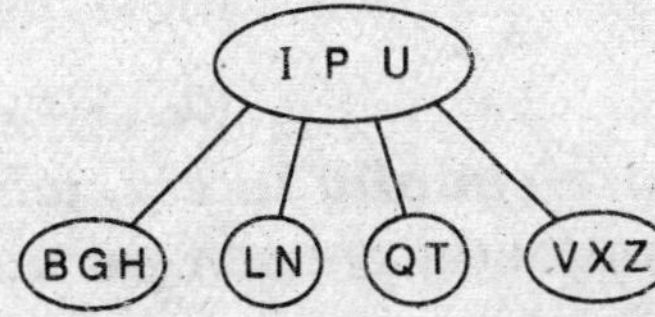

(d) None of the above

77. ***Let S be a stack of size n ≥ 1. Starting with the empty stack, suppose we push the first n natural numbers in sequence, and then perform n pop operations. Assume that Push and Pop operation take X seconds each, and Y seconds elapse between the end of one such stack operation and the start of the next operation. For m ≥ 1, define the stack-life of m as the time elapsed from the end of Push (m) to the start of the pop operation that removes m from S. The average stack-life of an element of this stack is:***

(a) $n((X + y)$
(b) $3Y + 2X$
(c) $n(X + Y) - Y$
(d) $Y = 2X$

78. ***A data structure is required for storing a set of integers such that each of the following operations can be done in (log n) time, where n is the number of elements in the set.***

I. Detection of the smallest element

II. Insertion of an element if it is not already present in the set

Which of the following data structures can be used for this purpose?

(a) A heap can be used but not a balanced binary search tree
(b) A balanced binary search tree can be used but not a heap
(c) Both balanced binary search tree and heap can be used
(d) Neither balanced binary search tree nor heap can be used

Answers : **74.** (b) **75.** (c) **76.*** (c) **77.*** (d) **78.** (b)

THE FOLLOWING INFORMATION PERTAINS TO Q. 79—80

In a permutation $a_1 \ldots a_n$ of n distinct integers, an inversion is a pair (a_i, a_j) such that $i < j$ and $a_i > a_j$.

79. What would be the worst case time complexity of the Insertion Sort algorithm, if the inputs are restricted to permutations of 1....n with at most n inversions?

(a) $\Theta(n^2)$
(b) $\Theta(n \log n)$
(c) $\Theta(n^{1.5})$
(d) $\Theta(n)$

80. If all permutations are equally likely, what is the expected number of inversions in a randomly chosen permutation of 1...n?

(a) $n(n-1)/2$
(b) $n(n-1)/4$
(c) $n(n+1)/4$
(d) $2n [\log_2 n]$

81. A program consists of two modules executed sequentially. Let $f_1(t)$ and $f_2(t)$ respectively denote the probability density functions of time taken to execute the two modules. The probability density function of the overall time taken to execute the program is given by:

(a) $f_1(t) + f_2(t)$
(b) $\int_0^t f_1(x) f_2(x)\, dx$
(c) $\int_0^t f_1(x) f_2(t-x)\, dx$
(d) $\max\{f_1(t), f_2(t)\}$

THE FOLLOWING INFORMATION PERTAINS TO Q. 82—83

Consider the following assembly language program for a hypothetical processor. A, B and C are 8 bit registers. The meaning of various instructions are shown as comments.

```
     Move B, # 0      ; B ← 0
     MOVE C, # 8      ; C ← 8
Z :  CMP C, # 0       ; compare C with 0
     JZX              ; jump to X if zero flag is set
     SUB C, # 1       ; C ← C − 1
     RRCA, # 1        ; right rotate A through carry by one bit.
```

Thus :
; if the initial values of A and the carry flag are $a_7 \ldots a_0$ and
; c_0 respectively their values after the execution of this
; instruction will be $c_0 a_7 \ldots a_1$ and a_0 respectively.

```
        JCY          ; jump to Y if carry flag is set
        JMP Z        ; jump to Z
Y :     ADD B, # 1   ; B ← B + 1
        JMP Z        ; jump to Z
X :
```

82. ***Which of the following instructions when inserted at location X will ensure that the value of register A after program execution is the same as its initial value?***

(a) RRC A, #

(b) NOP ; no operation

(c) LRC, A # 1 ; left rotate A through carry flag by one bit

(d) ADD A, # 1

83. ***If the initial value of register A is*** A_0, ***the value of register B after the program execution will be:***

(a) the number of 0 bits in A_0

(b) the number of 1 bits in A_0

(c) A_0

(d) 8

84. ***Consider the following circuit composed of XOR gates and non-inverting buffers.***

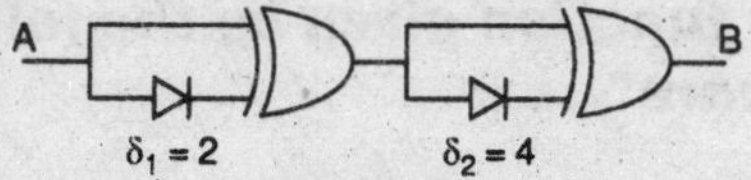

The non-inverting buffers have delays $\delta_1 = 2$ ***ns and*** $\delta_2 = 4$ ***ns as shown in the figure. Both XCR gates and all wires have zero delay. Assume that all gate inputs, outputs and wires are stable at logic level 0 at time 0. If the following waveform is applied at input A,***

how many transition(s) (change of logic levels) occur(s) at B during the interval from 0 to 10 ns?

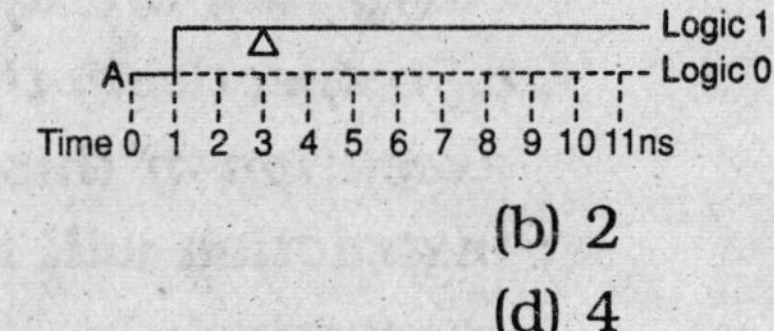

(a) 1 (b) 2
(c) 3 (d) 4

85. ***Consider the ALU shown below:***

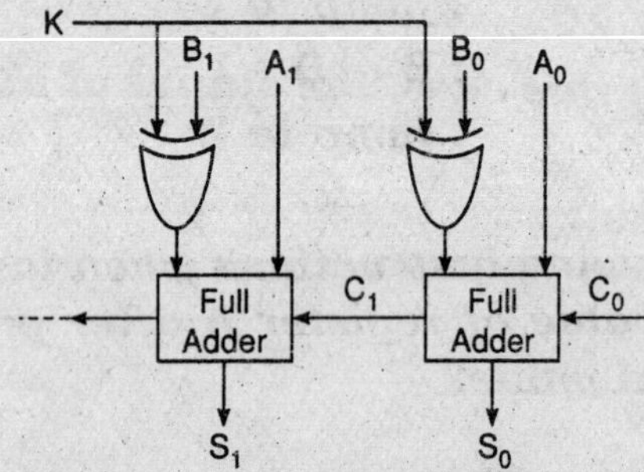

If the operands are in 2's complement representation, which of the following operations can be performed by suitably setting the control lines K and C_0 only (+ and – denote addition and subtraction respectively)?

(a) A + B, and A – B, but not A + 1
(b) A + B, and A + 1, but not A – B
(c) A + B, but not A – B, or A + 1
(d) A + B, and A – B, and A + 1

86. ***The literal count of a boolean expression is the sum of the number of times each literal appears in the expression. For example, the literal count of $(xy + xz')$ is 4. What are the minimum possible literal counts of the product-of-sum and sum-of-product representation respectively of the function given by the following Karna map? Here, X denotes "don't care"***

xy \ zw	00	01	11	10
00	X	1	0	1
01	Q	1	X	0
11	1	X	X	0
10	X	0	0	X

(a) (11, 9) (b) (9, 13)

(c) (9, 10) (d) (11, 11)

87. ***A 1-input, 2-output synchronous sequential circuit behaves as follows:***

Let z_k, n_k denote the number of 0's and 1's respectively in initial k bits of the input ($z_k + n_k = k$). The circuit outputs 00 until one of the following conditions holds.

- ***$z_k - n_k = 2$. In this case, the output at the k-th and all subsequent clock ticks is 10.***
- ***$n_k - z_k = 2$. In this case, the output at the k-th and all subsequent ticks is 01.***

What is the minimum number of states required in the state transition graph of the above circuit?

(a) 5 (b) 6

(c) 7 (d) 8

88. ***The following is a scheme for floating point number representation using 1 bits.***

Bit position 15 14 ... ... 9 8 0

s	*e*	*m*
Sign	**Exponent**	**Mantissa**

Let s, e and m be the number s represented in binary in the sign, exponent, and mantissa fields respectively. Then the floating point number represented is:

$$\begin{cases} (-1)^s (1 + m \times 2^{-9})\, 2^{e-31} \\ 0 \text{ otherwise} \end{cases}$$

if the exponent ≠ 111111

What is the maximum difference between two successive real number representable in this system?

(a) 2^{-40} (b) 2^{-9}

(c) 2^{22} (d) 2^{31}

Answers : **84.*** (c) **85.*** (d) **86.** (a) **87.*** (c) **88.*** (c)

89. *A piecewise linear function f(x) is plotted using thick solid lines in the figure below (the plot is drawn to scale).*

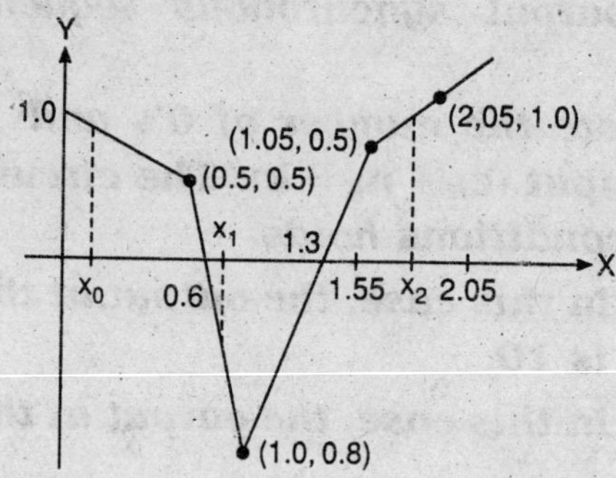

If we use the Newton-Rapson method to find the roots of $f(x) = 0$ using x_0, x_1 and x_2 respectively as initial guesses, the roots obtained would be:

(a) 1.3, 0.6, and 0.6 respectively

(b) 0.6, 0.6 and 1.3 respectively

(c) 1.3, 1.3 and 0.6 respectively

(d) 1.3, 0.6 and 1.3 respectively

90. *Consider the following system of linear equations:*

$$\begin{bmatrix} 2 & 1-4 \\ 4 & 3-12 \\ 1 & 2-8 \end{bmatrix}\begin{bmatrix} x \\ y \\ z \end{bmatrix} = \begin{bmatrix} a \\ 5 \\ 7 \end{bmatrix}$$

Notice that the second and the third columns of the coefficient matrix are linearly dependent. For how many values of a, does this system of equations have infinitely many solutions?

(a) 0

(b) 1

(c) 2

(d) infinitely many

Answers : **89.** (b) **90.** (b)

EXPLANATORY ANSWERS

1. $0^* (10^*)^* = 0^* (1^* 0^*)$

(a) $(1^* 0)^* 1^* = (1^* 0^*) 1^*$

(b) $0 + (0 + 10)^* = 0 + (0^* 1^* 0^*)$

(c) $(0 + 1)^* 10(0 + 1)^* = 0^* 1^* 10(0^* 1^*)$

Hence (d) is the correct answer

4. $1 + 2 + ... + n = \frac{n(n+1)}{2} = 0(n^2)$

8. $P(A/B) = \frac{P(A)\, P(B/A)}{\sum P(A)\, P(B/A)}$

So, value of $P(A/B) = P(A) = 1$

$$P(B/A) = P(B) = \frac{1}{2}$$

10. For larger values of y

$$P = P^* \frac{x}{i} = \frac{x}{i}$$

$$S = S + P \neq 1 + \frac{x}{i}$$

When $i < y$ and i++,

then, $$S = 1 + \frac{x}{i} + \frac{x}{i+1} + ...$$

$$= 1 + x + \frac{x}{2} + \frac{x}{3} + ...$$

Hence for larger value of y, the return value of the function f best approximates in $(1 + x)$

15. Number of page $= \frac{2^{32}}{2^{12}} = 2^{30}$

Here number of pages is much in number, so, chances to internal fragmentation due to size of pages is larger, then overhead is reduced.

16. 2's complement → 00000101 = 5

2's complement of 11100111 is 00011001 = 25

18. Let P denote the set of all non-empty strings of letters from M where, $M = \{\alpha, \beta, \gamma\}$,

we have $P = \{\alpha, \beta, \gamma, \alpha\alpha, \alpha\pi, \alpha\gamma, \dots \alpha\alpha\alpha, \alpha\alpha\beta, \dots\}$.

19. $$T(n) = \sum_{k=1}^{n} T(k-1)\,T(x)$$

$$T(n) = T(x)\,[T(0) + T(1) + \ldots\ldots + T(n-1)]$$

So, $$x = n - k + 1$$

24. In a Binary search tree, we see that left child is less than Right child.

Hence in order 0 2 4 3 1 6 5 9 8 7

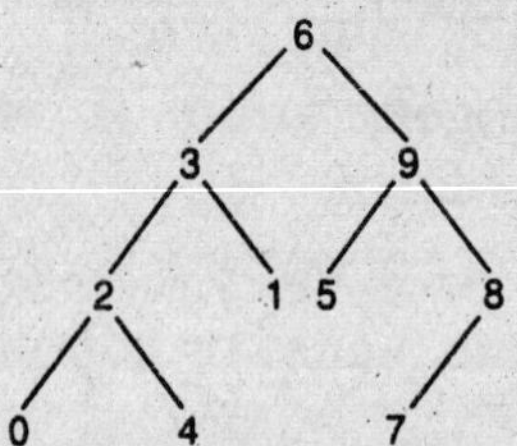

30. $(n + k)^m = \Theta(n^m)$, above k and m are constants

$$2^{n+1} = O(2^n)$$

32. TLB hit ratio = 96%

TLB access time = 1 ns

Virtual page hit ratio = 90%

Main memory access time = 10 ns

Hence, for no page faults Average time

= hit ratio × cache access time + (1 – hit ratio) × memory access time

$= 0.9 \times 1 + 0.1 \times 10 = 1.9 \text{ ns} \cong 2 \text{ ns}$

35. $x.f(1)$

$f(1)$ copy to f (int i)

So $i = 1$

print (2* i) = 2

Same as, $((P)y) \,.\, f(1);\ z \,.\, f(1) = 2$

36. By dynamic we take local value

$P(i + j)$, $x = i + j = 105$ (global value of i and j)

print $(x + 10) = 115$

print $(x) = 200 + 20$

= 220 (due to local value)

37. $P(i + j)$

$x = i + j = 105$ (global value of i and j)

print $(x + 10) = 115$

print $(x) = 105$

because static value store previous value stored at place of x.

38. If P = True, Q = false, R = True, then we find,

$$(T \cup F) \Rightarrow ((T \cup T) \wedge (F \cup F))$$
$$T \Rightarrow (T \wedge F)$$
$$T \Rightarrow F$$
$$F \cup F = \text{False (is not valid)}$$

41. This is three-address code generation. Three address code is a sequence of statement of the general form.

$$X : Y \text{ op} Z$$

where, X , Y and Z are name, const or compiler-generated temporaries op stands for any operator such as fixed or floating point arithmatic operation or a logical operator on boolean value data.

OR $\quad X : Y + Z$

$t_1 = Y$, $t_2 = t_1 + Z = Y + Z$

$$X = t_2 = Y + Z$$

42. $S \rightarrow TR$

$R \rightarrow + T$ {Print '+');} $R \mid \in$

$T \rightarrow$ num {print (num. val);}

44. $S \rightarrow iE\, t\, SS' \backslash a$

$S' \Rightarrow e\,S \mid a$

$E \rightarrow b$

This is left factor grammar

Thus we may expand S to ibt SS′ on input i and wait until ibtS has been seen to decide whether to expand S′ symbol $e\,S \mid \in$

45. Then $\quad L = (0 \mid 1)\, 01$

$$= (0 \mid 1)\,(0,\, 1)^*\, 0$$

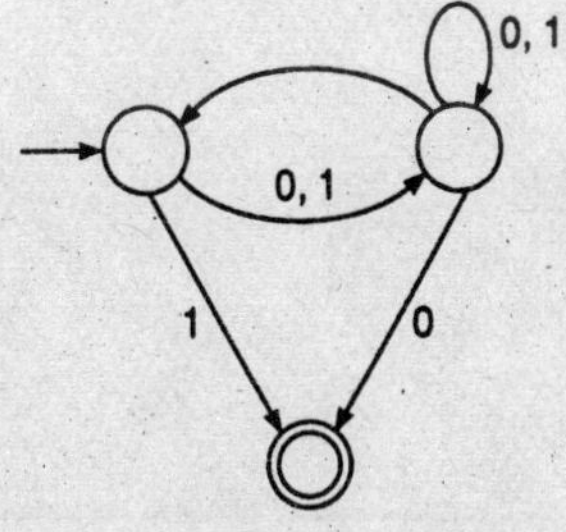

Changing the accepting state to non-accepting state and changing state and changing the non-accepting state to accepting state is known as h_1.

$$L_1 = (0 \mid 1)(0, 1)^*$$

$$= 0(0 \mid 1), (0, 1)^*$$

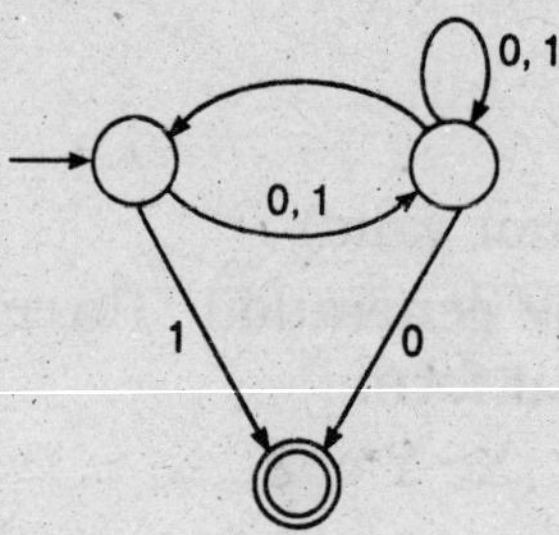

We find from both language L and L_1. So $L_1 \subseteq L$

49.

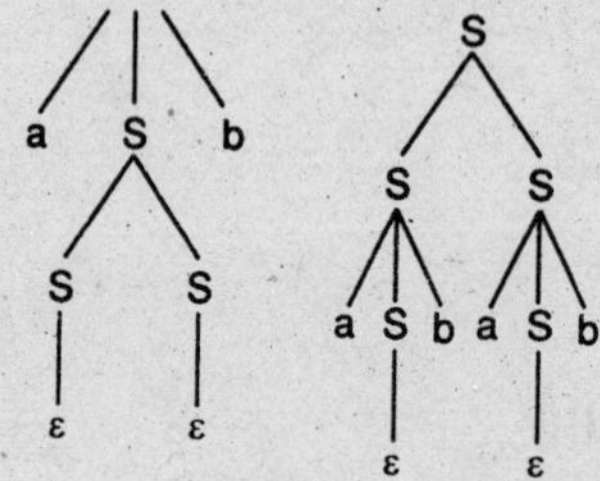

$S \to aSb \mid SS \mid \in$

Hence, S is ambiguous

So, we can find a deterministic finte state automation that accepts L(G).

50. According to question, S denote the set of seven bit binary strings in which the first, fourth and last bits are 1.

1 2 3 4 5 6 7

$\Rightarrow$ 1 0 0 1 0 0 1

So number of string in S that are accepted by M is one.

51. Given $|E| \leq 3|V| - 6$

We know from graph,

Number of edges $= \dfrac{n(n-1)}{2}$

(a) V = 3, E = 3

$|3| \leq 9 - 6 \to$ True

(b) V = 4, E = 6

$|6| \leq 12 - 6 \rightarrow$ True

(c) V = 5, $E = 10$

$|10| \leq 15 - 6 \rightarrow$ not true

(d) V = 6, E = 15

$|15| < |18| - 6 \rightarrow$ not true

So, minimum degree of G cannot be 5

52. Let $\sum = \{a, b, c, d, e\}$

$g(a) = 3$, $g(b) = 5$, $g(c) = 7$, $g(d) = 9$, $g(e) = 11$

$p_1 = 2$ (1st prime number)

$$f(s) = \prod_{i=i}^{n} p_i^{g(a_i)}$$

$$= 2^3 = 8$$

So, $h < s_1, \ldots s_n >) = \prod_{i=1}^{n} p_i^{f(s_1)} = 2^8\ 2^8\ 5^8$

53.

+	a	b	c
a	b	a	c
b	a	b	c
c	a	c	b

×	a	b	c
c	a	b	c
b	b	c	a
c	c	c	b

We can write from given expression

$a + a = b$, $a + b = a$, $a + c = c$
$b + a = a$, $b + b = b$, $b + c = c$
$c + a = a$, $c + b = c$, $c + c = b$
$a \times a = a$, $a \times b = b$, $a \times c = c$
$b \times a = b$, $b \times b = c$, $b \times c = a$
$c \times a = c$, $c \times b = c$, $c \times c = b$

$a \times x + a \times y = c$ ...(1)

$b \times x + c \times y = c$ ...(2)

First we see, these are the equation which give result c.

$a + c = c$
$b + c = c$
$c + b = c$

For equation (1), we find $a \times x = b\ x = b$ we find

$a \times x = a$ then $x = a$, $a \times y = c$, $y = c$, $x = a, b, c$

$a \times y = c$ then $y = c$, $a \times x = c$, $x = c$, $y = a, b$

$a \times y = b, y = b$

For equation (2), we find

$b \times x = b, c \times y = c,$ $b \times x = a$ then $x = c$

$x = a, y = a, b$ $c \times y = c$ then $y = a, b$

$b \times x = c$ then $x = b$ we find

$c \times y = b$ then $y = c$ $x = a, b, c$

$y = a, b, c$

So, total number of solution pairs (x, y) is 3.

54. $f: A \to B$ be an injective (one-to-one) function.

$A \to B$ means

$A \subseteq B$

Define $g: 2^A \to 2^B$ as : $g(C) = \{f(x) \mid x \in C\}$, for all subset C of A.

$g(C) \subseteq B$

Define : $n: 2^B \to 2^A$ as :

$h(D) = \{x \mid x \in A, f(x) \in D\}$, for all subset D of B

$2^B \subseteq 2^A$

$h(D) \subseteq 2^A$

$2(h(D)) \subseteq C$

55. For complete graph of 6 vertices number of perfect matching

$$= \frac{n(n-1)}{2} = \frac{6 \times 5}{2} = 15$$

56. $T(1) = 1$

$T(n+1) = T(n) + \lfloor \sqrt{(n+1)} \rfloor$ for all n 1

If $n = m^2 - 1$

$T(m^2) = T(m^2 - 1) + \lfloor \sqrt{2} \rfloor = 1 + 1 = 2$

$T(3) = T(2) + \lfloor \sqrt{3} \rfloor = 2 + 1 = 3$

$T(4) = T(3) + 2 = 5$

$T(5) = 5 + 2 = 7$

$T(6) = 7 + 2 = 9$

$T(7) = 9 + 2 = 11$

$T(8) = 11 + 2 = 13$

$T(9) = 13 + 3 = 16$

$T(10) = 16 + 3 = 19$

$T(11) = 19 + 3 = 22$

$T(12) = 22 + 3 = 25$

$T(13) = 25 + 3 = 28$

$T(14) = 28 + 3 = 31$

$T(15) = 31 + 3 = 34$

$T(16) = 34 + 4 = 38$

$T(m^2) = T(m^2 - 1) + \lfloor m \rfloor$

Put $m = 2$

$T(4) = T(3) + 1 = 4$

Put $m = 3$

$T(9) = T(8) + 1 = 13 + 1 = 14$

(a) $\frac{m}{6}(21m - 39) + 4$

Put $m = 2$, $\frac{2}{6}(42 - 39) + 4 = 5$

Put $m = 3$, $\frac{3}{6}(63 - 39) + 4 = 16$

Put $m = 4$, $\frac{4}{6}(84 - 39) + 4 = \frac{2}{3} \times 45 + 4 = 34$

(b) Put $m = 2$, $\frac{m}{6}(4m^2 - 3m + 5)$

$= \frac{2}{6}[16 - 6 + 5] = 5$

Put $m = 3$, $\frac{3}{6}[4 \times 9 - 3 \times 3 + 5] = \frac{1}{2}[32] = 16$

Put $m = 4$, $\frac{4}{6}[64 - 12 + 5] = \frac{2}{3}[57] = 38$

Hence, choice (b) satisfies the solution of $T(m^2)$

57. Let $n = 3$, and $k = 1$, $m = 3$

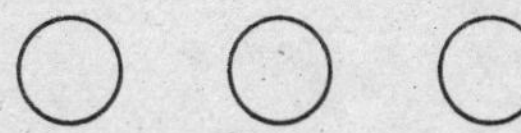

According to question, n is number of distinct bags.

Number of balls = 3, then number of ways balls be placed in 1 ways then, number of ways = $3 \times 2 = 6 = 3!$ ways.

If $k = 2$

Number of balls = $nk = 6$

We have chosen atleast k balls

Number of ways = one way

58. $\alpha = (\forall\ x)\ [P(x) \Leftrightarrow (\forall\ y)\ [Qxy \Leftrightarrow \neg\ Qyy]] \Rightarrow (\forall\ (x)\ [\neg Px]$

I_1 : domain the set of natural numbers

$Px = x$ is a prime number = 2, 3, 5, 7, 11, 13, ...

$Qxy = y$ divides x = means y is also prime number = 2, 3, 5, 7, 11, 13, ...

I_2 : $Px = x$ is composite number (*i.e.* not prime number)

= 4, 6, 8, 9, 10, 12, 14, ...

Qxy = 2, 3, 4, 5, 7, ... = mean all the numbers

From expression, we know, I_1 satisfies α, I_2 does not

59. We know that, if the four tense operators, P, F, H and G and following axioms:

$G(Q \rightarrow R) \rightarrow (GQ \rightarrow GR)$

$H(Q \rightarrow R) \rightarrow (HQ \rightarrow HR)$

$G - HQ \rightarrow Q$

$-H - GQ \rightarrow Q$

60. (S; ≤) is partial order in which S is reflexive, transitive and symmetric

According to question

$P(a)$ = True, $P(b)$ = False

$P(x) \Rightarrow P(y)$

If $P(x)$ then $P(y)$ and $a, y \in S$, satisfies $x \leq y$

So, $-P(x) \cup P(y)$

$\Rightarrow$ False $\cup$ False

$\Rightarrow$ False

So, $P(x)$ = False for all $x \in S$, such that $b \leq x$ and $x \neq c$.

62. $^*y = \&\ x = 5$

$x = {}^*\ y + 2 = 7$

$Q(x)$;

$z = x = 7$

$z = z + x = 12$

print $(z) = 12$

$^*\ y = x - 1 = 16$

print $(x) = 7$

print $(x) = 6$

66. Given, Date_of_Birth → Age

Age → Eligibility

Name → Roll_number, Roll Number → Name

Course_Number → Course_Name

Course_Name → Instructor

(Roll Number, Course_number) → Grade

From given relation,

Date_of_Birth → Eligibility (By transitively)

Course_Number → Instructor (By transitively)

After observing we see that, it is not in 3rd Normal form because in third normal form relation, every not prime attribute is non-transitively and fully dependent on the every candidate key.

In 2nd Normal form, all non-prime attributes are fully functionally dependent on the relation keys.

67. Window size = 5 packet

Packet size = 1000 bytes = 2^{10} (approx. 10 bits)

Window size = 5000 byte (13 bits approx.)

Transmission time = $5 \times 50 = 250\ \mu$ sec

Propagation delay = $200\ \mu$ sec

Total time = $250 + 200\ \mu$ sec = $450\ \mu$ sec

Maximum achievable throughput = $\frac{5000}{450} \times 10^6$ bps = 11.11×10^6 bps

68. According to question, length = 2 km = 2000 m

$\lambda = 10^7$ bps

$\upsilon = 2 \times 10^8$ m/s

$s = \upsilon t$

$t = \frac{2 \times 10^3}{2 \times 10^8} = 10^{-5}$ sec = $10\ \mu$ sec.

Total number of packets = $10^7 \times 10 \times 10^{-6}$

= 100 bits = 12 byte

73.

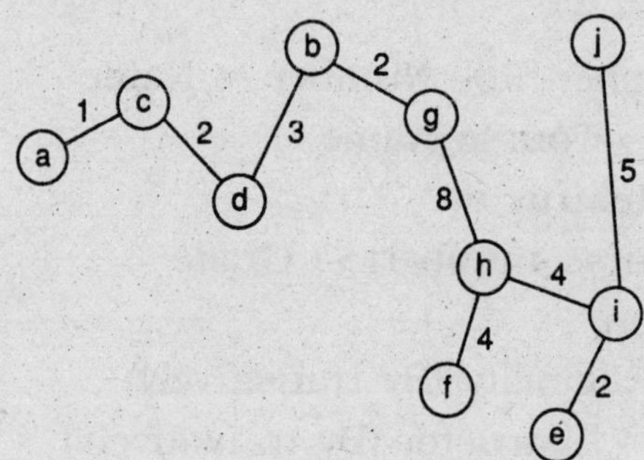

Spanning tree is minimum, when all weight assigned to its edges between two vertices where every vertex is connected.

∴ Height of minimum spanning tree

$$= 1 + 2 + 3 + 2 + 8 + 4 + 4 + 2 + 5 = 31$$

76. Initially, after inserting G.

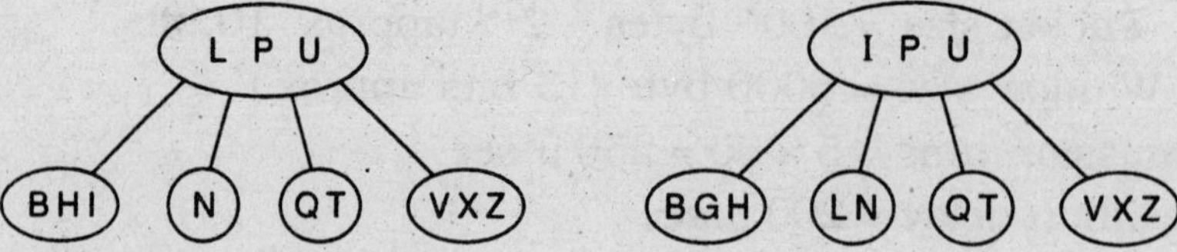

77. Push & Pop take time = 2X

Delay between one push and one pop = Y

So, average stack life of an element (m)

$$= \frac{2Xm + mY}{m} = 2X + Y$$

Hence the required answer is $y + 2x$

80. Expected number of inversion $= \frac{n(n-1)}{2}$

For randomly $= \frac{n(n-1)}{2} \times \frac{1}{2} = \frac{n(n-1)}{4}$

81. Probability density function of $f_1(t)$ and $f_2(t)$ is $= \int_0^t f_1(x)\, f_2(t-x)$

84. Delay $\delta_1 = 2$ ns

$\delta_2 = 4$ ns

at 1 ns transition logic 0 to logic 1.

at 2 ns some transition occur

at 4 ns some transition occur.

85. From figure (given in question):

If $k = 1$, $C_0 = 1$

$$S_0 = \overline{B}_0 \oplus A_0 \oplus C_0 = \overline{B}_0 \oplus \overline{A}_0$$
$$= A_0 \overline{B}_0 + B_0 \overline{A}_0$$
$$C_1 = \overline{B}_0 A_0 + (\overline{B}_0 \oplus A_0) C_0$$
$$= \overline{B}_0 A_0 + B_0 A_0 + \overline{A}_0 \overline{B}_0 = A_0 + \overline{A}_0 \overline{B}_0$$
$$S_1 = A_1 \oplus \overline{B}_1 \oplus C_1$$

If $k = 0$, $C_0 = 1$

$$S_0 = A_0 \oplus \overline{B}_0 \oplus 1 = A_0 \oplus \overline{B}_0$$
$$= A_0 B_0 + \overline{A}_0 \cdot \overline{B}_0$$
$$C_1 = A_0 B_0 + (A_0 \oplus B_0) = A_0 + \overline{A}_0 B_0$$

A + B and A − B and A + 1

87. $z_k = 00.....k$

$n_k = 1 + ...k$

$z_k + n_k = k,$

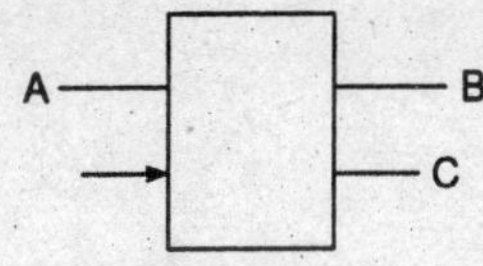

Number of transition state = $2^3 - 1 = 7$.

88. 15 14..................9 8.....................0

s	e	m
Sign	Exponent	Mantissa

s = signbit

e = exponent = 2^6 = 0 to 63

$m = 2^8$ = 0 to 255

Now floating point representation is

$$(-1)^s (1 + m \times 2^{-9})\, 2^{e-31} \text{ if the exponent} \neq 111111$$
$$(-1)^s (1 + 2^9\, 2^{-9})\, 2^{e-31} = (-1)^s (1 + 2^0)(2^{e-31})$$

If exponent is 111110 or 111101 then $e_1 = 62$

$e_2 = 61$

Then successive difference = 2^{31}.

2004

CS : COMPUTER SCIENCE AND ENGINEERING

Q. 1—30 carry one mark each

1. ***The goal of structured programming is to***
(a) have well indented programs
(b) be able to infer the flow of control from the compiled code
(c) be able to infer the flow of control from the program text
(d) avoid the use of GOTO statements

2. ***Consider the following C function***

```
void swap (int a, int b)
    { int temp;
          temp = a;
          a = b;
          b = temp;
    }
```

In order to exchange the values of two variables x ***and*** y***,***
(a) call swap (x, y)
(b) call swap (&x, &y)
(c) swap (x, y) cannot be used as it does not return any value
(d) swap (x, y) cannot be used as the parameters are passed by value

3. ***A single array A[1..MAXSIZE] is used to implement two stacks. The two stacks grow from opposite ends of the array. Variables top 1 and top 2 (top 1 < top 2) point to the location of the topmost element in each of the stacks. If the space is to be used efficiently, the condition for "stack full" is***
(a) (*top 1* = MAXSIZE/2) and (*top 2* = MAXSIZE/2 +1)
(b) *top 1* + *top 2* = MAXSIZE
(c) (*top 1* = MAXSIZE/2) or (*top 2* = MAXSIZE)
(d) *top 1* = *top 2* − 1

4. ***The following numbers are inserted into an empty binary search tree in the given order: 10, 1, 3, 5, 15, 12, 16. What is the height of the binary search tree (the height is the maximum distance of a leaf node from the root) ?***
(a) 2 (b) 3

(c) 4 (d) 6

5. ***The best data structure to check whether an arithmetic expression has balanced parentheses is a***

(a) queue (b) stack

(c) tree (d) list

6. ***Level order traversal of a rooted tree can be done by starting from the root and performing***

(a) preorder traversal (b) inorder traversal

(c) depth first search (d) breadth first searrch

7. ***Given the following input (4322, 1334, 1471, 9679, 1989, 6171, 6173, 4199) and the hash function x mod 10, which of the following statements are true ?***

(i) 9679, 1989, 4199 hash to the same value

(ii) 1471, 6171 hash to the same value

(iii) All elements hash to the same value

(iv) Each element hashes to a different value

(a) (i) only (b) (ii) only

(c) (i) and (ii) only (d) (iii) or (iv)

8. ***Which of the following grammar rules violate the requirements of an operator grammar ? P, Q, R are nonterminals, and r, s, t are terminals.***

(i) $P \rightarrow Q\ R$

(ii) $P \rightarrow Q\ s\ R$

(iii) $P \rightarrow \varepsilon$

(iv) $P \rightarrow Q\ t\ R\ r$

(a) (i) only (b) (i) and (iii) only

(c) (ii) and (iii) only (d) (iii) and (iv) only

9. ***Consider a program P that consists of two source modules M_1 and M_2 contained in two different files. If M_1 contains a reference to a function defined in M_2, the reference will be resolved at***

(a) Edit-time (b) Compile-time

(c) Link-time (d) Load-time

10. ***Consider the grammar rule $E \rightarrow E_1 - E_2$ for arithmetic expressions. The code generated is targeted to a CPU having a single register. The subtraction operation requires the first operand to be in the***

register. If E_1 and E_2 do not have any common subexpression, in order to get the shortest possible code

(a) E_1 should be evaluated first

(b) E_2 should be evaluated first

(c) Evaluation of E_1 and E_2 should necessarily be interleaved

(d) Order of evaluation of E_1 and E_2 is of no consequence

11. ***Consider the following statements with respect to user-level threads and kernel-supported threads.***

(i) Context switch is faster with kernel-supported threads

(ii) For user-level threads, a system call can block the entire process

(iii) Kernel-supported threads can be schedule independently

(iv) User-level threads are transparent to the kernel

Which of the above statements are true ?

(a) (ii), (iii) and (iv) only (b) (ii) and (iii) only

(c) (i) and (iii) only (d) (i) and (ii) only

12. ***Consider an operating system capable of loading and executing a single sequential user process at a time. The disk head scheduling algorithm used is First Come First Served (FCFS). If FCFS is replaced by Shortest Seek Time First (SSTF), claimed by the vendor to give 50% better benchmark results, what is the expected improvement in the I/O performance of user programs?***

(a) 50% (b) 40%

(c) 25% (d) 0%

13. ***Let R_1(A, B, C) and R_2(D, E) be two relation schema, where the primary keys are shown underlined, and let C be a foreign key in R_1 referring to R_2. Suppose there is no violation of the above referential integrity constraint in the corresponding relation instances r_1 and r_2. Which one of the following relational algebra expressions would necessarily procuce an empty relation ?***

(a) $\Pi_D (r_2) - \Pi_C (r_1)$ (b) $\Pi_C (r_1) - \Pi_D (r_2)$

(c) $\Pi_D (r_1 \bowtie_{C \neq D} r_2)$ (d) $\Pi_C (r_1 \bowtie_{C = D} r_2)$

14. ***Consider the following relation schema pertaining to a students database:***

Student(rollno, name, address)

Enroll(rollno, courseno, coursename)

where the primary keys are shown underlined. The number of tuples

in the Student and Enroll tables are 120 and 8 respectively. What are the maximum and minimum number of tuples that can be present in (Student * Enroll), where '*' denotes natural join?

(a) 8, 8 (b) 120, 8
(c) 960, 8 (d) 960, 120

15. ***Choose the best matching between Group 1 and Group 2.***

Group 1	Group 2
P. Data link layer	1. Ensures reliable transport of data over a physical point-to-point link
Q. Network layer	2. Encodes/decodes data for physical transmission
R. Transport layer	3. Allows end-to-end communication between two processes
	4. Routes data from one network node to the next

(a) P-1, Q-4, R-3 (b) P-2, Q-4, R-1
(c) P-2, Q-3, R-1 (d) P-1, Q-3, R-2

16. ***Which of the following is NOT true with respect to a transparent bridge and a router ?***

(a) Both bridge and router selectively forward data packets
(b) A bridge uses IP addresses while a router uses MAC addresses
(c) A bridge builds up its routing table by inspecting incoming packets
(d) A router can connect between a LAN and a WAN

17. ***The Boolean function*** $x'y' + xy + x'y$ ***is equivalent to***

(a) $x' + y'$ (b) $x + y$
(c) $x + y'$ (d) $x' + y$

18. ***In an SR latch made by cross-coupling two NAND gates, if both S and R inputs are set to 0, then it will result in***

(a) $Q = 0, Q' = 1$ (b) $Q = 1, Q' = 0$
(c) $Q = 1, Q' = 1$ (d) Indeterminate states

19. ***If*** 73_x ***(in base-x number system) is equal to*** 54_y ***(in base-y number system), the possible values of x and y are***

(a) 8, 16 (b) 10, 12
(c) 9, 13 (d) 8, 11

20. ***Which of the following addressing modes are suitable for program relocation at run time?***

(i) Absolute addressing *(ii) Based addressing*
(iii) Relative addressing *(iv) Indirect addressing*

(a) (i) and (iv) (b) (i) and (ii)
(c) (ii) and (iii) (d) (i), (ii) and (iv)

21. ***The minimum number of page frames that must be allocated to a running process in a virtual memory environment is determined by***

(a) the instruction set architecture
(b) page size
(c) physical memory size
(d) number of processes in memory

22. ***How many 8-bit characters can be transmitted per second over a 9600 baud serial communication link using asynchronous mode of transmission with one start bit, eight data bits, two stop bits, and one parity bit?***

(a) 600 (b) 800
(c) 876 (d) 1200

23. ***Identify the correct translation into logical notation of the following assertion.***

Some boys in the class are taller than all the girls

Note : *taller*(x, y) is true if x is taller than y.

(a) $(\exists x)$ (boy$(x) \rightarrow (\forall y)$ (girl$(y) \wedge$ taller $(x, y)))$
(b) $(\exists x)$ (boy$(x) \wedge (\forall y)$ (girl$(y) \wedge$ taller $(x, y)))$
(c) $(\exists x)$ (boy$(x) \rightarrow (\forall y)$ (girl$(y) \rightarrow$ taller $(x, y)))$
(d) $(\exists x)$ (boy$(x) \wedge (\forall y)$ (girl$(y) \rightarrow$ taller $(x, y)))$

24. ***Consider the binary relation:***

$S = \{(x, y) \mid y = x + 1$ ***and*** $x, y \in \{0, 1, 2, \ldots\}\}$

The reflexive transitive closure of S ***is***

(a) $\{(x, y) \mid y > x$ and $x, y \in \{0, 1, 2, \ldots\}\}$
(b) $\{(x, y) \mid y \geq x$ and $x, y \in \{0, 1, 2, \ldots\}\}$
(c) $\{(x, y) \mid y < x$ and $x, y \in \{0, 1, 2, \ldots\}\}$
(d) $\{(x, y) \mid y \leq x$ and $x, y \in \{0, 1, 2, \ldots\}\}$

25. ***If a fair coin is tossed four times, what is the probability that two heads and two tails will result?***

(a) 3/8 (b) 1/2
(c) 5/8 (d) 3/4

26. ***The number of different*** $n \times n$ ***symmetric matrices with each element being either 0 or 1 is: (Note: power***(2, *x*) ***is same as*** 2^x)

(a) power (2, *n*)
(b) power (2, n^2)
(c) power (2, $(n^2 + n)/2$)
(d) power (2, $(n^2 - n)/2$)

27. ***Let A, B, C, D be*** $n \times n$ ***matrices, each with non-zero determinant. If ABCD = I, then*** B^{-1} ***is***

(a) $D^{-1} C^{-1} A^{-1}$
(b) CDA
(c) ADC
(d) Does not necessarily exist

28. ***What is the result of evaluating the following two expressions using three-digit floating point arithmetic with rounding?***

(113. + −111.) + 7.51
113. + (−111. + 7.51)

(a) 9.51 and 10.0 respectively
(b) 10.0 and 9.51 respectively
(c) 9.51 and 9.51 respectively
(d) 10.0 and 10.0 respectively

29. ***The tightest lower bound on the number of comparisons, in the worst case, for comparison-based sorting is of the order of***

(a) n
(b) n^2
(c) $n \log n$
(d) $n \log^2 n$

30. ***The problems 3-SAT and 2-SAT are***

(a) both in P
(b) both NP-complete
(c) NP-complete and in P respectively
(d) undecidable and NP-complete respectively

Q. 31—90 carry two marks each

31. ***Consider the following C function:***

```
int f (int n)
{       static int i = 1;
        if (n > = 5) return n;
        n = n + i;
        i ++;
        return f (n);
}
```

The value returned by f (1) is

(a) 5 (b) 6

(c) 7 (d) 8

32. ***Consider the following program fragment for reversing the digits in a given integer to obtain a new integer. Let n = $d_1 d_2 \ldots d_m$.***

```
int n, rev;
rev = 0;
while (n > 0) {
        rev = rev * 10 + n % 10;
        n = n / 10;
}
```

The loop invariant condition at the end of the ith iteration is :

(a) n = $d_1 d_2 \ldots d_{m-i}$ and rev = $d_m d_{m-1} \ldots d_{m-i+1}$

(b) n = $d_{m-i+1} \ldots d_{m-1} d_m$ or rev = $d_{m-i} \ldots d_2 d_1$

(c) n ≠ rev

(d) n = $d_1 d_2 \ldots d_m$ or rev = $d_m \ldots d_2 d_1$

33. ***Consider the following C program segment:***

```
char p[20];
char *s = "string";
int length = strlen (s);
for (i = 0; i < length; i ++)
        p [i] = s [ length - i];
printf ("%s", p);
```

The output of the program is

(a) gnirts (b) string

(c) gnirt (d) *No output is printed*

34. ***It is desired to design an object-oriented employee record for a company. Each employee has a name, unique ID and salary. Employees belong to different categories and their salary is determined by their category. The functions getName, getId and computeSalary are required. Given the class hierarchy below, possible locations for these functions are:***

(I) getId is implemented in the superclass

(ii) getID is implemented in the subclass

(iii) getName is an abstract function in the superclass

(iv) getName is implemented in the superclass

(v) getName is implemented in the subclass

(vi) getSalary is an abstract function in the superclass
(vii) getSalary is implemented in the superclass
(viii) getSalary is implemented inthe subclass

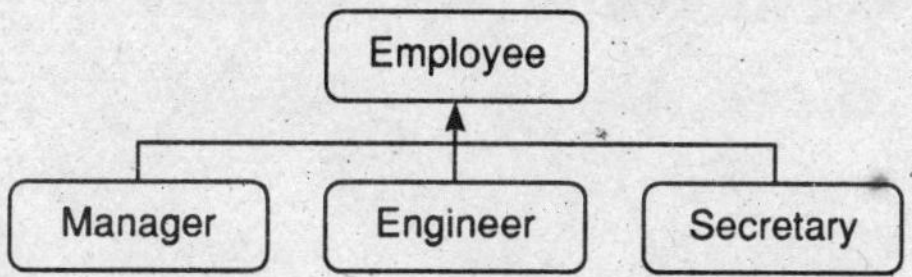

Choose the best design

(a) (I), (iv), (vi), (viii)
(b) (i), (iv), (vii)
(c) (i), (iii), (v), (vi), (viii)
(d) (ii), (v), (viii)

35. ***Consider the label sequences obtained by the following pairs of traversals on a labeled binary tree. Which of these pairs identify a tree uniquely?***

(i) preorder and postorder
(ii) inorder and postorder
(iii) preorder and inorder
(iv) level order and postorder

(a) (i) only
(b) (ii), (iii)
(c) (iii) only
(d) (iv) only

36. ***A circularly linked list is used to represent a Queue. A single variable p is used to access the Queue. To which node should p point such that both the operations enQueue and deQueue can be performed in constant time?***

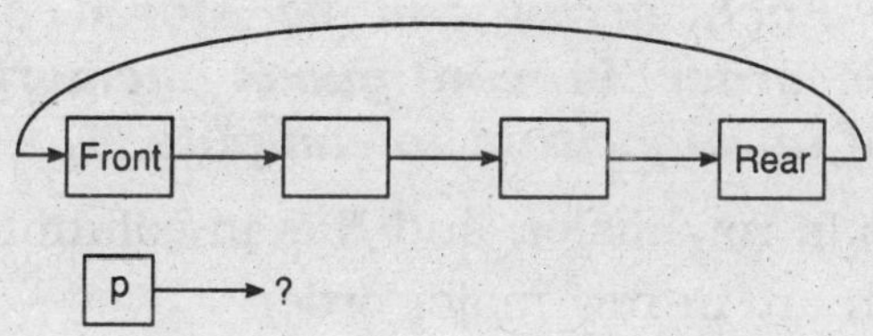

(a) rear node
(b) front node
(c) not possible with a single pointer
(d) node next to front

37. ***The elements 32, 15, 20, 30, 12, 25, 16, are inserted one by one in the given order into a maxHeap. The resultant maxHeap is***

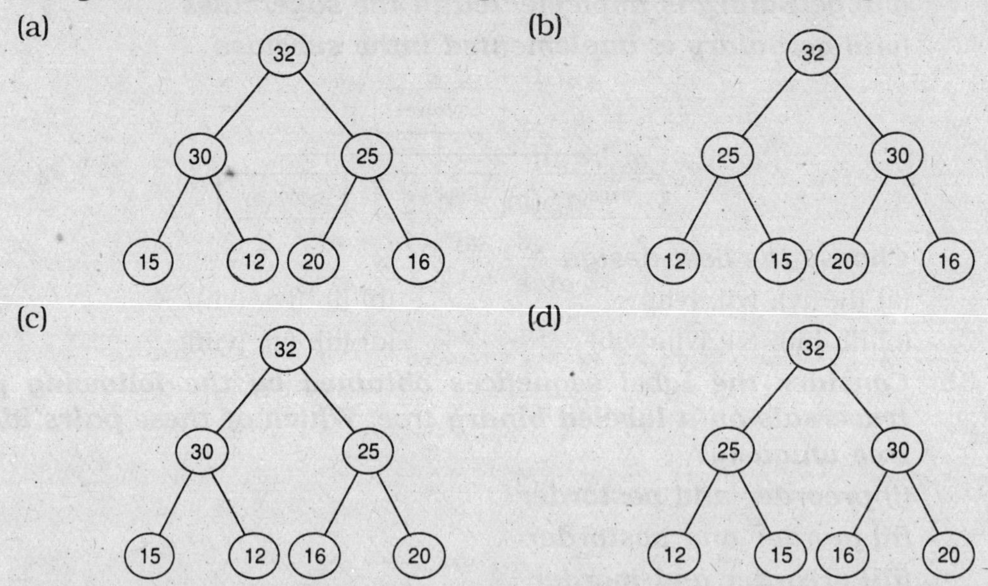

38. ***Assume that the operators +, −, × are left associative and ^ is right associative. The order of precedence (from highest to lowest) is $\wedge, \times, +, -$. The postfix expression corresponding to the infix expression* $a + b \times c - d \wedge e \wedge f$ *is***

(a) $abc \times + def \wedge\wedge -$ (b) $abc \times + de \wedge f \wedge -$

(c) $ab + c \times d - e \wedge f \wedge$ (d) $-+ a \times bc \wedge\wedge def$

39. ***Two matrices M_1 and M_2 are to be stored in arrays A and B respectively. Each array can be stored either in row-major or column-major order in contiguous memory locations. The time complexity of an algorithm to compute $M_1 \times M_2$ will be***

(a) best if *A* is in row-major, and *B* is in column-major order

(b) best if both are in row-major order

(c) best if both are in column-major order

(d) independent of the storage scheme

40. ***Suppose each set is represented as a linked list with elements in arbitrary order. Which of the operations among union, intersection, membership, cardinality will be the slowest ?***

(a) union only (b) intersection, membership

(c) membership, cardinality (d) union, intersection

41. ***Consider the following C program***

```
main ( )
{       int x, y, m, n;
        scanf ("%d %d", &x, &y) ;
        /* Assume x > 0 and y > 0 */
        m = x; n = y;
        while ( m ! = n)
            {       if (m > n)
                            m = m - n;
                    else
                            n = n - m;
            }
        printf ("%d", n);
}
```

The program computes

(a) $x \neq y$ using repeated subtraction

(b) x mod y using repeated subtraction

(c) the greatest common divisor of x and y

(d) the least common multiple of x and y

42. ***What does the following algorithm approximate? (Assume*** $m > 1$, $\varepsilon > 0$).

```
x = m;
y = 1;
while (x - y > ε)
    {       x + (x + y) / 2 ;
            y = m / x;
    }
print (x);
```

(a) $\log m$

(b) m^2

(c) $m^{1/2}$

(d) $m^{1/3}$

43. ***Consider the following C program segment.***

```
struct Cellnode {
        struct CellNode *leftchild;
        int element;
        struct CellNode * rightChild;
        } ;
```

```
int DoSomething (struct CellNode *ptr)
{
        int value = 0 ;
        if (ptr ! = NULL)
              { if (ptr - > left Child ! = NULL)
                        value = 1 + DoSomething (ptr - > left Child) ;
                   if (ptr - > right Child ! = NULL)
                        value = max (value,
                                  1 + DoSomething (ptr - > right Child ) ) ;
              }
        return (value) ;
}
```

The value returned by the function DoSomething when a pointer to the root of a non-empty tree is passed as argument is

(a) The number of leaf nodes in the tree

(b) The number of nodes in the tree

(c) The number of internal nodes in the tree

(d) The height of the tree

44. ***Suppose we run Dijkstra's single source shortest-path algorithm on the following edge-weighted directed graph will vertex P as the source.***

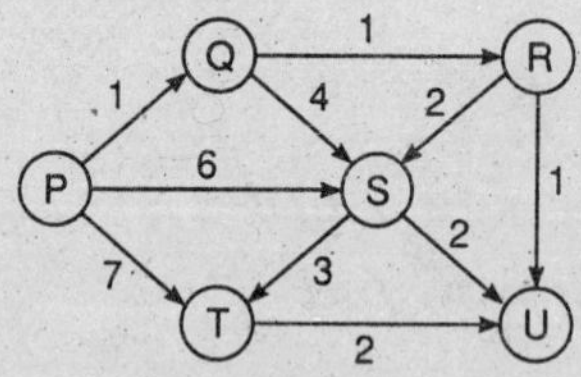

In what order do the nodes get included into the set of vertices for which the shortest path distances are finalized ?

(a) P, Q, R, S, T, U

(b) P, Q, R, U, S, T

(c) P, Q, R, U, T, S

(d) P, Q, T, R, U, S

45. ***Consider the grammar with the following translation rules and*** E ***as the start symbol.***

$$E \rightarrow E_1 \# T \{E.value = E_1.value * T.value\}$$

$$| \; T \{E.value = T.value\}$$

$T \rightarrow T_1$ & F { *T.value* = T_1*.value* + *F.value* }
| *F* {*T.value* = *F.value* }

F $\rightarrow$ *num* { *F.value* = *num.value* }

Compute E.value for the root of the parse tree for the expression: 2 # 3 & 5 # 6 & 4.

(a) 200 (b) 180
(c) 160 (d) 40

46. ***Consider the following set of processes, with the arrival times and the CPU-burst times given in milliseconds***

Process	Arrival Time	Burst Time
P1	0	5
P2	1	3
P3	2	3
P4	4	1

What is the average turnaround time for these process with the preemptive shortest remaining processing time first (SRPT) algorithm ?

(a) 5.50 (b) 5.75
(c) 6.00 (d) 6.25

47. ***Consider a system with a two-level paging scheme in which a regular memory access takes 150 nanoseconds, and servicing a page fault takes 8 milliseconds. An average instruction takes 100 nanoseconds of CPU time, and two memory accesses. The TLB hit ratio is 90%, and the page fault rate is one in every 10,000 instructions. What is the effective average instruction execution time?***

(a) 645 nanoseconds (b) 1050 nanoseconds
(c) 1215 nanoseconds (d) 1230 nanoseconds

48. ***Consider two processes P_1 and P_2 accessing the shared variables X and Y protected by two binary semaphores S_X and S_Y respectively, both initialized to 1. P and V denote the usual semaphore operators, where P decrements the semaphore value, and V increments the semaphore value. The pseudo-code of P_1 and P_2 is as follows:***

P_1 :

```
while true do {
    L1 : ............
    L2 : ............
    X = X + 1;
    Y = Y – 1;
    V(SX);
    V(SY); }
```

P_2 :

```
while true do {
    L3 : ............
    L4 : ..............
    Y = Y + 1;
    X = X – 1;
    V(SY);
    V(SX); }
```

IN order to avoid deadlock, the correct operators at L_1, L_2, L_3 and L_4 are respectively

(a) $P(S_Y)$, $P(S_X)$; $P(S_X)$, $P(S_Y)$ (b) $P(S_X)$, $P(S_Y)$; $P(S_Y)$, $P(S_X)$

(c) $P(S_X)$, $P(S_X)$; $P(S_Y)$, $P(S_Y)$ (d) $P(S_X)$, $P(S_Y)$; $P(S_X)$, $P(S_Y)$

49. ***A Unix-style i-node has 10 direct pointer and one single, one double and one triple indirect pointers. Disk block size is 1 Kbyte, disk block address is 32 bits, and 48-bit integers are used. What is the maximum possible file size?***

(a) 2^{24} bytes (b) 2^{32} bytes

(c) 2^{34} bytes (d) 2^{48} bytes

50. ***The relation scheme StudentPerformance (name, courseNo, rollNo, grade) has the following functional dependencies:***

name, courseNo → grade

rollNo, courseNo → grade

name → rollNo

rollNo → name

The highest normal form of this relation scheme is

(a) 2NF (b) 3NF

(c) BCNF (d) 4NF

51. ***Consider the relation Student (name, sex, marks), where the primary key is shown underlined, pertaining to students in a class that has at least one boy and one girl. What does the following relational algebra expression produce? (Note: ρ is the rename operator).***

$$\Pi_{name}(\sigma_{sex = female}(\textbf{Student})) - \Pi_{name}(\textbf{Student} \bowtie_{(sex = female \wedge x = male \wedge marks \leq m)} \rho_{n, x, m}(\textbf{Student}))$$

(a) names of girl students with the highest marks

(b) names of girl students with more marks than some boy student

(c) names of girl students with marks not less than some boy student

(d) names of girl students with more marks than all the boy students

52. ***The order of an internal node in a B⁺ tree index is the maximum number of children it can have. Suppose that a child pointer takes 6 bytes, the search field value takes 14 bytes, and the block size is 512 bytes. What is the order of the internal node?***

(a) 24 (b) 25

(c) 26 (d) 27

53. ***The employee information in a company is stored in the relation***

Employee (name, sex, salary, deptName).

Consider the following SQL query

```
select deptName
    from Employee
    where sex = 'M'
group by deptName
having avg (salary) >
        (select avg (salary) from Employee)
```

It returns the names of the departments in which

(a) the average salary is more than the average salary in the company

(b) the average salary of male employees is more than the average salary of all male employees in the company

(c) the average salary of male employees is more than the average salary of employees in the same department

(d) the average salary of male employees is more than the average salary in the company

54. ***A and B are the only two stations on an Ethernet. Each has a steady queue of frames to send. Both A and B attempt to transmit a frame, collide, and A wins the first backoff race. At the end of this successful transmission by A, both A and B attempt to transmit and collide. The probability that A wins the second backoff race is***

(a) 0.5 (b) 0.625

(c) 0.75 (d) 1.0

55. ***The routine table of a router is shown below:***

Destination	*Subnet Mask*	*Interface*
128.75.43.0	**255.255.255.0**	***Eth0***
128.75.43.0	**255.255.255.128**	***Eth1***
192.12.17.5	**255.255.255.255**	***Eth3***
default		**Eth2**

On which interfaces will the router forward packets addressed to destinations 128.75.43.16 and 192.12.17.10 respectively?

(a) Eth1 and Eth2 (b) Eth0 and Eth2
(c) Eth0 and Eth3 (d) Eth1 and Eth3

The following information pertains to Q. 56-57

Consider three IP networks *A*, *B* and *C*. Host H_A in network *A* sends messages each containing 180 bytes of application data to a host H_C in network *C*. The TCP layer prefixes a 20 byte header to the message. This passes through an intermediate network *B*. The maximum packet size, including 20 byte IP header, in each network is

A : 1000 bytes
B : 100 bytes
C : 1000 bytes

The networks *A* and *B* are connected through a 1 Mbps link, while *B* and *C* are connected by a 512 Kbps link (bps - bits per second).

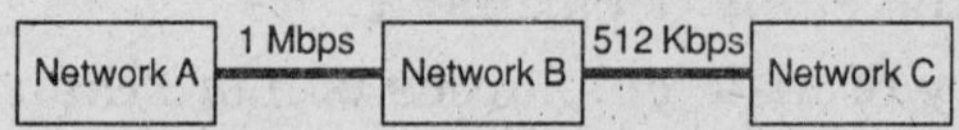

56. ***Assuming that the packets are correctly delivered, how many bytes, including headers, are delivered to the IP layer at the destination for one application message, in the best case? Consider only data packets.***

(a) 200 (b) 220
(c) 240 (d) 260

57. ***What is the rate at which application data is transferred to host H_C? Ignore errors, acknowledgements, and other overheads.***

(a) 325.5 Kbps (b) 354.5 Kbps

(c) 409.6 Kbps (d) 512.0 Kbps

58. ***A circuit outputs a digit in the form of 4 bits. 0 is represented by 0000, 1 by 0001, ..., 9 by 1001. A combinational circuit is to be designed which takes these 4 bits as input and outputs 1 if the digit $\geq$ 5, and 0 otherwise. If only AND, OR and NOT gates may be used, what is the minmum number of gates required?***

(a) 2 (b) 3

(c) 4 (d) 5

59. ***Which are the essential prime implicants of the following Boolean function?***

$$f(a, b, c) = a'c + ac' + b'c$$

(a) $a'c$ and ac' (b) $a'c$ and $b'c$

(c) $a'c$ only (d) ac' and bc'

60. ***Consider a multiplexer with X and Y as data inputs and Z as control input. Z = 0 selects input X, and Z = 1 selects input Y. What are the connections required to realize the 2-variable Boolean function f = T + R, without using any additional hardware?***

(a) R to X, 1 to Y, T to Z (b) T to X, R to Y, T to Z

(c) T to X, R to Y, 0 to Z (d) R to X, 0 to Y, T to Z

61. ***Consider the partial implementation of a 2-bit counter using T flip-flops following the sequence 0-2-3-1-0, as shown below.***

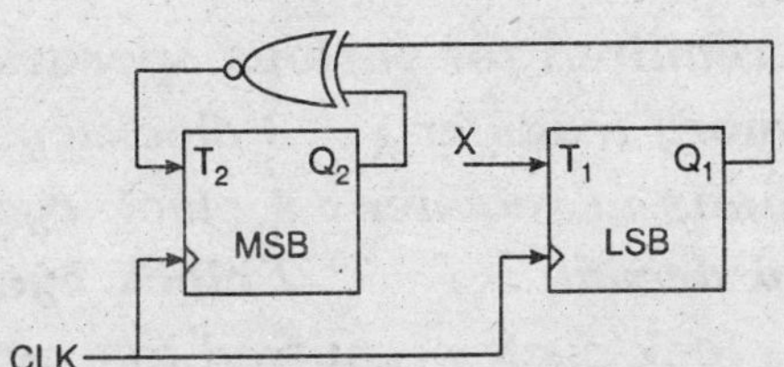

To complete the circuit, the input X should be

(a) Q'_2 (b) $Q_2 + Q_1$

(c) $(Q_1 \oplus Q_2)'$ (d) $Q_1 \oplus Q_2$

62. ***A 4-bit carry lookhead adder, which adds two 4-bit numbers, is designed using AND, OR, NOT, NAND, NOR gates only. Assuming that all the inputs are available in both complemented and uncomplemented forms and the delay of each gate is one time unit, what is the overall propagation delay of the adder ? Assume that the carry network has been implemented using two-level AND-OR logic.***

(a) 4 time units (b) 6 time units
(c) 10 time units (d) 12 time units

The following information perta ns to Q. 63-64

Consider the following program segment for a hypothetical CPU having three user registers $R1$, $R2$ and $R3$.

Instruction	*Operation*	Instruction Size (in words)
MOV R1, 5000	; R1 ← Memory[5000]	2
MOV R2, (R1)	; R2 ← Memory[(R1)]	1
ADD R2, R3	; R2 ← R2 + R3	1
MOV 6000, R2	; Memory[6000] ← R2	2
HALT	; Machine halts	1

63. ***Consider that the memory is byte addressable with word size 32 bits, and the program has been loaded starting from memory location 1000 (decimal). If an interrupt occurs while the CPU has been halted after executing the HALT instruction, the return address (in decimal) saved in the stack will be***

(a) 1007 (b) 1020
(c) 1024 (d) 1028

64. ***Let the clock cycles required for various operations be as follows:***

Register to/from memory transfer : 3 clock cycles

ADD with both operands in register : 1 clock cycle

Instruction fetch and decode : 2 clock cycles per word

The total number of clock cycles required to execute the program is

(a) 29 (b) 24
(c) 23 (d) 20

65. ***Consider a small two-way set-associative cache memory, consisting of four blocks. For choosing the block to be replaced, use the least recently used (LRU) scheme. The number of cache misses for the following sequence of block addresses is***

8, 12, 0, 12, 8

(a) 2 (b) 3
(c) 4 (d) 5

66. ***Let A = 1111 1010 and B = 0000 1010 be two 8-bit 2's complement numbers. Their product is 2's complement is***

(a) 1100 0100 (b) 1001 1100
(c) 1010 0101 (d) 1101 0101

67. ***The microinstructions stored in the control memory of a processor have a width of 26 bits. Each microinstruction is divided into three fields: a micro-operation field of 13 bits, a next address field (X), and a MUX select field (Y). There are 8 status bits in the inputs of the MUX.***

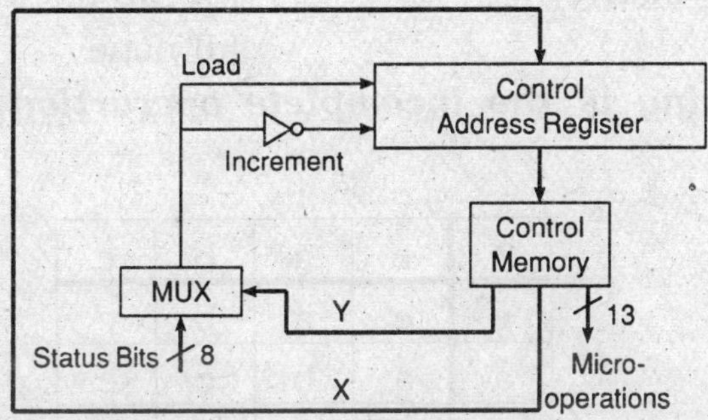

How many bits are there is the X and Y fields, and what is the size of the control memory in number of words ?

(a) 10, 3, 1024 (b) 8, 5, 256
(c) 5, 8, 2048 (d) 10, 3, 512

68. ***A hard disk with a transfer rate of 10 Mbytes/second is constantly transferring data to memory using DMA. The processor runs at 600 MHz, and takes 300 and 900 clock cycles to initiate and complete DMA transfer respectively. If the size of the transfer is 20 Kbytes, what is the percentage of processor time consumed for the transfer operation ?***

(a) 5.0% (b) 1.0%
(c) 0.5% (d) 0.1%

69. ***A 4-stage pipeline has the stage delays as 150, 120, 160 and 140 nanoseconds respectively. Registers that are used between the stages have a delay of 5 nanoseconds each. Assuming constant clocking rate, the total time taken to process 1000 data items on this pipeline will be***

(a) 120.4 microseconds (b) 160.5 microseconds
(c) 165.5 microseconds (d) 590.0 microseconds

70. ***The following propositional statement is***

$$(P \rightarrow (Q \vee R)) \rightarrow ((P \wedge Q) \rightarrow R)$$

(a) satisfiable but not valid (b) valid

(c) a contradiction (d) none of the above

71. ***How many solutions does the following system of linear equations have?***

$$-x + 5y = -1$$
$$x - y = 2$$
$$x + 3y = 3$$

(a) infinitely many (b) two distinct solutions
(c) unique (d) none

72. ***The following is the incomplete operartion table of a 4-element group.***

*	e	a	b	c
e	e	a	b	c
a	a	b	c	e
b				
c				

The last row of the table is

(a) c a e b (b) c b a e
(c) c b e a (d) c e a b

73. ***The inclusion of which of the following sets into***

S = {{1,2}, {1,2,3}, {1, 3, 5}, {1, 2, 4}, {1, 2, 3, 4, 5}}

is necessary and sufficient to make S a complete lattice under the partial order defined by set containment?

(a) {1} (b) {1}, {2, 3}
(c) {1}, {1, 3} (d) {1}, {1, 3}, {1, 2, 3, 4}, {1, 2, 3, 5}

74. ***An examination paper has 150 multiple-choice questions of one mark each, with each question having four choices. Each incorrect answer fetches -0.25 mark. Suppose 1000 students choose all their answers randomly with uniform probability. The sum total of the expected marks obtained by all these students is***

(a) 0 (b) 2550
(c) 7225 (d) 9375

75. ***Mala has a colouring book in which each English letter is drawn two times. She wants to paint each of these 52 prints with one of k colours, such that the colour-pairs used to colour any two letters are different. Both prints of a letter can also be coloured with the***

same colour. What is the minimum value of k ***that satisfies this requirement?***

(a) 9 (b) 8

(c) 7 (d) 6

76. ***In an*** $M \times N$ ***matrix such that all non-zero entries are covered in*** a ***rows and*** b ***columns. Then the maximum number of non-zero entries, such that no two are on the same row or column, is***

(a) $\leq a + b$ (b) $\leq \max \{a, b\}$

(c) $\leq \min \{M - a, N - b\}$ (d) $\leq \min \{a, b\}$

77. ***The minimum number of colours required to colour the following graph, such that no two adjacent vertices are assigned the same colour, is***

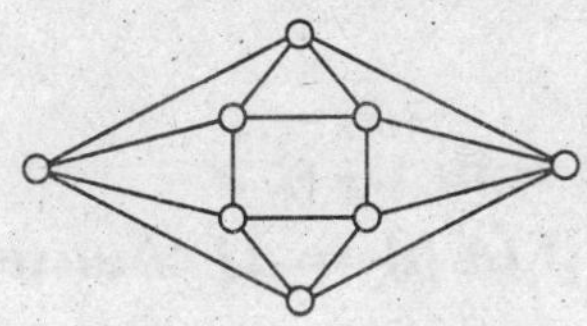

(a) 2 (b) 3

(c) 4 (d) 5

78. ***Two n bit binary strings,*** S_1 ***and*** S_2***, are chosen randomly with uniform probability. The probability that the Hamming distance between these strings (the number of bit positions where the two strings differ) is equal to*** d ***is***

(a) ${}^{n}C_{d} / 2^{n}$ (b) ${}^{n}C_{d} / 2^{d}$

(c) $d / 2^{n}$ (d) $1 / 2^{d}$

79. ***How many graphs on*** n ***labeled vertices exist which have at least*** $(n^2 - 3n)/2$ ***edges?***

(a) ${}^{(n\wedge 2-n)/2}C_{(n\wedge 2-3n)/2}$ (b) $\sum_{k=0}^{(n\wedge 2-3n)/2} {}^{(n\wedge 2-n)}C_k$

(c) ${}^{(n\wedge 2-n)/2}C_n$ (d) $\sum_{k=0}^{n} {}^{(n\wedge 2-n)/2)}C_k$

80. ***A point is randomly selected with uniform probability in the X – Y plane within the rectangle with corners at (0, 0), (1, 0), (1, 2) and (0, 2). If p is the length of the position vector of the point, the expected value of*** p^2 ***is***

(a) 2/3 (b) 1
(c) 4/3 (d) 5/3

81. ***Let $G_1 = (V, E_1)$ and $G_2 = (V, E_2)$ be connected graphs on the same vertex set V with more than two vertices. If $G_1 \cap G_2 = (V, E_1 \cap E_2)$ is not a connected graph, then the graph $G_1 \cup G_2 = (V, E_1 \cup E_2)$***

(a) cannot have a cut vertex
(b) must have a cycle
(c) must have a cut-edge (bridge)
(d) has chromatic number strictly greater than those of G_1 and G_2

82. ***Let A[1, ..., n] be an array storing a bit (1 or 0) at each location, and f(m) is a function whose time complexity is θ(m). Consider the following program fragment written in a C like language:***

```
counter = 0;
for (i = 1; i < = n; i ++)
    {       if (A [i] == 1) counter ++;
            else {f (counter) ; counter = 0 ; }
    }
```

The complexity of this program fragment is

(a) $\Omega(n^2)$ (b) $\Omega(n \log n)$ and $O(n^2)$
(c) $\theta(n)$ (d) $o(n)$

83. ***The time complexity of the following C function is (assume n > 0)***

```
int recursive (int n) {
    if (n == 1)
            return (1) ;
    else
            return (recursive (n - 1) + recursive (n - 1) );
}
```

(a) $O(n)$ (b) $O(n \log n)$
(c) $O(n^2)$ (d) $O(2^n)$

84. ***The recurrence equation***

$$T(1) = 1$$
$$T(n) = 2T(n-1) + n, \; n \geq 2$$

evaluates to

(a) $2^{n+1} - n - 2$ (b) $2^n - n$

(c) $2^{n+1} - 2n - 2$ (d) $2^n + n$

85. ***A program takes as input a balanced binary search tree with n leaf nodes and computes the value of a function g(x) for each node x. If the cost of computing g(x) is min {no. of leaf-nodes in left-subtree of x, no. of leaf-nodes in right-subtree of x} then the worst-case time complexity of the program is***

(a) $\Theta(n)$ (b) $\Theta(n \log n)$

(c) $\Theta(n^2)$ (d) $\Theta(n^2 \log n)$

86. ***The following finite state machine accepts all those binary strings in which the number 1's and 0's are respectively***

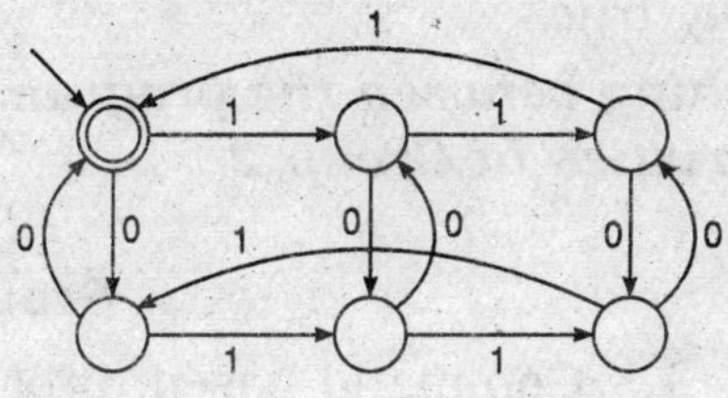

(a) divisible by 3 and 2 (b) odd and even

(c) even and odd (d) divisible by 2 and 3

87. ***The language*** $\{a^m b^n c^{m+n} \mid m, n \geq 1\}$ ***is***

(a) regular

(b) context-free but not regular

(c) context sensitive but not context free

(d) type-0 but not context sensitive

88. ***Consider the following grammar*** G:

$S \rightarrow bS \mid aA \mid b$

$A \rightarrow bA \mid aB$

$B \rightarrow bB \mid aS \mid a$

Let $N_a(w)$ ***and*** $N_b(w)$ ***denote the number of a's and b's in a string w respectively. The language*** $L(G) \subseteq \{a, b\}^+$ ***generated by G is***

(a) $\{w \mid N_a(w) > 3N_b(w)\}$

(b) $\{w \mid N_b(w) > 3N_a(w)\}$

(c) $\{w \mid N_a(w) = 3k, k \in \{0, 1, 2, \ldots\}\}$

(d) $\{w \mid N_b(w) = 3k, k \in \{0, 1, 2, \ldots\}\}$

89. ***L_1 is a recursively enumerable language over Σ. An algorithm A effectively enumerates its words as $w_1, w_2, w_3, \ldots$ Define another language L_2 over $\Sigma \cup \{\#\}$ as $\{w_i \# w_j : w_i, w_j \in L_1, i < j\}$. Here # is a new symbol. Consider the following assertions:***

S_1 : L_1 is recursive implies L_2 is recursive

S_2 : L_2 is recursive implies L_1 is recursive

Which of the following statements is true?

(a) Both S_1 and S_2 are true

(b) S_1 is true but S_2 is not necessarily true

(c) S_2 is true but S_1 is not necessarily true

(d) Neither is necessarily true

90. ***Choose the best matching between the programming styles in Group 1 and their characteristics in Group 2.***

Group 1	Group 2
P. Functional	1. Command-based, procedural
Q. Logic	2. Imperative, abstract data types
R: Object-oriented	3. Side-effect free, declarative, expression evaluation
S: Imperative	4. Declarative, clausal representation, theorem proving

(a) P-2, Q-3, R-4, S-1

(b) P-4, Q-3, R-2, S-1

(c) P-3, Q-4, R-1, S-2

(d) P-3, Q-4, R-2, S-1